MATTERS OF FACT IN JANE AUSTEN

MATTERS

OF

FACT

IN

JANE

AUSTEN

History, Location,
and Celebrity

JANINE BARCHAS

The Johns Hopkins University Press
Baltimore

Johns Hopkins Paperback edition, 2013
9 8 7 6 5 4 3 2 1

The Johns Hopkins University Press
2715 North Charles Street
Baltimore, Maryland 21218-4363
www.press.jhu.edu

The Library of Congress has cataloged the hardcover edition of this book as follows:
Barchas, Janine.
  Matters of fact in Jane Austen : history , location, and celebrity / Janine Barchas.
    pages cm
  Includes bibliographical references and index.
  ISBN 978-1-4214-0640-4 (hdbk.)—
  ISBN 1-4214-0640-3 (hdbk.)—
  ISBN 978-1-4214-0731-9 (electronic)—
  ISBN 1-4214-0731-0 (electronic)—
    1. Austen, Jane, 1775–1817—Knowledge—History.   2. Austen, Jane, 1775–1817—
Knowledge—Geography.   3. Austen, Jane, 1775–1817—Knowledge—Genealogy.
4. Austen, Jane, 1775–1817—Family.   5. Setting (Literature)   6. Names in literature.
7. England—In literature.   8. Literature and history—Great Britain—History—19th
century.   9. Literature and society—England—History—19th century.   I. Title.
  PR4038.H5B37 2012
   823'.7—dc23   2012000022

A catalog record for this book is available from the British Library.

ISBN-13: 978-1-4214-1191-0
ISBN-10: 1-4214-1191-1

*Special discounts are available for bulk purchases of this book. For more information,
please contact Special Sales at 410-516-6936 or specialsales@press.jhu.edu.*

To Isaac and Madison

CONTENTS

ACKNOWLEDGMENTS

Writing in Austin on Austen has allowed me to accumulate a whole new set of debts to family, friends, colleagues, institutions, and generous experts who assisted in person and from afar.

First, I want to thank Jocelyn Harris, whose suggestions, teachings, and support have been crucial to this project. Her copious annotations on immature versions of nearly every chapter always improved and clarified—precisely because in her generosity she never pulled any punches.

I also benefitted greatly and gratefully from scholars in Austin whose proximity made them easy targets for a myriad of requests, but whom I would have sought out regardless. Michael Charlesworth offered needed expertise on all things Wentworth Castle, as well as a tour of that landscape garden which proved a highlight of the research process. Lance Bertelsen found that he could not hide from my Austen queries even in his own office, from which I emerged with many a borrowed book and idea. William Scheick generously took his editorial pen to my prose, sharpening and clarifying.

Colleagues near and far read sections of chapters or listened to nascent ideas, offering suggestions or directing me to related materials that I might never have discovered on my own. I am grateful to Samuel Baker, Linda Bree, Kevin Bourque, Thora Brylowe, Stephen Clarke, Susan Allen Ford, Alan Friedman, James Garrison, Susan Heinzelman, Thomas Keymer, Juliet McMaster, Lisa Moore, Cedric Reverand, and the anonymous reviewers at *Eighteenth-Century Life* and *Review of English Studies*. Specific thanks are due to Elizabeth Scala, for repeated steerings in Chaucer studies; to Brian Boyd, for first directing me to Nabokov's papers in the New York Public Library; to Peter Sabor, for judicious nudgings on *Evelyn* and Burney; to Kathryn Sutherland, for corrigenda on two chapters; to Sandy Lerner, for information about toll scarves; to John LaFave, for trial access to the Burney Newspaper database; and to Patrick Eyres, for organizing a magical conference at Wentworth Castle, which featured real as well as intellectual fireworks.

A special shout-out is also due to those persons who, for several years, enthusiastically supported my project with resources and energies above and beyond their job descriptions: Molly Schwartzburg, Cline Curator of Literature at the Harry Ransom Research Center; Lindsey Schell, English Literature and Women's Studies Librarian at the University of Texas Libraries; and Elizabeth Cullingford, Chair of my English Department. In addition, Daniel Brown, the force behind the *Bath in Time* website, helped locate rare maps and images at different stages of the project, while Anne Buchanan, Local Studies Librarian at Bath Central Library, assisted in dating a key map's features.

The earliest experiments to test the ideas of this book took place in the classrooms of the University of Texas, particularly in my "Jane Austen on Page and Screen" seminars for Plan II and my "Jane Austen on Location" classes for the Oxford Summer Program, housed at Brasenose and Wadham Colleges. Clever undergraduates in these classes reaffirmed the Möbius strip of research and teaching. Particular thanks are due to Teel Liddell, whose intelligence animated multiple classes, and Katherine Hysmith, my undergraduate research apprentice for four glorious months of enhanced productivity.

One of the pleasures of working on Jane Austen has been the opportunity to also engage with a large number of her readers outside of traditional academic settings. Both the Jane Austen Society of North America and the Jane Austen Society of Australia have made me feel very welcome in their vibrant company. I especially want to thank Marsha Huff, Joan Ray, Elizabeth Steele, Susannah Fullerton, Kerri Spennicchia, and Gail Parker for facilitating opportunities of engagement and exchange.

During its fragile nascent phase, this project was generously supported by an American Council of Learned Societies Fellowship as well as a University of Texas Faculty Research Assignment in 2007–8. A Humanities Research Award from the College of Liberal Arts helped defray incidentals and travel during the last stages of the research. The illustrations in this book were made possible by a University of Texas at Austin Subvention Grant awarded by President William C. Powers, Jr. The project was shepherded through the final stages of production by the most supportive of editors, Matthew McAdam, and copyeditor Barbara Lamb, who proved a lioness of exactness.

Sections of Chapters 2, 3, and 5, now revised and extended, appeared in earlier forms in the following publications, respectively: "Mapping *Northanger Abbey*: Or, Why Austen's Bath of 1803 Resembles Joyce's

Dublin of 1904," *Review of English Studies* 60.245 (2009): 431–59; "The Real Bluebeard of Bath: A Historical Model for *Northanger Abbey*," *Persuasions* 32 (2010): 115–34; and "Hell-Fire Jane: Austen and the Dashwoods of West Wycombe," *Eighteenth-Century Life* 33.3 (2009): 1–36. In addition, a handful of pages from the Introduction are reworked from an article entitled "Artistic Names in Austen's Fiction: Cameo Appearances by Prominent Painters," *Persuasions* 31 (2009): 145–62.

Finally, and most importantly, I acknowledge that without the assistance of Isaac and Madison Barchas—suppliers of sustenance, purveyors of hope, and critics of Jane Austen in their own right—it would not have been possible to write any part of this book.

ABBREVIATIONS

DNB   *Oxford Dictionary of National Biography*. Oxford: Oxford University Press, 2004. On-line.

E   *Emma*. Ed. Richard Cronin and Dorothy McMillan. *The Cambridge Edition of the Works of Jane Austen*. Cambridge: Cambridge University Press, 2005.

J   *Juvenilia*. Ed. Peter Sabor. *The Cambridge Edition of the Works of Jane Austen*. Cambridge: Cambridge University Press, 2006.

Letters   Le Faye, Deirdre. *Jane Austen's Letters*, 3rd ed. Oxford: Oxford University Press, 1995.

LM   *Later Manuscripts*. Ed. Janet Todd and Linda Bree. *The Cambridge Edition of the Works of Jane Austen*. Cambridge: Cambridge University Press, 2008.

MP   *Mansfield Park*. Ed. John Wiltshire. *The Cambridge Edition of the Works of Jane Austen*. Cambridge: Cambridge University Press, 2005.

NA   *Northanger Abbey*. Ed. Barbara M. Benedict and Deirdre Le Faye. *The Cambridge Edition of the Works of Jane Austen*. Cambridge: Cambridge University Press, 2006.

P   *Persuasion*. Ed. Janet Todd and Antje Blank. *The Cambridge Edition of the Works of Jane Austen*. Cambridge: Cambridge University Press, 2006.

P&P   *Pride and Prejudice*. Ed. Pat Rogers. *The Cambridge Edition of the Works of Jane Austen*. Cambridge: Cambridge University Press, 2006.

S&S   *Sense and Sensibility*. Ed. Edward Copeland. *The Cambridge Edition of the Works of Jane Austen*. Cambridge: Cambridge University Press, 2006.

MATTERS OF FACT IN JANE AUSTEN

"History, real solemn history" in Austen

"I can read poetry and plays, and things of that sort, and do not dislike travels. But history, real solemn history, I cannot be interested in. Can you?"

"Yes, I am fond of history."

"I wish I were too. I read it a little as a duty, but it tells me nothing that does not either vex or weary me. The quarrels of popes and kings, with wars or pestilences, in every page, the men all so good for nothing, and hardly any women at all—it is very tiresome: and yet I often think it odd that it should be so dull, for a great deal of it must be invention. The speeches that are put into the heroes' mouths, their thoughts and designs—the chief of all this must be invention, and invention is what delights me in other books." (*NA*, 109–10)

To A SIGNIFICANT EXTENT, Jane Austen creates her novels out of the "real solemn history" dismissed here by her heroine Catherine Morland in favor of "invention." Family tradition has it that, in contrast to the naïve Catherine, Austen's own reading in history "was very extensive" and "her memory extremely tenacious."[1] In fact, scholars continue to find moments in Austen's fictions that reward knowledge of events and people from the English historical record. Emerging from the number of such discoveries in recent years is a historical specificity to Austen's work that sits uneasily astride her long-standing reputation for timelessness and transparency. In spite of a universality that lies at the heart of Austen's appeal, her plots, brimful of historically suggestive names and locations, often flow from historical fact. Austen, in short, may play confidently with the tantalizing tension between truth and invention that characterizes the realist novel. This book examines that tension in her work.

By unearthing Austen's historical references to real-world locations, events, and celebrity families in her fiction, I aim to resituate her work nearer to the stout historical novels of her contemporary Sir Walter Scott, or even the encyclopedic reach of modernist James Joyce, than to the narrow domestic and biographical readings that still characterize much of Austen studies. If I can prove that her fictions persistently allude to real people and locations—from high-profile politicians and

1

outrageous Regency celebrities to important locations and events in England's war-torn history—such historical allusions may offer new insights into her novels and creative process. Austen's unique reception history has led to a unique ahistoricism in critical approaches to her work. Unlike Shakespeare, Scott, or Joyce, Austen was not popular in her own lifetime. Her first posthumous flush of popularity, in the wake of Richard Bentley's 1833 reprintings, left her Victorian audience unable or unwilling to decipher her allusions to the celebrity gossip and political history of her turn-of-the-century era. Like those Victorian critics who first celebrated her genius, we still read Austen out of time. Ironically, her supposed timelessness has fed her continuing popularity, making Austen the perfect object for the ahistoricism of highly theoretical scholars and popular readers alike. While both types of readers have offered tremendous insights into her work, it is time to reexamine Austen through the historical methodologies routinely applied to other great writers. Building upon the claims and discoveries of a recent generation of critics attuned to Austen's historical reach, I want to join the perennial challenge to that lingering image of Jane Austen as a cloistered rectory daughter, innocent of larger social and political events—a somewhat misogynistic popular misconception that stubbornly refuses to die. Instead, I see Austen as an active participant in what historians now describe as the emergence of celebrity culture. By situating Austen more concretely in her contemporary milieu, and by heeding her own clues to history, I hope to prove, ironically, that she was even more modern than today's "Cult of Jane" allows.

In 1923, Austen's first serious editor, R. W. Chapman, was already sensitive to problems posed by her historical specificity. On the one hand, he knew that "Jane Austen was singularly scrupulous in her regard for accuracy in those parts of her fiction which were grounded on fact—such as dates and places."[2] He even acknowledges that she worked with calendars and "took great pains to make her dates mutually consistent." Concerts in her Bath novels fall "always on the right days of the week," for example.[3] On the other hand, he omitted editorial notes about historical accuracy from his edition, warning how she "clings to reality in a way which might argue poverty of invention." Even though Chapman dismisses such critiques as "absurd," he seems acutely aware that any editorial apparatus indexing the historical facts in Austen might mar her reputation for imaginative achievement.[4] Wordsworth had indeed objected to Austen for being a mere copyist, judging her pictures as too close to life to qualify as art because not "clarified, as it were, by the pervading light of imagination."[5] Chapman's cautious reluctance to annotate Austen's historical method may have been his way of defending her status as an imaginative genius.

Now, with Austen's reputation robust enough to withstand recognition of her scrupulous realism, recent scholarship is starting to acknowledge her abiding interest in history. This book therefore makes grateful use of the cornucopia of scholarly findings about Austen's local deployment of historical moments and facts, all the while leaning upon her strong editorial legacy. Partly by corralling prior scholarly insights about local allusions and historical references, I hope to demonstrate anew the profound historicism and geographical specificity that cut across her work. In spite of the mature scholarly impulse to overcome Chapman's reluctance and historicize Jane Austen to her own time in modern editions, her gestures toward an earlier British history—her historiography, as it were—remain comparatively ring-fenced into footnotes and individual readings. While biographers and critics acknowledge Austen's understanding of history, citing as evidence for early reading habits her own juvenile "History of England," as well as her marginalia in a copy of Oliver Goldsmith's *History of England* (1771), an inclination to interpret her fictions through her biography, rather than her knowledge of history, persists.

Consider, for example, the history of Wentworth Woodhouse in Yorkshire: the estate dates back to at least the thirteenth century, when Robert Wentworth married a rich heiress named Emma Wodehouse. Their Yorkshire family so prospered that in 1611 its senior line achieved a baronetcy under James I, while the sister of this first baronet married the heir of the wealthy D'Arcy family. The eldest son of that same first baronet was Thomas Wentworth, Earl of Strafford, the ill-fated minister of Charles I. When he came into the family estate of Wentworth Woodhouse in 1614, it was already worth £6,000 per annum, a sum judged in an 1815 history book as "a very ample patrimony at that time."[6] When Thomas Wentworth was executed as part of the king's final and desperate attempt to appease Parliament, the Wentworth Woodhouse estate was confiscated. With the Restoration, however, it was returned to Strafford's eldest son, William Wentworth. But when William died without issue in 1695, the family wealth transferred to the children of his sister, Anne Wentworth, wife to the head of the Watson family. In December 1750, when Charles Watson, heir to these princely estates, succeeded his father as the second Marquess of Rockingham, he became one of the wealthiest peers in England. His annual income for that year is calculated at over £20,000, "which probably at least doubled over the following thirty years."[7] Charles Watson-Wentworth, having added his mother's maiden name to his own, was twice elected prime minister of England, but he died unexpectedly in 1782, just after his second election, childless at age fifty-two. The sudden extinction of the Marquessate of Rockingham meant that the combined fortunes of the Woodhouses, Wentworths, and Watsons transferred to the next of kin, the Fitzwilliams, during Jane Austen's girlhood.

I am not the first to notice how a summary history of one of England's most prominent political families features the standout names of protagonists from *Pride and Prejudice* (hero Fitzwilliam Darcy), *Emma* (heroine Emma Woodhouse), *Persuasion* (heroine's married name is Anne Wentworth), and even Austen's fragmentary novel *The Watsons* (so named by her nephew in 1871 because it focuses on a Watson family). In 1953, Donald Greene reflected on the "interesting 'coincidences'" between these historical names from the peerage and those in Austen's fictions.[8] He also suggested that in the juvenilia "names of great families are even more frequent and more obvious" (Greene, 1021). Yet even Greene may have underestimated the manner in which English history, particularly eighteenth-century history, suffused and inspired Austen's choices of names and settings. Austen's deep concentration on the history of the Wentworth family extends much further than Greene traced, perhaps because he was hindered by the politics of historiography in his day. Building upon Greene's initial insight into Austen's methodology, her profound historical awareness, and her daring use of famous names from the peerage, I explore how wider notions of English history might further enrich an interpretation of Austen's method as well as challenge established readings of her work. In the case of Austen's enduring interest in the Yorkshire Wentworths, for example, a broader historical context for that family not only connects a greater number of her fictions than Greene aligns but may also solve a specific interpretive conundrum within Austen scholarship by fixing a more precise date to the composition of *Lady Susan*.

Austen's deployment of famous names presupposes a celebrity culture, a phenomenon that scholars have now accepted as active in her time. Since Leo Braudy's book *The Frenzy of Renown: Fame and Its History* (1986), which surveyed fame as a historical constant from Alexander the Great to Marilyn Monroe, the history of celebrity culture has come under closer scrutiny by scholars. According to theater historians, the first generation of celebrities emerged in Britain in the 1660s, when actresses and mistresses orbiting the court of Charles II attained a star status that was aggressively promoted beyond their theatrical performances and public appearances.[9] This emergent celebrity culture was fully operational by the 1690s, with flamboyant portraits, especially those by Peter Lely, enjoying wide circulation as engravings. Additional printed fare, from naughty broadsheets to fully endorsed autobiographies, also fanned the flames of fame. Ambulance-chasing booksellers and publishers, including most famously the "unspeakable" Edmund Curll, spurred on a thriving print market for gossip in the popular press of the eighteenth century, exploiting, stimulating, and even creating the condition of being much talked of that is the defining feature of celebrity. True celebrity, as opposed to temporary notoriety or local fame, implies a far-reaching reputation, a condition that outpaces and outlasts local gossip. In his "Introduction" to *Romanticism and Celebrity Culture, 1750–1850*, Tom Mole contends that the Romantic period "witnessed a slow, diffuse, but significant shift in the nature of fame."[10] For the purposes of considering Austen's fascination with high-profile names, either of these new starting points for modern celebrity—whether 1660 or 1750—allows her access to an emergent multimedia phenomenon now hailed as celebrity culture. The "deep eighteenth century," as Joseph Roach labels this period of emergence, brought us the "it" factor.[11] I argue that Austen, in her choices of famous names and settings, dared to reference the "abnormally interesting people" of her past and present whom we now term celebrities.[12] Rather than eschew celebrity associations, Austen embraced memories conjured up by her redeployment of famous names, apparently delighting in upending and redirecting established associations. Most importantly, the enormous creative energies that, as I will show, Austen put into the siphoning off of celebrity appeal may reflect her authorial ambitions for the type of audience she wished to court with her fiction. As an artist, Austen seems to have been keen to prove her skill in terms of recognizable plays on the social field of her time.

If Austen's stories are a hybrid of fact and fiction, history and story, they may anticipate the work of Sir Walter Scott in ways not yet fully recognized. While scholars generally credit Sir Walter Scott with the invention of the so-called proper historical novel, Austen may, in her own unique manner, have pioneered a prototype. Large cultural debates about the nature of history at the turn of the century prepared readers for what Scott undertook with his brand of historical fiction. Similarly, Austen delicately crafted a hybrid of history and the novel, anticipating in a subtle way what Scott accomplished in a more direct, blunt manner. In his journal, Scott disparaged his own approach when comparing it to Austen's: "The Big Bow-wow strain I can do myself like any now going; but the exquisite touch which renders ordinary commonplace things and characters interesting from the truth of the description and the sentiment is denied to me."[13] Scott's self-deprecating comparison may tacitly acknowledge how Austen's work—with its shared allusions to, as I will show, England's medieval history and Yorkshire Wentworths—quietly mirrors his own historical mastiff.

No reader of this book can be more resistant to my approach than I was at the start of my project. As a student of the eighteenth century, I felt distracted while rereading Austen's novels by many bits of historical trivia, including parallels to famous eighteenth-century personages. At first I dismissed such echoes of my eighteenth-century interests as coincidences, forcing myself to put them aside as out of step with Austen's contemporary Regency world. For example, in the context of eighteenth-century studies, the mention of a rich Mr. Allen in Bath, the horticultural emphasis of a story called *Evelyn*, or the appearance of odious Dashwoods, whose misguided "improvements" to their landscape garden mark their villainy, all initiate associations with famous families from English history that I dutifully shook off. Eventually I began to question my repeated dismissals of such supposed historical coincidence: was my knowledge of the eighteenth century truly such a hindrance, or might it be a help? Only Greene, a fellow eighteenth-century scholar, treats such coincidences in Austen's names as genuine and serious historical references.

Yet Peter Knox-Shaw's recent book *Jane Austen and the Enlightenment* (2004) shows how much Austen absorbed of eighteenth-century literature and philosophy through her extensive reading. If, I asked myself, Jane Austen was a keen student of eighteenth-century culture, an amateur historian of a prior age as well as an acute observer of her present, might her references to an immediate past have gotten lost in the hyperspecialization of academic discourse, in which Austen—born in 1775, writing actively in the 1790s, and not published until 1811—is most often written about by experts specializing in nineteenth-century literature? Since Austen's fame lay relatively dormant until Richard Bentley reprinted her works in 1833 as part of his *Standard Novels* series, did the well-documented delay in her initial popularity muffle some of Austen's references by further widening the gap between her novels and the historical facts and events that she reworked? When the *Literary Gazette*, in response to Bentley's reissues, reviewed Austen's work in 1833, her stories were, as William Galperin observes, nostalgically lamented as "absolute historical pictures" of a bygone era.[14] If Austen already seemed that remote in 1833, might she be better understood in the context of the history and events of the late eighteenth century? My exploration of these questions, which challenge the temporal categories of my profession while also probing Jane Austen's historical method, generated this book.

Historicizing and Mapping Austen

Luckily, Austen scholarship has come a long way since 1917, when Reginald Farrer praised the "hermetically sealed" worlds of Austen's fictions as "always concerned only with the universal, and not with the particular." Austen, rejoiced Farrer, "can never be out of date, because she never was in any particular date."[15] Now, a century later, a thriving industry in the historicizing of Jane Austen exists—and along three dimensions: contextual reconstructions, editorial interventions, and theoretical historiographies. The first category includes the many fine scholarly works devoted to a range of important contextual topics, from landscape aesthetics and economics to turn-of-the-century consumer culture, the navy, and the theater—each providing a detailed historical context for a Regency view of Austen's works.[16] Collections such as *Jane Austen in Context* (2005) and *A Companion to Jane Austen* (2009) bundle scholarly essays on medicine, painting, architecture, clergy, food, education, money, rank, and politics—providing a panoramic historical context.[17] In the popular market, too, books such as *What Jane Austen Ate and Charles Dickens Knew: From Fox Hunting to Whist* respond to the general reader's desire to responsibly heed the Regency details of her novels.[18] To all this is almost-daily added historical data on the Web, where nothing is considered too insignificant for the true devotee—from recipes of the foods Austen ate to patterns for the dresses she wore and the quilt she helped to sew. No matter how focused or ambitious, these historical reconstructions are of a piece, sharing in the belief that a material and historical context of her time will illuminate or enrich an interpretation of Austen. That faith is most palpable in the village of Chawton itself, where the Jane Austen House Museum and the scholarly library at the recently restored Chawton House embody the historical and material impulse behind Austen studies.

As for historically responsible editing, Vivien Jones demonstrated in the notes and commentary to her Penguin edition of *Pride and Prejudice* just how far the editing of Austen had come by 1996. As she explains, prior generations of critical emphasis on the universality of Austen's themes, her so-called "timelessness," prevented annotation.[19] In the 1970s, fifty years after Chapman, Tony Tanner still argued that extensive notes were unnecessary since "references to topical events or other writers" "are almost totally suppressed" and "the overall impression given by the book is of a small section of society locked in an almost timeless present in which very little will or can change."[20] Tanner's edition offered only four explanatory notes to the whole of *Pride and Prejudice* under the auspices of tenderly preserving that transparency.

Jones, on the other hand, saw the need for historically informed annotations to unlock Austen's wit. In one such annotation, she identifies the "jokey" allusion to Sir Joshua Reynolds (1723–92), the era's greatest portraitist, in the name of the Pemberley housekeeper, Mrs. Reynolds, who takes the heroine on a tour of the estate's portrait "gallery."[21] While informative annotations have grown exponentially in modern editions, editors remain cautious about attaching historical allusions to Austen's choice of names. For example, although Paula Byrne convincingly evidences the contemporary stage pedigree of the names Crawford and Yates, thus showing how Austen flaunts her concrete theatrical knowledge in a novel that stages a play, these names are not glossed in subsequent editions of *Mansfield Park* as likely invoking famous actors.[22] John Wiltshire, for example, still maintains that Austen's reference to "Mr. Repton" in the same work is "a rare, though not unique, use of a historical person in [Austen's] novels."[23] Even the best of Austen's modern editors, in other words, remain hesitant about her ability to reference real people. This is understandable in light of an Austen family tradition that protested against the influences of specific personalities and people upon her work.

Mrs. Ann Barrett, who professed to have befriended Jane Austen during the Chawton years, famously recollected how the author resisted the easy identification of her characters with real people: "I am much too proud of my own gentlemen ever to admit that they are merely Mr A. or Major C."[24] Both the touch of pride and the telling "merely" in Austen's denial allow for a possible equivocation about a charge that Henry Austen feels compelled to defend his sister against in his biographical notice of 1817: "She drew from nature; but, whatever may have been surmised to the contrary, never from individuals" (*P*, 330). Although Jane prevaricates and Henry exaggerates, neither tells an outright lie—not exactly. Austen, who plucked so many of her character names from the ancestral trees of genuine families, was not satirizing "individuals" in the sense of describing particular people whom she knew or knew of, but building her stories out of names and locations that resonated with popular national and local history. Nonetheless, the subtlety of her historical process must have made it difficult, at a time when the Romantics so prized original genius, to stave off accusations of copying too much from life. Writing in the unique space between the immediacy of the satirical tell-all literature of the eighteenth century and the temporal remove made possible by the historical novel of the nineteenth, Jane Austen created, I hope to show, hyperrealistic, historically based fictions that combine elements of both types.

As a result of a scholarly reticence that has dutifully aligned itself with family tradition, local tracings of likely celebrity or historical personages remain scattered across scholarly articles on different Austen-related topics, rather than gathered together for a reader to judge her demonstrable and consistent historicism. Nonetheless, the increasing number of recent articles that place interpretive pressure on a leading name or identify a celebrity portrait in Austen's fictions suggest an emergent historicism in Austen studies.[25] Such sensitivity to historical resonances does not insist myopically upon her characters as "merely Mr A. or Major C." or deny Austen her artistry, as Henry feared. Austen certainly did not write mere romans à clef. The manner in which she folds the historical associations of her stories' settings into the minute realism for which she has long been famous merely widens the scope of her ambition, enhancing her extraordinary accomplishment and daring. I contend that part of her daring realism rests precisely upon her choices of historical names for her characters. While her family fearfully and repeatedly stressed how she wanted "to create not to reproduce," Austen as an artist may show herself at her most creative and ambitious as a historian-turned-novelist.[26]

Over the last fifteen years or so, fresh acknowledgments of Austen's historicism have begun to change the course of Austen studies. In 1998, Devoney Looser hailed a more historical turn in an essay entitled "Reading Jane Austen and Rewriting 'Herstory.' "[27] Celebrating (perhaps slightly prematurely) that "the critical heyday of Austen's ahistoricism is now happily behind us," Looser welcomed a new wave of criticism in which "Austen as a writer concerned with history has arrived."[28] Her own work does much to realize this promise, for Looser examines "how Austen positioned her texts in relation to historiographical trends and to historical novels," in order to reveal the gendered attitudes prevalent in Austen's day with regard to history's uneasy relationship to fiction.[29] Similarly, William Galperin, in *The Historical Austen* (2003), examines the historical mediation of her novels, even tendering a chapter on Austen as a "chronicler of the everyday" and a "historian" reacting to the shoplifting trial of her aunt.[30] Galperin vigilantly pivots between Austen's own historical impulses and those he identifies in readers who nostalgically consume her stories, mixing recorded responses to Austen with his assessment of the author's personal stance toward the past. He particularly attends to moments of fictional retrospection in light of the appreciative nostalgia for the world depicted in her stories. In their separate ways, Looser and Galperin each emphasize how the new "philosophical history" inaugurated by Robertson and Hume was of particular interest to Austen as a reader. Remarkably, both stay far clear of the events-based schoolbook history eschewed by Catherine Morland, probing Austen's novels not for historical personages or events but for larger historical gestures and sympathies.

Looking back on this same topic in 2009, Looser rightly assumes a tone of accomplishment: "Nowadays it may seem difficult to fathom, but Jane Austen was once branded an ahistorical writer."[31] This is because, in the wake of Looser and Galperin, others have taken to examining Austen "in reference to things that are old," in relation to "the past and its remembrance (or suppression)," and in light of "relics," both architectural and corporal, found in her stories.[32] Among the many critics examining Austen's views toward history and historical events, a few have begun to take note of historical allusions in her "choice of character names," observing, for example, how Sir Walter alludes to the Strafford family in *Persuasion*, while in *Emma* "the name Fairfax resonates of the civil war parliamentary commander, and in case we miss the point, her father turns out to be a valiant army officer."[33] Interestingly, however, even those who attend to Austen's historical sensitivity do not tend to see such leading names as evidence of a larger historical method. Daniel Woolf, for example, concludes that "Wentworths and Fairfaxes aside, her pages are not full of references to historical characters."[34] Yet a historical approach to Austen's choice of surnames may prove essential to a fuller understanding of the social and artistic implications of her work. Looser, too, laments that "even in *Northanger Abbey*, in which history is commented on directly as a written form . . . there are few explicit references to historical events."[35] I hope to lessen such critical disappointment by unearthing many more "explicit" historical allusions, tracing patterns among Austen's choices of names as well as settings that point to a sustained historical method.

When it comes to spotting patterns, Franco Moretti has brought the mapping of novels back into vogue with his *Atlas of the European Novel, 1800–1900* (1998). Although Moretti readily admits to his critics that his approach is "not really geography . . . but rather *geometry*," his spatial diagrams of the plots of nineteenth-century novels, including Austen's, have forced scholars to reconsider spatial practices in fiction.[36] While my own mapping method in this book is strictly geographical—using, for example, old maps of Bath and environs to track Austen's characters through the roads of *Northanger Abbey* as they appeared in 1803— Moretti's diagrammatic insights hold for my own approach: "Not that the map is itself an explanation, of course: but at least, it offers a model of the narrative universe which rearranges its components in a non-trivial way, and may bring some hidden patterns to the surface."[37] When applied to Austen, any insistence upon the importance of maps and spatial relationships resembles, surprisingly, the approach of her earliest editors. According to Kathryn Sutherland, Chapman assiduously mapped locations and dates in the novels, working through suggestions from Arthur Platt and Frank MacKinnon. Chapman's folder of *Emma* materials includes "a sketch in Platt's hand" of the major residences in the novel as well as calculations for distances, such as that between Highbury and the Kingston road.[38] In such a manner Chapman tracked carriage rides in *Emma* and penciled the places and street names mentioned in *Mansfield Park* on the back of a wartime list of British prisoners.[39]

Similarly, Vladimir Nabokov probed the minutely mapped surfaces of Austen's fiction in the 1950s. In the margins of his battered teaching copy of *Mansfield Park*, Nabokov observed Austen's handling of temporal and spatial distance. There and in his lecture notes, he drew charts, maps, and diagrams, made lists of dates and character names, and calculated distances, incomes, or ages from the numerical information provided by Austen. Guided by Austen's descriptions, he mapped the grounds at Sotherton Court, sketched a barouche to determine the spatial arrangements of the characters in a carriage, and laid out the rooms of Mansfield with architectural confidence. He also sketched maps of England, including a small one in the top corner of his copy's opening page, noting the locations of both real and imaginary places mentioned in the text, such as "Portsmouth," "Huntingdon," "Hampshire," "London," "MP." [40] Moretti-like, Nabokov triangulated the presumed location of Mansfield Park from the stated distances to real-world cities: "120 m" between MP and Portsmouth, "50" from Portsmouth to London, and "70 m" from London to MP. He calculated from specifics of the story that the year of the "main action" was "1808," explaining in his lecture how he arrived at this date: "The ball at Mansfield Park is held on Thursday the twenty-second of December, and if we look through our old calendars, we will see that only in 1808 could 22 December fall on Thursday."[41] As a committed lepidopterist and naturalist, Nabokov even underlined the varieties Austen assigned to her trees, annotating in pen, then pencil, the scattered references to fruits, plants, and landscape features.[42] Nabokov's annotations may be deeply personal, marking his peculiar interests and curiosities as a fellow artist, but their quantity insists upon his professional assessment that all her details are meaningful. In light of Chapman, Nabokov, and Moretti, my own use of maps to reveal patterns in Austen's art is, admittedly, not entirely new. What I offer is a synthesis of the individual conversations currently emerging about early celebrity culture, about mapping novels, and about Austen's profound interest in history—conversations that have not yet had a chance to fully engage with one another's findings.

Two critics whose major contributions to the recovery of a historical Austen should not be overlooked are Marilyn Butler and Roger Sales. Butler's *Jane Austen and the War of Ideas* was, in 1975, a timely and necessary jolt to the entrenched view of Austen as a sheltered reader and myopic thinker. With feminist rhetoric that sharply diverges from Greene's conservative historicism, Butler similarly challenged the cloistered view of Austen, providing a larger ideological context for her novels. Butler's argument that Austen, too, should be read in the context of the age's political polemics against the excesses of Revolutionary and Napoleonic France made her book a landmark in Austen criticism. Nearly twenty years later, in *Jane Austen and Representations of Regency England* (1994), Roger Sales builds upon Butler's ambitious argument to protest, yet again, the continued scholarly pinioning and Victorian whitewashing of Austen. Sales insists upon Austen's open rather than clandestine engagement with, in particular, Regency presentations of masculinity, dandyism, and sexuality. Sales's account of the Regency crisis as a time uniquely troubled by uncertainties—generated by royal scandal and disease, celebrity affairs, healthcare restructuring, and wartime violations of local rule—paints a more complex and gritty picture of Austen's Regency world than seemed previously imaginable. Sales also insists upon Austen's knowledge of specific celebrities, including some who were discussed for their vices rather than their virtues.

Finally, still another valuable source on history, celebrity, and Jane Austen is the recent body of work on the cult of Jane herself. Since 2000, a number of books have examined the rise of Austen's popularity, the history of her scholarship, and the historically determined perceptions of her.[43] What I learned from the books that seize upon our modern cultural assessment of Jane Austen and *her* historical place in literary history confirmed my belief in reading and writing as historically determined acts. This, in turn, added to my growing sense of her fictions as similarly influenced by the historical pressures of her own time. After all, the dominant culture of celebrity that produced these books was firmly, if newly, in place when Austen wrote—even if the readership that awards Jane Austen superstar status and tirelessly tracks her biography does not always recognize that she, too, may have enjoyed reading about famous people.

Habits of Mind

If many of the names of Austen's fictional characters invoke famous families and their histories, this demands a habit of mind. Might this then also be visible in her letters? Unfortunately, if Jane Austen's letters ever contained references to the high-profile families whose names she borrowed for her fictions, Cassandra surely burned them in the purge that left posterity with a censored and narrow cache of correspondence. Although surviving letters cannot, therefore, be expected to contain celebrity gossip, I believe they do, obliquely, support the idea that Austen would be likely to invest her fictional names with allusive importance, since they show how she habitually scrutinized the names of those around her for suggestive combinations. Already in her very first surviving letter, written in January 1796, when Jane was twenty-one, she finds humor and significance in a name: "What a funny name Tom has got for his vessel! But he has no taste in names, as we well know, and I dare say he christened it himself" (*Letters*, 2). That ship was the *Ponsborne*, in which Cassandra's fiancé, the Rev. Tom Fowle, was about to depart for the West India campaign with Lord Craven. In response to Cassandra's likely anxiety about the long voyage and campaign ahead—and indeed the sad news of Tom's death at St. Domingo would come in the spring of 1798—Jane resorts to characteristic humor to put her older sister at ease.[44]

Family witticisms about names occur frequently in the letters. For instance, in a breezy letter to Cassandra, written in January of 1801, Jane muses on the expectation of promotions for their sailor-brothers Frank, awaiting transfer to another ship, and Charles, an officer on the *Endymion*: "Eliza talks of having read in a Newspaper that all the 1st Lieut:^{s} of the Frigates whose Captains were to be sent into Line-of-Battle ships, were to be promoted to the rank of Commander—. If it be true, Mr Valentine may afford himself a fine Valentine's knot, & Charles may perhaps become 1st of the Endymion" (*Letters*, 75). Mr. David Valentine was then first lieutenant on the *Endymion*. Since a "Valentine's knot" is a colloquial euphemism for a wedding, Austen plays off the idea that a promotion to commander might enable or inspire Mr. Valentine to marry and leave his post conveniently vacant for Charles. Similar wordplay occurs in a subsequent letter, when Austen complains about the dye of several new and refurbished gowns, lashing out at a Southampton tradesman with a jibe on his name: "As for Mr Floor, he is at present rather low in our estimation; how is your blue gown?—Mine is all to peices.—I think there must have been something wrong in the dye, for in places it divided with a Touch.—There was four shillings thrown away" (*Letters*, 143). The low blow at Mr. Floor resembles the bons mots in "Love and Freindship," that earlier piece of absurdist comedy written at age fourteen. As Peter Sabor observes, Austen puns there on the "staves" of a barrel as akin to the stays of a woman's corset when she invents "Gregory Staves a Staymaker" (*J*, 138 and 443).

Name and word games were popular in the Austen household. The correspondence comments on guessing baby names ("My Mother was some time guessing the names") and mentions passing the time devising "riddles" and "conundrums" for her young nephews (*Letters*, 139–40 and 150).[45] Even as an adult, Jane continued to exchange charades and word puzzles with Cassandra. When she writes to Crosby & Company in the spring of 1809 to complain of their not having followed through on the publication of her manuscript *Susan*, she picks the penname "M^rs. Ashton Dennis" so that she can defiantly close her letter with a play on her false initials: "I am Gentlemen, &c &c/ MAD" (174). Conversely, her poem "On the marriage of Mr. Gell of East Bourn to Miss Gill" takes delight in a ceremony that will alter only the vowel of the woman's surname (*LM*, 253). A genuinely clever pun makes explanation redundant. Although Jane's first surviving letter conveniently quips "what a funny name," we cannot expect all her name play to be as blatantly glossed. Sometimes, therefore, it is impossible to know for certain if the joke is implied or accidental: "Sweet Mr Ogle. I dare say he sees all the Panoramas for nothing" (*Letters*, 248).

It is revealing of Austen's habits of mind that, in two cases of self-conscious riffing on the names of those around her, she immediately shifts to thinking about her own fictions, as if such name games bring to mind her own modus operandi as author. Take for example, the letter in which Jane plays with the name of Knight and wonders about a new novel by Mary Brunton: "It gives me sincere pleasure to hear of Mrs Knight's having had a tolerable night at last—but upon this occasion I wish she had another name, for the two *Nights* jingle very much.—We have tried to get Self-controul, but in vain.—I *should* like to know what her Estimate is—but am always half afraid of finding a clever novel *too clever*—& of finding my own story & my own people all forestalled" (*Letters*, 186). The sequence of ideas hints at a possible connection between the act of playing on a person's name and Austen's nagging fear that her novels will not be deemed original enough. Had she perhaps heard how a character named Mr. Wentworth appears in *Self-Control* (1811)? Was that, too, part of the reason she worried about "finding my own story & my own people all forestalled" in a "clever novel" like Brunton's?[46] A similar progression recurs just after the publication of *Pride and Prejudice*, when, in writing to Cassandra of the new governess employed by their brother Edward, she follows a pun with the decision to reveal her authorship to their niece Anna:

Miss Clewes seems the very Governess they have been looking for these ten years;—longer coming than J. Bond's last Shock of Corn.—If she will but only keep Good & Amiable & Perfect!—Clewes & [sic] is better than Clowes.—And is not it a name for Edward to pun on?—is not Clew a Nail?—Yes, I beleive I *shall* tell Anna—& if you see her, & donot dislike the commission, you may tell her for me. (*Letters*, 205)[47]

Even if the gap between the governess's name and her own anonymity is not bridged by punning, that Austen scrutinized even ordinary names for linguistic quirks and associations, a family habit apparently shared by Edward, cannot be doubted. Even cousin Eliza shared in this family trait: "I saw in the Papers this very Morning that one of Mrs. Wynch's Sons is Married to Miss Perfect of West Malling—[I ho]pe the Lady does justice to her name."[48]

Often, too, when Jane Austen writes about other people's fictions she comments upon invented names. For instance, her exchange with Cassandra about Hannah More's novel *Coelebs in Search of a Wife* (1809) delineates her own preference for the unpretentious name:

> I am not at all ashamed about the name of the Novel, having been guilty of no insult towards your handwriting; the Dipthong I always saw, but knowing how fond you were of adding a vowel wherever you could, I attributed it to that alone—& the knowledge of the truth does the book no service;—the only merit it could have, was in the name of Caleb, which has an honest, unpretending sound; but in Coelebs, there is pedantry & affectation.—Is it written only to Classical Scholars? (*Letters*, 172)

Typically again, after reviewing and annotating Anna Austen's literary manuscript, she similarly comments on that author's choice of names and their implications. "Lesley *is* a noble name," Austen writes, "but the name of Rachael is as much as I can bear" (*Letters*, 275 and 276).[49] Another one of Anna's names is singled out for praise: "The name of Newton-Priors is really invaluable!—I never met with anything superior to it.—It is delightful.—One could live upon the name of Newton-Priors for a twelve-month.—Indeed, I do think you get on very fast" (284). She even dismisses the criticism of others about Anna's work as insensitivity to her choices of names and what they signal: "We have no great right to wonder at his not valueing the name of Progillian. *That* is a source of delight which he hardly ever can be quite competent to" (277). Even though Jane Austen's true opinion of Anna's literary efforts remains obscured by irony, in reading works by others she scanned the names of characters for creativity, meaning, and "delight." If this was her habit, might she not have hoped that her readers would do the same?

Maggie Lane, author of *Jane Austen and Names* (2002), a booklet devoted to the Christian names found in the later novels, has suggested that Austen, like any parent, picked even first names for her creations based on their accumulation of cultural associations.[50] John Wiltshire at first disagrees, arguing that "nothing in particular attaches to a first name in Jane Austen."[51] He urges that what Lane calls Austen's "limited palette" of first names simply reflects customary English practices.[52] Nonetheless, even Wiltshire makes exceptions, insisting that in the case of *Mansfield Park* the name of Edmund "may have special significance" after all.[53] Thus critics and readers oscillate between wanting to invest interpretive significance in a particular Austen name and fearing that such investment runs counter to the nature of her realist art.

This critical unease recently met with another strong challenge as regards the names and historical puns in the juvenilia, particularly the "The History of England," which was written, scholars agree, when Austen was fifteen. Recognizing that "a preoccupation with wordplay and hidden meanings is a recurring feature," Annette Upfal suggests that the portraits which Cassandra drew into her sister's historical satire are encoded with veiled meaning.[54] In their edition of "The History of England" for the Juvenilia Press (2009), Christine Alexander and Upfal expand upon the claims of Jan Fergus, who initially suggested in 1995 that a few of Cassandra's small oval miniatures might resemble members of the Austen family. In this manner, Cassandra may not only mock the impoverished style of illustration found in Goldsmith's *History*, her sister's acknowledged satirical target, but may do so by depicting real people in the Austen circle.

Upfal and Alexander support their thesis, which claims resemblances for all of Cassandra's illustrations, with computer imposition of extant family silhouettes and portraits upon Cassandra's drawings. Based on these comparisons, they argue that Austen's summary discussion of kings and queens was comically interpolated with recognizable portraits of namesakes: brothers Edward, Henry, and James Austen, for example, stand in for Edward VI, Henry V, and James I, respectively. Similarly, cousins Mary Lloyd and Edward Cooper may have served Cassandra as models for Mary I and Edward IV. Where first names are not a match for the collaborating sisters to pun on, resemblance alone must argue for an encoded family reference. Upfal and Alexander insist that this is so with the images of Mary, Queen of Scots, and Elizabeth I, which they match to the profiles and portraits of young Jane and her mother. Upfal overreaches when she assigns "brutal" intent behind a Schiller-like juxtaposition of a sympathetic portrait of Jane as Mary with "the hostile image" of "Mrs. Austen caricatured as Elizabeth, her evil foe and persecutor," ignoring how Jane's tendency toward irony might imply precisely the opposite.[55] Irrecoverable family dynamics aside, Upfal and Alexander's imposition of real portraits upon those drawn into the story unearths a family habit of layering English historical figures upon the present. I trace in Jane Austen's fictions this selfsame habit of historical imposition with words, although I consistently stress the public, rather than private, meanings resulting from her reworkings of "real solemn history" in her stories.

Private Family History

Although I fault some biographical criticism for cordoning off the meaning of Austen's art, I readily confess to exploring her life for contact points with famous personages and distant locales—even those she is not known to have visited. With certain locations, such as Bath and Lyme, I stress her personal knowledge of a place and its history. As Park Honan remarks of Austen's early time in Bath, house hunters and visitors notice things that may go unobserved by long-time residents.[56] Her own travels, as Honan reasons, inspired her talent for description. Whenever biography does not place her in a setting or landscape, family history often does. As Greene pointed out for the Yorkshire Wentworths, distant family connections link Jane Austen "through the Leighs and Cravens" to the Fitzwilliams and the Wentworths (Greene, 1019). Even such "remote connections" may have given Austen a personal reason to interest herself in certain famous families (1019). In the case of the infamous Sir Francis Dashwood, whom I discuss in the context of *Sense and Sensibility* in Chapter 5, his sister Rachel married Robert Austen of Kent, a distant relation of the Austens. Similarly, Ralph Allen's building projects in Bath (discussed in Chapter 2) intersected with the investment schemes of Mrs. Austen's great-uncle the Duke of Chandos. In such cases, too, Jane Austen may have so valued her small personal stake in another family's history that these connections did not appear so very "remote."

As Greene explains for the Wentworths of Wentworth Woodhouse, Jane Austen's mother's family, the Leighs of Adlestrop, were a collateral branch of the Leighs of Stoneleigh, occasionally dubbed "loyal Leighs" and ennobled for their part in the Royalist cause during the Civil War. The Leighs thus could imagine themselves as having partly avenged the death of Thomas Wentworth, the original Earl of Strafford. In addition to sharing the Royalist politics of Wentworth Woodhouse, the Leighs were connected by marriage to its Watson branch through Eleanor Watson, sister to Thomas Watson Wentworth, the first of the Watsons to inherit the vast estate. Eleanor Watson, daughter of Anne Wentworth and Lord Rockingham, married a Lord Leigh of Stoneleigh. Jane Austen visited the "almost impossibly grand house" of Stoneleigh Abbey with her mother and sister in July of 1806.[57] "Stoneleigh appealed," writes Park Honan, "to her sense of history and continuance." In light of Austen's confident fictional descriptions of a wide variety of estates and her modest knowledge of such places through her extensive reading, it may be an overstatement to claim, as does Honan, that Stoneleigh was "the only house on the grandest English scale that she could feel connected with." Yet, he is surely right to notice how "along with Godmersham Park it was a main source for her ample fictional mansions."[58] Fresh from their years of renting in Bath and facing an uncertain and threadbare future, the Austen women must have been wide-eyed before the opulent galleries of inner rooms displaying "ancestors in their ornate frames against dark paneling."[59] Although, according to family lore, she had already begun *The Watsons* and may have finished her fair copy of *Lady Susan* as early as its 1805 watermark allows, Jane Austen had yet to write her other novels starring characters whose names seem similarly plucked from the ancestral galleries of great estates. Surely the visit to Stoneleigh heightened her interest in the grandeur and history of such places.

The unplanned stay at Stoneleigh in July of 1806 arose from much talk of family trees and lineage, which, irrespective of personal connections, may have fed Austen's interest in genealogy and history more generally. When the Austen women arrived at Adlestrop, in Gloucester, to visit Mrs. Austen's first cousin, the Rev. Thomas Leigh, they heard of the death of their relative the Hon. Mary Leigh, a life tenant of Stoneleigh Abbey for twenty years who had never married. With her death, the Stoneleigh branch died out and, since various other Leighs in their own Adlestrop branch of the family had also passed away, Thomas Leigh thought himself the legal owner of Stoneleigh. "Advised to take possession quickly, he persuaded the Austens to accompany him into Warwickshire."[60] Under the provisions of an ambiguous will left by the last Lord Leigh, Mrs. Austen also hoped that her brother, Mr. James Leigh Perrot, might gain a life interest in the estate. In other words, the grand portrait gallery of Stoneleigh seemed about to make room for Jane's uncles and cousins. As Greene remarks, "the unusual terms of the last Lord Leigh's will caused a great deal of searching of pedigrees before it could be decided which member of the Leigh family was heir to Stoneleigh" (Greene, 1019–20). Ultimately, Stoneleigh did fall to Thomas Leigh, after extensive discussion of family trees in which the Watson-Wentworth connection must have featured. These discussions of the Leigh family tree in 1806 were also surely not the first time that Mrs. Austen spoke to her daughters about their ancestry.

Sir Samuel Egerton Brydges provides the most extreme case of pedigree-searching in the Austen circle, especially for his claims on the Chandos peerage. Mrs. Austen's great uncle, James Brydges, was created the first Duke of Chandos in 1719. The duke had married Cassandra Willoughby, which may explain the profusion of Cassandras among their descendants in the Leigh family, as well as young Jane Austen's interest in the Willoughby name. The Chandos peerage officially became extinct in 1789, but Egerton Brydges "fought an epic battle to establish the claim to it," on behalf of first his elder brother and then himself (Greene, 1020). Although Egerton Brydges officially lost this fight when the case was decided against him in 1803 in the House of Lords, he continued through to 1834 to style himself "Baron Chandos of Sudeley," an affectation known to Jane Austen (1020). As Greene points out, Jane Austen's early awareness of Egerton Brydges and his genealogical combat is virtually assured by the fact that he was the brother of Mrs. Lefroy, born Anne Brydges—Jane Austen's principal friend and neighbor during the years at Steventon. Indeed, Egerton Brydges developed such an interest in the genealogy of the peerage that in 1808 he extensively revised and edited the "standard edition" of Arthur Collins's *The Peerage of England*. Greene remarks of Collins, the original compiler of the eight-volume *Peerage*, how "No one ever loved a lord more" (1021). But Egerton Brydges, by all accounts, was a match for Collins in his tireless and tiresome devotion to the filigreed detailing of the peerage. Greene observes how in a letter of 1798 Jane Austen already belittles "Egerton's" style as vacuous, remarking that she was spared disappointment because, unlike her father, she "expected nothing better" (*Letters*, 22). The name of Austen's obsequious Mr. Collins in *Pride and Prejudice*, a straightforward allusion to the newly reedited *Peerage* of 1808, probably mocks her own would-be relative's genealogical obsession.

Austen's choice of name for her most fusty example of snobbery, Lady Catherine de Bourgh, suggests a comical association with Egerton Brydges, calculated to keep herself at an ironic distance from such sycophantic men. The name of de Bourgh may poke fun at the privilege of the nobility from within, for, as Collins informs readers of his *Peerage*, the name Brydges was "anciently written Brugge, Bruges, Burgh, Brigge, &c."[61] Egerton Brydges himself claimed that his "male stock" was "baronial from the Conquest; ascending . . . to Johannes De Burgo (Monoculu), founder also of the House of De Burgh."[62] Thus, Austen's own relations claimed a kind of de Bourgh pedigree. If Austen's critical portrait of the obnoxious Lady Catherine de Bourgh targets Mrs. Lefroy's brother and his supercilious insistence to all who would listen that his ancestors came from the grand house of De Burgh, such an allusion was a dangerous game for a single woman whose own future in 1813 depended largely upon her family's good will and its network of "high" connections. Do other names in Austen incur such personal risk?

Reading Jane Austen like James Joyce

A borrowed name risks looking like a pun, especially when the author plays with the frisson between a new identity and the old. Lest anyone dismiss Austen's sport with historical names as a mere game, I would like to point out that her fondness for puns and suggestive names was shared by lightweights such as Shakespeare and Joyce. Samuel Johnson observed of Shakespeare's puns that even "a quibble, poor and barren, gave him such delight that he was content to purchase it by the sacrifice of reason, propriety, and truth."[63] Austen never sacrifices verisimilitude to a clever pun or historical allusion. I believe that, instead, a major part of her realism resides in the names and facts that she lifts from history. To make use of a name from a legend, newspaper, or printed book for one's fiction is surely a different authorial gesture from assigning characters the names of relatives and friends, as Austen's biographers believe she did.

James Joyce, for instance, unabashedly consulted city directories and encyclopedias, a habit that enhanced his powerful reputation as a strategic rewriter and cunning punster. His puns on names do not appear to cause any critical embarrassment—quite the contrary. Stuart Gilbert, for example, in his diary entry for 1 January 1930 approvingly recording how Joyce composed *Finnegans Wake*, or what was then called *Work in Progress*:

> At last J. J. has recommenced work on W. in P. Five volumes of the
> Encyclopedia Brit. on his sofa. He has made a list of 30 towns, New

York, Vienna, Budapest. . . . Whenever I come to a name (of a street, suburb, park, etc.) I pause. J. thinks. If he can Anglicise the word, i.e., make a pun on it . . . the name or its deformation [are recorded] in the notebook. Thus 'Slotspark' (I think) at Christiana becomes Sluts' park. He collects all queer names in this way and will soon have a notebook full of them.[64]

Just as acceptable, surely, is the parallel vision of Jane Austen, surrounded not merely by copies of the *Baronetage* and *Peerage* but also by works such as Repton's *Observations* (with its great list of famous patrons), contemporary biographies and histories, or an atlas and a newspaper or two, busily constructing lists of names that she could, as Joyce would, put into play in her fictions. But scholars deal in facts, not visions. Nor can they look to any single publication or print relic as a proposed key to all Austen mythologies. I therefore attempt to substantiate in every chapter the manner in which Austen might have learned of the historical information invoked by a particular name or setting. At times, this print trail leads to a modest expansion of the materials Austen is assumed to have read.

Joyce's Trieste library is a much-prized resource at the Harry Ransom Research Center. While a parallel collection of Austen's books does not survive (she sold her books at auction prior to the move to Bath[65]), scholars have long assumed her voracious reading habits, constructing likely reading lists from her literary allusions and the many books and authors mentioned in her letters. A few association copies and even a handful of books with her marginalia survive.[66] Jane Austen's annotations to her brother James's copy of Oliver Goldsmith's *History of England* (1771) in four volumes, in particular, have long given rise to specific claims about her politics and historical savvy.[67] In addition, Jane Austen herself counted "500 Volumes" in her father's teaching library at Steventon in January 1801.[68] Because the advertisement, found by Robin Vick, mentions only "200 volumes of Books" sold from the Steventon parsonage a few months later, many books may have been retained in the move to Bath—with her brother James possibly keeping a share when he took over the parsonage.[69] Even after shifting to Chawton cottage in July 1809, where she had access to her brother Edward's library, Austen joined a local book club and "gloried in its eclectic stock."[70] Based upon this evidence of access to a wide range of books, Jane Austen's healthy knowledge of history is gaining acceptance.[71]

To all this, we can now add the more than a thousand titles in the *Godmersham Park Library Catalogue*.[72] The relatively recent availability of this inventory, on loan to the Chawton House Library, has extended the list of specific books to which Austen likely had access. *Godmersham Park Library Catalogue* newly provides Austen scholars with data about specific authors and editions in her environs—supporting with specific titles our growing appreciations of her knowledge of history. Although it is not considered an exhaustive inventory of the Knight family library in Kent during Austen's lifetime (it is presumed to have been compiled in the 1860s), it is the only such surviving list of specific Austen-circle holdings. The catalogue is, of course, more barometer than proof. It reflects family interests on certain topics, rather than proffering a key specific to Austen—since a book's mere presence among the inventory cannot guarantee that she read it. Yet the Godmersham library's wide holdings in histories of all sorts—ancient and modern, national and local, biographical and geographical, naval and parliamentary—surely expand the measure of history that Austen might possibly have known, read, or heard about. Incidentally, the catalog lists surprisingly little fiction. Austen possibly consulted many of these books during her visits to Godmersham Park, where she relished that library's "quiet."[73] In the following chapters, I do gesture to specific Godmersham titles. Even where individual books cannot offer proof, the sheer number of titles in the Godmersham catalog on historical subjects, on travel in England, on landscape gardening, on national antiquities, on naval voyages and admirals, and on the lives of famous and "illustrious" persons consistently reinforces my local assertions about Austen's probable knowledge of British history, famous locations, and celebrity culture.

I argue that Jane Austen, like Joyce, not only *names* her fictional characters with uncanny historical precision but *maps* them with equal care through historical settings. In her advice to Anna Lefroy, Austen states that location is another key consideration for the novelist: "Lyme will not do. Lyme is towards 40 miles distance from Dawlish & would not be talked of there" (*Letters* 268). In this same letter, dated 10–18 August 1814, she approvingly comments that "Russel Square is a very proper distance from Berkeley S^t" but warns: "Better not leave England. Let the Portmans go to Ireland, but as you know nothing of the Manners there, you had better not go with them. You will be in danger of giving false representations. Stick to Bath" (269). In a follow-up letter, Austen assumes that even Anna's fictional locations are modeled upon real places:

"Is not the Cottage taken from Tollard Royal?" (276). In her poetry, too, Austen charts journeys through real-world settings with astonishing accuracy, as Janet Todd and Linda Bree point out in their notes to "See they come," a poem written in 1806 to celebrate the marriage of Frank Austen to Mary Gibson.[74]

Just as *Thom's* directory was famously indispensable to Joyce in recreating the layout of the streets and environs of 1904 Dublin when he lived in Paris, because it allowed him to check the accuracy of his memory as well as invent with authority, so too did Austen have at her disposal publications that could have helped hone her accuracy about setting. John Cary's *New Itinerary* (1798), for example, indexed distances, locales, inns, and roads—a veritable Google Maps of Austen's day.[75] A slightly older version, *Cary's New and Correct English Atlas: Being a New Set of County Maps from Actual Surveys* (1787), is listed among the Godmersham inventory.[76] When it came to tracking the residences of aristocratic families, the 1780s and '90s saw cheap directories such as *The Treble Almanack*, which listed addresses for hotels and surgeons along with the homes of the rich and famous, giving columns for their "*Town Residence*" and "*Prim.[ary] Country Residence*." For example, one 1786 almanac lists "William Wentworth, | Strafford, [V. Wentworth] | 1711 | St. James's-square, | Wentworth Castle, *Yorksh*."[77] The existence and format of such almanacs also confirms that Austen was by no means singular in her attentions to aristocratic celebrity. In addition to being able to consult maps of England in the form of books, almanacs, and atlases in private and public libraries, Austen might also have relied upon loose printed maps, toll scarves, or popular souvenir charts, as well as her own limited experience traveling through many of the southern counties, where most of her fictions are set.[78]

When Austen was uncertain, she asked others to fact-check locations—just as Joyce would. For example, while composing *Mansfield Park*, she prodded Cassandra to do some reconnoitering on her travels: "If you c^d discover whether Northamptonshire is a Country of Hedgerows, I sh^d be glad again."[79] Austen's request tantalizingly resembles James Joyce's question to a Dublin aunt in a letter from Paris, written while he was finishing *Ulysses*: "Is it possible for an ordinary person to climb over the area railing of no 7 Eccles street, either from the path or steps, lower himself down from the lowest part of the railing till his feet are within 2 feet or 3 of the ground and drop unhurt? I saw it done myself by a man of rather athletic build. I require this information in detail in order to determine the wording of a paragraph."[80] David Lodge drew on this same letter to exemplify novelistic methodology, observing that just as Samuel Richardson worried that his characters "do too much in the time" and Henry Fielding consulted almanacs for 1745 when writing *Tom Jones*—just so does the modernist, who "moves cautiously from the real to the fictional world, and takes great pains to conceal the movement."[81] Virginia Woolf's famous dictum that Jane Austen is of all great writers the hardest to catch in the act of greatness conveys just how perfectly Austen hides her art inside the glassy, unrippled realism of her novels. In the 1830s, another fellow novelist, Thomas Lister, had already remarked that Austen was "too natural" for the critics: "They did not consider that the highest triumph of art consists in its concealment; and here the art was so little perceptible that they believed there was none."[82] I hope that this book exposes some of Austen's hidden artistry.

Austen's historical approach to writing, tracked in my own book through her choices of surnames and settings, defies a neatly compartmentalized argument. As shown in her long-standing fascination with the Yorkshire Wentworths, Austen's interests in historical families and locations often spanned decades, leaving their marks upon a number of her works drafted and revised in overlapping ways. As much as possible, I have nonetheless tried to cluster Austen's historical interests to conform to the dominant custom of discussing her novels individually. However, my discussion of Austen's major novels cannot offer balance: with one chapter attentive to *Lady Susan*, two chapters on *Northanger Abbey*, and one each on *Evelyn*, *Sense and Sensibility*, and *Persuasion*, I leave several of Austen's major novels relatively unexplored. While I am convinced that *Emma*, *Pride and Prejudice*, and *Mansfield Park* would benefit from the same approach—indeed, the names of their protagonists readily yoke to the history of the Wentworth family—a single study cannot exhaust all of the historical references and topographical clues found in Austen's oeuvre. Rather than attempt to voice the final word on Austen's fact-infused fiction, I hope that the following case studies and clusters will begin to deepen an appreciation of Austen as a local and national historian, leading to additional explorations by others.

With these caveats in place, I begin the next chapter by expanding upon Donald Greene's initial insights into the Wentworth line of names. Greene's crisply political characterization of Austen's interest in the Whig side of the Wentworth family from Wentworth Woodhouse ignores their Tory cousins at nearby Wentworth Castle, a branch whose history may help date the contested composition of *Lady Susan*. In the two chapters that follow I show how contemporary maps of Bath can expose the historical allusions behind Austen's precisely timed routes for characters in *Northanger Abbey*. These local rereadings suggest further similarities between Austen's method and that of the modernist James Joyce. Scholars take James Joyce's boast that turn-of-the century Dublin might forever be reconstructed from the details in his *Ulysses* extremely seriously—more seriously, it is certain, than anyone takes the descriptions of Bath in Austen's *Northanger Abbey*, written a century earlier. Joyce also bragged that the puzzles of *Ulysses* would keep scholars scrambling for centuries. Given Austen's similar penchant for wordplay, historical accuracy, and cartographic precision, scholars may be even further behind schedule on solving her puzzles—even as we celebrate the two-hundredth anniversary of Austen's initial publications.

CHAPTER ONE

"Quite unconnected"

The Wentworths and *Lady Susan*

JANE AUSTEN ASKS one of her most sycophantic and unreliable characters to inoculate her against celebrity culture. In her own era, the name of Wentworth was so famous that its mere mention enabled, as one eighteenth-century newspaper columnist put it, "Admission to the Intimacy of the Great." Knowing, as she must have, that any astute reader would connect the hero of *Persuasion* with the Wentworth family, she disclaims. She has Sir Walter Elliot sneeringly dismiss any link between Capt. Frederick Wentworth, the story's self-made naval officer, and the highborn Wentworths from Yorkshire, who held titles such as the Earl of Strafford: "Mr. Wentworth was nobody, I remember, quite unconnected; nothing to do with the Strafford family. One wonders how the names of many of our nobility become so common" (*P*, 26). By placing the requisite disclaimer in the mouth of Sir Walter, however, Austen keeps her own tongue firmly in her cheek. Sir Walter is notoriously unreliable— a narcissistic fop who lacks judgment. Despite, or perhaps because of, Sir Walter's blunt assertion, the name of Wentworth so flagrantly invites contemporary associations that the upending of those expectations becomes part of the story's appeal. When Austen names her landless sailor for one of the nation's most prominent landholding families since 1066, she winks knowingly at her reader.

Donald Greene accurately ascertained the irony behind Sir Walter's sneer. He traced the additional names of Fitzwilliam, Darcy, Woodhouse, and Watson to occupants of Wentworth Woodhouse in Yorkshire, showing how Austen repeatedly borrows for her protagonists' surnames fraught with Wentworth clout. His tracings of the prominent appearances of so many Wentworth-related names across Austen's works demonstrates what must have been all too obvious in Austen's day. Greene focuses in particular on the politics of *Pride and Prejudice*, where the hero's name, Fitzwilliam Darcy, amalgamates two branches of the Wentworth family of Whigs. Although his findings offer important insights into Austen's method and political savvy, Greene found only half of her Wentworth-family references—only those from the Whig side. He omitted to take into account their Tory cousins at nearby Wentworth Castle, in whom I argue Austen was just as keenly interested. When modern critics, most notably Patrick Parrinder, redeploy Greene's findings, they also therefore see only "the strong Whig associations" of "Austen's names."[1]

This chapter reconstructs Jane Austen not only as someone informed by contemporary celebrity culture but also as an author promiscuous in her borrowings across the political spectrum. It redirects Greene's argument, outlining the neglected history of the Tory families at Wentworth Castle and tracing that history's impact on a few of Austen's fictions. When Austen wrote *Persuasion*, the last three Wentworth men to carry the title Earl of Strafford, a title that had died out in 1799, were all Tories residing at Wentworth Castle (not at Wentworth Woodhouse). The name of the last and most recent Earl of Strafford—and there lies the true rub of Sir Walter's remark—was Frederick Wentworth. In addition to resonating with the story of *Persuasion*, which celebrates a fictional Frederick Wentworth's rise from obscurity, specific moments in the history of Wentworth Castle may also inform squabbles among Vernons over a family castle in *Lady Susan*. In real life the Vernon branch of the Wentworth family inherited Wentworth Castle in 1803, after a confused legal fracas that followed the death of Frederick Wentworth, third Earl of Strafford. Suggestive parallels between Wentworth Castle fact and Austen's Vernon-centered fiction may even pinpoint a date for the contested composition of *Lady Susan*.

The century-long rivalry between the Tory and Whig sides of the high-profile Wentworths had finally abated when Austen wrote *Persuasion*, itself an investigation of family dynamics and dynasties. Starting in the 1710s, the nation had closely watched Tory and Whig cousins vent their political spleen on the battleground of their landscaped gardens, where increasingly elaborate structures took part in an escalating game of architectural one-upmanship reported on by almost every travel writer and aesthetician who visited Yorkshire. Just such unique and unhappy family tension makes, as Tolstoy famously remarked, for the type of fraught dynamic that intrigues the novelist. The Tory branch of the Wentworths, resentful at not inheriting the family estate at Wentworth Woodhouse in 1695, purchased nearby Stainborough Hall in 1708. Decades of "improvements" turned this park and residence, which in 1731 was rechristened Wentworth Castle to denigrate the mere House of their Whig cousins, into a model landscape garden. Horace Walpole hailed the house itself as representing "the most perfect taste in architecture"[2] (fig. 1.1). Major renovations to the Wentworth Castle estate were duly answered with elaborate improvements to nearby Wentworth Woodhouse, shaping English garden design through one family's political rivalry[3] (fig. 1.2). The competitive landscaping at these neighboring estates, the bulk of which took place between 1710 and 1790, was a prolonged endeavor that occurred on a grand scale and in the national spotlight. And while the Whig branch of this family did indeed dominate contemporary political debates during that time, their celebrity cousins at Wentworth Castle remained makers of manners in their own right well into Austen's adulthood. It was in 1791, when Austen was in her teens, that the Wentworth Castle estate and titles were inherited by an obscure gentleman from Dorset named Frederick Wentworth. When she reached her late twenties, it became the property of young Frederick Vernon, after a heated Wentworth family dispute. The historical circumstances surrounding this contested transfer of Wentworth wealth resemble those in *Lady Susan*, which features at least two characters named Frederic Vernon as well as a dispute over a family castle.

Only an expanded Wentworth context—including travel guides, books on landscape gardening, the society pages of contemporary newspapers, and perhaps even pamphlets peddling scandal—might explain, as Greene's austere emphasis on Whig politics cannot, why "the quiet Tory daughter of a quiet Tory parson" seems to name so many of her heroes for, as Greene thinks, Whig greats.[4] That is, only the larger historical context of these two neighboring estates in Austen's day can reveal why a writer who apparently sets her family-centered stories exclusively in the villages and towns of southern counties would reach repeatedly for Yorkshire politicians as a naming source. That larger context shows how Austen may not restrict her concern with *history* to what Catherine Morland disparages as "real solemn history," but expand her gaze to a wider swathe of human experience now termed *cultural history*. Her more expansive appreciation of history seems to have delighted in Wentworth celebrity well beyond parliamentary politics.

Wentworth Fame

In the long eighteenth century, both political branches of the extended Wentworth family, not just the Whig occupiers of Wentworth Woodhouse, enjoyed pride of place among the "abnormally interesting people" now

WENTWORTH CASTLE.
(GENERAL VIEW)
YORKSHIRE

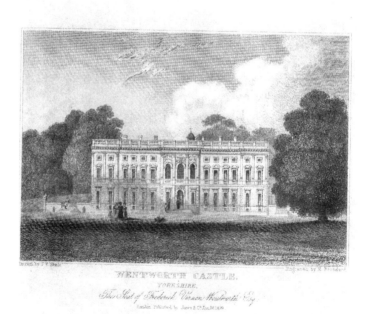

WENTWORTH CASTLE.
YORKSHIRE.
The Seat of Frederick Vernon Wentworth Esq

FIGURE 1.1. "Wentworth Castle, Yorkshire. The Seat of Frederick Vernon Wentworth Esq." Engraved by R. Brandard, after a drawing by J. F. Neale. Published in Jones's *Views of the Seats* (1829). Private Collection.

WENTWORTH HOUSE,
YORKSHIRE.

FIGURE 1.2. "Wentworth House, Yorkshire." Engraved by J. Henshall, after a drawing by J. P. Neale. Published in Jones's *Views of the Seats* (1829). Harry Ransom Center, The University of Texas at Austin.

termed celebrities.[5] The newspapers and tabloids of Austen's day reported on the doings of all the politically and socially active Wentworths, feeding a market for copies of the portraits by Reynolds and Gainsborough of individual family members, both Whig and Tory, which circulated as popular prints and celebrity pinups.[6] This is not to say that all that glittered among the Wentworths was gold (as I show momentarily), but even infamy is a type of fame. During the war-strewn era in which Jane Austen lived and wrote, anyone aware of current events would have been bombarded with mentions of high-flying Wentworths, "even if," as Park Honan reports of Jane Austen, "one was not reading every scrap of news for items about two naval brothers."[7]

In the literary realm, too, the name of Wentworth was starting to accumulate associations beyond those of the minor poet Wentworth Dillon, fourth Earl of Roscommon (1637–85)[8]—nephew of Thomas Wentworth, the first Earl of Strafford—due to the sexual scandals of poetry's latest celebrity bad boy, Lord Byron. In January of 1815, Byron married

"Quite unconnected": The Wentworths and *Lady Susan*   31

Annabella Milbanke (1792–1860), *suo jure* Baroness Wentworth. The marriage was followed within the year by salacious scandal of incest and neglect involving his half sister, Augusta Mary (1783–1851), who was the daughter of his father's second wife, Amelia D'Arcy. Thus Byron's own acute celebrity further increased the piquancy of these Wentworth-family names during precisely the year that Austen composed *Persuasion*.[9] Even so, Byron did not spark Jane Austen's interest in the Wentworths.

Her fascination with the romance and pedigree of the Wentworth family tree began as a child. Jane Austen was not yet seven when Prime Minister Charles Watson-Wentworth, head of the Wentworth Woodhouse estate, died suddenly and without an heir in 1782, passing his vast fortune to his cousins, the Fitzwilliams. At age ten, Jane wrote a mock entry for the saying of marriage banns between a "Jane Austen of Steventon" and an imaginary "Henry Frederick Howard Fitzwilliam of London" in her father's parish registry.[10] To the budding writer, the glam of a Fitzwilliam offered the antithesis of a plain Jack Smith (whom she marries in another fantasy entry). A few scholars have provocatively parsed the fantasy name, noting that Austen recycles its constituent parts in her fictions. For example, Elizabeth Jenkins points out that the name Henry appears prominently in *Mansfield Park*, Frederick in *Persuasion*, Howard in *The Watsons*, and Fitzwilliam in *Pride and Prejudice*.[11] When taken together, however, the name may audaciously link the famous Henry Frederick Howard (1608–52) with the newly enriched Fitzwilliams. The real Henry Frederick Howard, heir to three of the oldest and premier earldoms in the peerage, secretly married Lady Elizabeth Stuart (d. 1674) against the express wishes of the king, who had intended for her to marry another.[12] As punishment, the couple was first confined at Lambeth but eventually pardoned. Their marriage was long and happy. Thus young Jane, writing clandestinely in her father's book, may further brighten the shine on the recent Fitzwilliam windfall with the romance of a historic elopement and, just for good measure, three of the kingdom's oldest titles. Whatever the specific intention or prompt behind her historical amalgam, written at so young an age, Jane's mixing of history and celebrity in the creation of a grand "Henry Frederick Howard Fitzwilliam" seems part of a juvenile romantic fantasy.

Evidently, young Jane continued to breathe Wentworth atmosphere, for at thirteen she penned a comic story featuring a Miss Wentworth, entitled "Sir William Mountague, an Unfinished Performance." The slightly bawdy tale ends dramatically when the fickle young rake, fond of shooting and of women, enquires about a "fair Unknown." The tantalizing reveal of the girl's legendary name literally ends the story: "Miss Wentworth . . . . Finis" (*J*, 49; the ellipses are original). These early appropriations of Wentworth fame by a young girl cannot yet resemble the mature political act that Greene interprets *Pride and Prejudice* to be, even though the parish book entry may demonstrate Austen's budding sympathy for the Stuarts, which took root, critics stress, in her annotations to Goldsmith's *History* and blossomed in "The History of England" soon thereafter.[13] Yet these fictional gestures, too, are precociously suffused with history and with the romance of political intrigue, titles, and wealth. How astonishing that for the next three decades Austen actively nurtured and embellished her childhood fascination with the Wentworth family, plucking name after name from its venerable ancestral tree for so many of her later stories.

Partly because Austen tracked Fitzwilliam history from so early an age, her focus on the Wentworth family may concern personality as much as politics—celebrity as well as schoolbook history. Again and again, Austen takes from the ancient branches of the Yorkshire Wentworths, which boasted the old names of D'Arcy, Wodehouse, Wentworth, and even Bertram—which she deploys for her protagonists in *Mansfield Park*. The ancient name of Ferrars, too, which features prominently in *Sense and Sensibility*, is also mentioned by Joseph Edmondson, author of *The Present Peerages* (1785), as part of the Saxon ancestry of the Wentworth family, along with "the Lords D'Arcy of the North."[14] But when Greene funnels all such ancient names toward Austen's near-contemporaries at Wentworth Woodhouse, the Watsons and Fitzwilliams, he focuses only on the Whig branch of this politically prominent family. As Arthur Collins records in a lengthy entry for "Wentworth, Earl of Strafford" in his *Peerage*, the Wentworth cousins who lived only six miles away at Wentworth Castle naturally share these same ancestors.[15]

Greene's Historiography

Prompted by the resemblances between Austen's choice of names for her characters and the family trees of the nobility, Donald Greene asks, "Was there a copy of Collins' *Peerage* in the Steventon rectory library?" (Greene, 1021). Although Greene's question is rhetorical, the *Godmersham Park Library Catalogue* now provides an answer of sorts. The Knights of Godmersham armed themselves not just with one *Peerage*, but with at least five copies published between 1753 and 1810 in multiple formats: in octavo they owned "Peerage of England 4 vols London 1735," "Peerage of England 2 vols London 1769," and "Peerage 3 vols London 1769," while in the smaller duodecimo format they had a "Pocket Peerage 2 vols London 1790" and "Peerage 2 vols 1810." They also owned a "Baronetage 3 vols 1804" in duodecimo. If the Knights, whose peerage peering never approached that of the obsessive Brydges, were representative of a healthy concern with rank in the family circle, there must have been a copy (or two) to hand even in Steventon.

Greene ponders with Johnsonian understatement the "interesting 'coincidences'" suggested by the overlap between Austen's novels and the peerage, speculating about what this might reveal of her "milieu and her social attitudes" (Greene, 1017). Citing some of the old Austen family connections to the nobility, Greene insists on the importance of Jane Austen's own social status in her portrayal of the social elite, stressing her certain knowledge of her family's modest connections to the peerage. Thus he shows how Austen reflects on the peerage from within rather than critiqing from outside. He names several "great men in Whig political circles" from the extended Wentworth family who "caught Jane Austen's fancy": William Wentworth Fitzwilliam (1748–1833), Robert D'Arcy (1718–78), and Charles Watson Wentworth (1730–82), the prime minister who died when Austen was six (Greene, 1018 and 1017). Greene concludes that "Jane Austen is being consciously political in her novels" when she selects these names, and he interprets these choices as ironic, locating "in the arrogant possessors of the great Whig names of Fitzwilliam and D'Arcy a satire on aspects of Whiggism" (1026). Although I want to correct the myopia of Greene's own Whiggism, he does identify an extraordinary realism through which, contrary to Austen's reputation in 1953 as an isolated spinster, he argues that she confidently engages "the world around her" (1025).

In spite of Greene's modest disclaimer that he offers only "a few facts and speculations" in "a very cursory study of the family names in her writing," his article in the high-profile pages of *PMLA* should have caused a paradigm shift in Austen studies (Greene, 1017). After all, Greene proposes a politically audacious and edgy Austen who selects nomenclatures that play with contemporary politics, daring to engage the high-profile ideologies associated with noble titles, both extinct and extant. But although Greene chides "those who still think of Jane Austen as a naïve and gentle spinster, ignorant of the world outside the walls of a country rectory," he nonetheless tucks away the magnitude of what is at stake in a footnote, the one place where he allows himself to deviate from a marked scholarly restraint (1025). In the tradition of Augustan satire, Greene's splenetic footnote risks outshouting the central text. Too lengthy to quote in its entirety, his footnote opens with a volley of Janeite spleen that must suffice here to indicate the high-stakes implications for a revolutionary recharacterization of Austen in 1953: "The notion that Jane Austen was preternaturally innocent of the world of affairs still persists and still has to be combated. It is true that the characters of her novels do not continually talk about the Napoleonic War, any more than the ordinary person removed from the scene of battle continually talked about the Second World War. But the Napoleonic War is there, nevertheless" (1025). In the light of continuing efforts to resist the enduring Victorian portrait of a cloistered Austen, Greene's aim in 1953 seems strikingly contemporary. Even within the last decade, scholars such as Jocelyn Harris, Peter Knox-Shaw, and Brian Southam have had to insist upon Austen's keen engagement with her larger intellectual and political milieu, especially war and naval matters, each arguing more vehemently than the last against her presumed innocence of worldly events. Greene's vehemence was ahead of its time.

Surprisingly, the field prepared by Greene in 1953 failed to raise a large crop of followers. This is all the more remarkable since the availability of Greene's essay was not limited to one issue of *PMLA*: Ian Watt included it in a 1963 collection of essays on Jane Austen, where it kept company with commentaries by Lionel Trilling and Kingsley Amis.[16] Frequent citations suggest that Greene was read and acknowledged, although most scholars pursued the rhetorical question about whether the Austen family library contained a probable copy of Collins, enthusiastically thumbing through *The Peerage of England* to view such names as Willoughby, Ferrars, Musgrave, Dashwood, and many others identified by Greene as part of Austen's audacious verisimilitude. Because Greene encouraged what he termed the "fascinating pastime" of perusing the *Peerage*, critics routinely acknowledged the aristocracy in general, or Collins specifically, as "a useful naming source for Jane Austen."[17] Even so, Collins's *Peerage* has virtually punctuated Austen studies with a full stop rather than providing an intellectual link to Austen's larger political, social, and historical concerns. While scholarly source studies continue to find the names of Austen's characters elsewhere in isolated print sources, from novels to obituaries, these findings have not yet been united into a methodological model.[18] Only by calibrating such data with Greene's and with each other, however, might it be possible to chart larger patterns among her choices of names and those of her contemporaries.

For instance, Sir Walter Scott, who reviewed and admired the story of Emma Woodhouse, likewise reaches imaginatively for the Yorkshire Wentworths. A year after *Persuasion* was published, Scott opened *Ivanhoe* (1819) in an "ancient" forest near Sheffield whose remains were "still to be seen at the noble seats of Wentworth," thus animating the "chief scene" of his historical fiction with Wentworth renown.[19] That a shared cultural referent, in this case the famous Yorkshire Wentworths, found its way into the works of two contemporaries is not all that remarkable in light of the celebrity status of these Wentworths. But for scholars and editor to habitually follow up on such references to places and people in Scott but not in Austen seems odd—an editorial double standard suggestive of a difference in their historicity that may prove false.

Biographers did follow Greene's lead. John Halperin's *Life of Jane Austen* (1984) prominently includes a "Partial Pedigree of Jane Austen, Devised by Donald Greene" and, in tandem with Greene, chips away at the "placid, pleasant, and benign" Austen of family legend.[20] The pedigree even includes a note that, thirty years later, still shows Greene insisting upon debunking the "myth" of Austen's secluded spinsterhood by showing "her family's connections with nobility and even royalty, with the worlds of politics, learning, and high society."[21] Other biographers prefer to link Austen's name choices to the surnames of individuals in her own life or family history. Jon Spence, a biographer willing to cross the boundaries between fact and fiction, declares in *Becoming Jane Austen* (2003) that she chose names in homage to family and friends:

> By 1794 Jane's habit of using names to allude to her sources of inspiration was well-established, and the network of Leigh and Brydges connections receives a tribute in her use of some of their names in every novel: Brandon, Middleton and Willoughby in *Sense and Sensibility*; Bennet and Bingley in *Pride and Prejudice*; Tilney in *Northanger Abbey*; Ross in *Mansfield Park*; Woodhouse, Knightley, and Fairfax in *Emma*; Wentworth, Carteret and Dalrymple in *Persuasion*; even in the unfinished work we find Musgrave in *The Watsons* and Brereton in *Sanditon*.[22]

Yet biographical links do not rule out larger artistic purposes. Just because a Willoughby or a Brandon existed in Jane Austen's extended family, or an Elliot and a Palmer circulated among her acquaintances, interpretation should not grind to a halt. While no one disputes that Austen's life fed her work, the literariness of her fiction, especially when written with the express aim of publication, must not be cordoned off by biographical fact. An overreliance on biography risks confining Austen to a coterie audience, attracted merely to minor details of her life.

Greene's own emphasis on Austen's personal relationship to the British aristocracy may, in fact, have prompted consequent scholarly resistance to his findings. His emphasis upon biography inadvertently exposes an uncomfortable truth about Austen's own elitism. For, in spite of Greene's progressive scholarly reading, details about Austen's active interest in her "distant relationships with . . . noble families," particularly the Wentworths, make her appear less modern. For instance, take the manner in which Greene cites a letter to Cassandra written during a visit to relatives in Kent in 1808: "It is pleasant to be among people who know one's connections and care about them" (Greene, 1019). The original context of the letter stresses fond familiarity over rank, for Austen follows it with "& it amuses me to hear John Bridges talk of 'Frank'" (*Letters*, 138). But Greene quotes it as evidence of Austen's delight in her lofty "connections" to the elite, aligning her implicitly with the lord-loving Sir Walter Elliot or his self-absorbed daughter Mary Musgrove, who insists upon taking precedence over her mother-in-law, rather than with the stoic Anne Elliot or the defiant Elizabeth Bennet. Perhaps because Greene stresses that "Jane Austen was related, if distantly, to many of the nobility" he dampened his impact on readers in the 1950s and 1960s, decades during which both town and gown sought emancipation from past social conventions (1019). Greene documents Austen's fascination with the peerage so extensively that he confirms her psychological investment in an outmoded value system. It is ironic that, by insisting ambitiously upon Austen's wider knowledge of the world, Greene still made that knowledge appear old-fashioned.

There is nothing fuddy-duddy, however, about the manner in which, as Greene reveals, *Pride and Prejudice* sails dangerously close to the political wind with the name of its hero. For, not only does Austen combine two prominent branches from the Wentworth family tree, Fitzwilliam and D'Arcy, but she implies that the maiden name of Lady Catherine de Bourgh and her sister Lady Anne Darcy, who jointly broker an arranged marriage for their children, is Fitzwilliam. Their father held the earldom from which the de Bourgh and Darcy pride presumably stems.

Colonel Fitzwilliam, their nephew and Darcy's cousin, is the younger son of the present earl, their brother. As Greene notes, at the time when Austen wrote *Pride and Prejudice*, "there was one, and only one, earl in the British realm whose family name was Fitzwilliam—the Whig magnifico, nephew of Rockingham and heir to his wealth and influence, one of the leaders of the 'coalition Whigs' whose political position was so important to Great Britain in the dangerous years of the French Revolution" (Greene, 1024–25). In the light of Edmund Burke's famous "Letter" of 1796, addressed to the "Noble Lord" known as William Wentworth Fitzwilliam, Mr. Collins's description of Fitzwilliam Darcy as "one of the most illustrious personages in this land" allows scant room for Austen's usual irony (*P&P*, 402). As Greene points out, the real Earl Fitzwilliam had several sisters and daughters, making Austen's story of the hushed-up seduction of young Georgiana Darcy by Mr. Wickham potentially out of bounds.

Although Greene is right about Austen's daring political allusion in *Pride and Prejudice* to the Fitzwilliam family at Wentworth Woodhouse, his account of Austen's interests in this family of Whigs, which he labels ironic in order to accord with known Austen family politics, is politically one-sided. Greene ignores luminaries from the Wentworth family's Tory side—their disenfranchised cousins who lived six miles away at Wentworth Castle. In fairness to Donald Greene, who reckons the brand recognition of Austen's names strictly in the political realm, Thomas Wentworth's legacy was largely obliterated by Whig propaganda that belittled his political activities. Michael Charlesworth is adamant in defense of the earl's contributions to English landscape gardening, architecture, and politics, arguing that few Tory politicians of that era "suffered more from the neglect and slighting brought about by the domination of British history by Whig historiography."[23] Even in modern history books "he is invariably characterized in the words of his political enemies."[24] Late eighteenth-century prejudice against this Earl of Strafford as a power-grabbing upstart remains so dominant that the *Oxford Dictionary of National Biography* still scolds him for "always importuning the court for some honour or promotion," complaining that Wentworth's "seemingly unbridled ambition coupled with his hauteur antagonized many."[25] Such ingrained historical prejudice surely caused Greene (and those who do take up his findings) to miss how Wentworth Castle history also informs *Persuasion* and *Lady Susan*. It is necessary, therefore, to relate some of that ignored Wentworth family history before returning to Austen's use of it for her fictions.

Rivalry between Wentworth Woodhouse and Wentworth Castle

The family rivalry between the Whig and Tory branches of the Wentworths started in 1695, when William Wentworth, the second Earl of Strafford, died without issue. Through Anne Wentworth, William's sister and widow to Edward Watson, second Baron Rockingham, the estate of Wentworth Woodhouse passed to her son, Thomas Watson, and thus newly into the Watson family. Upon his inheritance, Thomas added his mother's maiden name to his own. The transference of ancient Wentworth property out of the family name via well-married female kin did not go unprotested. In fact, the Watson family's inheritance of Wentworth Woodhouse initiated a contest within the Wentworth clan that lasted for about a century. The earldom had indeed become extinct with William's death in 1695, but his cousin, Thomas Wentworth (1672–1739), inherited the lesser title of Lord Raby (fig. 1.3). As the transfer of that title suggests, he was the Wentworth family's surviving male heir, who had built his financial and political ambitions upon legitimate expectations of inheritance.

When the Wentworth wealth and family lands passed, instead, through the female line into the Watson family, Thomas Wentworth felt cheated out of his inheritance. Contemporary historian Nicolas Tindal (1687–1774) explains Wentworth's justified resentment: Thomas Wentworth "was the surviving head of the family of Wentworth-Woodhouse, in Yorkshire, but by a dispute between his father and the late earl of Strafford, cut off from the estate."[26] The family "dispute" was of a political nature, and the decision to shift the estate to the Watsons a likely means of safeguarding the Whig loyalties at Wentworth Woodhouse. Consequently, Thomas Wentworth redoubled his efforts at political promotion in the hope of eventually reclaiming his wealth and status. His ambitions were partially fulfilled in 1711, when, after having risen to high political office, including several ambassadorships under William III and Queen Anne, he officially became the first Earl of Strafford of the so-called Second Creation, a promotion that revived especially for him the title made famous by his grandfather. At the same time, he also received the lesser

FIGURE 1.3. Portrait of Thomas Wentworth, first Earl of Strafford
(1672-1739). By John Simon, after Charles D'Agar, published by
Edward Cooper. Mezzotint, c. 1725. © National Portrait Gallery,
London.

title of "Viscount Wentworth of Wentworth-Woodhouse," an honor that
added to the confusion and family strife since the physical estate by that
same name would continue to be owned by the Watsons and, though
them, the Fitzwilliams.

Three years before his promotion to Earl of Strafford, Thomas Wentworth purchased Stainborough Hall, near Barnsley in Yorkshire. Stain-

borough proved an ideal platform for Wentworth's retaliatory ambitions, partly because of its tantalizing proximity to Wentworth Woodhouse, a mere six miles away. A "very judicious marriage" to an heiress worth £60,000, together with the spoils of high office, allowed for the improving of his new country estate with features befitting his restored rank and wealth.[27] However, when the sudden death of Queen Anne in 1714 forced Thomas Wentworth into retirement and virtual exile at his Yorkshire estate, his Whig cousins resumed the lead in politics. Wentworth then turned his political energies and frustrations into a massive redesign of his house and landscape garden, building a large-scale forest garden dotted with experimental features. In 1723, when he used an agent to secretly purchase a piece of land mortgaged to Watson, Wentworth's code name for Watson was Vermin. As Charlesworth observes, the moniker evidences the animosity and family rivalry spurring on the "spate of building activity" at both locales.[28] As a symbolic rejoinder to those who had usurped his family's medieval name and estate, Wentworth built a mock castle on Stainborough's highest ground. One of the earliest such follies in England, the castle structure led him to rename the whole of his estate Wentworth Castle—a transparent rebuke to the mere "House" of his relatives down the way (one can still see structures on the rival estate from the top of the folly). He also remodeled the main house in accordance with a Baroque design, to which his son, William Wentworth (1722–91), added a Palladian extension. The Wentworths wanted, as one modern family historian puts it, to "cock a snook" at their cousins with these projects.[29] The proximity of these rival estates led to decades of architectural one-upmanship—assiduously tracked by a nation obsessed with trends in landscape design.

The feud extended across generations, for when Thomas Watson-Wentworth died in 1723, his son, who bore the same name, "unleashed his desire for the ostentatious cultural display that had been held in check for so long by his father."[30] Promptly, the owners of Wentworth Woodhouse launched an architectural "counter-attack" with a gargantuan Palladian expansion begun by architect Henry Flitcroft, though not finished until 1772. The remodeling of Wentworth Woodhouse—with its 1,000 windows, 365 rooms, and wings spanning 600 feet across, which gave the house the longest façade in England—"dramatically visualised the rivalry," which remained, as Patrick Eyres explains, "primarily ideological," positioning Whig against Tory.[31] Over the years, each estate added further monuments to its gardens, challenging its neighbor's aesthetics, politics, and patriotism by means of ornamentation and inscriptions. At Wentworth Castle, the second Earl of Strafford updated and augmented his father's grounds, cultivating a fashionable taste for the picturesque into a bold experimental landscape on a grand scale. By 1791, he had expanded upon his father's love of follies and views with "an extraordinary sham-city, whose walls extended for several miles" along a ridge of hills directly in front of Wentworth Castle.[32] By 1800, Wentworth Castle, purchased in 1708 and actively remodeled by father and son, had become an extraordinary match for the Whig monuments and architectural grandeur at nearby Wentworth Woodhouse.

Although Austen is not known to have ever ventured into Yorkshire, the celebrated landscape rivalry at Wentworth Woodhouse and Wentworth Castle could easily have caught her eye in print. From the 1730s onward, Wentworth Woodhouse and Wentworth Castle synthesized contemporary garden aesthetics by taking, in turn, the role of antithesis to the other's latest thesis. Their dialectic gardening made the Wentworths a focal point for historians, travel writers, and aestheticians, with prints of both estates circulating widely in books and magazines. Scholars such as Alistair M. Duckworth have long argued that books about landscape aesthetics formed part of Austen's extensive reading since girlhood.[33] The Wentworth estates are pictured in famous collections of views such as *Vitruvius Britannicus* (1739) and William Watts's *The Seats of the Nobility and Gentry* (1779–86), both of which are listed in the *Godmersham Park Library Catalogue*. Humphry Repton, whom Austen mentions by name in *Mansfield Park*, reported on his work for the Wentworths in *Observations on the Theory and Practice of Landscape Gardening* (1803). Travel literature about the north of England included verbal descriptions of the Wentworth estates in popular works by, among others, Arthur Young, Britton and Brayley, Frederick Atkinson, Richard Warner, Henry Skrine, William Watts, William Camden, William Mavor, and William Gilpin.[34]

Most notably, Horace Walpole represented Wentworth Castle as the epitome of refinement in the encomium that closes *The History of the Modern Taste in Gardening* (1771):

> If a model is sought of the most perfect taste in architecture, where grace softens dignity, and lightness attempers magnificence; where proportion removes every part from peculiar observation, and delicacy of execution recalls every part to notice; where the position is the most

happy, and even the colour of the stone the most harmonious; the vir-
tuoso should be directed to the new front of Wentworth-castle: the result of the same elegant judgment that had before distributed so many
beauties over that domain, and called from wood, water, hills, prospects
and buildings, a compendium of picturesque nature, improved by the
chastity of art.[35]

Although Walpole only gestures here to a comparison with Wentworth
Woodhouse, he wrote privately of the "litter and bad taste" at the neighboring estate, sneering in a letter to Richard Bentley that the propor-
tions there were so grandiose that even the obelisks on the bowling green
looked "like a Brobdignag nine-pin-alley."[36] While Arthur Young famously
concurred with Walpole, the scales of comparison between the two estates tipped back and forth with shifts in popular tastes.

William Gilpin, predictably enough, favors the picturesque in his
Observations (1786), a work listed among the many books on English
landscape in the *Godmersham Park Library Catalogue*.[37] Objecting to
the "want of simplicity" in the design of Wentworth Woodhouse, he concludes that "on the whole, I was not much pleased with any thing I saw
here."[38] As for the nearby grounds of Wentworth Castle, which he views
from the "eminence" of its central hill, Gilpin allows that "the scene all
together is grand," even though he dismisses Strafford's mock castle as
"no ornament" up close.[39] By 1795, Henry Skrine found defects of excess
in both estates. Although Skrine deems each house sufficiently suffused
with grandeur, he finds that the "wings" of the expanded Wentworth
Woodhouse push it out of proportion.[40] He also critiques the gold-
painted windows of the Earl of Strafford's "great pile of building," reasoning that gilding, barely "admissible in such a house as Chatsworth,"
was out of keeping with the architectural modernity of Wentworth
Castle.[41] In 1802, Richard Warner (a prolific travel writer whose guidebook on Bath the Austens owned) diverges from Skrine by applauding
the grandeur of Wentworth Woodhouse. After devoting twenty ecstatic
pages in his blog-like guidebook to the pictures and internal trimmings
of Wentworth Woodhouse, Warner contentedly judges its "extensive
park," which he measures very conservatively at 1600 acres, "consistent
with the magnificence and expense which reign *within*."[42] Claiming that
the views "would exhaust" his "powers of description," he eventually re-
signs himself to summary, offering a panoptic judgment that resembles
Elizabeth's admiration for Pemberley: "It is difficult to say whether the

beauty of nature, the efforts of art, or the operations of taste, are to be most admired. . . . We had no hesitation in pronouncing it to be the finest place we had ever seen."[43] When Warner next turns to the garden monuments and "park of Wentworth-Castle," he finds its outdoor features comparatively "heavy and tasteless," lamenting that the natural loveliness of the place is "injured in the injudicious attempt to add a beauty to them by artificial trifles; such as *made ruins*, Chinese temples, &c."[44] In sum, no matter which landscape was judged superior, by Austen's day it remained impossible to consider one estate without the other.

Austen and Wentworth Castle

Thus the name of Wentworth was synonymous in Austen's culture with the long-standing landed privileges of one of the oldest, richest, and most politically prominent families in England. The vast Yorkshire estates of Wentworth Woodhouse, where the deer herd had roamed uninterrupted since 1066, and of Wentworth Castle, so excessively praised by Walpole, *both* epitomized landed wealth. Brian Southam acknowledges how such "aristocratic associations" eventually bring Wentworth "up to the mark as a son-in-law" at the novel's close—when Sir Walter, "assisted by his well-sounding name," finally feels able "to prepare his pen with a very good grace for the insertion of [Anne's] marriage in the volume of honour."[45] What already reads like a wry joke at the expense of Sir Walter's snobbery gains further significance for any reader aware of the two opposing Strafford lines in the Wentworth family—one Whig and one Tory, one old and one comparatively new.

Through Sir Walter's sneer, Austen calls attention to the genuine Wentworths at the same time that she ostensibly separates *Persuasion's* invented people from those in the real world. With characteristic irony, Austen's initial disclaimer, spoken after all by a dislikable snob, prompts a reader to reconsider the real-world Wentworths more thoroughly. While Sir Walter's Whiggish disdain likely recalls Thomas Wentworth (1593–1641), the original Earl of Strafford, contemporary history allows another, and nearer, association. While the Strafford earldom of Wentworth Woodhouse died out in 1695, their Tory cousins at Wentworth Castle reacquired it in 1711. When Austen wrote *Persuasion*, the last Earl of Strafford had recently died at Wentworth Castle, in 1799. He was named—just like Austen's valiant captain—Frederick Wentworth.[46]

Frederick Wentworth (1732–99) of Henbury in Dorsetshire became the third (and last) Earl of Strafford in 1791, when William Wentworth died without issue. That the real Frederick Wentworth, who grew up in reduced circumstances in Dorset, gained Wentworth Castle as well as the lofty earldom and other titles, may even gloss the meteoric rise of Austen's sailor. The papers for March and April 1791, when Austen was fifteen, were full of the news: "Frederick Thomas Wentworth who succeeds the late Earl of Strafford as Baron Raby of Raby Castle in the county of Durham, is the only surviving heir to these titles, though three of his ancestors preceding the late Earl had six-and-twenty children."[47] The real Frederick Wentworth's surprising elevation from humble beginnings occurred, like that of his fictional namesake, against all odds.

In 1799, when the elite Strafford earldom ended with the death of this Frederick Wentworth,[48] the properties of Wentworth Castle became involved in a "confused legal situation."[49] "After several twists and turns," Wentworth Castle passed, via Frederick Wentworth's sister Augusta Ann Hatfield Kaye (née Wentworth), who died in 1802, to her seven-year-old nephew Frederick William Thomas Vernon (1795–1885), the second son of Henry Vernon, of Hilton Park in Staffordshire.[50] Between 1799 and 1803, the legal entanglements and financial negotiations that took place among Strafford's descendants involved claims from various individuals: the recalcitrant Lady Strafford, widow of the elder Frederick; her persistent sister-in-law, Mrs. Kaye; the irate parents of young Frederick Vernon; and some distant Irish relatives, named Conolly, who staked their own claim during the confusion and even moved into Wentworth Castle for a few months during 1802. Eventually a settlement was reached, and the Vernon household, headed by young Frederick's father and "The Hon. Mrs Vernon," took possession of the estate on their son's behalf in October 1803.[51] In 1804, the boy-heir Frederick Vernon officially changed his name to Vernon-Wentworth to seal the hard-won deal. While young Frederick remained underage, Wentworth Castle was known as the home of his parents, the Vernons.[52]

Austen's epistolary story *Lady Susan* concerns a Vernon family, formerly of "Vernon Castle," and a young Frederic Vernon deprived of this rightful inheritance by a selfish aunt (*LM*, 9). I believe Austen may have written *Lady Susan* during the contentious years that Wentworth Castle passed into the hands of the Vernons. Although the novella survives in a fair copy on paper watermarked 1805, it was not published until 1871—over half a century after the author's death. In spite of the material evidence of an 1805 watermark and the mature subject of a mother's sexual jealousy of her teenage daughter, opinions about the possible dates of the manuscript's original genesis and composition differ greatly. While Chapman worked from the "presumption that an original manuscript was composed not long after the date of the paper," subsequent critics stress the difference between genesis and fair copy.[53] Deirdre Le Faye tentatively suggests that Austen "possibly starts writing *Lady Susan*" as early as November of 1793.[54] Brian Southam observes that the date of composition is what likely led the Austen family to belittle is as a "betweenity," a work written during the transition between the juvenilia and the mature novels.[55] Southam therefore nudges the date of composition significantly forward from 1793, with a reminder that Austen's known work habits, which included saving paper for several years, also allow for significant alterations to the manuscript even during fair-copying. He puts forth the possibility that Austen wrote the abrupt summary "Conclusion" during fair-copying after 1805. Various critics accept Southam's logic, including the editors of *Lady Susan* for the Juvenilia Press, who strongly maintain a dating in two parts. They urge that while Jane Austen wrote the bulk of her epistolary novella "about the time the later juvenilia pieces were revised," she likely concluded it after 1805.[56] At one time, Marilyn Butler pressed for a much later dating in her Oxford *Dictionary of National Biography* (2004) entry for Jane Austen, suggesting that because *Lady Susan* resembles Maria Edgeworth's "Tales of a Fashionable Life," Austen wrote it after May 1809.[57] Terming it one of the "Chawton novels," Butler allowed 1810–12 as a possible window of composition.[58]

Although Janet Todd and Linda Bree are careful not to date *Lady Susan* too definitively in their introduction to the Cambridge edition of the *Later Manuscripts*, the decision to include the text at the start of that volume rather than at the close of the *Juvenilia* hints at their leanings toward a relatively late date. They stress the possibility, first put forth by Q. D. Leavis, that Eliza de Feuillide served as "a real-life source" for the character of Lady Susan, thus tying its inspiration to events between 1795 and 1797 (*LM*, li). They do allow that "Butler's late dating has something to recommend it, perhaps less for the supposed indebtedness to Edgeworth than for the obvious sophistication of the novella's content and technique" (xlix). If all critical opinion is taken together, the span of roughly a decade and a half, from 1793 to at least 1809, leaves little to cling to by way of placing Austen's epistolary novella securely within her development as a writer. But if the names in *Lady Susan*, along with its plotted squabbles over a fictional castle in Staffordshire, actually invoke the Vernon branch of the Wentworth family, whose original estate at Hilton Park was in Staffordshire, historical events might help resolve the contest over the date of Austen's composition.

These same historical events also suggest a link between *Lady Susan* and *Persuasion*, again forged from a name: Frederick Vernon-Wentworth. In 1795, the Vernons had named their second son Frederick Thomas William in honor of all three Earls of Strafford, with the then-current earl taking pride of place. The implied expectation was that this younger son would inherit his namesake's estate. Even though the will of Frederick Wentworth's sister, Mrs. Hatfield Kaye, honored this original expectation by leaving Wentworth Castle to young Frederick Vernon after her death in 1802, the Vernons were unable to take possession until at least October 1803 due to legal irregularities across several generations of wills and entailments. Lady Strafford's staunch opposition to on old will of her husband's apparently enflamed this legal confusion, causing further delay. Only when Frederick Vernon's name was officially changed to Vernon-Wentworth in 1804 were these legal uncertainties publicly resolved. In *Lady Susan*, Austen echoes the dispute over Wentworth Castle's transfer in her fictional account of Vernon Castle, where a younger son in the Vernon family, also named Frederic, is wholly denied the family estate by a proud aunt. In Austen's story, the aunt actually victimizes multiple Frederic Vernons, as well as her daughter, Frederica Vernon. The real-world legal name-change of Frederick Vernon to Vernon-Wentworth may thus also link Austen's concerns in this early novel, *Lady Susan*, with her last, *Persuasion*. Historical circumstances bridge the imaginative leap from the name Frederic Vernon to Frederick Wentworth simply because it reflects a shift in nomenclature adopted by an actual person. In both these novels, then, Austen may be recalling the actual history of Wentworth Castle.

As *Lady Susan* is not among Austen's better-known works, I should explain how the Vernon name and a family castle appear at that story's psychological center. The story's "predatory heroine" is the "bewitching" but amoral Lady Susan Vernon, recent widow of Frederic Vernon,[59] and "victimizing mother" to their daughter, Frederica, a teenage innocent.[60] Austen's epistolary story is told from different perspectives within the Vernon family, with some letters scorning Lady Susan as "the most accomplished coquette in England" and others, penned by Lady Susan herself, deriding those who would meekly display "all the Vernon Milkiness" (*LM*, 8 and 29). We learn that Lady Susan fell out of favor with the otherwise kindly Vernon family years earlier over the sale of Vernon Castle, said to lie in Staffordshire. Because of Lady Susan's interference, it was sold out of the Vernon family when, under financial pressures, her husband was "obliged to sell it" (9). Frederic's bachelor-brother Charles was eager to step in and buy the old family home with his self-made banking fortune, but Lady Susan "did not let Charles buy Vernon Castle," in case her "Husband's Dignity should be lessened by his younger brother's having possession of the Family Estate" (9 and 10). Her justification is purely selfish: "What benefit could have accrued to me from his purchasing Vernon?" (10). Years later, Charles's wife, Catherine, cannot forgive her sister-in-law for an interference that has deprived her young son, poignantly named Frederic Vernon after his duped uncle, of his birthright.

The real-world legal conflict between Frederick Wentworth's sister and his widow, "each of whom resented 'the immense riches' obtained by the other," was also "a kind of sub-plot, a hot dispute." [61] Lady Strafford lived in good health until 1811, and her husband had apparently "put the interests of his sister, another Wentworth, before those of his wife," quietly settling his estates upon a deserving sibling in reduced circumstances without ever informing his ambitious and spirited spouse. As a result, Frederick Wentworth's will in favor of his unassuming sister came as a shock to Lady Strafford, described by her sister-in-law as a "greedy" woman who "wants to carry too much into her own family."[62] The feisty protagonist of *Lady Susan* and that story's resentment between Vernon sisters-in-law over a castle match this genuine dispute with pitch-perfect tone, even while Austen inverts the plight of the historical Fredericks with characteristic irony.[63] In Austen's novel the husband becomes the dupe while his young nephew, the boy-heir Frederic Vernon, suffers as the innocent victim of his aunt's selfish machinations. Even the Irish cousins, the Conollys, who boldly moved into Wentworth Castle in 1802 so as to claim right of possession but were outflanked by their well-connected English relatives, are possibly invoked through the maiden name of the Mrs. Vernon in Austen's story, which is De Courcy.[64] Did the relative transparency of the Vernon family reference prevent Austen from pursuing publication? Does the further delay to 1871, so long after her death, reflect how the Vernons continued to own Wentworth Castle well into the next century?

Bracketing its impact upon *Lady Susan*'s public release, the history of

Wentworth Castle challenges current assumptions about Austen's imaginative process. In the case of *Lady Susan*, scholars suggest that Austen based her psychological portrait of Lady Susan upon members of her extended family, Mrs. Craven and Eliza de Feuillide in particular.[65] But even the *possibility* that the larger plot and family dynamics depicted in Austen's epistolary novel about the Vernons play with a public scandal well outside of her own circle allows for a wider set of influences upon her art. Since these Wentworthian influences would appear to connect Austen's texts—from the juvenilia to *Persuasion*—they offer exciting new avenues for scholarly exploration.

Vernon Infamy

The Vernon branch of the family at Wentworth Castle made headlines long before their squabbles over the estate in 1802. In the 1740s, one of the children of the first Earl of Strafford, Lady Henrietta Wentworth, had married yet another Henry Vernon, of Hilton Park in Staffordshire. As Collins records, by means of this marriage the Vernon name entered the family tree of Wentworth Castle, preparing the way for young Frederick Vernon's eventual inheritance.[66] Lady Henrietta and Henry Vernon had many children, including a daughter named Henrietta, after both parents; their eldest son, also Henry, would become Frederick Vernon-Wentworth's father. As a granddaughter and niece of earls, the beautiful Henrietta Vernon (bap. 1745–d. 1828) grew up the epitome of privilege and style. At the impetuous age of nineteen, she married a handsome man fourteen years her senior, Richard Grosvenor, first Earl Grosvenor (1731–1802). In spite of the liberal dose of pink in Thomas Gainsborough's famous painting of Henrietta as a young bride in 1766, the marriage did not prove rosy, largely due to Grosvenor's habits of excessive gambling and whoring (fig. 1.4). When young Henrietta sought solace in the company of the king's brother, the Duke of Cumberland, her husband discovered them in flagrante delicto and took his wife to court, using a trove of racy letters exchanged between the duke and Henrietta to secure £10,000 in damages. These letters, including "Her Ladyship's Letters to the Hon. Miss Vernon, Maid of Honor to the Queen," were reproduced (and imitated) in the popular press, linking the Vernon scandal with racy private letters in the popular imagination.[67] The trial made Henrietta the target of moralizing anti-adultery tracts, as well as doggerel verse, satirical prints, and bawdy broadsheets[68] (fig. 1.5). Although nicknamed

FIGURE 1.4. Portrait of Henrietta Vernon, Lady Grosvenor, c. 1766-67 (oil on canvas), by Thomas Gainsborough. Private Collection / The Bridgeman Art Library.

"the Cheshire Cornuto," Grosvenor's own infidelities precluded a divorce, and for the next thirty years he contented himself with an official separation, paying his estranged wife an annuity of £1200.[69] The Grubstreet press continued to hound Henrietta Vernon, now soiled by her identity as Lady Grosvenor, long after feasting upon her humiliations during the public trial, a scandal that was all the juicier for involving a royal.

The pursuit of Henrietta by the age's paparazzi proved so unrelenting that even Austen, born four years after the trial, grew up with newspapers listing Lady Grosvenor's known escorts, enumerating the precise

FIGURE 1.5. "Lady Harriot Grosvenor" (a.k.a. Henrietta Vernon). Anonymous print, dated 1770. © Trustees of the British Museum.

box that she had secured for the opera, or reporting which ladies had merely stood beside her at assemblies.[70] As late as 1788, public fascination with Henrietta Vernon, though by now a mature woman in her forties, continued unabated, as evidenced by London's *Morning Post and Daily Advertiser* on 11 June: "Lady Grosvenor yesterday attended the Impeachment as a Peeress in her own right. Lady Worsley was also an auditress. The chaster part of the female company did not seem highly satisfied with these unexpected visitors—but some of the younger senators cast many a wanton smile." The "Impeachment" attended by Henrietta was that of Warren Hastings, former governor of Bengal, whose prolonged trial before the House of Commons was a star-studded event tracked closely by the Austens, who claimed personal connections to Hastings and expressed relief at his acquittal.[71] When Austen was seventeen, the newspapers gleefully revealed the location of a modest country cottage that Henrietta, now forty-seven, had rented to escape the public view: "Lady GROSVENER and Capt. PORTER have taken a cottage *orne* within half a mile of Acton, where they intend to pass the summer."[72] When Austen was twenty-two, George Cruikshank still poked fun at the old scandal in his cartoon *The Enraged Politician* (1799), which features clues to Grosvenor House and a headline that reads "The Trial of L. G. for Adultry." Only in 1802, with the death of Richard Grosvenor, was Henrietta allowed to marry her lover, becoming Mrs. Porter. The mixture of romantic tragedy and sordid gossip lingering around the high-profile name of Vernon at the same time that other Vernons in the family dispute over a castle also matches the tone of *Lady Susan*, which centers on the attractions of "a Lady no longer young" yet still so alluring that she manages to turn the heads even of married men (*LM*, 11). Austen's epistolary format, with its central conceit of private letters by Vernon women, may further summon the ghosts of this old Vernon scandal. Thus might Austen in *Lady Susan* neatly conjure up with a single surname two real-world Vernon events whose namesakes battle out parallel conflicts in her story: on the one side, parental forces protect the interests of young Frederic Vernon, while on the other, an aging Vernon beauty in high society still attracts notice and even sympathy although branded a female rake.

Lady Susan, in spite of surviving as a completed manuscript, has never had its due. Still dismissed as, at best, a piece of precocious juvenilia or an epistolary throwback to Richardson, this astonishing account of the cruelties that a mother can inflict upon her own daughter is a tour de force of characterization. Critical neglect of *Lady Susan* is all the more remarkable for its being a finished novel, rather than another fragment, and for surviving as a fair copy in the author's own hand on paper dated 1805, the year Austen turned thirty. If the fiery Vernon tug-of-war over Wentworth Castle served as inspiration for the plot of *Lady Susan*, perhaps this short work, whose genesis would then date to the period just after the death of Mrs. Kaye in 1802, could finally take its rightful place among Austen's mature, if still early, fiction. Honan correctly describes the novella as far more subversive and important than critics have acknowledged.[73] Also, if this early manuscript draws on the same family legacy as does her last finished novel, her own ironic description of her work as preoccupied with "3 or 4 Families in a Country Village" may, instead, point to a single family in the national spotlight (*Letters*, 275).

Only after the late date of 1871 then, only when the Austen family allowed publication of *Lady Susan*, might scholars and readers have recognized how Austen circled back to the Vernons in *Persuasion* after plucking so many additional names from its ancient family tree: Fitzwilliam, D'Arcy, Ferrars, Bertram, Woodhouse, Watson, Vernon, and of course Wentworth itself. In this context, even the name of Rushworth in *Mansfield Park* resonates with Wentworth history, since an influential historian by that name wrote a popular account of the trial of the executed Thomas Wentworth, first Earl of Strafford. The so-called Rushworth Papers were available as a massive edition on large paper that is listed among the folio books in the *Godmersham Park Library Catalogue* as "Rushworth's Collections 8 vols London 1721."[74] For anyone familiar with that work, the association may doom the marriage in *Mansfield Park* between a Bertram (a Wentworth family name) and a Rushworth from the start. That *Emma* includes the historic name of the famous parliamentary general Fairfax, Strafford's nemesis, has been noted by others; that this name, in light of the historic parade of Wentworth-related personages across Austen's novels, stirs the visceral and unwarranted dislike that Emma Woodhouse bears for poor Jane Fairfax befits an emerging Wentworth-logic.[75] And when, in *Pride and Prejudice*, Austen mentions the arrival of a Mr. Bingley with "a large fortune from the north of England," perhaps she gestures to Baron Bingley, the Yorkshire neighbor just to the north of the Fitzwilliams and Wentworths, who owned handsome Bramham Park nearby (*P&P*, 3).[76]

Even Austen's juvenilia, which include "A Collection of Letters" featuring a handful of names recycled in later novels, mention surnames such as Neville and Bernard, which are associated with Raby Castle, yet another property belonging to Thomas Wentworth, the later first Earl of Strafford and Lord Raby. Although Donald Greene recognizes that in the juvenilia the "names of great families are even more frequent and more obvious" and identifies the central Gowers of Austen's *Evelyn* as a reference to the "Marquesses of Stafford and Dukes of Sutherland," he does not connect these Gowers with the Wentworths and Vernons via their family trees.[77] If the links between these names crisscross her work with historical associations, Austen routinely returned to Wentworth family history in the way that a poet willingly submits to the confines of a sonnet, finding sport in creating new utterances within a set structure. From the names of Fitzwilliam, Wentworth, and Vernon in the family's present to those of Woodhouse, Bertram, and D'Arcy from their distant past, Austen's fictions may be still more profoundly suffused with historical allusions than anyone, including Greene, realized. With the addition of each Wentworth-linked surname, the intertextual allusions across her fictions look increasingly deliberate.

If Austen tugs on the coattails of Wentworth celebrity, she is not the first or last to do so. In 1765, Hugh Kelly (1739–77), an editor of *Court Miscellany; or, Ladies New Magazine*, used the pseudonym Matilda Wentworth for contributions to a periodical dedicated to "Anecdotes of the Court," so as to "hold up the Character of many of the highest Rank, either for Ridicule or Imitation." Advertisements lured buyers with the mystique of the Wentworth name in small caps, "By MATILDA WENTWORTH," adding "of Piccadilly" for apparent comic effect. Fronted by the Wentworth name, the magazine grandly promises "Admission to the Intimacy of the Great."[78] A few years later, just when the Rockingham Whig party under Charles Watson-Wentworth as prime minister had formed, Edward Bancroft (1744–1821) published a far more serious novel in three volumes called *The History of Charles Wentworth, Esq.* (1770).[79] In Dublin, just before a "Miss Wentworth" entered Austen's juvenilia, there appeared an anonymous epistolary novel entitled *The New Eloisa; or, The History of Mr. Sedley and Miss Wentworth. In a Series of Letters. By a Lady* (1781), which reflects on "the wicked world of gaiety" and mentions "select parties" thrown by a Lady Wentworth.[80] Mary Brunton's novel *Self-Control* (1811), a "runaway success" that went into three editions in the first year, features a prominent cameo by a Mr. Wentworth.[81] By April of 1811, Austen had not yet been able to locate a copy of *Self-Control* yet worried that she would find it *"too clever"* and "my own story & my own people all forestalled."[82] Such works appear desirous of capitalizing on Wentworth fame, titillating audiences with the possibility of a story's connections to a celebrity family that was no stranger to scandal and dispute. While Austen's Capt. Frederick Wentworth may stand out as far more robust and legitimate than these other fictional allusions, even Sir Walter Scott situates his stories among the Wentworths. Not only does he literally place *Ivanhoe* (1819) in a Wentworth forest, in *Rob Roy* (1817) he includes a love interest named Diana Vernon along with a protagonist named Campbell—both prominent names on the Wentworth Castle tree.[83] None of these other publications engage the Wentworth names as if innocent of their larger celebrity. Surely Jane Austen is no innocent either.

What of the Non-Wentworth Names?

Much yet remains to be said about the manner in which the history of the real-world Wentworth clan brings Austen's early and late work into closer proximity and historical relief, but I shall not attempt to fill that large void here. Although I return briefly to the Wentworths in my final chapter, on *Persuasion*, I do not explore the full interpretive impact of Wentworth family history across all of Austen's fictions. While I am greatly indebted to Greene's original insights, I neither duplicate his tight historiographical method nor continue his specific line of inquiry concerning the Wentworth string of Whig characters. I have lingered on Greene's groundbreaking argument, amplifying Austen's allusions to this family with the history of Wentworth Castle, in order to illustrate the need for a wider interdisciplinary lens when reconstructing cultural contexts for Austen's choice of names. Books such as Collins's *Peerage* are not enough. Moreover, not all of Austen's names and protagonists point north to Yorkshire, even though the many that do testify to an astonishing consistency of method and artful allusion.

While the long Wentworth line of names already assuages critical disappointment about a dearth of explicit historical references in Austen, it may still seem possible to lament, as Woolf does, that "Wentworths and Fairfaxes aside, her pages are not full of references to historical characters."[84] Is Austen's fixation on Wentworth history unique or representative of her method? Throughout the remainder of this book, I suspect Austen of applying the same type of historical filter to her choices of non-Wentworth names. If, as Austen so memorably asserted, "an artist cannot do anything slovenly," her other choices must be equally pregnant (*Letters*, 20). Following this logic, I next explore the interpretive consequences for historical and celebrity associations invoked by other clusters of names in her fiction. Wherever possible, I also heed Austen's many small clues to her characters' geographical location. As the story of Wentworth Castle illustrates, a family name may be intricately bound up with the history of their physical estate. In fact, Austen's attention to particular family histories often goes hand in hand with an interest in landscape and garden design. Influenced by the modern expansion of the rubric of history, and relying upon the extensive body of research into Austen's knowledge of such diverse matters as landscaping, local and national history, the navy, economics, literature, travel, and contemporary events, I follow her signposts to real-world historical events and places, arguing that her texts consistently draw on historical people and locations.

In the next chapter, I focus on the twin cases of mistaken identity that activate the plot of *Northanger Abbey*. Escorted to Bath by a kindly Mr. and Mrs. Allen, the heroine promptly gets mistaken for the Allen heir. In turn, the Allens, a modestly well-to-do country couple, are thought vastly rich. These catalysts for Austen's plot have never been investigated with an eye to a historical explanation because being mistaken for an heiress neatly fits the gothic model that *Northanger Abbey* decidedly spoofs. But Austen's fiction has an unacknowledged basis in historical fact, for Bath's largest private fortune, belonging to a genuine Mr. and Mrs. Allen, was in transition during precisely the years that Austen drafted her novel (her sister pointed to 1798 and 1799). The wealth amassed by Bath entrepreneur Ralph Allen (bap. 1693–1764) and held by a niece for more than three decades was just then reverting to obscure Allens living in the country. These historical circumstances warrant a fresh look at *Northanger Abbey*, where the many encoded references to Ralph Allen's architectural legacy reveal a historical specificity to Austen's method that rivals the meticulous attention to setting associated with James Joyce.

CHAPTER TWO

Mapping *Northanger Abbey* to Find "Old Allen" of Prior Park

BEFITTING A BOOK filled with fakes and follies, *Northanger Abbey* starts with a misconception. Almost instantaneously upon her arrival in Bath, the unpretentious Catherine Morland gets mistaken for an heiress. It is not just the buffoonish young John Thorpe who makes this error but also, largely due to Thorpe's influence, the seasoned General Tilney— all because of something suggested by a name. The surname these men seize upon is not Catherine's own but that of her guardians in Bath, a Mr. and Mrs. Allen. The reader knows Mr. Allen to be a comfortable landowner "who owned the chief of the property about Fullerton," the small fictional Wiltshire village where the Morlands live (*NA*, 9). His wealth, in other words, is relative and confined to that locale. The narrator reveals in the opening chapter that the childless Allens head for Bath to treat Mr. Allen's "gouty constitution," kindly taking along young Catherine, the daughter of their local clergyman (9). Yet when these rather ordinary Allens arrive in Bath with their young charge, men such as Thorpe assume "Old Allen is as rich as a Jew" and that Catherine is his goddaughter and the likely heir to his vast fortune (59).

This assumption has legs, if made during the years that Austen drafted her novel (her sister pointed to 1798 and 1799). It is possibly significant that Austen never provides her Allens with first names, keeping them at a deliberate remove, for the Allen surname, common enough in Britain as a whole, was in the context of turn-of-the-century Bath particularly potent. Ralph Allen (bap. 1693–1764), postal entrepreneur, philanthropist, former mayor, stone mogul, and builder of Prior Park, with its renowned landscape garden, had arguably been Bath's most famous historical personage (fig. 2.1). His was not a narrow sort of celebrity. Ralph Allen was a nationally recognized figure and often referred to simply as "the Man of Bath."[1] Without question this Mr. Allen was Bath's richest inhabitant to date. Significantly, the real-world Allen fortune that he had amassed

FIGURE 2.1. Print of Ralph Allen dated 1754, engraved by J. Faber, after a drawing by T. Hudson. *Bath in Time*, Bath Central Library Collection.

was in transition during the novel's composition. The immense wealth that had been held for over three decades by a distant niece, Gertrude Tucker, reverted back to the Allen family name upon her death in 1796.

Catherine's case of mistaken identity by association, as it were, is the understood catalyst for the novel's plot, since the notion that she is the Allens' heir explicitly motivates both Thorpe's initial pursuit as well as

General Tilney's subsequent invitation to Northanger. Such a conjecture about a young woman's sudden wealth from distant relations is, of course, a recurrent feature in the gothic tales that Austen satirizes. Because being mistaken for an heiress seems a typically melodramatic scenario for a gothic heroine, Thorpe's and the General's motivations have never been investigated with an eye to a historical explanation. But *Northanger Abbey* mocks rather than imitates the gothic novel. And Austen's own story has a basis in fact, characteristically offering her peculiar brand of realism as the antidote to gothic fiction. The real-world Mr. and Mrs. Ralph Allen of Bath had passed the bulk of their vast fortune to their favorite niece, Gertrude Tucker.[2] Under her two married names Gertrude lived for many years at Prior Park, until 1796. That year she too died childless, causing the estate to transfer to another branch of the Allen family (to the heirs of the sons of Ralph Allen's brother, Philip Allen), in line with the rules of inheritance law. There appears to have been some minor mystery about this transfer, partly because the distant Allens who inherited the remaining fortune did not move into the family mansion at Prior Park. Relatively unknown in Bath, these remote Allens apparently preferred country life. During all the years that Austen resided in Bath, Prior Park's future remained uncertain; it was eventually sold out of the family in 1807, after Austen had moved away.

Thorpe's tawdry solicitousness toward Catherine is transparently motivated by the assumption that she will inherit the vast riches of *an* Allen fortune. I think that Austen suggests that Thorpe believes it to be *the* Allen fortune, just then in transition. Like Wickham and Willoughby, Thorpe is a rakish member of the predatory species *homo economicus.* General Tilney, "misled by Thorpe's first boast of the family wealth," plays to this same type when he invites Catherine to Northanger in a transparent attempt to hijack her presumed fortune for his son (*NA*, 261). The joke is on them, since Austen reveals that her Allens from Fullerton have no connection whatsoever to the Allens of Bath. Thorpe's predation upon Catherine in the hurly-burly of the Bath marriage market is decidedly generic, and his actions, so typical of the rake-as-obstacle in any romance, do not cry out for immediate explanation through an Allen-Allen connection. Yet the rapidity and inanity of his targeting the daughter of a mere country clergyman, one who, while not strictly poor, harbors no wealthy prospects, are explained by specific historical events of the 1790s. These events are slyly reinforced by Austen's gestures to the name and memory of Ralph Allen throughout the story of *Northanger Abbey.*

The ubiquity in Georgian and Regency Bath of the lingering memory of the late Ralph Allen cannot be exaggerated. Along with Beau Nash and the two architects named John Wood (the Elder and the Younger), Ralph Allen was, indeed remains, among Bath's most famous and foundational inhabitants. He figures in Bath's history as the prime mover of the eighteenth-century wealth, vision, and city planning that raised the city from a slovenly seventeenth-century village with waters for the sick to a metropolitan spa and tourist destination. His name is associated with the pinnacle of Bath's prosperity, a heyday of trade and glamour that was drawing to a close when Austen composed *Northanger Abbey*.[3] A better understanding of the Bath-centered reputation of Ralph Allen recovers the comedic force and social satire embedded in Tilney's and Thorpe's mistaken assessment of the heroine. More specifically still, a knowledge of the high-profile architectural elements in the Bath landscape most directly associated with Allen, particularly his gardens at Prior Park and his so-called Sham Castle, exerts an influence upon a reading of specific scenes in the text, scenes that deftly take us past these famous places. For with a cartographer's precision, Austen navigates her characters through Bath's turn-of-the-century landscape, emphasizing Catherine's ignorance of the mistakes made by Thorpe and General Tilney with implied views of the real-world Allen's visible legacy. These historical circumstances warrant a fresh look at *Northanger Abbey*, where the many encoded references to Ralph Allen's architectural designs reveal a historical specificity to Austen's method that rivals the cartographic exactitude of modernists such as James Joyce.

Bath and *Northanger Abbey*'s Composition and Sale

The connection my argument makes between *Northanger Abbey*'s plot and its astonishing precision about Bath's history and urban landscape touches upon the work's composition and publication. Relative to the complex debates about Austen's others novels and their multiple bouts of revision, the history of *Northanger Abbey*'s composition is fairly uncontroversial. Cassandra records in her much-cited memorandums of 1817 that "North-hanger Abbey was written about the years 98 & 99," and Deirdre Le Faye refines this period to, tentatively, August 1798 to June 1799.[4] These dates roughly coincide with Austen's recorded visits to Bath in 1797 and again in 1799, although other short visits may, some suggest, have occurred as early as 1794, or even 1790.[5] The Austen family had relatives in Bath and eventually moved there as part of Mr. Austen's retirement in 1801, taking up residence at No. 4 Sydney Place. This is where, scholars agree, Jane Austen probably put the finishing touches to her manuscript, initially called *Susan*. With regard to family, the young Jane Austen enjoyed a distant as well as an immediate connection to Bath. Her mother's great uncle was James Brydges, Duke of Chandos (1674–1744), a near-contemporary of Ralph Allen's and co-sponsor of John Wood's Bath. Knowledge of her own family history thus already secures Austen's awareness of Ralph Allen, since it overlaps a great deal.[6]

All scholars accept that the bulk of *Northanger Abbey* was written prior to 1803, when Austen first offered the manuscript for sale under the title of *Susan*. Then a full-time resident of Bath, the twenty-seven-year-old Austen received £10 for the copyright, saw the novel advertised as "In Press," but never, to her dismay, saw it actually published.[7] Her brother Henry bought back the original manuscript from Crosby & Company in London sometime in 1816 with an evident intention to help his sister publish it. She then altered her heroine's name to Catherine and penned a brief advertisement. This advertisement accompanied the novel under the still-different title of *Northanger Abbey*, which scholars presume to be Henry's and Cassandra's choice, when it was posthumously published in December 1817 (the cited date is 1818), six months after the author's death on 18 July 1817. The consensus of scholarly opinion is that Austen, who was growing increasingly ill from the autumn of 1816 onward, did not extensively revise her 1803 manuscript, both because she lacked the time and because all the historical references in the final novel predate that year. The mapping of Austen's cartographic details reinforces this standard view, suggesting that Austen wrote in the company of Bath as it looked to her in 1797 and 1799 and possibly slightly beyond—through her first years of residence at Sydney Place, from 1801 to 1803. To the extent that the novel's own physical and historical setting likely reflects the time of its composition, I agree with Marilyn Butler that "*Northanger Abbey* is essentially a work of the late 1790s."[8]

My emphasis on the novel's deliberate mapping of Bath may, however, gloss one minor sticking point in its publication history, namely her nephew James Edward Austen-Leigh's assertion, made in his *Memoir*, that the original sale of the manuscript in 1803 had been "to a publisher in Bath."[9] Gilson suggests a "Mr. Cruttwell" as the likely Bath conduit to Crosby & Company in London and points to an advertisement for a pamphlet about the trial of Mrs. Jane Leigh Perrot, Austen's aunt who was accused of shoplifting, that names both firms.[10] In light of this connection, Gilson grants, quoting the *Memoir*, that "it is possible that the first overtures for *Susan* were in fact made in Bath."[11] Anthony Mandal similarly allows that "the Bath connection is quite likely a valid one," suggesting that Crosby's "provincial links" to publishers in the West Country might have enabled Cruttwell to serve as "the channel through which Austen approached Crosby and Co."[12] In 1803, the year of *Susan's* sale, the Austen family resided at Sydney Place, making an approach to a prominent local publisher about a story set in Bath appear logical. The Cruttwell family also had strong ties to Sherborne, a country parish contiguous with the one from which Mr. Austen had just retired. This further strengthens the possibility that the Austens knew, or knew of, the Cruttwells and so began enquiries with them.[13] If sending an unsolicited manuscript to a London publisher seemed daunting to the young Jane Austen—and certainly her father's cold-call on Thomas Cadell in London via letter had not yielded any results in 1797—then calling on a Bath-based firm with family connections to their previous community would have been an appealing alternative, especially when such a visit might be made in person. If, as Gilson suggests, Austen approached the Cruttwell establishment in 1803, she dealt with Richard Shuttleworth Cruttwell, who took over his father's business in 1799. Yet, as Gilson is aware, all the Cruttwells were primarily printers and not, strictly speaking, publishers—though they owned shares in several local newspapers, including the *Bath Chronicle*, and were "one of the earliest publishers to issue local guides."[14]

If the nature of Cruttwell's output and business dealings are carefully considered, perhaps Austen's choice to approach this firm reveals an intended audience for *Susan*. Occasionally, the Cruttwells of Bath did print book-length works "for the author" or "for the editor," suggesting that the firm was willing to dabble in book publishing as long as the author bore the printing costs. The Cruttwells were also worth approaching for their London network alone, as evidenced by the many respectable London booksellers mentioned in their imprints. But perhaps the salient feature of their business interests concerns the fact that Cruttwell owned Bath's local newspaper and issued guides. This might have made him particularly receptive to the manner in which the manuscript of *Susan* made use of local history and geography. While Cruttwell's was in the business of printing novels for other publishers, it published much local news and indigenous fare. Perhaps Austen thought of *Susan* in this light—as slightly journalistic, a fictionalized guidebook of sorts. Perhaps Cruttwell, as both Gilson and Mandal imply, declined but pointed the way to Crosby's in London. To preserve the author's anonymity, her brother Henry's banking agent, William Seymour, it has been suggested, transacted the actual sale to Crosby.[15] The significance of these speculations about Cruttwell's initial involvement for my own place-centered argument of *Northanger Abbey* is transparent. If Austen initially consulted a Bath-based firm about her debut novel—and it is Gilson, with Mandal's approval, who points to Cruttwell's as the most likely establishment—it greatly increases the chance that she targeted a reader familiar with Bath's landscape and local lore.

A presumed Bath-savvy audience explains why *Northanger Abbey* devotes little or no space to any direct description of sights in Bath. Instead, Austen drops the names of Bath's streets and locales into her story in what one historian calls "an amiable taking-it-for-granted manner."[16] Austen, who knows Bath well, does indeed tacitly assume a kindred familiarity in her reader. Banking on Bath's popularity as a tourist destination, she might have assumed a great deal even from a London audience. Yet, her smallish mentions of streets differ from the wide-angled descriptions in, for example, Frances Burney's *Evelina* (1778), a known favorite of Austen's. Partly set in Bath, *Evelina* describes features of interest to a London reader, including the dominant view of Ralph Allen's estate as seen from the city's center: "The Crescent, the prospect from it, and the elegant symmetry of the Circus, delighted me. The Parades, I own, rather disappointed me; one of them is scarce preferable to some of the best paved streets in London, and the other, though it affords a beautiful prospect, a charming view of Prior Park and of the Avon, yet wanted something in *itself* of more striking elegance than a mere broad pavement, to satisfy the ideas I had formed of it."[17] Burney's fault-finding descriptions, voiced by her young heroine, are those of the tourist. Although Austen's heroine is similarly new to Bath, *Northanger Abbey*, by contrast, offers scenery from a local's "taking-it-for-granted" point of view. It never has to mention, we shall see, Prior Park by name. Austen coyly practices a synecdoche of description that allows a mere part to stand for the whole. The reader's assumed topographical knowledge of Bath includes the structures along the city's skyline that were so strongly associated with the real-world Mr. Allen, particularly his estate of Prior Park and his so-called Sham Castle. These well-known Allen landmarks, highly visible along the edges of "Bath's amphitheatrical setting" from almost every street mentioned in the novel, watch over Austen's characters.[18] As one 1799 guidebook observed, "Prior Park, and its embellishments, form a pleasing scene for the rambling eye, while you are walking over the parades, or passing along Great Pulteney-street."[19] Austen assumes that a reader's knowledge of Bath, helped along by the telltale name of Allen, will conjure up his buildings and gardens in the landscape of her scenes. To overlook these famous features of Bath's landscape, the visible evidence of the Allen fortune in Austen's day, is to miss much of Austen's artistic subtlety in *Northanger Abbey*.

"The Man of Bath" and Squire Allworthy

Ralph Allen's wealth was remarkable both because it was utterly self-made and because it was rarely begrudged. In Pope's terms, "low-born" Allen came to remote Bath to obtain the position of salaried deputy postmaster in 1712.[20] He soon secured the right "to farm the cross-post, and the bye-way post" in such a manner that the regional mail did not need to go, as was customary, via London.[21] His entrepreneurial postal scheme involved great risk, including an outlay of £6,000 annually for the rights, but paid huge dividends. Determined to prevent fraud in his subcontractors, Allen proved a meticulous and fair-dealing businessman and "in time realized profits in the order of £12,000 per year."[22] Allen primarily invested these profits in large swathes of land in and around Bath, including its stone quarries. Eventually, this investment strategy gave Allen a near-monopoly on Bath's local stone, putting him in a position to encourage the city's growth. He did not stimulate urban development merely to line his own pockets, being known, in fact, for the reverse. He bought out his competitors so as to keep the price of stone low and encourage further urban beautification and expansion. Allen was also widely hailed as a generous philanthropist, giving freely to the poor (over £1,000 annually) and funding a number of benevolent projects with donations of stone and labor, such as Bath General Hospital.

The jewel of the Allen empire was the Palladian mansion at Prior Park (fig. 2.2). The house was built by John Wood, the Elder, starting in the 1730s. It had a grand imposing façade and enjoyed breathtaking vistas of Bath from its vantage point at the top of a hillside just southeast of the city. But Prior Park was built on a hilltop "not only to see all Bath but for all Bath to see."[23] The house on the hill's crest and its elegant sloping gardens, which rolled toward town, were intended as visible markers of

FIGURE 2.2. Popular 1750 print of Prior Park, by Anthony Walker. *Bath in Time*, Bath Central Library Collection.

Bath's prosperity. To achieve maximum visual impact, Allen employed major talent in the design of his landscape garden. He initially sought the advice of Alexander Pope, with William Kent weighing in on subsequent improvements. Over the years Allen added structures and satellite buildings to these grounds. Most widely known, perhaps, is the copy of a much-admired Palladian bridge, whose original was designed by Pembroke, constructed in the 1750s to stretch over a sculpted pond at the bottom of the Prior Park garden. But there were also some lesser-known touches. For example, Mrs. Allen began construction on a grotto in the 1740s, possibly under the influence of Pope's passion for such garden features (Boyce, 115). Over the Ralph Allen years a pinery, a cascade, an octagonal stone hut, an outdoor room called the Grass Cabinet, a "sham bridge," a Gothic Temple, serpentine walks and a serpentine lake, a pair of gatehouses, and various other embellishments sprouted up on the sloping lawns facing Bath.[24]

In addition to building notable architectural monuments at Prior Park, Allen also turned his home into "a centre of hospitality and culture."[25] Many of England's literati, politicians, and artists came to stay with the Allens at Prior Park. Thomas Gainsborough, who lived in town, visited the Allens, along with celebrity-painter William Hoare and James Quin, who apparently brought David Garrick. Alexander Pope, in particular, relied heavily upon the friendship and hospitality of Ralph Allen. Pope wrote much of the expanded *Dunciad* at Prior Park and on one memorable visit even brought Martha Blount. The Allens frequently hosted such literary figures as Sarah and Henry Fielding, and also had Samuel Richardson to stay. Well-known clergy and politicians stopped by, including William Warburton, William Pitt the Elder, and Sir John Ligonier. Royalty, too, came to visit, including the young Princess Amelia. Prior Park was part of the eighteenth-century literary scene, even when the authors did not come in person. Richardson wrote Allen for advice on the manuscript of his continuation of *Pamela*, while Sterne sent two copies of *Sermons of Mr. Yorick* to Prior Park.[26] "The mounting fame of both mansion and master," recounts Benjamin Boyce, turned Prior Park itself into a tourist site, "the object of curiosity to all strangers who came to Bath." The Allens proved so inundated with tourists that they "set Thursday as the time in each week when sight-seers might be admitted."[27] In brief, Allen's literary and political network at Prior Park had given the place a national profile. Although a natural part of a literary-minded novel, *Northanger Abbey*'s many explicit references to Fielding, Pope, Richardson, and other eighteenth-century greats, dovetail nicely with Bath's own history.

By Austen's time, Ralph Allen had not only served as host to literary giants, he had personally played a role in the history of the early novel, that is, as a model for Squire Allworthy in *Tom Jones* (1749). Fielding, a most frequent guest at Prior Park, evidently wrote part of the story there. Fielding's picture of a benevolent squire who lives on a vast estate in Somerset without an heir (Ralph Allen's only son, George, had died in infancy) was widely hailed as an homage to the generous and kindhearted Allen. Later, Fielding also dedicated *Amelia* (1751) to his friend and benefactor.[28] From the start of *Northanger Abbey*, Austen refers to *Tom Jones* obliquely, quipping, for example, that the Morlands in Fullerton knew not one family "who had reared and supported a boy accidentally found at their door—not one young man whose origin was unknown" (*NA*, 9).[29] She even mentions *Tom Jones* by name, although not wholly favorably since she allows her rake to condemn it with his praise. Thorpe so much approves of *Tom Jones* that he measures all other novels against it: "Novels are all so full of nonsense and stuff; there has not been a tolerably decent one come out since Tom Jones, except the Monk" (43). Thorpe, who soon rails against Burney's *Camilla* (1796), a novel for which Austen was an original subscriber, by saying "I took up the first volume once and looked it over, but I soon found it would not do," may be in the habit of reading only the beginnings of books (43). His literary opinion likely does not matter much. Yet it was precisely the opening chapters of *Tom Jones* that were scrutinized most closely for Fielding's fictionalized portrait of Allen.

In light of this association, local Bath lore regularly conflated Allen and Allworthy. One nineteenth-century print depicts the ivy-bedecked mausoleum at nearby Claverton, where Allen lies interred: it is inscribed "Mausoleum of Ralph Allen, the Squire Allworthy of Tom Jones" (fig. 2.3).[30] If a reading of *Tom Jones* activates an awareness of the rich and benevolent Ralph Allen in Bath, talk of the novel may account for, or at least clue the reader into, Thorpe's sudden change of itinerary for the next day's outing. For, just prior to the mention of *Tom Jones*, Thorpe proposes to take Catherine for a ride in his open carriage, declaring, "I will drive you up Lansdown Hill to-morrow," a popular destination that promises a scenic drive along the high ground leading to Bristol (*NA*, 42). The subsequent small talk about the excellences of *Tom Jones*, however, seems to influence his proposed itinerary, for on the following day when he and his sister arrive, rather suddenly, to take Catherine for a ride, their declared destination is instead Claverton Down.

Despite Thorpe's implication and Catherine's half-hearted agreement that such was his intention all along, Claverton Down is in precisely the opposite direction from the promised Lansdown Hill:

> "What do you mean?" said Catherine, "where are you all going to?"
> "Going to? why, you have not forgot our engagement! Did not we agree together to take a drive this morning? What a head you have! We are going up Claverton Down."
> "Something was said about it, I remember," said Catherine, looking at Mrs. Allen for her opinion; "but really I did not expect you." (*NA*, 57)

Catherine does not protest the change in direction and, in fact, seems too flummoxed by the brazenness of the party and the novelty of a carriage outing with a young man to assert herself. Possibly Thorpe's radical change of direction, from Lansdown Hill in the northwest to Claverton

FIGURE 2.3. Nineteenth-century print of the "Mausoleum of Ralph Allen, the Squire Allworthy of Tom Jones." *Bath in Time*, Bath Central Library Collection.

Down in the southeast, is intended as a geographical clue to the influence of the Allen estate of Prior Park on Thorpe's motivations, for Thorpe's radically revised route will now lead them straight to the gates of Prior Park.

Prior Park, the Sham Castle, and Mapmaker Mr. Thorpe

It is in direct sight of the Prior Park gates that Thorpe first speaks about "Old Allen" and his money. Poor Catherine, unlike Austen's Bath-savvy reader, seems utterly oblivious to Thorpe's geographical innuendo. Because contemporary maps of Bath tended to extend their shelf life by anticipating planned developments, thus forecasting Bath slightly, multiple charts are essential in any mapping of *Northanger Abbey*. Using plans of Bath from 1794 and 1808 to roughly bookend the novel's possible dates of composition, it is possible to trace Thorpe's route and topographically gloss the encoded conversation that occurs during this drive (figs. 2.4 and 2.5).

Austen has the awkward pair start off in "silence" from Pulteney Street, where the Allens and Catherine reside. From that address the most direct route to the Claverton Down Road would take her characters from the corner of Pulteney Street and Sydney Place onto the quiet rural track that throughout the 1790s still lay across the open meadows connecting the Bathwick development to the parish of Widcombe. This road ran roughly parallel to the Avon and would eventually be straightened out to become Darlington Street (the 1794 map names it Sackville Street, a provisional name that was never actually used for the finished project). After the completion of the Kennet and Avon Canal portion, which dissects Sydney Gardens, shown in the 1808 map, the extension of Darlington Street would direct traffic smoothly between the river and the canal. The first boat trip along the Sydney Gardens portion of the canal took place in June 1810, so even the 1808 map anticipates the canal's completion.[31] Just after passing through the Turnpike Gate, any carriage traveling along this road would be forced to come to a stop right in front of the Prior Park Gate, where a sharp left turn would place the party immediately on the Claverton Down Road.[32] Not only does this road offer the most direct route to their declared destination, but both maps show that through to at least 1808, straightened or not, it still offered the relative privacy of rural scenery craved by both John Thorpe and James Morland, who accompanies Thorpe's sister Isabella in a second carriage.

With confident precision, Austen allows that "a silence of several minutes succeeded their first short dialogue" (*NA*, 59). Although Thorpe has already boasted in a prior scene that his horse travels, come rain or shine, at a nippy ten miles per hour, the text again calculates their exact rate of progress in the thoughts of an ironic narrator, focalized by Catherine, who observes of the calm horse that "its inevitable pace was ten miles an hour" (59). Thorpe's boast and Catherine's ironic acceptance, of course, defy a reader's belief, since this rate of speed was barely sustained by seasoned professionals, such as the coach that will take Catherine home at the novel's end, and only on clear days and good roads. Indeed, the Allen fortune, made from a postal route's optimized efficiency, nicely belies Thorpe's ambitious calculations for his mere gig. Austen puts the lie to Thorpe in the earlier scene when James contradicts his estimate of ten miles per hour for their trip from Tetbury to Bath: Thorpe insists they covered twenty-five miles in 2.5 hours, while James says it was twenty-three miles in 3.5 hours (this would give their true speed as 6.57 miles per hour). The map confirms that the distance from the top of Pulteney Street to Prior Park is no more than three-quarters of a mile, which, even

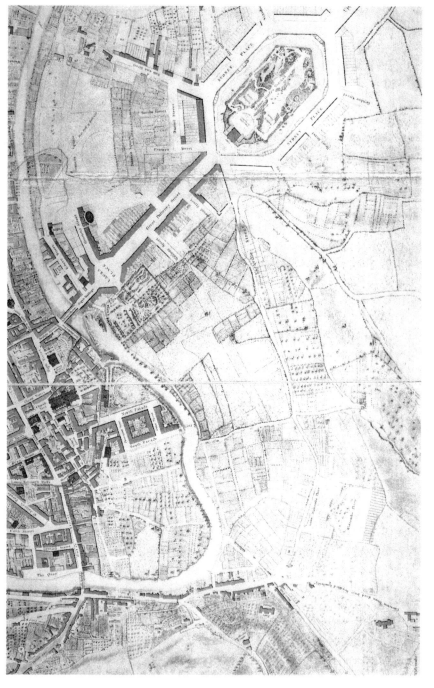

FIGURE 2.4. Detail of the Bathwick area in one of the most detailed maps of the time, "The City of Bath," by Charles Harcourt Masters (1794). Reprinted with minor revisions in 1808 (see figure 2.5). *Bath in Time*, Bath Central Library Collection.

FIGURE 2.5. Detail of the Bathwick area in the 1808 version of "The City of Bath," by Charles Harcourt Masters. *Bath in Time,* Bath Central Library Collection.

at the slower rate given by James, would take a carriage under seven minutes to traverse. Austen's unusual redundancy about likely rates of speed ensures that any reader familiar with Bath can mentally calculate how "several minutes" of silent progress may be all that is necessary to have Catherine brought from the fictional Allens in Pulteney Street to the gates of the real-world Allen home at Prior Park.

It is likely, then, in full view of the old Allen estate that Thorpe, perhaps at the sharp turn onto Claverton Down Road, "abruptly" breaks the silence with his crude inquiry into Catherine's relationship to the Allens. "A silence of several minutes succeeded their first short dialogue;—it was broken by Thorpe's saying very abruptly, 'Old Allen is as rich as a Jew—is not he?' Catherine did not understand him—and he repeated his question, adding in explanation, 'Old Allen, the man you are with'" (*NA*, 59). Since the scenic road "up Claverton Down" then travels steeply uphill with Prior Park on the right, the entire exchange about the Allens takes place in a carriage that is slowly edging Ralph Allen's grounds at Prior Park:

> "Oh! Mr. Allen, you mean. Yes, I believe, he is very rich."
> "And no children at all?"
> "No—not any."
> "A famous thing for his next heirs. He is *your* godfather, is not he?"
> "My godfather!—no."
> "But you are always very much with them."
> "Yes, very much."
> "Aye, that is what I meant. He seems a good kind of old fellow
> enough, and has lived very well in his time, I dare say; he is not gouty
> for nothing." (59–60)[33]

Although Catherine, newly arrived in Bath, remains troublingly unaware of the significance of their locale during this odd interrogation, any reader who knows the landscape cannot remain innocent of the Allen-Allen link—and neither, surely, does Thorpe.

Cruttwell's *New Bath Guide* recommends a scenic airing up Claverton Down for all who would enjoy "a delightful prospect of the city of Bath." It adds that "To the right as you ascend this Down, is a seat that belonged to the late Ralph Allen, esq."[34] While Catherine's naïve gaze is probably turned toward the delightful urban prospect on their left, Thorpe presumably ogles his financial prospects on the right. This is not to say that Austen implies that Thorpe must believe Mr. Allen to be Ralph Allen, dead for over three decades even in the first draft of *Susan*—although that level of stupidity would nicely lard his buffoonery—but merely that his timing and line of enquiry suggest that he mistakes Catherine for the heir to an Allen fortune with Bath connections. Perhaps he hopes that the day's proximity to Prior Park will set loose some acknowledgment of a family association on Catherine's part. Claverton Down road, of course, also aims directly at nearby Claverton, where stands the mausoleum of "Ralph Allen, the Squire Allworthy of Tom Jones" (see fig. 2.3). Austen enhances Thorpe's conversation with a choice of setting that winks at and rewards those in the know about Bath. Her street names are not casual throwaways to mark the urban setting generally, but compact clues that ironically highlight what the characters are looking at—or, in Thorpe's case, even thinking.

If Jane Austen maps her fictional characters with uncanny precision, she may have gleaned this impulse from another cartographer in her family. A map of the island of St. Helena published in 1816 by the Hydrographic Office bears this note: "The N.W. Bank of Soundings by Captain F. W. Austin R.N. in 1808" (fig. 2.6). In spite of the spelling variation, this map of the island is indeed based upon the painstaking coastal measurements, or "soundings," taken by Jane Austen's seafaring brother Frank (Francis William Austen), a ship captain in the Royal Navy at that time.[35] Although the date of this particular map takes us beyond the completion of *Susan*, the existence of Frank's chart of St. Helena (he also made other charts) suggests the larger cartographic sensibility that surrounded the Austens. Jane herself, we know, had the necessary knowledge of Bath to be precise. Starting in 1801, she lived at No. 4 Sydney Place, on that very intersection with Pulteney Street from which Thorpe's carriage departs. Not only had the long months of active house-hunting in Bath, as Park Honan observes, sharpened her eye for details of distance and location, she must have traveled the same route to the Claverton Down Road on numerous occasions and therefore need not have owned a stopwatch to measure, with the naval precision of her brother Frank's soundings and charts, that a mere "several minutes" would suffice to take a gig from her own home directly to the gates of Prior Park.[36]

Before returning to the concrete mapped movement of Austen's characters, I would like to insert one minor speculative observation about a particular brand of map. In Austen's time, Bath's population, which swelled to about 33,000 during the season, constituted a clientele keen on works about the place itself. Due to its heavy tourist constituency,

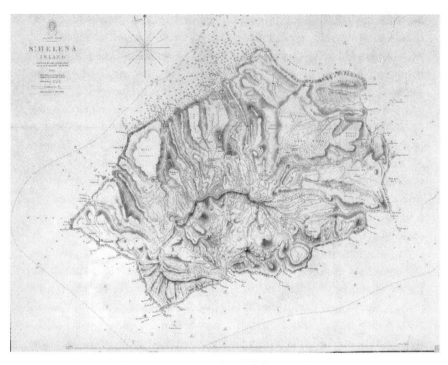

FIGURE 2.6. Map of the island of St. Helena published in 1816 by the Hydrographic Office, based upon "Soundings by Captain F. W. Austin R.N. in 1808." Harry Ransom Center, The University of Texas at Austin.

Bath's print market in local products enjoyed a lively trade in maps of all sorts. Some ladies' fans even came equipped with maps of the city center and pictures of local buildings (fig. 2.7). Cruttwell's guides, too, could be purchased for one price without a map and a slightly higher price with a "plan" of the city. For example, the title page of Cruttwell's *The Strangers' Assistant and Guide to Bath* (1773), another of their early guidebooks, lists two prices: "*One Shilling*" for the book alone and "*One shilling and Sixpence*" if purchased "with a Plan of Bath." *The Strangers' Assistant* appends a list of related works sold separately. This list includes a cheap and compact map of the city center as well as another that was so detailed and far ranging that it cost the same as Cruttwell's guidebook-with-plan. This meticulous map of Bath and its environs is the work of a man named Thorpe: "A MAP of Five Miles round the City of BATH, on a Scale of One Inch and a Half to a Mile, reduced from an actual Survey made by THOMAS THORPE, with Alterations & Improvements to the present Time. Pr. 1s. 6d."[37] One 1773 map that fits this advertisement's description is shown here (fig. 2.8). Updated and shrunken versions of this same circular map, with or without mention of Thorpe as the original designer, appeared in editions of *The Original Bath Guide* through the 1820s.[38]

In 1742, Thomas Thorpe had drawn up a map of Bath and its environs so comprehensive that it remained the gold standard for all maps with a radius of multiple miles for, at least, the next half century. The original map's sheer bulk, as well as its list of subscribers, implies that Thorpe's creation was not aimed at the mere tourist. Mowbray Green describes Thorpe's survey as a watershed moment in the history of Bath's topography: "The map, 39 inches in diameter, is perhaps one of the most valuable contributions which we possess, not only to the topography, but also to the history of the time. The names of many of the owners of the country houses are noted, and the two spandrel corners on the left of the map are occupied by an alphabetical list of the subscribers."[39] Thorpe's map was originally published in multiple sheets: "Mr. Thorpe published an actual survey of the city and five miles round; wherein are laid down all the villages, gentlemens seats, farm houses, roads, highways,

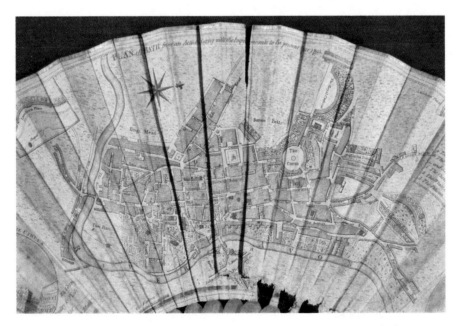

FIGURE 2.7. Detail from plan of Bath fan, "From an Actual Survey with the Improvements to the present year 1793." *Bath in Time*, Private Collection, Bath.

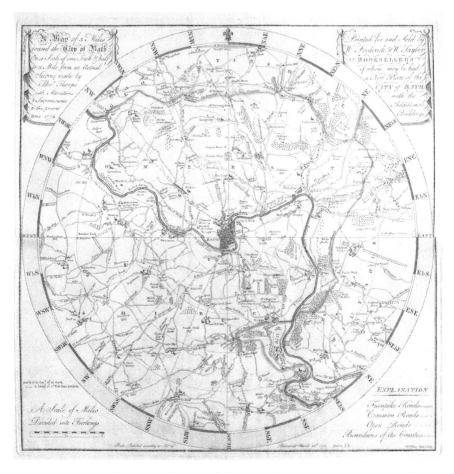

FIGURE 2.8. "A Plan of 5 Miles Round the City of Bath On a Scale of one Inch & half to a Mile from an Actual Survey made by Tho:ˢ Thorpe with Alterations & Improvements to the present time 1773." *Bath in Time*, Bath Central Library Collection.

rivers, watercourses, and all things worthy of observation, in ten sheets, circular."[40] The advertisements in Cruttwell's guidebooks already confirm that for many decades Bath's best maps for tourist consumption continued to be based upon Mr. Thorpe's well-known original, and often prominently declared this heritage in their imprints and advertisements. At least as late as 1787, maps of Bath and its environs, those not limited to the inner city, continued to pay homage to Thorpe: "Improved Map of the Villages, Roads, Farm-Houses, & c., Five Miles round the City

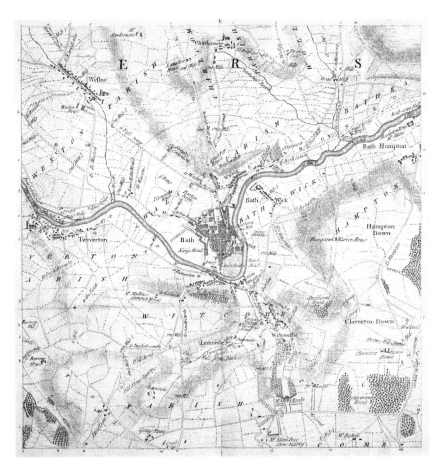

FIGURE 2.9. Detail of the original 1742 "Plan of Bath and 5 Miles Surrounds,"
by Thomas Thorpe. *Bath in Time*, Bath Central Library Collection.

of Bath; by T. Thorpe and others. London. 1787."[41] Since Thorpe's map
dates to the heyday of Ralph Allen, the Prior Park estate, Allen holdings,
and even his quarries, were dutifully listed in the original[42] (fig. 2.9).
These same features continue to appear on the subsequently updated
(and compact) Thorpe-brand of maps still sold in Austen's time. The
existence and longevity of Thorpe's maps, of course, begs the question of
whether Austen names her topographically active rake for a well-known
surveyor and mapmaker. Perhaps the name of Thorpe is itself a clue to
her readers to pull out their updated copy of Mr. Thorpe's map of "five
miles round" and follow his namesake around Bath's landscape. In this
context, the suggestion that Austen initially consulted Cruttwell's, an es-

tablishment familiar with the Thorpe maps and incentivized to approve of any gimmick that reminded readers of related products, has luster.

Whether or not she gestures to an actual map of Bath by a Mr. Thorpe, Austen repeats her map trick the next time John Thorpe takes Catherine out in his carriage. On this occasion the fictional Thorpe's lure is the promise of Blaise Castle beyond Clifton, which he describes in false terms:

> "Blaize Castle!" cried Catherine; "what is that?"
> "The finest place in England—worth going fifty miles at any time to see."
> "What, is it really a castle, an old castle?"
> "The oldest in the kingdom."
> "But is it like what one reads of?"
> "Exactly—the very same."
> "But now really—are there towers and long galleries?"
> "By dozens."
> "Then I should like to see it." (*NA*, 83)

As Austen's modern editors routinely point out, in reality Blaise Castle was neither "old" nor "real" and encompassed but one small open-air room. Built in 1766 by Thomas Farr, a sugar merchant from Bristol, Blaise Castle was a typical folly, a faux Gothic castle built to enhance the view from Farr's house. This eye-catcher was also located at Henbury and not, as Thorpe has it, at Kingsweston. It had three round towers triangulated around one central circular room, which was used to entertain the occasional visitor on outdoor excursions. The whole effect of Farr's summer house is not unlike a fanciful picnic area in Disneyland and nothing like the genuine castle Catherine imagines and Thorpe promises. As Marilyn Butler notes, the discussion of Blaise Castle "seems a clear case where Austen advantages those of her readers who have topographical and architectural knowledge."[43] The cartographic cleverness of Austen's ensuing scene extends, however, beyond knowledge of Blaise Castle alone.

Thomas Farr's Blaise Castle was, in fact, erected in imitation of a prominent folly in Bath built a decade earlier by Ralph Allen. Like Austen's heroine, Ralph Allen was fond of the Gothic and added in 1755 to his Palladian achievements at Prior Park a fake Gothic castle on the crest of Bathwick Hill facing the city center (see Boyce, 225–26). Colloquially dubbed "Ralph Allen's Sham Castle" the structure was a classic garden folly, an architectural trompe l'oeil to fool the likes of a visitor just like Catherine. From a distance the whimsical façade deftly impersonated a medieval castle, complete with a gothically pointed central archway, a pair of round towers with cross cutouts, and a castellated silhouette (fig. 2.10). The sham castle was Allen's response to the emerging interest in the Gothic. Boyce points to a fake Gothic "ruin" at Stowe, built some years previous, as a project "Allen must have known" (225). Quick to recognize this trend as an "opportunity" to make the city of Bath more picturesque and enhance tourism with "a Gothick Object," Allen asked none other than William Pitt, "another enthusiast for Gothic supplements to Palladian triumphs," to enlist for him the help of that "Great Master of the Gothic," Sanderson Miller (225 and 226). As Boyce notes, Wood senior was no longer alive to protest the placing of a bogus Gothic behemoth prominently along his delicately planned Palladian skyline. Allen's motivation was, however, characteristically public-minded. The sham castle, Boyce explains, "was not built, one must understand, to ornament the vista from Prior Park," from which the structure would barely be visible. "This was one of Mr. Allen's benefactions (and Mr. Pitt's) to Bath

FIGURE 2.10. Steel engraving of Ralph Allen's Sham Castle, published by W. Everitt in 1844. *Bath in Time*, Bath Central Library Collection.

FIGURE 2.11. "Sham Castle from the North Parade Bridge," a print c. 1850. *Bath in Time*, Bath Central Library Collection.

and the world's travelers" (226). Boyce documents the prominence of the sham castle on the top of the hill, from where it "looked down upon the Terrace Walk and the Parades to charm all visitors to Bath" (226). Maps and views of Bath well beyond 1803 confirm the lack of surrounding structures that might impede the prominent view of its blazing white façade against the green hill from almost anywhere along the eastern sweep of Bath, which up to that date remained, with the notable exception of the Bathwick development where the Austens (and the fictional Allens) resided, bounded by the curvature of the Avon (figs. 2.11 and 2.12). In Austen's day, the Sham Castle, in fact, peered over this suburban development. Although a restoration project in 1921 possibly tidied and repaired Allen's "strange building" to excess, making a faux medieval castle look disturbingly new, even today, when it ornaments a private golf course, it remains a noteworthy architectural oddity.[44]

Allen's garden folly ironically illuminates Catherine's enthusiasm for Gothic piles, and especially her desire to see Blaise Castle. Allen's Sham

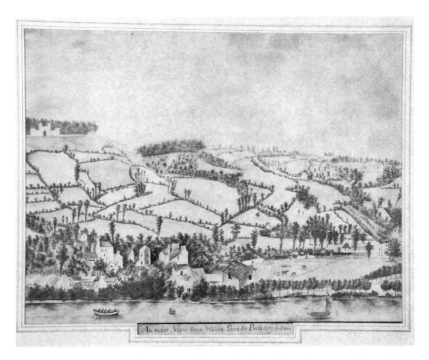

FIGURE 2.12. View of Hills surrounding Bath from Sham Castle on left to Prior Park on right, dated 1789. Pen and ink drawing by John West. © Victoria Art Gallery, Bath and North East Somerset Council / The Bridgeman Art Library.

Castle figures in the exchanges about Blaise not only because it may have served as its impetus and model but also because its location atop Bathwick Hill made it visible from the very street where the heroine starts her quest for a Gothic "edifice like Udolpho" (*NA*, 85). Catherine's eagerness to see Blaise Castle blinds her to the castle on the hill near her own doorstep on Pulteney Street. Her address is, of course, around the corner from the one that was Austen's own between 1801 and 1804. From No. 4 Sydney Place, the Austens probably saw the Sham Castle daily from their upstairs windows. In 1848, James Tunstall records how the Sham Castle still "stands conspicuously on the slope of the hill" and includes a picture of it in his book that could indeed serve as an apt illustration for Ann Radcliffe's novel (fig. 2.13).[45] For a reader knowledgeable about Bath, the fact that Thorpe would take Catherine "fifty miles" to see something that can essentially be seen from where they start reconfirms his misleading influence. A view of the Sham Castle closer to the novel's 1803 date of sale is shown in "The Sydney Hotel" (1805), by Jean Claude Nattes,

THE SHAM CASTLE.

FIGURE 2.13. "The Sham Castle." Book illustration from James Tunstall's *Rambles about Bath and Its Neighbourhood* (1848). *Bath in Time*, Bath Central Library Collection.

likely the same "Mr Claude Nattes" hired in 1785 to instruct young Cassandra and Jane "in the ladylike accomplishment of pencil portraiture"[46] (fig. 2.14). Nattes's plate confirms the visual proximity of Allen's folly to the fictional Allens's residence on Pulteney Street. As seen from the Sutton Street intersection at the forking of Sydney Place with Pulteney Street, Nattes's view of 1805 shows the castle on the hill visible behind the garden wall of the Sydney Hotel, a structure begun in 1796 that now houses the Holburne Museum. Austen charts the progress of Thorpe's carriage down Pulteney Street with notable precision, naming each relevant intersection toward Pulteney Bridge on their way into town—to take, eventually, the road north toward Clifton. Thus Austen marks her

FIGURE 2.14. Sham Castle as seen in the background of "Sydney Hotel," by Jean Claude Nattes (1805). *Bath in Time*, Bath Central Library Collection.

characters' slow and steady retreat from one sham castle as they aim toward another.

Through the symbolic intervention of the Tilneys, Catherine momentarily turns "round" to face the correct way. Catherine, of course, is preoccupied by thoughts of the Tilneys, whom she believes have forgotten all about their promise to take her on a country walk:

> To feel herself slighted by them was very painful. On the other hand, the delight of exploring an edifice like Udolpho, as her fancy represented Blaize Castle to be, was such a counterpoise of good, as might console her for almost any thing.
>
> They passed briskly down Pulteney-street, and through Laura-place, without the exchange of many words. Thorpe talked to his horse, and she meditated, by turns, on broken promises and broken arches, phaetons and false hangings, Tilneys and trap-doors. As they entered Argyle-buildings, however, she was roused by this address from her companion, "Who is that girl who looked at you so hard as she went by?"
>
> "Who?—where?"

"On the right-hand pavement—she must be almost out of sight now."
Catherine looked round and saw Miss Tilney leaning on her brother's
arm, walking slowly down the street. She saw them both looking back
at her. (*NA*, 85)

The street names in this passage allow us to track their straight line of
progress down the length of Pulteney Street, through the offset square of
Laura Place, and onto Argyle Street, where they pass by the Tilneys, who
are walking in the opposite direction along the "Argyle-buildings," which
line both sides of the bridge.

Any map of the area will confirm that none of the characters has yet
moved out of the corridor that extends behind them and aims toward
Bathwick Hill. Miss Tilney, who has not forgotten her, is thus proceeding directly toward the very destination that Catherine's hopes are set
upon, namely, a sham castle—the one on the hill at Pulteney Street's end.
Yet even when she turns round to look at Miss Tilney, Catherine fails to
see, or recall,[47] the castle so near to hand, a fact that enhances the irony
of her blindness to the double sham of Thorpe's ruse and Allen's fake
castle. Even today, although nestled amid the thick mature plantings on
Bathwick Hill, Allen's Sham Castle remains visible from the corner of
Pulteney Bridge and the Grand Parade, the very spot where Catherine
turns round but loses sight of the Tilneys as Thorpe turns sharply to
the left and "she was herself whisked into the Market-place" (*NA*, 85).
A few paragraphs onward, Catherine, still smoldering with outrage at
Thorpe's trickery, consoles herself: "Blaize Castle remained her only comfort; towards *that*, she still looked at intervals with pleasure" (86). In
fact, Austen's string of street names tracts Catherine moving directly away
from Blaise's close twin. Although comically blind to her surroundings
in Bath, Catherine does gain insight into Thorpe's true character during their carriage ride. Symptomatic of his lessening efficacy is that they
never even reach the fakery of Blaise.

What Happened to the Real Allen Fortune?

Throughout it all, Thorpe and his sister remain convinced that Catherine is the Allen heir. Their hints to this effect are many, but one major
instance makes the case. After Isabella hastily secures her engagement
to Catherine's brother, James Morland, she disingenuously laments her

own unworthiness due to her lack of fortune. Catherine mistakes her meaning for something romantic:

> "Indeed, Isabella, you are too humble.—The difference of fortune can be nothing to signify."
> "Oh! my sweet Catherine, in *your* generous heart I know it would signify nothing; but we must not expect such disinterestedness in many. As for myself, I am sure I only wish our situations were reversed. Had I the command of millions, were I mistress of the whole world, your brother would be my only choice." (*NA*, 121–22)

Isabella does not suffer under the apprehension that the Morlands enjoy "the command of millions," although she will be disappointed by Mr. Morland's financial proposals to his son James. As the slanted wink of the italics stresses, Isabella compares her own situation to Catherine's—and suggests that, one day, her friend will be "mistress of the whole world." This assumption is far from silly.

Cruttwell's *New Bath Guide* helps uncover the reasons for the Thorpes' suspicions. In Austen's day, Cruttwell's *Guide* was as much a local directory to the homes of the rich and famous as a standard travel manual for tourists. It records in 1795, for example, that Prior Park once "belonged to the late Ralph Allen esq; but now to the Rev. Stafford Smith" at the same time that it points out how it lies "to the right as you ascend" Claverton Down.[48] Updated yearly, the *Bath Guide* tracks any change of ownership or residents at Prior Park through the time of *Northanger Abbey*'s composition. Augmented by modern biographies, the *Bath Guide* explains why, in the late 1790s in particular, the identity of the heir to the Allen fortune became suddenly complicated and increasingly vague, allowing for the type of confusion about the heirs of "old Allen" that Austen's plot manipulates.[49] The "Rev. Stafford Smith," is Martin Stafford Smith, the second husband of Gertrude Tucker, the real-world "favorite niece" of Ralph Allen's who had, after the death of Allen's widow in 1766, inherited all his properties. In 1745, the year in which the central action of *Tom Jones* also takes place, Gertrude, then aged nineteen, had married her uncle's friend, William Warburton (1698–1779), a man thirty years older than herself.[50] They lived at Prior Park with the Allens and had a son named Ralph, "the child of Warburton's old age" and "a sort of grandson" to his namesake (Boyce, 297 and 231). After inheriting the property at the death of Ralph Allen's widow in the late 1760s, the

Warburtons moved out of Prior Park for a time, letting the house to an Irish peer and selling the furniture and contents to meet the £60,000 of total liquid legacies that Allen had so generally bequeathed to others. With the annual rental value of the Allen real estate alone amounting to at least £4,000 per annum, the Warburtons probably calculated that time would restore their ability to refurnish. Although "legal impediments" prevented the outright sale of land, the Warburtons may also actively have avoided diminishing the landed holdings that would eventually pass to their son, Ralph (296). Unfortunately, the young heir presumptive died unexpectedly of consumption in his twenties. The age difference in her marriage soon also left Gertrude a widow. In the 1780s, Gertrude returned to live again at Prior Park, so the *Bath Guide* lists it as occupied by Mrs. Warburton during the 1780s. Gertrude was now a widow with an estate slowly restored to splendor, but no heir. When she reached her early fifties, however, she must have set all the tongues in Bath wagging by marrying the Rev. Martin Stafford Smith, a clergyman about twenty years her junior.[51] This Mrs. Smith was thus not "an every day Mrs. Smith" or a "poor widow" in Bath "barely able to live," but a veritable Wife of Bath who married her choice of Jenkins (*P*, 171). Prints of the time identify Prior Park as "The Seat of Mrs. Smith" (fig. 2.15).

Since the true Allen heir, born Gertrude Tucker, had already changed names twice, by the start of the 1790s, the Allen-Tucker-Warburton-Smith legacy had become fairly complicated. In 1796, Mrs. Smith of Prior Park died, aged sixty-eight, having outlived her son and heir as well as a disagreeable brother and all her cousins of that same generation. Starting in 1797, the year of Austen's first recorded visit to Bath, Prior Park gained a new occupant and was relisted in the *Bath Guide* as the home of Lord Hawarden, a distant relation of the original Ralph Allen.[52] But although Hawarden—husband to the daughter of Ralph Allen's brother, Philip—would live there for some years, his wife Mary did not inherit the estate. For, in the end, the fortune fell to her elder brother's children, reverting back to the Allen name. The descendants of Ralph Allen's nephew, also called Ralph Allen (the eldest son of Phillip Allen), were the ones who sold Prior Park in 1807 and maintained part of the estate well into the twentieth century. In other words, although Lord Hawarden occupies Prior Park when Austen's Thorpe drives by with Catherine, everyone in the neighborhood knows him to be bound to a new set of Allens (his brother-in-law's son) who will, backed by all the forces of primogeniture and inheritance laws, succeed to the property.

FIGURE 2.15. "Prior Park in Somersetshire, the Seat of Mrs. Smith." This plate is dated 1 September 1785. *Bath in Time*, Bath Central Library Collection.

From 1797 through 1807, Prior Park's fate lay in the hands of Allens who lived in the nearby countryside but who, because all eyes for decades had been trained on Gertrude living up on the hill, were decidedly less well known than their ancestors. *Northanger Abbey* was begun at the front end of this window, the start of the presumed hype and a time when all of Bath must have been Allen-spotting at the assembly rooms. Thorpe's mistake is not as buffoonish as it seems.

We must assume then that Thorpe feels emboldened by these particular circumstances when he swaggers round Bath and brags to General Tilney, who, in his turn, sees an opportunity for his son Henry to snatch the soon-to-be-wealthy Catherine instead. Only these circumstances explain why the ever-cynical General acts on the mere "rhodomontade" of a nobody such as Thorpe (*NA*, 256). The General knows this same context. His response to the name of Allen is just as Pavlovian as Thorpe's. As a result, the General's invitation to Catherine to join them at Northanger Abbey is as transparent a machination as Thorpe's carriage rides. This is where Austen deftly turns the tables on her situation comedy, switching back and forth between the gothic and the realistic. For just as General

Tilney proves to be mistakenly under the spell of the name of her chaperones, the Allens, Catherine seizes upon the name of his home with a similarly absurd set of assumptions: "With all the chances against her of house, hall, place, park, court, and cottage, Northanger turned up an abbey, and she was to be its inhabitant. Its long, damp passages, its narrow cells and ruined chapel, were to be within her daily reach, and she could not entirely subdue the hope of some traditional legends, some awful memorials of an injured and ill-fated nun" (143–4). In the lingering context of Bath, which boasts at its center a prominent and ancient Gothic abbey of its own, Catherine's wide-eyed impatience "for a sight of the abbey" is as absurd as was her desire to travel to distant Blaise to see a faux castle (164). Identical edifices surround her in her current location of Bath. Indeed, Ralph Allen's estate at Prior Park is, of course, named for the priory that was the offshoot of Bath's abbey. The historic name of Allen, again, unlocks both the General's mistake and Catherine's folly.

Not only does Northanger Abbey not live up to Catherine's immature hopes, but General Tilney eventually discovers his error and abruptly sends her home. She is forced to travel alone the "seventy miles" by post to her home in Fullerton, pained by an ignorance of how she has offended (*NA*, 233).[53] At the novel's close the narrator explains, somewhat unnecessarily for a reader who has read the clues in Bath's landscape, the chain of events that led to the General's mistake. This is when we are told that "John Thorpe had first misled him" about Catherine and her family (254). Thorpe's pride in commandeering Catherine's attentions had led him to inflate accounts of her father's estate: "as his intimacy with any acquaintance grew, so regularly grew their fortune" (254). In addition, he told the General of Catherine's expectations from the Allens: "The ten or fifteen thousand pounds which her father could give her, would be a pretty addition to Mr. Allen's estate. Her intimacy there had made him seriously determine on her being handsomely legacied hereafter; and to speak of her therefore as the almost acknowledged future heiress of Fullerton naturally followed. Upon such intelligence the General had proceeded; for never had it occurred to him to doubt its authority" (255). In the context of Bath in Austen's time, "the absolute facts of the Allens being wealthy and childless" were, indeed, not to be doubted (255). False calculations, we are told, "had hurried him on. That they were false, the General had learnt from the very person who had suggested them, from Thorpe himself, whom he had chanced to meet again in town" (255).

Thorpe's corrective retelling of events to the General leaves the reader with one final clue that the Allens of Bath, the descendants of Ralph Allen, were the family that both Thorpe and the General had in mind: "The terrified General pronounced the name of Allen with an inquiring look; and here too Thorpe had learnt his error. The Allens, he believed, had lived near them too long, and he knew the young man on whom the Fullerton estate must devolve. The General needed no more" (256). Thorpe's reconstituted logic about their length of residence in Fullerton reveals, once and for all, the fatal error behind his initial calculations. If these country Allens have indeed resided "too long" in Fullerton, they cannot be related to Ralph Allen's family from Bath.

Reconsidering the Style of *Northanger Abbey*

Precise knowledge of Bath matters, of course, in *Persuasion*, too. In that novel, as Jocelyn Harris and Keiko Parker have pointed out, "location matters, because the level of habitation in Bath calibrates neatly to rank."[54] "Upward," Parker and Harris demonstrate, indicates social as well as topographical elevation in *Persuasion*, so that Sir Walter at Camden Place emblematically "looks down on Bath from almost the highest point in the city."[55] In that novel too, then, knowledge of the cartography of Bath is amply rewarded: "The Crofts lodge in Gay Street, not so far enough down as to discourage Sir Walter and Elizabeth from visiting them, but not so high as to make their address a challenge. Sir Walter disdains Mrs. Smith for living in Westgate Buildings at the actual and symbolic low end of Bath."[56] *Persuasion*, as we know from the precise dating of the first draft, was begun on 8 August 1815, more than a decade after Austen left Bath to settle, eventually, at Chawton. There is no record of Austen ever having returned for a subsequent visit. Her memory and residual knowledge of Bath's topographical ups and downs in *Persuasion* are extraordinary, a match for the spatial precision of *Northanger Abbey*.

Even with prior knowledge of *Persuasion*'s particulars, however, the cartographic precision of *Northanger Abbey*'s setting as well as its time-specific context will likely take some by surprise, as it did me during the course of my research. Its playful use of the transfer of the Allen inheritance in the 1790s makes the novel seem unexpectedly rooted in Bath's social events, as well as its spaces, at the turn of the century. If Austen wrote her text between 1798 and 1803 with these bits of Allen family history in mind, what did she think upon rereading it in 1816, after Henry bought it back for her? Did she fear that nearly a decade and a half had erased from memory much of this historical context for even a reader from Bath? She hints at this in a disclaimer penned in 1816, which was to accompany the published text (in 1818 it appeared at the front as the author's "Advertisement"): "Some observation is necessary upon those parts of the work which thirteen years have made comparatively obsolete. The public are entreated to bear in mind that thirteen years have passed since it was finished, many more since it was begun, and that during that period, places, manners, books, and opinions have undergone considerable changes" (NA, 1). Apparently this caveat alone was insufficient. She thought substantial revision essential, for after years of delay she did not forward it straight to her publisher with this disclaimer attached, but in March of 1817 shelved the text once more: "Miss Catherine is put upon the Shelve for the present, and I do not know that she will ever come out;—but I have a something ready for publication, which may perhaps appear about a twelvemonth hence. It is short, about the length of Catherine."[57] A "something" else of similar length and similar precision about Bath, namely *Persuasion*, was deemed ready, while *Catherine* was after all that time still judged unripe. Thirteen years had made some "parts" seem "obsolete." What parts? What did she want to change?

I cannot shake off the notion that Austen may have failed to recognize how a lapse of so many years had actually expanded rather than narrowed the appeal of her 1803 manuscript. When she implied a need for substantial revision in 1816 and reshelved the manuscript, she may have acted on a fear that her youthful fidelity to events in the late 1790s needed updating. She was wrong; that her story has been read and enjoyed outside of the context of the Ralph Allen legacy for two hundred years proves as much. Ironically, the loss of certain original historical events from cultural memory forced readers to generalize their interpretations and see how Austen addresses larger questions about genre, history, and the gothic. Still, like the story's heroine, Austen's readers—just as she feared—have been habitually blind to the interpretive significance of Bath's local landscape and the name of Allen in *Northanger Abbey*.

Such blindness is of long standing, since in 1897 one critic, Austin Dobson, already lamented the novel's sparse mode of describing Regency Bath:

> Personally, we could have willingly surrendered a good deal of the
> clever raillery about Mrs. Radcliffe for a little more of Beau Nash's

old city, which Miss Austen knew so thoroughly. But her nice sense of artistic restraint does not admit of this. Her characters turn out of the right streets into the right crescents and cross the right crossings, as they would have done in real life, but of the topography of Bath itself, where the author lived so long, there is not as much in the whole of *Northanger Abbey* as there is in one chapter of *Humphry Clinker*.[58]

While Dobson rails against "that Boeotian Bookseller of Bath" whose pathetic "phrenological conditions" left him so "infatuated with Mrs. Radcliffe" that it made him "insensible" to the value of the manuscript he had purchased but failed to publish, he too judges Austen by standards not her own.[59] Of course, *Northanger Abbey* had received scant reviews in 1818, and by the time fuller treatments appeared in the mid-nineteenth century, Ralph Allen was still less of a force in people's minds. Bath had come to be associated with Beau Nash instead, or even William Beckford. Our own continued blindness to Austen's unique use of local context and space is even more excusable, since centuries of expansion in Bath have crowded out the locales indicated by Austen's text, although it is a remarkable boon to Austen readers that both Prior Park and Allen's Sham Castle still survive. Now, perhaps, we can address the novel's physical setting differently and enhance our reading of *Northanger Abbey* by appreciating, among its many other artistic features, its precious time capsule of a moment in Bath's history.

What began as a realistic approach to local scenery and events had, over the decade and a half that it lay neglected in the basements of Cruttwell's and Crosby & Company, unexpectedly evolved. In 1803 Austen's picture of Bath's geographical and social scene may indeed have been provincial, the work of a youngish author. An 1803 publication date might have made the novel regional in scope. But in 1818, through a lucky series of accidents, *Northanger Abbey*'s publication marked, perhaps, a new type of historical realism. Lest I be misunderstood and my own reader fear, like Jane Austen herself, that minute attention to the novel's hyperspecificity about place and its time-specific events threaten to take away from the universality of Austen's literary achievement in *Northanger Abbey*, I point again to James Joyce's *Ulysses*. Joyce's picture of 1904 Dublin testifies to the fact that adhering closely to the ephemera of a specific place and former time does not make a work parochial or old-fashioned. Nor, of course, does a text's place of publication mark it as courting merely a local audience, for *Ulysses* was first printed in Paris in 1922. The twist is that Joyce's project, written from self-imposed exile, was self-consciously retrospective, while Austen's was written on location and in the present. *Northanger Abbey*'s minuteness—its attention to maps, distances, and rates of speed—anticipates Joyce's much-admired technique. But its picture of 1803 Bath resembles his 1904 Dublin in method only due to circumstances outside the author's control. I could not, in other words, make precisely the same claim about Joycean resemblance if Austen's novel had been published in 1803, as the author originally desired. Surely the wry-witted twenty-something who sold *Susan* but never saw it in print would have relished the paradoxical benefits that an unwanted delay brought to her novel.

CHAPTER THREE

Touring Farleigh Hungerford Castle and Remembering Miss Tilney-Long

ESPITE ITS JOYCEAN precision about place, *Northanger Abbey* is "routinely regarded as the clumsiest and least controlled of Austen's novels."[1] Critics still revisit old complaints that the two-part structure awkwardly merges two types of parody, Bath novels and gothic novels, and that these disparate techniques "never coalesce into a satisfactory whole."[2] Marilyn Butler explains how critics continue to "suspect the book does not hang together as it stands" because "it moves jerkily between the social comedy of the Bath scenes and the gothic burlesque of the shorter sequence at Northanger Abbey."[3] Already one dividend of the historicist Allen reading, then, is a gain in thematic unity between the novel's two parts, since both sections can now be seen to hinge upon the power of misconception. The mistake over Catherine's identity in the first volume only becomes more marked in light of the later Radcliffe-induced distortions at the abbey. Nonetheless, I have left the later episodes at the abbey relatively unexplored. I shall now pay similar attention to history and location during Catherine's visit to the Tilneys, so as to further test the novel's unity of purpose and historical method, responding to the hoary complaint that the novel's two halves are disjunct.

Although the fictional location of Northanger is said to lie in Gloucester, "a few hours" from Bath, I argue that this story's plot and core imaginings never leave the city's environs, personages, or history (*NA*, 233).[4] This is a Bath-centered novel through and through. But whereas the first volume essentially interpolates Bath's recent history—that of the eighteenth-century Allens, their building projects, and immense fortune—Austen's second volume folds in the more distant history of a ruling landed family of Bath during the time of Henry VIII. In other words, while the first half of *Northanger Abbey* comments on contemporary Bath and the city's immediate past, the second half deploys the city's medieval history with a flashback appropriate to the gothic reading and preoccupations of its heroine. Rather than a botched fusion of disparate styles, *Northanger Abbey* is a one-two punch at the use of history, near and far, in the modern novel.

As I will show, most of Austen's historical source material for *Northanger Abbey* can be found within seven miles of Bath's city center. The episode at Northanger ranges figuratively as far as Farleigh Hungerford Castle, which is exactly the same distance from Bath as that traveled by John Thorpe's carriage on his botched attempt to get to Blaise Castle. As Austen describes the distance traveled by Catherine and Thorpe's disappointed party in uncharacteristically redundant fashion, readers knowledgeable about Bath may find themselves speculating about the existence of an alternate tourist destination that Thorpe could have aimed at with greater success. The picturesque ruins of Farleigh (or Farley) Hungerford Castle, with its bloody history of murder and poison, of wives locked in tall towers, of letters found in old furniture, and of mysterious coffins on view, provide not only a nearby example of "an old castle . . . like what one reads of" that Catherine is so eager to see but also a possible real-world model for events at Northanger (*NA*, 83) (figs. 3.1 and 3.2). The similarities between Farley fact and Northanger fiction should not be dismissed as mere coincidence. Given the popularity of Farleigh Hungerford Castle as a tourist site near Bath, Austen likely visited the ruined castle in person. It certainly features prominently in a Bath guidebook owned by her family and annotated in her hand. The history reported in this and other popular guidebooks map onto *Northanger Abbey*'s plot with surprising accuracy, especially onto Catherine's darkening suspicions about the death of Mrs. Tilney. Indeed, the close resemblance between Catherine's fantasies of General Tilney as a wife killer and the reality of the crimes committed by Farleigh Castle's most notorious residents suggest that Austen finds the gothic in genuine history, slyly demonstrating that real-world events can be as bizarre as gothic invention.

Just as Thorpe's delusions about Catherine's presumed wealth had a basis in fact, so too are Catherine's gothic fantasies borne out by Bath's history. By appealing to history, Austen challenges the gothic novel not merely with its own tropes, imitated from the pages of fellow novelists such as Ann Radcliffe, but with her own consistently realistic approach. Farleigh Hungerford Castle, which, like nearby Prior Park, is now an English Heritage site, has simply been overlooked as another background source for Austen's first novel. With genuine historical points

P.b 9, April 1785, by S. Hooper .   Sparrow Sculp.

Farley Castle , Somersetshire .

FIGURE 3.1. "Farley Castle, Somersetshire." Published 9 April 1785, by
S. Hooper. Private Collection.

of reference for the gothic added to the fictional models mentioned in
the story itself, *Northanger Abbey* may further modify our assessment of
Austen's historical method.

Parts of that method may have been so au courant that Austen insisted upon some retuning after publication was delayed for more than a
decade. In her "advertisement," written in 1816 after the manuscript's re-
trieval, Austen warns readers how the interval of thirteen years between
composition and publication has dulled her mentions of people and
things. Growing increasingly ill, Austen is known to have made only one
sweeping change before her death: before shelving the manuscript, she
altered her heroine's name from Susan to Catherine. Critical consensus
points to another novel entitled *Susan*, published during the interval, as
the catalyst for that single and singular alteration. Accepting this, I examine the significance of Austen's particular choice of substitute in light
of the celebrity status of a young debutante who, in that same interval,
had become the nation's richest and most-discussed marriage prize. Her
name was Catherine Tilney-Long.

FIGURE 3.2. "Part of Farley Castle, Somersetshire." Engraved and published by J. Storer, after a drawing by S. Prout, 1 April 1812. Private Collection.

Seven Miles from Bath

Austen's Mr. Thorpe dangles the lure of Blaise Castle before his naïve prey as he takes Catherine in his gig northward on the road toward Clifton. Although I glossed this scene in Chapter 2, here again are the essential facts. Not only does Blaise Castle lie twenty miles northwest of Bath—so impossible a distance for a daytrip in a mere one-horse gig that the party never reaches it—but Thorpe describes it in false terms:

> "Blaize Castle!" cried Catherine; "what is that?"
> "The finest place in England—worth going fifty miles at any time to see."
> "What, is it really a castle, an old castle?"
> "The oldest in the kingdom."
> "But is it like what one reads of?"
> "Exactly—the very same."
> "But now really—are there towers and long galleries?"

"By dozens."

"Then I should like to see it." (*NA*, 83)

As previously explained, Blaise Castle was neither "old" nor "real," but a small garden folly built in 1766. Although at least one contemporary guidebook aggrandizes the folly, describing it as "a Gothic castellated building" with "stately turrets" named after St. Blasius for his association with "an ancient chapel" formerly occupying the spot, it amounted to but one open-air room fit only for picnics.[5] The estate's neoclassical manor house, also called Blaise Castle after the quirky folly, was newer still—so much so that in 1797, the year of Austen's first recorded visit to Bath, it remained under construction for banker John Harford. I explained in the previous chapter that Blaise was modeled upon Bath's own Sham Castle. However, from Catherine's starting point in Pultney Street it is not only possible to see the twin folly built by Allen but also to set out for a genuine castle relatively nearby. One real medieval castle *does* exist within the reach of the day's outing—Farleigh Hungerford. That Thorpe does not take Catherine to this nearby tourist destination that so perfectly fits her gothic expectations enlarges his idiocy and, consequently, emboldens Austen's irony.

Austen provides further clues to distance. The group fails even to get halfway to Blaise, because after "exactly an hour coming from Pulteney-street" they have traveled "very little more than seven miles," finding themselves "within view of the town of Keynsham" (*NA*, 87 and 86). Here they reluctantly recognize that they must abort the outing to Blaise and "turn round," back toward Bath (87). In the context of Austen's precision about location elsewhere in *Northanger Abbey*, her seemingly gratuitous details about distance in this scene look significant. For a start, Keynsham boasted a genuine twelfth-century abbey, which was connected to the Brydges family and the early dukes of Chandos, to whom, in turn, Austen was related though her mother's family.[6] Their stopping within view of Keynsham Abbey's genuine Gothic ruin likely compounds the irony of their not reaching the faux-Gothic folly at Blaise many miles off (164 and 165). But why also mention that they traveled just seven miles? The party's "view" of Keynsham already provides sufficient information to calculate just how far along the northern road the characters have traveled, making a reference to their journey of "seven miles" a bit redundant. What could be significant about a distance of "very little more than seven miles" from their starting point?

A swivel of the compass point seven miles round Bath suggests an answer. If these same seven miles had been traveled in the opposite direction, to the southeast rather than northwest, it would have taken the party to a genuine castle capable of fulfilling even Catherine's ambitious expectations of gothic gore. Although this castle lies just beyond the confines of Mr. Thorpe's original "Map of Five Miles round the City of BATH," his touchstone map does help to establish our bearings (fig. 3.3). As this detail from Thorpe's original 1742 map shows (note how the thick line marks the county border, not a route), the short southward road to "Farly Castle" proffers a virtual smorgasbord of castles and abbeys, both fake and genuine, of the sort that Catherine craves, since in addition to Farley Castle two more sites might satisfy the gothic-minded along that road. First, at Midford stands another contemporary faux-Gothic castle, comparable to the Sham Castle and Blaise.[7] The road next leads through "Charterhouse Hinton," home to an abbey with ties to Farleigh Hungerford Castle, as I shall explain. The very guidebook owned by the Austens during their residence in Bath confirms these additional points of interest en route to nearby Farleigh—constituting a virtual Gothic Row for tourists.

The remains of Farleigh Hungerford Castle stand in what guidebooks, then as now, describe as "one of the most rural and picturesque spots within a wide radius of Bath"—worth visiting for "its antiquity, its importance, and the beautiful romantic scenery with which it is encompassed."[8] At "about seven miles distant" from the city of Bath, the castle lies "within the compass of a summer day's ramble."[9] Built in the fourteenth century on a piece of land that derives its name "from the *fairness* of its *leys*, or meadows," Farleigh Castle was home to the Hungerford family for about three hundred years, from 1369 to 1686.[10] Three centuries of residence at the castle by the Hungerford family ended at the close of the seventeenth century, when Sir Edward Hungerford, known as "the spendthrift," was forced to sell the family home to pay his debts.[11] Sir Edward's sale of the property in 1686 virtually finished the castle's days as a habitable residence, although the sister of the poet Lord Rochester, the notorious Restoration rake, is said to have lived there for a few years with her husband, Henry Baynton.[12] In 1705 the castle was "sold for salvage," resulting in a slow dismemberment that "over the next 30 years" saw it "systematically reduced to ruin for its materials."[13] The deteriorating ruin became a popular tourist destination for day-trippers from Bath and, after its chapel was repaired in 1779 by a distant Hungerford relation, slowly grew into "a sort of repository for curiosities," its walls bedecked with medieval armor and the dilapidated structure filled with fanciful furnishings of a prior age[14] (fig. 3.4). By 1801, a typical guidebook urges a visit to "Farley-Castle" as "a rich treat to the antiquary."[15] This tourist site, but a short ride or long walk from Bath, is the only genuine "old castle" in Bath's landscape within both "a day's ramble" and Austen's expressly stated range of "seven miles."

The story of Farleigh Hungerford Castle and the family who resided there for so long rivals any Radcliffe plot in bodice-ripping drama and murderous intrigue. Hungerford history at the castle starts with "one of the most renowned barons of the time," whose riches at Farleigh "awakened the jealousy" of Richard II. "A series of heroes of the same noble family" succeeded this patriarch, including "a knight of great martial achievements" whose "romantic character" combined his reputation for piety with fearlessness in battle.[16] While one Hungerford was celebrated as a hero of Agincourt, another was "tried, condemned, and executed for treason" during the Wars of the Roses.[17] The colorful Hungerford family tree also includes a woman hanged for murdering her first husband and

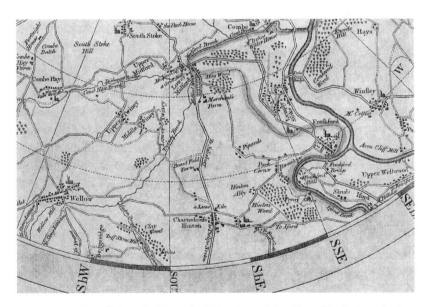

FIGURE 3.3. Detail from "A Map of 5 Miles Round the City of Bath On a Scale of one Inch & half to a Mile from an Actual Survey made by Thos. Thorpe with Alterations & Improvements to the present time 1773." *Bath in Time*, Bath Central Library Collection.

FIGURE 3.4. "Farley Castle & Chapel." Published January 1823 for Sir R. C. Hoare. *Bath in Time*, Bath Central Library Collection.

burning his body in the castle's kitchen oven. Another Hungerford, rumored to have killed his wives by poison, was beheaded for treason and witchcraft. Coupled with a location that fits within the distance covered by the touring party, even a sketchy history of Farleigh Hungerford Castle reveals the inanity of Thorpe's choice of remote Blaise as his destination. For anyone familiar with Bath's tourist sites, the comedy of Austen's novel resides partly in its send-up of this local history.[18]

Murders at Farleigh Hungerford Castle

Most descriptions of Farleigh Hungerford Castle focus on two Tudor-era scandals that fed local lore for centuries. The earlier of these took place in the castle kitchen, a domestic space that Austen mentions half a dozen times in *Northanger Abbey*. In fact, at Northanger the kitchen delineates history, marking the boundaries between old and new: "With the walls of the kitchen ended all the antiquity of the Abbey" (*NA*, 189). In the winter of 1518, Sir Edward Hungerford I married a widow named Agnes

Cotell, who "had previously been married to a certain John Cotell, possibly Sir Edward's steward." Although the Cotells were, by all accounts, materially comfortable, Agnes evidently saw an opportunity to improve her situation: "On 26 July 1518, two of her servants, 'by the procurement and abetting of the said Agnes,' strangled John at Farleigh castle with his own linen neckerchief."[19] Trial records show that "the body of the said John [was] put into a certain fire in the furnace of the kitchen in the castle of Farley . . . and did burn and consume" his remains. Six months later, by now the new Lady Hungerford, Agnes coolly received these two servants at the castle, "well knowing that they had done the murder aforesaid."[20] Locally, the murder was an open secret, but Agnes and her hired killers remained unprosecuted while the powerful Sir Edward, her new husband, lived. After Sir Edward died in 1522, however, all three were speedily hanged at Tyburn in London for the crime.

Given the kitchen-centered murder in Farleigh Hungerford's past, General Tilney's preoccupation with improvements to "the ancient kitchen of the convent, rich in the massy walls and smoke of former days," which he has stocked with every modern convenience, especially with efficient "stoves and hot closets," begins to sound perverse (*NA*, 188–89). After news of thousands of troops starving on the European battlefield for want of supplies had shocked the British home front in 1804, an army general's interest in his kitchens would become standard. But if this detail had been written prior to 1803, when *Susan* was supposedly "finished," General Tilney's interest in stoves may point, if obliquely, to Hungerford history. Austen is also atypically specific when she identifies the General's fireplace as "a Rumford," a brand associated with the latest and most efficient stoves named for their designer, a Bavarian Count (165). Farleigh Castle's macabre history of incineration renders even "The Comforts of a Rumford Stove" rather sinister.[21] It may be coincidental that any tour of Farleigh Hungerford Castle emphasizes, like Miss Morland's tour of Northanger, the outlines of the old kitchen and servants' quarters still visible in the vestigial remains of the castle walls, while stories of murder, oven burnings, and domestic intrigue seize the imagination. Even so, the dark comedy of *Northanger Abbey* may deepen to black in the shade of Hungerford history.

The Hungerford who received "the greatest attention of local gossip" was a wife killer by the name of Lord Walter Hungerford, executed, at age thirty-seven, in 1540.[22] James Tunstall, author of a popular nineteenth-century guidebook, describes this bizarre episode in terms that closely resemble Catherine's mistaken fantasies about General Tilney, identifying Walter Hungerford as "something of a Bluebeard." "Three wives in succession complained of his cruel treatment," with the third piteously petitioning then-king Henry VIII that she was "imprisoned" in a tower where her "lord" continued to try to "poyson" her.[23] Sir Walter, intent upon remarrying for increased wealth and political position, might have succeeded in his sequence of murderous schemes were it not for this third wife Elizabeth, who, aided by local villagers, defied his incessant attempts to kill her by poison.

Elizabeth was the daughter of the well-connected Lord Hussey, a court favorite when Sir Walter married her in 1532. Through his father-in-law's recommendations, Sir Walter rose in the esteem of Henry VIII's court, became an agent of Thomas Cromwell, and gained the one-time title of Baron Hungerford of Heytesbury. But as Hussey's political star faded, so did Sir Walter's fondness for the daughter. Elizabeth wrote to Cromwell in 1539 that she was "continually locked in one of my Lord's towers in his castle . . . these three or four years past."[24] She claimed that she was being poisoned upon her husband's order, had been reduced to drinking her own urine, and that without the charity of the country women who "brought me to my great window, in the night, such meat and drink as they had," she would have starved to death.[25] Tradition has it that Elizabeth remained imprisoned for four years in what consequently became known as the Lady Tower of the castle, visible in the background of this 1785 print of the chapel (fig. 3.5). Her imprisonment ended when Henry VIII felt Sir Walter's insolence directed at him and simply beheaded the nuisance. On 28 July 1540, both Cromwell and Sir Walter were executed on Tower Hill, Cromwell for treason, a move Henry VIII came to regret, and Sir Walter for the additional charges of witchcraft and homosexuality. Elizabeth, "the lady in the tower," remarried after Sir Walter's death, happily this time, to a man with whom she had at least four daughters.[26]

Walter Hungerford's first wife, and probably his initial victim, had been named Susan.[27] Austen's original title for her manuscript, for the eventual *Northanger Abbey*, was of course also *Susan*. A coincidence? Or was the initial choice of name for the heroine intended to signal her vulnerability? Susan is a common enough name, and one that Austen seems to have favored, as she used it also in *Lady Susan* and again in *Mansfield Park*, for Fanny's little sister. As Maggie Lane and John Wiltshire have cautioned, a ubiquitous first name may not be interpretively

FIGURE 3.5. "Farley Chapel, Somersetshire." Published 9 April 1785, by
S. Hooper. Private Collection.

significant.[28] But surnames in *Northanger Abbey* are a different matter.
Just as the mundane names of Thorpe and Allen gain significance when
looked at in the light of Bath's recent history, so do several other surnames cry out for more extensive analysis in relation to a Tudor-centered
past. Mrs. Tilney's maiden name, Drummond,[29] for example, conjures
up another medieval family of nobility.[30] The history of the Drummond
family during this early period is likewise packed with political intrigue
and sexual scandal.[31] Similarly, the name Tilney also reached the zenith
of its political currency in the reign of Henry VIII, when a series of calculated "marriages allied the Tilneys to virtually every important family in the country, including the royal family."[32] Given the setting of a
medieval abbey, the family names of Tilney and Drummond may allow
Austen to balance her novel's mock-gothic dimensions with a quiet set
of historical references to genuine political mayhem. Indeed, Austen's
imagined General Tilney seems to embody both Hungerford brutality
and Tilney ambition. If so, he may combine the criminal lore of Farleigh
Hungerford with the political cunning of the powerful Tilneys in order
to set their associations with the Tudor court against the allegiances of

the real-world Drummonds, a family historically allied with the claims of the Stuarts.[33]

In the extended context of English political history then, to marry a Tilney to a Drummond is to ignore the internal strife and religious conflicts between the houses of Tudor and Stuart. From a young age, Austen showed Stuart sympathies, as evidenced by her "History of England." Her choice of historically evocative names may not only flag her sympathies for the off-page character of Miss Drummond but mark the union between the General and his bride as ill-fated and antagonistic from the outset, a marriage between opposites. Whatever the intended implications, by imagining a loveless marriage between a "cruel" Tilney and a rich Drummond, a union designed to maximize wealth and social position that ends tragically in an abbey confiscated by Henry VIII, Austen does not stray far from the history books (*NA*, 185).[34]

Of course, by virtue of being an abbey, Northanger already conjures up the violent dissolution of the monasteries that passed such buildings into private hands. The fictional Tilneys, as well as being linked to Tudor courtiers through their historical name, are tied to Henry VIII through their home's history. Patrick Parrinder laments that "*Northanger Abbey* is silent about the Tilney family's history," judging the "deliberate omission" as "typical of Austen's fiction." Yet, Parrinder too recognizes how "names like Northanger Abbey and Donwell Abbey invoke the medieval, monastic past."[35] Catherine learns of "Northanger Abbey having been a richly-endowed convent at the time of the Reformation, of its having fallen into the hands of an ancestor of the Tilneys on its dissolution, of a large portion of the ancient building still making a part of the present dwelling although the rest was decayed, or of its standing low in a valley, sheltered from the north and east by rising woods of oak" (*NA*, 144). Austen's cryptic history of her imaginary Northanger Abbey teasingly matches in certain details the genuine history of the buildings on the Farleigh Hungerford estate, which included, in addition to the castle, a medieval abbey acquired in the wake of the dissolution as well as a manor house built from the stones of its ruins. The abbey land owned by the Hungerfords also included portions of a famous stretch of wood visible even in Thorpe's map, where it is labeled Hinton Wood and shown lying just "north and east" of the abbey. This was just the type of so-called hanger of trees from which the name North-hanger Abbey, as Cassandra spelled it, is ostensibly derived.[36]

The genuine abbey annexed to the Hungerford estate after the dissolution of the monasteries was nearby Hinton Abbey, or Hinton-Charterhouse, two miles closer to Bath along the route that leads south from the city to Farleigh Hungerford Castle. Historians in the early nineteenth century describe how the abbey was originally founded in the early thirteenth by Ela, Countess of Salisbury, to honor the memory of her husband.[37] It became the residence of a "very severe" order of Carthusian monks, who "abstained entirely from flesh" and lived "in silence, solitude, and prayer."[38] General Tilney's eating of meat with virtually every meal, and even "cold meat" on a Sunday "between morning and afternoon service," may comment wryly on the monastic abstinence and self-denial associated with the generic histories of many abbeys, irrespective of the possible link to Hinton Abbey (NA, 195). That Northanger Abbey designates, specifically, a Carthusian Charterhouse is suggested by the "traces of cells" pointed out to Catherine (188). Architectural historian Nikolaus Pevsner seizes upon this detail, even though he judges Austen "without exception vague, when it comes to describing buildings."[39] Nonetheless, it is Pevsner who points out that the evidence of cells "would indicate a Charterhouse" since non-Carthusian orders of monks used dormitories, but only, he hesitates, "if Jane Austen knew archaeology."[40] Austen may not have been an archaeologist, but she was a keen historian of Bath's locations, with, in this instance, access to the specific history of Farleigh Hungerford, where the abbey was a Charterhouse whose "Carthusian monks" did indeed sleep in cells.[41]

Austen's historical allusions so blend into the mimetic landscape of the realist novel that many become virtually untraceable. As Thomas Lister observed as early as 1830, Austen's strategy of self-effacement means that she may be "too natural" for those critics who demand that artistry show itself.[42] Then again, how subtle are Austen's historical allusions to the tumultuous medieval period that culminated in the reign of Henry VIII, when she houses characters named Tilney and Drummond in a medieval abbey obtained during the dissolution of the monasteries? When she names her heroine's female companions Eleanor and Isabella, using old-fashioned spellings of names associated with medieval queens?[43] Or, when her plot culminates in the marriage of a Henry to a Catherine? Critical agreement about how Northanger Abbey spoofs, specifically, Radcliffe's gothic recipe for novel-writing has possibly prevented us from looking for other sources of inspiration.[44] Radcliffe's exotic and historically remote settings permitted, even fostered, a reader's complacency about the relative security of modern English life (although, comically enough, not for Catherine Morland). Perhaps Austen gestures to the history of this genuine locale in Bath to respond to the implied social smugness of Radcliffe's treatment of old and new—foreign violence juxtaposed with an English reader's domestic safety—by warning of the internal, rather than external, threats to polite society. For generations, Austen scholars have shown how *Northanger Abbey* critiques an all-too-easy contrast in Radcliffe between the secure world of the reader and the perilous violence outside it. Although Peter Knox-Shaw recently narrowed the perceived gap between Radcliffe and Austen, arguing that Radcliffe, too, acknowledges "the threat of recidivism" when she shows "a precarious order haunted by a violent past," A. Walton Litz representatively asserts that "Catherine's belief in a violent and uncertain life lurking beneath the surface of English Society is nearer the truth than the complacent conviction, shared by the readers of Mrs. Radcliffe, that life in the Home Counties is always sane and orderly."[45] In her clues to England's violent history, Austen may be offering concrete reasons for Catherine's fears.

"Farley Castle" as Tourist Site in Austen's Time

Knowledge of Farleigh Hungerford Castle and its local history, including its annexation of Hinton Abbey, was widespread in Austen's day, with Bath guidebooks describing the castle grounds as a popular destination for day-trippers from the city. Mentions of "Farley Castle," a variant that dominates in Austen's time, as a local curiosity and tourist destination are ubiquitous, with different aspects of the experience emphasized in different books, from seasonal pocket companions such as *The New Bath Guide* to Rev. Richard Warner's elegant *Excursions from Bath* (1801). For example, while *A Picturesque Guide* (1793) stresses the site's "savage state of desolation," John Collinson details the tombs and monuments significant to the antiquary in his three-volume *History and Antiquities of the County of Somerset* (1791).[46] One issue of the *Weekly Entertainer*, with a relatively late date of 11 March 1816, even offers up a poem inspired by a visit—aptly named "Lines suggested on viewing Farley Castle, in Wiltshire" and signed "W.B.T."—that points to the "ruin'd edifice, in ivy bound!" as a memento mori.[47] A guidebook listed among those in the *Godmersham Park Library Catalogue* similarly stressed in 1792 the site's picturesque appearance: "the gateway, and three towers, covered with ivy, still rear their ruined heads."[48] When recorded history reveals similarities between Sir Walter Hungerford's poisoning of his wife (indeed, probably all three wives) and Catherine's morbid fantasies about General Tilney, local knowledge lends additional irony to Catherine's supposed flights of imagination.

In the year Austen began *Susan*, dated by Cassandra to 1798, *The New Bath Guide* also records a curiosity at Farleigh Castle not unlike the one that her heroine imagines awaits discovery in the "immense heavy chest" at the abbey, that is, a secret stash of letters hidden in a particular piece of castle furniture (*NA*, 167). "In the chapel," states the guidebook, "stands a chest of old armour, brought from the castle, on opening of which were found three original letters written by Oliver Cromwell." Two of these letters were "lent to a gentleman who never returned them," while the last was "preserved in a frame by the woman who shews the chapel."[49] As late as 1876, James Tunstall confirms that Cromwell's framed letter remains on display at Farleigh, repeating the story of its being found in an "old chest in the castle."[50] While the letter has since been removed, several guidebooks, including *The New Bath Guide* for 1798, proffer a transcription:[51]

> SIR, I am very sorye my occasions will not permit me to return to you as I would. I have not yet fully spoken with the gentleman I sent to wait upon you; when I shall doe itt I shall be enabled to be more particular, being unwilling to detaine youre servant any longer. With my service to youre Lady and family, I take leave, and rest Youre affectionate servant,
>
> July 30, 1652.   O. CROMWELL
> For my Honnerd Frind Mr. Hungerford the Elder, These.[52]

The disappointingly dull domestic nature of the note, an empty thank-you carried by a waiting servant, suggests that Cromwell's signature alone, rather than the letter's substance, prompted its preservation and guidebook hype.

As Austen's contemporaries would have known, however, this author is not the Cromwell whose political connections with Farleigh Hungerford Castle tie him to the dramatic imprisonment of Elizabeth Hungerford. This is not signed by Thomas Cromwell, that much-feared and cruel minister of Henry VIII who was executed with Sir Walter Hungerford, but by Oliver Cromwell, the regicidal leader of the Commonwealth over a century later. Since both Cromwells were controversial, the orthography of either would be worth preserving. And yet the discovery of "old letters" in a chest of this medieval castle seems distinctly less dramatic when written by Oliver rather than Thomas Cromwell. Similarly, Catherine's "fearful curiosity" about a mysterious chest and her wide-eyed delight in finding inside a "precious manuscript" ends in comical disappointment about the relative newness of the documents (*NA*, 168 and 174). The paper found by Catherine in Northanger furniture proves to be nothing more than a contemporary washing list that, in terms of humdrum content, comically resembles Oliver Cromwell's note of apology. Austen's scene, with its parallel discovery of documents that prove unexpectedly modern, not only repeats a generic gothic trope from another novelist but also reenacts real events at Farleigh Castle—as if Austen sets history up to compete with Radcliffe. Austen could have read about the Cromwell letter in a book such as *The New Bath Guide*. Or, perhaps, as a tourist led round by "the woman who shews the chapel," she saw the original firsthand.

If Austen toured Farleigh Hungerford Castle, when might she first have visited? As Austen lived in Bath for several years before the sale of *Susan* in 1803, she might have been influenced by an outing to Farleigh Hungerford Castle, which Meehan explains was accessible from Bath by foot, especially if "shortened by way of 'Brass Knocker' Hill."[53] Deirdre Le Faye's *Chronology* allows for much sightseeing even during Austen's earlier visits to Bath in 1797 and 1799.[54] During her first visit in November and December of 1797, however, the weather was gloomy and rainy, hardly conducive to a ride or walk of about seven miles.[55] By contrast, the later visit, in 1799, occurred during the months of May and June, which set the "family party" on many long walks and outings around Bath's countryside. Seasonal weather therefore makes it likely that Austen's first day-trip to Farleigh Hungerford Castle, if indeed she ventured there, occurred during the summer of 1799. Most significantly, during their time in Bath the Austens actually owned the popular guidebook that introduces a visit to Farleigh Hungerford Castle as "a rich treat," judges some of its monuments as "most choice," and provides further details that match Catherine's visions and experiences at Northanger—namely, Rev. Richard Warner's *Excursions from Bath*, published in the same year that the Austens moved to Bath permanently.[56] A copy of Warner's guidebook acquired during their residence in the Bathwick development is inscribed "Geo: Austen 4 Sydney Terrace 1802" and "J. Austen Southampton 1807."[57] The volume contains the additional rarity of marginalia in, quite possibly, Jane Austen's own hand.[58] Perhaps Austen's father purchased one of Bath's latest guidebooks to orient his daughters, so fond of walking, to the countryside around their new home. Whether gift or purchase, the book is a definitive link between Austen and the tourist industry around Farleigh Hungerford. Warner's schematic roadmap to Farleigh Castle labels both Midford Castle and Hinton-Charterhouse Abbey as notable sites along the way, further verifying the folly of Thorpe's choice of outing for Catherine.[59]

In the more than ten pages that Warner devotes to Farleigh Castle, he emphasizes how a visit can become an important history lesson when "remains of ancient days awaken curiosity" and "entice the mind to sober reflection, and to a fair estimate of our present state."[60] He lauds the "chapel of the castle" as "nearly perfect," stressing some of the site's "curious monuments," particularly "the magnificent monument which stands in the center of the chapel, and is, perhaps, one the finest *morsels* of the kind in England."[61] The monument consists of white marble effigies of Sir Edward and Lady Margaret Hungerford (1596–1648 and 1603–72), which also featured in several early nineteenth-century prints of Farley Castle (fig. 3.6). Like Warner, Catherine also focuses in the family chapel one Sunday morning on "the sight of a very elegant monument to the memory of Mrs. Tilney, which immediately fronted the family pew. By that her eye was instantly caught and long retained; and the perusal of the highly-strained epitaph, in which every virtue was ascribed to her by the inconsolable husband, who must have been in some way or other her destroyer, affected her even to tears" (*NA*, 195). In possible imitation of Warner then, Catherine constructs a pathos of place through the inscriptions and monuments of her surroundings.

Even more uncanny is the manner in which the "ruined chapel" of Catherine's imagination, where she hopes to find evidence of "some traditional legends" and further "awful memorials" at Northanger (*NA*, 143 and 144), resembles the spooky and crumbling crypt under the ruined chapel at Farleigh Castle as described by Warner in the guidebook on the Austens' shelves: "The crypt, or vault, under this chapel, exhibits a very extraordinary family party, the pickled remains of eight of the Hungerfords, ranged by the side of each other, cased in leaden coffins, and assuming the forms of Egyptian mummies, the faces prominent, the shoulders swelling out into their natural shape, and the body gradually tapering towards the feet."[62] Most of these curious family coffins, what

FIGURE 3.6. "The Chapel at Farley Castle near Bath." Early nineteenth-century print. *Bath in Time*, Bath Central Library Collection.

one 1816 visitor termed "the cold relics of an ancient clan," still remain on view today for visitors who similarly descend the stairs into the lower crypt[63] (fig. 3.7).

After identifying the Hungerford family thus on display, guidebook veteran Warner recommends one macabre activity: "One of the full-sized leaden coffins has a perforation on the right shoulder, through which a stick may be introduced, and the embalming matter extracted; this appears to be a thick viscous liquid, of a brown colour, and resinous smell and consistence; the flesh is decomposed by the admission of the air, but the bones still retain their soundness."[64] Catherine also imagines inspecting the coffin of Mrs. Tilney, which she conjectures may be occupied by a mere "waxen figure" (*NA*, 196). She demands the physical proof of death that, according to Warner, awaited visitors to Farleigh Hungerford: "Were she even to descend into the family vault where her

FIGURE 3.7. The crypt at Farley Castle, 1846. *Bath in Time,* Bath Central Library Collection.

ashes were supposed to slumber, were she to behold the coffin in which they were said to be enclosed—what could it avail in such a case? Catherine had read too much not to be perfectly aware of the ease with which a waxen figure might be introduced, and a supposititious funeral carried on" (196). Is Catherine following the directive in Warner's book when she thinks of descending, with determined step, into the Tilney vault to put her suspicions to the test? This passage is often cited as a direct allusion to Radcliffe, whose *Mysteries of Udolpho* prominently feature a wax substitute: "the figure before her was not human, but formed of wax."[65] My point is not that the existence of a possible real-world referent replaces the obvious literary allusion but that it reinforces Catherine's fears, mocked by Henry, that the Gothic novel reflects a reality of sorts. Austen cements the Gothic in fact.

Thankfully, there is no proof that Austen herself poked the decomposing Hungerford remains with a stick during any visit to Farleigh Castle. Her signature and marginalia in the family copy of Warner's guidebook, however, suggests that she knew of this "choice" sight for any fan of the gothic, located about seven miles from Bath. Irrespective of a visit in person, Austen's spoof of gothic fiction resonates with Bath's genuine history. Catherine's gothic fantasies may not be, after all, utter nonsense. Instead, their resemblance to actual historical events and relics at Farleigh Castle expose Austen's ironic project and elevate the ambitions of her early fiction. Resemblances to these real situations would also add to the humor of her story. If Austen bests the fantasy of a Radcliffe novel with her own brand of hyperrealism, she may be showing readers that the choicest truths make for the strangest fictions.

Discussions of History in *Northanger Abbey*

Only a few pages after Catherine's mental descent into the "family vault," Henry Tilney reacts in revulsion when he catches her in his mother's former bedroom, where Catherine is self-indulgently brooding on her evolving suspicions that his father murdered his mother. He appeals to her common sense: "If I understand you rightly, you had formed a surmise of such horror as I have hardly words to—Dear Miss Morland, consider the dreadful nature of the suspicions you have entertained. What have you been judging from?" (*NA*, 203). The obvious implication is that Catherine, like Don Quixote, misjudges the world through the lens of fiction.

Yet, when Henry's chastising minisermon maintains his father's innocence through a further appeal to British history, his argument that Christians simply do not murder their wives, is neatly contradicted by Bath's local history:

> Remember the country and the age in which we live. Remember that
> we are English, that we are Christians. Consult your own understand-
> ing, your own sense of the probable, your own observation of what
> is passing around you—Does our education prepare us for such
> atrocities? Do our laws connive at them? Could they be perpetrated
> without being known, in a country like this, where social and literary

intercourse is on such a footing; where every man is surrounded by a neighbourhood of voluntary spies, and where roads and newspapers lay every thing open? Dearest Miss Morland, what ideas have you been admitting? (*NA*, 203)[66]

Admittedly, Henry argues a "now versus then" as well as a "reality versus fiction" position. Even so, the passage in which Catherine, her cheeks wet with "tears of shame," reacts to this speech by running to her room, "completely awakened" and sensible of the "absurdity of her curiosity and her fears," looks different in the light of parallels with Farleigh Hungerford Castle's history and its resulting touristic appeal (203 and 204). I agree with the critical consensus that recognizes how "touches of irony" separate Austen's point of view from her hero's. Peter Knox-Shaw judges the speech as sardonic: "His harangue is lightened, as it develops, by touches of irony that gradually rid his rite of exorcism of its Panglossian air."[67] The novel, after all, eventually comes round to validate Catherine's assessment of the General: "Catherine, at any rate, heard enough to feel, that in suspecting General Tilney of either murdering or shutting up his wife, she had scarcely sinned against his character, or magnified his cruelty" (256). Long before her narrator's closing gloss, however, Austen can rely upon local knowledge of Farleigh Hungerford Castle to place a wedge between Henry's speech and her novel's treatment of history.

By Henry's own logic, Farleigh Hungerford Castle's real-world history would prove rather than dispute the General's guilt. If Henry takes "comfort in the 'probable,'" as Galperin puts it, his convictions about the historical purity of English husbands are utterly misplaced.[68] It is not Catherine's reading of novels that is at fault but Henry's own *mis*-reading of history. Of course, such things having occurred hundreds of years earlier does not make General Tilney any more or less likely to have killed his wife. Henry's logic that history proves his father's innocence is flawed, and yet the inverse argument, that history insures his guilt, would be equally naïve. Austen's scene interrogates history's sway over the present. Whatever the cause of Mrs. Tilney's illness and death, local history supports only the possibility of murder; it does not confirm it. As Peter Knox-Shaw points out, Henry fails to convince with his appeal "to what we would now call 'the public sphere', to a lively culture sufficiently powerful, in view of developed infrastructure and press, to breach the walls protecting privilege and secrecy."[69] As with the mix-up about the Allens, Austen trusts readers familiar with Bath to heed her clues to distance and setting, allowing them the thrill of unearthing her historical sources and of finding the gothic not in yet another piece of make-believe but in the real world.

In the light of Austen's deft refashioning of local and national history throughout *Northanger Abbey*, the scene on Beechen Cliff, in which Catherine, Henry, and Eleanor talk about history books, may also gain in importance. Here Catherine complains that reading history is tedious. With typical teenage logic, she articulates her strong preference for the "invention" of novels and plays: "But history, real solemn history, I cannot be interested in. Can you?" (*NA*, 109). The Tilneys, whose family name is so historically significant, predictably resist, and Eleanor replies: "Yes, I am fond of history" (110). Catherine insists, however, that pure history is "tiresome" reading:

> "I wish I were too. I read it a little as a duty, but it tells me nothing that does not either vex or weary me. The quarrels of popes and kings, with wars or pestilences, in every page; the men all so good for nothing, and hardly any women at all—it is very tiresome: and yet I often think it odd that it should be so dull, for a great deal of it must be invention. The speeches that are put into the heroes' mouths, their thoughts and designs—the chief of all this must be invention, and invention is what delights me in other books."
>
> "Historians, you think," said Miss Tilney, "are not happy in their flights of fancy. They display imagination without raising interest. I am fond of history—and am very well contented to take the false with the true." (110)

As critics such as Devoney Looser and Marilyn Butler point out, Catherine unwittingly "becomes a participant in the still-running philosophical dialogue . . . carried on in the later 1790s" that positioned romance novels against historical works, aligning the novel with frivolous female readers and works of history with the serious accomplishments and elevated taste of men.[70] Knox-Shaw adds that the scene specifically engages with David Hume's essay "On the Study of History," with its appeal to "female readers" and its defense of historians who embellish speeches.[71] The edition of the "Essays Moral & Political" listed in the *Godmersham Park Library Catalogue* ("Edinboro 1742") indeed includes "On the Study of History."

The familiarity of the debate about "the utility of reading history" might also allow Austen to echo Samuel Johnson when the dialogue between Catherine and Miss Tilney replays a famous exchange recorded in Boswell's *Life*, another book Austen is presumed to have read.[72] In the presence of Gibbon, Johnson dared to dismiss most of history as "conjecture," insisting that his audience should "consider how very little history there is; I mean real authentic history. That certain Kings reigned, and certain battles were fought, we can depend upon as true; but all the colouring, all the philosophy of history is conjecture."[73] Perhaps in her heroine's parallel logic and the phrase "real solemn history" Austen deliberately echoes Johnson's "real authentic history." Because Catherine is the loser in her argument with Miss Tilney, Austen may indeed, as others have suggested, show a fondness for the new "philosophy of history," whose proponents she tracked.[74] But Austen also removes the slight redundancy in Johnson's phrase to mix it, possibly, with the "solemn history" that characteristically opens Radcliffe's *Sicilian Romance* (1790).[75] If Austen amalgamates expressions by Johnson and Radcliffe on history, her phrase "real solemn history" nicely mixes a sober insistence upon facts with the gothic point of view—just as she blends Bath history with gothic tropes in her own novel.

Bracketing her manifold allusions to other books, Austen's own work narrows the perceived gap between history and novel reading, between writers of fact and fiction. Austen writes just as Sir Walter Scott is about to emerge with overwhelmingly successful hybrids of history and fiction. While Austen, through the naïve Catherine, gives voice to a standard opposition in this scene, her larger offering of a novel saturated with references to Bath's local history and sprinkled with national politics through character names such as Drummond and Tilney defies this distinction for the more knowing reader. Rather than embellish history with fiction— for as Catherine rightly observes, "speeches that are put into the heroes' mouths" constitute the "invention" of historians—Austen takes delight in the reverse, infusing her Bath novel with historical facts to create, perhaps, her own prototype of the so-called historical novel.

The earlier salvo in *Northanger Abbey* against the overvaluation of mere distillers of history emerges, in light of Austen's historical specificity, as a possible attempt to seize the cultural authority of the traditional historian for the novelist: "And while the abilities of the nine-hundredth abridger of the History of England . . . are eulogized by a thousand pens,—there seems almost a general wish of decrying the capacity and undervaluing the labour of the novelist, and of slighting the performances which have only genius, wit, and taste to recommend them"

(*NA*, 31). Perhaps in this early passage Austen already throws down the gauntlet to historians, protesting a false, and falsely gendered, opposition between their work and that of the novelist. Her "labour" as a novelist remakes, as does her contemporary Scott, historical fact into realist fiction. While writers of official histories insisted on facticity, popular culture narratives, including celebrity accounts in Austen's time, delighted audiences with unbounded and sometimes transgressive blends of fact, rumor, innuendo, and even raw invention. With one particular change that Austen made to her manuscript in later years, it may be possible to see her deploy celebrity culture as a type of glue between history and invention.

The Change from *Susan* to *Catherine*

As discussed in Chapter 2, Austen ran up against the historical currency and immediacy of her own approach when the publication of *Northanger Abbey*, already "finished" in 1803, was unexpectedly delayed. In her prefatory caveat, written in 1816, Austen asks that "the public are entreated to bear in mind that thirteen years have passed since it was finished, many more since it was begun, and that during that period, places, manners, books, and opinions have undergone considerable changes" (*NA*, 1). Given that *Susan* was the name of the manuscript as originally "finished" and sold in 1803, the change in the first name of the heroine, from Susan to Catherine, is the only updating of her novel that Austen is known to have completed herself.[76] Scholars agree that the final title of *Northanger Abbey* was the editorial decision of Henry and Cassandra but that the initial substitution of *Catherine* for *Susan* was Austen's own. She refers to her manuscript as "Miss Catherine" in the previously mentioned letter dated March of 1817.[77] In the wake of R. W. Chapman, critics agree that the appearance of an anonymous novel called *Susan* in 1809 persuaded Austen to make that change.[78] However, while the desire not to appear to duplicate or reference novels published in the interim seems a viable reason to abandon the name Susan, it does not fully gloss Austen's substitution of *Catherine*. Why opt for Catherine? The generic fit of that name with the tropes of gothic fiction has not, as was true for the case of mistaken identity linked to the Allen name at the novel's start, given rise to further inquiry. Since Austen's historically allusive names elsewhere in this text attest to her precision in such choices, the reputation of an illustrious woman named Catherine Tilney, who came to sudden prominence in 1805, assumes possible significance.

Two years after the original sale of *Susan*, a fifteen-year-old named Catherine Tilney-Long (1789–1825), living with her family at Whaddon, just twelve miles southeast of Bath, became one of the richest women in England and the most sought-after prize in the nation's marriage market. Her father, born Sir James Long (1736–94), had assumed the additional surname of Tilney (also spelled Tylney) in 1767, when he became Earl Tilney upon the death of his father. His family, who resided for decades in Whaddon, Wiltshire, just five or six miles east of Farleigh Hungerford Castle, were referred to as the Tilney-Longs or the Tilneys and traced their connections back to the famous Tudor Tilneys. The earl did have a splendid and "almost regal" estate near London, called Wanstead, to which "he never once, in all the years of their wedded life, took his wife to visit, fearing that [she] might wish, if she saw it, to live there."[79] Gilpin confirms the beauty of the place when he contrasts the "want of simplicity" of Wentworth Woodhouse with "lord Tilney's house at Wanstead" in the *Observations*.[80] Nonetheless, Tilney preferred his country residence near Bath. He lived there quietly until his death in 1794, an event that transformed his infant son, James Tilney-Long, into the richest baby in the kingdom.

In 1805, this family heir, young Catherine's little brother, died unexpectedly at the age of eleven. While certain titles held by the Tilneys expired with her brother's death, fifteen-year-old Catherine inherited "the immense estates, real and personal, amounting to £25,000 a year, and nearly £300,000."[81] An eyewitness recorded the impact that this vast inheritance had on the reputation and charms of Catherine Tilney-Long: "At the time I allude to, the country rang with the fame of Miss Tilney Long, her beauty, her accomplishments, and her immense fortune being the theme of all male tongues."[82] By 1811, Catherine was attracting such high-profile suitors that she became the subject of at least three satirical illustrations by George Cruikshank. For example, *Princely Piety, or the Worshippers at Wanstead* (1811), a plate for *The Scourge*, shows the petite heiress on a fantastic throne receiving her many mercenary admirers, including even the Duke of Clarence, later William IV, who attempts to impress her in his new admiral's uniform. Behind him stands the famous actress Dorothy Jordan, the duke's recently jilted paramour and mother of his children, who pours a chamber pot, or jordan, over him in protest, raining their children down in a filthy stream over his head. Mrs. Jordan, in fact, appears as a victim in the background of all three of Cruikshank's images about the celebrity of Miss Tilney-Long, for, as Cruikshank shows in the broadside *The R----l Lover* (1812), the duke was known to have abandoned Mrs. Jordan in order to propose marriage to the rich Miss Tilney-Long[83] (fig. 3.8). Although his suit was unsuccessful, he never returned to the arms of the famous actress.[84] Since, as Roger Sales and Jocelyn Harris each suggest, the celebrity scandal of Jordan's abandonment by the duke, including his cruel removal of their children from her care, was already a high-profile Regency event familiar to Austen, the inadvertent role of Catherine Tilney-Long in the breakup would have been part of that knowledge.[85]

In 1803, before these high-profile events took place, Austen's use of the name Tilney had merely been a soft historical reference to an ancient family prominent at the time of Henry VIII, a minor historical allusion in keeping with the book's gothic theme. Perhaps reports of rich Tilney descendants who lived in nearby Whaddon, not too far from Farleigh Hungerford Castle, first suggested the allusion. The Tilney estate of Wanstead was, incidentally, the childhood home of Cassandra Willoughby (1670–1735), the supposed ancestor of Mrs. Austen, whose stepfather, Sir Josiah Child, took his new family to live there.[86] Indeed, Cassandra Willoughby's half-brother, Richard, became the Earl of Tylney in 1731.[87] Through this series of tenuous family connections, Austen might even have felt a personal interest in the Tylney/Tilney name. Regardless of what sparked her interest, when Austen changed the Christian name of her heroine from Susan to Catherine in 1816, she created a character who, by becoming Catherine Tilney at the story's close, invokes a specific and more contemporary debutante. While, as I speculated earlier, there is a slim chance that the choice of the name Susan originally signaled the vulnerability of her heroine, the substitution of *Catherine* increased contemporary celebrity associations. This simple but sweeping change updates the novel considerably, enriching the irony of the initial confusion about the heroine's Allen-associated wealth by making her share her eventual married name with England's richest and most talked-about teenager.[88]

Unfortunately, this updated allusion had a similarly short lifespan. Miss Tilney-Long's fate proved a tragic cautionary tale, one not yet known to Austen in March 1817, the last time that she refers to her book as "Miss Catherine." By then Austen could only have heard, along with all of En-

FIGURE 3.8. "The R----l Lover, or, The Admiral on a Lee Shore." Satirical broadsheet published by S. W. Fores, 1812. © Trustees of the British Museum.

gland, that Miss Catherine Tilney-Long had married the handsome William Wellesley Pole, fourth Earl of Mornington (1788–1857) and nephew of the Duke of Wellington. At the time of her marriage in March 1812, Catherine's estates in Essex and Hampshire were "said to be worth considerably over £1 million a year," a hundred times the splendor of the fictional Mr. Darcy.[89] This annual income explains why Catherine felt entitled to turn down even the Duke of Clarence, a refusal Cruikshank celebrates in *The Disconsolate Soldier; or, Miss Long ing for a Pole* (1811) and again in *The R----l Lover*. But her chosen husband's extravagant lifestyle slowly depleted both her wealth and her happiness. Pole-Tilney-Long-Wellesley, for so he renamed himself, steadily exhausted Catherine's vast fortune, laying waste to the large estate at Wanstead and ruining his wife both financially and emotionally. In 1822 the house was sold to pay his debts, and in 1823 he would abandon Catherine and their children to elope with another man's wife. In 1825 Catherine would die, disillusioned and universally pitied.

But in 1816, when Austen altered her heroine's name, these events had not yet occurred, and she could reinforce her happy marriage ending with an allusion to a contemporary social spectacle. Catherine Tilney had only recently been the nation's leading bachelorette, projecting an image of privilege that lingered through the early years of her brilliant marriage:

> I well remember how gay and happy she looked the last time I saw her at a ball, seated at the top of the room like a *little queen*, with all her attendant worshippers full of smiles and compliments, and jealously vying with each other in administering the sweetest dose of flattery to the great heiress. She was not so pretty as her sister Diana, though a pleasing looking fairy creature, and who might, under other circumstances, and *by other men*, have been loved for herself alone. Her marriage was a great grief to her amiable mother.[90]

These reminiscences, published in 1835, gain poignancy through the narrator's knowledge of subsequent events that Austen could not have foreseen but that make the speaker of this anecdote sigh, "Alas! poor victim of *man's selfishness!*"[91] In 1816, it is still only the picture of Catherine as the former belle of all Bath balls that the marriage of Austen's Catherine to a Tilney can conjure up. Thus, with one simple, easily executed change, an alteration already demanded by the publication of another work entitled *Susan*, Austen updates her ending by alluding to the more recent news of Catherine Tilney's vast inheritance and high-profile marriage. I believe that this allusion would have been entirely deliberate. The national profile of Catherine Tilney-Long, coupled with Austen's tendency to use celebrity names for their lingering associations, makes it difficult to imagine that Austen resisted these associations or simply failed to see the consequence of the change from *Susan* to *Catherine*. With the change in the first name, the marriage-ending of Austen's novel elevates the fictional Catherine Tilney to the symbolic status of the richest peeress of the realm. In her "advertisement," Austen laments that other aspects of her story, such as the case of the mistaken identity involving the Allens perhaps, could not be so easily updated.

Austen appears to have made discriminate name changes in other manuscripts as well. As Linda Bree and Janet Todd observe, Austen can be seen to fuss over and adjust the names of her characters in her surviving manuscripts:

> The manuscript of "Catharine" shows Austen still hesitating about how to name her heroine—"Kitty," her first thought, is crossed out on a number of occasions (including the title), and "Catharine" inserted in its place—while the Petersons become the Percivals and the Barkers the Barlows; it is startling to see such changes taking place in the course of fair-copying, presumably from a worked-out draft (though something similar also happens in "Lady Susan," when the name "Alicia" for Lady Susan's friend is clearly written over something else). "The Watsons" shows more radical changes of mind, not only about names but about locations. Only after she began did Austen decide she would write about the town of "D." in Surrey rather than the town of "L" in Sussex, that one of the Watson sisters, Penelope, is husband-hunting in Chichester rather than Southampton, that the name Charles should not be used for the local "single man in possession of a good fortune" but should be kept for the little boy Charles Blake, that Captain Hunter and not Captain Carr would be the soldier distracting Miss Edwards from thoughts of Sam Watson, who loves her.[92]

Bree and Todd appraise these adjustments as if these handwritten changes disappointed their expectations: "Many novelists, as we know, begin with a resonant name or location and work their fictions around it as a starting point; the manuscripts show that this tactic was not Jane Austen's way of working."[93] Their disenchantment with the inorganic nature of Austen's creative process seems at odds with the proof of constant and deliberate adjustment that the manuscripts unearth. Their own fine evidence shows how Austen invests great effort in the names of her characters, carefully tweaking even her minor characters and locales. The changes to fair copies, in particular, which may have occurred when rereading a "finished" manuscript after an interval of months or years, suggest that, as the world changed around her, Austen altered names and locations in her fictions to keep her historical allusions or celebrity references current.

Bree and Todd worry that Austen's method differs from that of other novelists, implying that because she changed some names in her manuscripts, names in general do not matter to Austen's creative process. Surely these changes prove rather than disprove that Austen identified artistic or interpretive difference between a Captain Carr and a Captain Hunter, whatever that difference might be. What if Austen did indeed "begin with a resonant name or location"? I have already argued how the novel starts with the resonant name of Allen, a name activated by the specific history of Bath. By changing her heroine's first name to Catherine, Austen exchanges a name selected between 1798 and 1803 for another one that had become equally, if differently, apt by 1816. Being forced to change her book's title, Austen embraces a contemporary allusion in a new name for her heroine, swapping a name plucked from a history book for one to be found in contemporary newspapers. That this change ends her novel, with its medieval setting and allusions, with the marriage of a Henry to a Catherine would surely also not have been lost on her. In a story that swings like Foucault's pendulum between old and new, Austen's substitution shows her confident flexibility and creativity in the face of changes around her, rather than any hesitation or uncertainty.

Revisions in an author's own hand do not diminish the artistic value or integrity of a text's creative outcome. It is no longer held that, in order for a literary work to be great, it must spring forth fully formed by a divine muse from the authorial brain, as Milton claimed for *Paradise Lost*. Austen herself mocked authors who laid claim to literary talent by writing fast: in 1809 she drily suggests that a particular novel "must be very clever, because it was written as the Authoress says, in three months" (*Letters*, 166). Brian Southam terms the thoroughness of Austen's revisions "a triumph of rethinking."[94] Of course, the reality of Austen's revisions remains a messy and inky business, as the manuscripts attest. We should not judge Austen's alterations to her own manuscript, however, as if self-editing or polishing constitutes a mark of weakness in an author. Of the manuscript of *The Watsons*, its blots and crossed-out passages, Bree and Todd remark that, "like a novelist working her way through a narrative she is not quite sure how to move forward," whereas *Sanditon*'s blot-free writing "represents a skilled professional."[95] They assess *Sanditon* as "generally more confident than 'The Watsons': the narrative moves forward smoothly, with many fewer corrections."[96] By the same logic, Ernest Hemingway, who allegedly rewrote the last paragraph of *A Farewell to Arms* close to a hundred times, would be labeled timid and inauthentic.

Admittedly, a fondness for fair copy over so-called foul papers has many precedents in the history of edition, where good looks have often led good editors astray. In Chaucer studies, for example, it is this same instinct that famously allowed the handsome and well-preserved manuscript of the *Canterbury Tales* known as Harley 7334 to enjoy "a prominence that was textually undeserved."[97] The Harley 7334 manuscript, "written in one clear, handsome book-hand of the XV century" and graced with such embellishments as rubricated headers and illuminated capitals at the start of each tale, projected an authority that was eventually unmasked as a "deceptive smoothness and fluency."[98] In 1908, editor W. W. Skeat definitively questioned Harley 7334's misleading aura of textual confidence, terming it "faulty and treacherous."[99] In the case of *Sanditon*, Bree and Todd are right to stress that "we can never known whether Austen would have gone back and rewritten more extensively had she been fit enough to do so," acknowledging that thirteen years separates *The Watsons* from *Sanditon*.[100] Deirdre Le Faye calculates that *The Watsons* was "probably" begun in the year 1804, whereas Austen "start[ed] writing *Sanditon*" on 27 January 1817.[101] This is, coincidentally, the same temporal distance as lies between *Susan* and *Catherine*. Compared to the manuscript of *The Watsons*, which may show years of intermittent revision and updating, *Sanditon* is an unedited and fragmentary first draft to which Austen, had she lived, would have returned. She apparently did so with all her texts. Death, not genius, keeps things tidy.

A preference for an uncluttered initial expression over re-inked thoughts implicitly appeals to the editorial doctrine of "original intention," although that editorial policy was formed with multiple print editions in mind and with the understanding that the interventions of compositors and editors could silently recalibrate a text's direction during the printing process. This doctrine of original intention still makes sense when a manuscript, whether surviving or imagined, differs significantly from the printed text of a first edition, where a heavy-handed editor might have intervened. Strong belief in the value of original intention can lead to projects of recovery. The application of this editorial doctrine to an author's own orthographic passes through their work-in-progress, long before any print editions ever existed, however, is extreme.

I linger on this bit of editorial theory because any study of the interpretive implications of Austen's names, including the doctoring of her own manuscripts in this regard, needs to allow for the years, even decades, of delay in publication to which the author was a pained witness. Such delays generated interpretive complications. As the "advertisement" and the renaming from *Susan* in 1803 to *Catherine* in 1816 shows, Austen corrected and updated her manuscripts with an eye to interim events, avoiding unintentional connections to new publications and weaving in topical irony by means of adjustments in name or location. Such changes would be entirely in keeping with the original intention of a manuscript *if* that intention were to comment, even in part, on current events and their historical precedents. If she meant much of her fiction to be topical, as I suggested is the case with the allusions to the Allen inheritance, all such polishing of the facets of her manuscripts may reflect and refract changes in the world around her. As the clock ticked, the wittiness of her fiction relaxed and needed rewinding or tightening. Eventually the name Kitty caught the interpretive light rather differently than the more formal Catharine. Also, the town of "D." in Surrey rather than the town of "L." in Sussex emerged as the new location to hint at when gesturing, perhaps, toward a fashionable new trend. "It is remarkable," observes Nikolaus Pevsner while inventorying the trendy seaside towns linked to specific characters in the novels, "how exactly Jane Austen could recognize and analyse the craze of her years for new seaside resorts."[102] Such targeted specificity about what was chic, vulgar, or last season would have required frequent retuning.

Time similarly affects the reader's response to Austen and her choice of names. Although most of Austen's fiction was fixed in print just after her death, her casual allusions to historical people and places continue to reflect interpretation differently for succeeding generations of readers. Indeed, many of the names in her novels, such as Marianne Dashwood or Frederick Wentworth, have become so famous in their own right as to shine from within, casting a Janeite shadow over the genuine personages and celebrities, now as forgotten as Catherine Tilney-Long, who held these names during Austen's lifetime. Jane Austen was admitted into the pantheon of celebrated British writers somewhere in the middle of the nineteenth century. In October 1845, the high-profile reviewer George Henry Lewes already mentioned Austen in the same breath with Shakespeare, Cervantes, Molière, Goethe, Fielding, and Scott. In an unsigned review in *Fraser's Magazine* in December 1847, Lewes praised Austen's "marvellous dramatic power" and her "truth in the delineation of life and character," declaring that "Fielding and Miss Austen are the greatest novelists in our language."[103] It was this review that supposedly inspired Charlotte Brontë to read *Pride and Prejudice*. By 1859, David Masson, a prominent Victorian scholar, would confidently sum up Austen's position in the literary landscape in *British Novelists and Their Styles*: "All in all . . . the best judges unanimously prefer Miss Austen to any of her contemporaries of the same order. They reckon her [works] as not only better than anything else of the kind written in her day, but also among the most perfect and charming fictions in the language. I have known the most hard-headed men in ecstasies with them."[104] If general acceptance of Austen occurred somewhere between Lewes's anonymous endorsement in 1847 and this grand encomium by Masson in 1859, Austen's works waited roughly forty years before being read with great regularity and seriousness alongside other canonical early novelists.

In the world of art history, there exists the so-called forty-year rule of perspective promulgated by Max Friedländer, the man who famously explained why "forgeries must be served hot."[105] Friedländer showed how it takes four decades or so for the clichés of the period in which a forgery was painted to reveal themselves fully to the modern eye. In other words, forty years, according to Friedländer, is precisely how long it takes to gain true distance from a work of art. While in the visual arts forty years endows the viewer with greater confidence about authenticity, in the case of Austen four decades distanced readers from her more particular contemporary references. As is true in painting, time changed the appearance of Austen's art. Not all of such changes were a gain.

In the remaining chapters, I continue to resituate Austen's historical allusions and celebrity references. In the next, I track Austen's sustained interest in the life and work of John Evelyn, the Restoration landscaper. Evidence of Evelyn's legacy remained, literally, writ large upon the English landscape in Austen's day, although the aesthetic movements promulgated by Brown, Repton, Gilpin, and others had shifted or felled

Evelyn's characteristic avenues and straight lines. New editions of Evelyn's famous *Sylva* revived interest in his work and life. While romanticism challenged Evelyn's rigidly geometric aesthetic, he continued to be celebrated for his forward-thinking tree-planting campaign, which, a century later, was still providing England's "wooden walls" with lumber during the Napoleonic wars. The attention Austen pays to John Evelyn emerges early in her juvenilia, not merely through one key name or a narrow concern with garden aesthetics but in a prodigious number of interlinked historical references. In *Sense and Sensibility*, Austen's interest in the personal history of John Evelyn widens still further to include additional remnants of the Civil War and Restoration.

"The celebrated Mr. Evelyn" of the *Silva* in Burney and Austen

IT IS A TANTALIZING COINCIDENCE that both Frances Burney and Jane Austen prominently deploy the name Evelyn in their earliest fictions. After reading *Evelina* (1778), which features a Mr. Evelyn as the namesake and grandfather of its eponymous heroine, the young Austen, a great admirer of Burney, wrote a piece of juvenilia about a rural idyll called "Evelyn," as well as a "A Collection of Letters" in which a Mr. and Mrs. Evelyn make brief cameo appearances. Both Burney and Austen, I argue, deliberately invoke the famous Restoration garden designer John Evelyn (1620–1706) in their early writings (fig. 4.1). Evelyn's best-known work, *Silva* (1664), was a well-known horticultural classic about tree planting that, in the wake of an elegantly illustrated edition in 1776 and further reissues in 1786 and 1801, enjoyed a resurgence of popularity during the final quarter of the century, when Burney and Austen wrote their Evelyn-centered stories. That both authors, although born several decades apart, each read the popular *Silva* during their youth is not, in and of itself, entirely surprising. In the 1780s, young William Wordsworth was brought up on *Silva*, too, reading a well-worn copy of the second edition in the Hawkshead Grammar School Library.[1] What is significant for an understanding of Austen's emerging historicism in *Evelyn* is the manner in which Burney may have provided her with a model for imbuing fiction with historical fact. Although Galperin rightly insists that "Jane Austen is not Frances Burney," the juvenilia and first published texts of both authors invoke the memory of John Evelyn in equal measure.[2] In that overlap, they share a creative approach to recycling history, even if their specific application of the memory of Evelyn differs.

Burney's *Evelina*, with a central garden motif that repeatedly gestures to John Evelyn, shares Austen's interest in landscape history and flair for suggestive names—indeed, may have partly inspired these. In the open-

FIGURE 4.1. Print of John Evelyn, after the portrait by Sir Godfrey
Kneller. © National Portrait Gallery, London.

ing pages of *Evelina*, Burney invokes the celebrated John Evelyn in a
character named Mr. Evelyn as well as, throughout the novel, with her
heroine's visits to extant London gardens, toured in rough chronological
order of their design. While the young Austen, like Burney, embeds fictional characters by the name of Mr. and Mrs. Evelyn in one of her earliest stories, it is her "imaginary village" of Evelyn, the title character of a
piece of juvenilia written in 1792, that functions as the most transparent
reference to the famous Mr. Evelyn of *Silva* (*J*, 482n2). Austen, as I will
show, adapts as well as adopts from Burney. Long after writing *Evelyn*,
Austen remained under the sylvan influence of John Evelyn, in *Sense*

and Sensibility (1811). In the emblematic landscapes of that novel, a story begun around 1795, Austen reengages *Silva*. In that mature novel's discourse about trees and aesthetics, Austen expands and deepens the increasingly rich intertextual relationship between the sylvan-focused career of Evelyn and her fiction. While Burney solely plays off of Evelyn's reputation as a Restoration garden designer—a reputation Austen doubtless knew to judge from her own youthful spoofs of gardening styles in *Evelyn*—Austen builds upon this historical figure in other ways too, adding further traces from the Restoration era to the names and story of *Sense and Sensibility*. Austen's early and prolonged attentions to John Evelyn bespeak Austen's ever-deepening interest in English history. In this chapter, I track these cascading influences and garden-associated borrowings from Evelyn's *Silva* to *Evelina* and onward to Austen's *Evelyn* and *Sense and Sensibility*. A close study of Burney's earlier allusions to John Evelyn, as expressed in a novel that is known to have influenced Austen acutely, reveals some of the literary and historical material from which Austen molds her own unique approach. Promising to return to Austen in due course, I start then with the career of the real-world Mr. Evelyn and its relationship to Burney's *Evelina*.

The Real Mr. Evelyn and His *Silva*

John Evelyn was primarily celebrated throughout the eighteenth century for his pioneering work on tree cultivation, published originally in 1664 as *Sylva, or A Discourse of Forest-Trees, and the Propagation of Timber in His Majesty's Dominions*.[3] Shortened in the vernacular to *Sylva*, or *Silva*, the book intended to encourage tree planting after the devastation and deforesting that took place during the Civil War. *Silva* was a learned botanical instruction manual in which Evelyn encouraged the landed gentry to restore England's denuded landscape: "I did not altogether compile this work for the sake of our ordinary Rustics, meer Foresters and Woodmen, but for the benefit and diversion of Gentlemen and persons of Quality, who often refresh themselves in these agreeable toils of Planting and Gardening."[4] The elegant rhetoric of *Silva*, which turned the planting of trees into a patriotic and privileged moral imperative, created the gentleman gardener while helping to restore Britain's important source of timber. The poet Robert Southey, who composed "Evelyn's Memoirs" for the *Quarterly Review* in 1818, would call *Silva* "one of the few books in the world which completely effected what it was designed to do."[5] In the dedication to Charles II at the front of the second edition, Evelyn could boast that more than "two Millions of Timber-Trees" had already been planted.[6]

Throughout the eighteenth century "Mr. Evelyn's Silva" continued to be praised. Wotton, the classical scholar, allegedly proclaimed that "it outdoes all that Theophrastus and Pliny have left us on that subject."[7] Evelyn's reputation, however, was not limited to scholars. Everyone knew of the renowned Mr. Evelyn, whose refracted fame was appropriated by a wide range of literary works on nature. For example, the poetry of Abraham Cowley continued to be published with an old bookseller's notice that deferred even in literary matters to "the judicious Mr. Evelyn's opinion," whose reputation for "veracity, judgement in Poetry, and skill in gardening" could be trusted.[8] In fact, any knowledge of Cowley (the poet had been Evelyn's friend and the supplier of a preface to *Silva*) practically guaranteed knowledge of Evelyn, since Cowley's poems refer to him so often. The *Godmersham Park Library Catalogue*, for example, lists two editions of "Cowley's works" ("London 1684" in folio and "2 vols London 1772" in octavo) that included the frequently reprinted "The Garden," expressly dedicated "To J. Evelyn, Esquire," and "Verses to Mr. Evelyn."[9] Irrespective of knowledge of Cowley's poetry, the name *Mr. Evelyn* at the time of *Evelina*'s publication in 1778 still conjured up the famous Restoration author of *Silva*, even though his work had first appeared more than a hundred years before. Encomia about Mr. Evelyn's *Silva* not only span the eighteenth century but also extend far into the next, with Sir Walter Scott continuing to gesture in *Kenilworth* (1821) to "the celebrated Mr. Evelyn, whose 'Silva' is still the manual of British planters."[10]

Today, John Evelyn is better known as the prodigious diarist whose recordings of Restoration life are frequently compared with those of Samuel Pepys. Since *Evelina* is essentially an urban diary, a diarist might make a fine referent for an epistolary novel. However, the publication of *Memoirs Illustrative of the Life and Writings of John Evelyn* did not take place until 1818. Although some claim that the *Memoirs* transformed Evelyn's reputation "almost overnight" from that of "a minor worthy into one of the most famous of all seventeenth-century Englishmen," the rhetoric of sudden "transformation" exaggerates Evelyn's change in status, even as "minor worthy" underestimates his renown at the time of *Evelina*'s publication in 1778.[11] This is because, in 1776, Dr. Alexander Hunter's publication of a luxuriously illustrated "fifth" edition of Evelyn's

Silva placed the book again at the foreground of horticultural literature about the British landscape. Although at least four editions, each
expanded by Evelyn, had appeared between 1664 and 1706, it was the
richly illustrated edition of 1776 that "gave it renewed popularity" just
prior to the publication of *Evelina*.[12] In fact, Simon Schama believes that
Hunter's republication of Evelyn's *Silva* in 1776, rather than the original 1664 text, "would truly revolutionize British sensibilities about the
woodlands."[13] Hunter's new edition of *Silva* was such a watershed book
that, for Schama, Evelyn's fame and impact after the 1776 edition rivaled
his influence during the whole of the previous century, marking a "re-
birth of sylvan patriotism."[14] Schama observes that the subscription list
of Hunter's edition was dominated "by the greatest and grandest among
the Whig nobility," quipping that "subscription to the Hunterian *Silva*
was a requirement of fashion."[15] The Godmersham library met these as-
pirant qualities with a copy of Hunter's edition of "Evelyns Silva York
1776" in quarto. Whether revived reverence for Evelyn was bona fide or
à la mode, Evelyn's name was a household word among the gentry by
1778 precisely because, in an age when the popular passion for gardening blossomed into national obsession, every landowner with claims to
elegance invariably owned a copy of *Silva*.

While Hunter's 1776 edition reasserted *Silva*'s status as essential to
the gentleman planter, the preferred arrangement of plantations had dras-
tically altered since 1664. It his original *Silva*, Evelyn had introduced
into the English landscape lexicon the term *avenues*, a Continental practice of planting long straight lines of trees at equal distance from one
another along formal rides, driveways, and main roads.[16] Striving for formalist elegance and symmetrical precision, Evelyn dictated the optimal
distance between various types of trees for the creation of "*Walks*," or
avenues. When it comes to limes, for example, he recommends a distance of "eighteen *foot*" if the soil is "rich" and "fifteen, or sixteen" if only
ordinary.[17] He also champions horizon-reaching lengths of crisply-kept
hedges, shrubs, and evergreens in a chapter on fences and quickthorn,
or "Quick-Set" hedges, those useful natural dividers planted, or set, with
live cuttings of hawthorn. Incidentally, Jane Austen's letters suggest that
her family applied Evelyn's preferred hedging method, for in the late
spring of 1811, she reports to Cassandra on the prosperity of the "young
Quickset hedge" along with the exciting discovery of an apricot in one of
their new fruit trees.[18] However, while gardening methods and even the
popularity of some varieties of plants remained relatively static, design

did not. Britain's new generations of landscape architects had already re-shaped many of England's formal avenues and clipped shrubberies into natural-seeming serpentine curves, Brownian clumps, and picturesque (dis)arrangements. In spite of changes in popular aesthetics, *Silva* still helped readers select trees fit to grow in the different soils and climates across Britain, especially since Hunter's notes to the 1776 text enhanced it with information about new varieties. The popularity of Hunter's elegant republication, which would lead to further editions in 1786, 1801, and 1812, may have prompted Burney to flaunt the Evelyn family name so prominently at the start of her fiction, thus fertilizing her first novel and its garden metaphors with Evelyn's revived fame.[19]

Hunter prefaces his 1776 edition of *Silva* with a long "Life of John Evelyn," which lionizes Evelyn and places his opus within the context of a moral and political career. Detailed biographical information about the famous Evelyn is not needed to recognize the dominant garden metaphor behind his appearance in *Evelina*. However, knowledge of his association with the royal family, London's public spaces, and French landscape aesthetics do pay further dividends in Burney's novel (as well as Austen's work). As Hunter records in his minibiography, Evelyn was a devout Royalist and well-acquainted with court culture. He spent his twenties among the exiled court in France, where he married Mary Browne, the only daughter of Charles I's ambassador, Sir Richard Browne of Sayes Court in Deptford, whose estate Evelyn eventually purchased.[20] In 1647, Evelyn subsequently returned to England, where "public affairs induced Mr. Evelyn to live very retired at Sayes-Court," meaning that his well-known loyalties forced him into quiet country life.[21] Among his earliest publications were translations from the French, including the popular *French Gardener* (1658). In the context of contemporary politics, however, even a gardening text could provoke debate about French or English superiority. As Hunter notes, most of the later editions added a corrective retort: "The English Gardener Vindicated," by John Rose, "Gardener to King Charles II." John Rose (1619–77), rumored to have grown England's first pineapple, would work with Evelyn on a number of publications and gardening projects and, in spite of his defensive posturing in print, would help bring the French formal style to England's elite gardens.[22] After the Restoration, Evelyn reentered politics, or as Hunter puts it, "the active scenes of life." Authoring the first serious English treatise on urban pollution, *Fumifugium* (1661), Evelyn dedicated himself to the improvement of urban life, serving on committees about "the sick and wounded" during the "war with the Dutch" in 1664, and tending to improvement of city sewers, major building projects, and London's redesign after the Great Fire.[23] "In the year 1662," records Hunter, "when the Royal Society was established, Mr. Evelyn was appointed one of the first Fellows and Council," while his *Silva* was the very first work officially published by the Society.[24] Thus Evelyn had the "well-fare of the nation" in mind, argues Hunter, when he wrote *Silva*. In light of the editorializing paratexts and notes to Hunter's edition, the name of Evelyn in *Evelina* invokes civic duty, loyalty, and elite society—as well as a particular garden aesthetic.

Burney's *Evelina*

Burney begins *Evelina; or, The History of a Young Lady's Entrance into the World* (1778) with the minihistory of a fictional Mr. Evelyn, the heroine's maternal grandfather.[25] An opening volley of letters about this deceased Mr. Evelyn passes between the oldest characters in the book, Mr. Arthur Villars and Lady Howard, who respectively reside at the country estates of Berry Hill and Howard Grove. Given the age and pastoral settings of the writers, the tragic history revived by this starting exchange hints at a postlapsarian Eden—a world, in other words, that already evokes a garden past. Under the guise of exchanging long-kept secrets between close friends, Villars and Howard convey essential family background about the heroine's parentage and social predicament. Only after the telling of the marital tragedies of Evelina's grandparents and parents does the title character write her story in her own words, in the form of epistles to her elderly guardian, Reverend Mr. Villars. From the novel's outset, Burney draws attention to the classic problem of how family history bears upon the individual. Her metaphors are transparently biblical: the history of Mr. Evelyn, whose name simultaneously evokes the gardens of England's recent past and an echo of Paradise, discloses the book's original sin—now carried by his namesake Evelina, whose name means, literally, *little Eve*.

Burney's brief history of Mr. Evelyn, bedecked with puns and suggestive names, imparts vital knowledge of the heroine's family tree—its *Evelyn* or *line of Eve*. Mr. Evelyn, a "young man of excellent character," fell tragically in love with a "low-bred," "vulgar and illiterate" tavern waitress whose infatuating beauty blinded him to her coarse intellect.[26] "Too weak to resist the allurements of beauty," Mr. Evelyn commits the sin of a judgment misled by aesthetics. The new Mrs. Evelyn adds insult to injury when she induces her husband "to abandon his native land, and fix his abode in France." Mr. Evelyn "survived this ill-judged marriage but two years," dying, presumably, of a consumptive regret and a festering "shame and repentance" (1:6). Because of his wife's ill character, Mr. Evelyn assigns the legal guardianship of his infant daughter to his tutor, Mr. Villars. At age eighteen, however, Miss Evelyn is returned to Paris, to a mother who has remarried to a rich Monsieur Duval. As the surname suggests, the Duvals prove "unnatural" and fiendish parents, who attempt to force Miss Evelyn to marry a distant relative against her will, prompting her rashly to elope with the dashing Sir John Belmont, whose own name inflects his libertinism with a risqué pun (1:3). Soon after the secret marriage, Belmont, disappointed in his expectations of a fortune, cruelly disowns both wife and newborn child (heroine Evelina) by tearing up their marriage certificate, the only legal proof of the union. Miss Evelyn, who can now no longer lay claim to being Lady Belmont, dies, leaving her baby girl to be raised by Mr. Villars, in imitation of herself.

Since this girl, too, is unable to claim her rightful family name and since the taking of her mother's surname would be tantamount to broadcasting her bastard status, she is dubbed Evelina Anville. Her pseudonym, more or less, rearranges the letters in her first name, itself a derivation of *Evelyn*. The Christian name that she retains not only confirms her matriarchal heritage but also neatly evokes the mother of all mothers. At the novel's start, Evelina has blossomed into a young woman of about sixteen, having been raised within the sheltered pastoral enclave of Berry Hill. Because Villars also reared her mother and educated her grandfather, his responsibility for this third generation—after both Mr. and Miss Evelyn made bad marriage choices under his influence—suggests a dangerous continuity with the past. After this operatic back-story, Evelina awkwardly finds her way through London society. Her story, which spans roughly a year, ends happily, if predictably, when she claims her rightful identity as Miss Belmont, only to relinquish the name almost immediately upon being married to the virtuous man of her choice, Lord Orville. Thus, in *Evelina* Burney breaks the tyranny of history and celebrates the triumphant individualism for which the eighteenth-century novel genre is known.[27]

I rehearse Burney's plot so minutely to point out that in a novel about a heroine's quest to regain her rightful name and identity, names become vitally significant. The heroine's name is, as Margaret Anne Doody puts it, "a crucial problem."[28] In many ways, Burney's treatment of names is typical of much eighteenth-century fiction (and this is where Austen diverges). The novel genre's increasing ordinariness, its generic realism, continues to partake in Burney of an old cratylic tradition in which the hidden innateness or truthfulness of proper names is assumed. The term derives from Plato's dialogue *Cratylus*, in which the eponymous character successfully argues that names express the nature of their bearers, as opposed to the view that names are, like most words, conventional or accidental designations for things. The literary tradition of connecting names and character traits articulated by Plato has deep roots in ancient times and practices. This cratylic tradition is still upheld by the eighteenth-century novel in names such as Mr. Allworthy, Mrs. Slipslop, Fanny Goodwill, Lovelace, Clarissa, Grandison, Betsy Thoughtless, and many others. In this manner, eighteenth-century novels routinely encouraged the scrutiny of names for clues to characterization. Laurence Sterne famously spoofs even this feature of the early novel, creating in *Tristram Shandy* (1759-67) a narrator accidentally christened with a name abhorred by his father and consequently plagued by his family's cratylic faith that this marks him for disaster. Suggestive nomenclatures do not operate in this old way in Austen—whose names, borrowed from history rather than invented, requisition Herodotus even more than Cratylus. While Austen places the same interpretive pressure on her names, she does so with a difference.

Precisely because of the tradition of cratylic reading, Burney's explicit and unrelenting emphasis throughout *Evelina* on the importance of names emboldens me to claim that neither the young Jane Austen nor any other attentive contemporary could have missed the allusion to the real-world Mr. Evelyn in the novel's opening gambit about the Evelyn legacy, which invokes both biblical and English gardens in the personal history that recounts the derivation of Evelina's name. Not only does the plot hinge upon whether the heroine may legitimately assume a particular name, but cratylic nomenclatures abound throughout the text, including, for example, the fiendish Mme. Duval and the indiscriminate Mr. Lovel. Eighteenth-century novel readers were schooled in a habit of scrutinizing names for hints of characterization (Austen enthusiastically took up this habit, as I showed in the Introduction). Even Evelina's pseudonym *Anville* seems calculated to yield to such ciphering, since it neatly pairs with *Orville*, the man marked as the heroine's match from the outset. The name *Anville* may also suggest the heroine's indelible virtuous core, since she is the fixed object against which, in the smithy of society, other characters are forged into shape.[29] That Miss Anville is ultimately united with an ore-full man named Orville reinforces the puns and all-around wordplay.

Together, *Evelina*'s prolonged Edenic metaphors, the cratylic emphasis it places on names, and the prominence of the heroine's namesake and grandfather Mr. Evelyn help invoke the real John Evelyn—gardener, botanist, and advocate of city planning. Given the novel's thematic emphasis on history, from the biblical to the personal, it is no coincidence that Evelina's progress through London offers a virtual history lesson in English garden design, illustrating with concrete urban examples a gradual departure from the formal French style favored by Evelyn. Many of the trials faced by Evelina, literal descendant from the line of Eve, or Eve-lyn, take place in the old and new gardens of London—from the formal grounds of St. James's Park and Kensington Gardens to the pleasure gardens of Vauxhall, Ranelagh, and Marylebone. Although Evelyn by no means designed all these urban spaces, his reputation as an old-style planter of trees and planner of cities informs the manner in which city parks function as an emblematic Eden in Burney's urban story.

Within a day of her arrival in London, Evelina visits St. James's Park, which she criticizes as an "uneasy" London landscape. As befits the timing of this early scene in the novel, St. James's is the oldest of London's royal parks. Purchased as swamp by Henry VIII in 1532 and drained by James I around 1603, it was redesigned and opened to the public by Charles II during Evelyn's lifetime, probably in consultation with him. Evelyn's occasional partner, John Rose, had official charge of the park's design and maintenance. The redesign reflected the king's enthusiasm, cultivated in exile, for the French formal style. St. James's Park, even in 1778, therefore remained marked by the straight lines and formal *avenues* for which Evelyn, coiner of the term, became known. Country-bred Evelina remarks on the strangeness of this urban garden when compared to the "open" vistas and parks familiar to her in rural England: "We . . . walked in the Mall in St. James's Park, which by no means answered my expectations: it is a long straight walk, of dirty gravel, very uneasy to the feet; and at each end, instead of an open prospect, nothing is to be seen but houses built of brick" (1:30).[30] Evelina's "uneasy" ramble in St. James's Park may reflect historical associations, since the park became a notorious hangout for London's whores and a site of sexual lewdness during the Restoration, as Rochester's infamous poem "A Ramble in St. James' Park" (1672) makes clear. Reforms in 1766 remained ineffective in curbing the "indecent practices in St. James Park," raising perennial complaints about the "playing and betting at unlawful games, bathings, and running of races naked, &c., particularly on the Sabbath Day," well into the 1770s.[31] Thus, in connection with John Evelyn's memory and contemporary reputation, St. James's is as postlapsarian a garden as London can offer. To clinch Burney's extended allusion to the garden of Genesis, the heroine is suddenly struck in St. James's Park by "how much everybody was dressed," especially London's women (1:30). After Burney repeats the archaic expression, "the ladies were so much dressed," to stress the comparison to Eve's nakedness, Evelina recognizes she must "*Londonize*" herself and soon sports the hastily gathered fig leaves of store-bought clothing.

Evelina, an Eve adrift, is soon redirected to Kensington Gardens, a royal garden of later design only recently open to a select public when the novel was published in 1778.[32] "Mrs Mirvan," writes Evelina when describing the disappointing visit to St. James's Park, "says we are not to walk in the Park again next Sunday, even if we should be in town, because there is better company in Kensington Gardens" (1:30). This move from St. James's Park to Kensington Gardens shifts *Evelina* into the next generation of British landscape design. This may seem an odd claim, since Kensington Gardens were initially laid out in 1691 by Henry Wise (1653–1738) and Charles Bridgeman (d. 1738) for William III. Like John Evelyn, Wise and Bridgeman were inclined to the formalist style and, in honor of the new Dutch king of Britain, added an extensive Dutch garden to the usual allotment of French parterres, Italian-inspired orangeries, and long avenues. Decades later, however, around 1730, Kensington Gardens had been reshaped to fit an evolving and "softening" British landscape aesthetic under the direction of Queen Caroline, wife of George II. With the help of an older Bridgeman, the queen molded the garden into the form it retained in Burney's day. She opened the area by annexing a large section from Hyde Park, creating walks that radiated outward from a circular pond. Two large lakes gained irregularities that newly broke with the practice of straight canals, wet versions of avenues, which had dominated the water features of formal garden scapes. Ditches or sunken fences, rather than the hedges or traditional fencing recommended by Evelyn's *Silva*, deformalized the park further. This design trick, which removed the need for unsightly fences while still separating grazing animals from vulnerable plantings, would become known as the ha-ha. It revolutionized the appearance of England's countryside, allowing the softer, fenceless aesthetic of Burney's and Austen's age to flourish. Kensington Gardens, popularly considered the birthplace of the ha-ha, may proffer the key to that "open prospect" so praised by Evelina. Thus Mrs. Mirvan's insistence that Kensington Gardens offers a more fashionable locale than St. James's Park redirects the reader to value a more open, up-to-date, garden plan—something increasingly British and less foreign.

Of all the London gardens Evelina visits, she predictably prefers those that stray from the straight walks, hedged spaces, and long avenues associated with the French-influenced aesthetic of her grandfather's namesake, John Evelyn, whose choices Burney tags as tragically flawed. Burney singles out Ranelagh, the most modern of the so-called pleasure gardens, for particular praise by her heroine: "It is a charming place and the brilliancy of the light, on my first entrance, made me almost think I was in some inchanted castle, or fairy place, for all looked like magic to me" (1:50–51). Ranelagh opened on 5 April 1742 as an elite rival to the popular Vauxhall. By 1778, Vauxhall was apparently an institution in decline, for when Evelina admits to the Branghton girls and Mr. Smith that she has not yet been to Vauxhall and "Marybone" gardens, Burney condemns it through the praise of her most transparent poseurs: "No!—God bless me!" proclaims Mr. Smith, "you really surprise me,—why Vauxhall is the first pleasure in life!—I know nothing like it" (2:106). Vauxhall also does not meet with the final approval of Evelina, who judges its gardens as still too closely aligned with the outdated aesthetic associated with Evelyn: "The Garden is very pretty, but too formal; I should have been better pleased, had it consisted less of strait walks" (2:117). As Evelina implies, Vauxhall, too, dated back to the 1660s, when, as the New Spring Gardens, it was little more than an alehouse with a small yard to which Pepys, for instance, occasionally retreated by boat across the Thames. Under the ownership of entrepreneur Jonathan Tyers, who would run the gardens for almost four decades starting in 1727, the grounds were expanded. Tyers transformed Vauxhall into a pleasure garden of elaborate symmetrical design, making it look, if compared to the open plan of Kensington Gardens, rather dated in 1778. While wilderness ringed Vauxhall, any visit focused on its long promenades and avenues, quadrangular groves bisected by straight paths, temples, concert venues, and boxes for dining. The more elaborate entertainments, especially the musical performances, took place in spaces that continued to adhere to Evelyn's formalist recipe. The novel's backhanded praise of Vauxhall by the coarse Miss Branghton proves transparently tongue in cheek: "For my part," said Miss Branghton, "I like it because it is not vulgar" (2:120). Burney's ironic dismissal of Vauxhall does not merely rank it low among London's gardens in accordance with contemporary taste but condemns it explicitly as "too formal" and "strait," qualities that continue to invoke the heroine's namesake Mr. Evelyn, whose flawed Frenchified aesthetic underlies the novel's original sin.

Evelina's climactic visit to Marylebone, or Marybone, Gardens, where she loses her way and ends up, astonishingly, walking arm in arm with two prostitutes, brings her full circle back to the biblical temptation in the symbolic garden where the novel began. For a moment it seems as if Evelina's burgeoning sexuality, together with its fragile affinity with money and the social currency of rank in the marriage market, risks eliding itself with the dangerous commodification of femininity transacted by common prostitutes. Evelina's initial visit to St. James's Park, a bower of iniquity during the Restoration, may presage the incident in Marylebone Gardens. Evelina's visits to London's gardens consistently threaten to reenact an original temptation whenever these spaces embody Evelyn's old aesthetics. Like the other gardens condemned by Burney, Marylebone bore the visual markings of a Restoration heritage. A pleasure garden from about 1650, it was originally nothing more than a few bowling greens adjoining a popular tavern, also frequented by Pepys. Enlarged by 1730, Marylebone was briefly famous for fireworks between 1772 and 1774, the presumed window in which the events of *Evelina* take place. Having closed in 1776, Marylebone was unlikely to suffer from Burney's implied censure of its clientele in 1778. All that Evelina, now an experienced garden visitor, remarks is that Marylebone "is neither striking for magnificence nor for beauty" (2:193).

For Burney, who lived at a time when the walled, hedged, and highly symmetrical French-style gardens, parterres, and avenues of the last century were steadily being softened and supplanted by the evolving English taste for openness and a natural-seeming irregularity, the name *Evelyn* smacks of an outdated and artificial sensibility still visible in those London spaces dating to the Restoration, when a king reared in exile on French aesthetics returned to the throne. That Burney's Mr. Evelyn proves victim to appearances and a false aesthetic, being "too weak to resist the allurements of beauty," absconds for the shame of it to France, and dies leaving behind a widow whose Francophile enthusiasm corrupts her native English tongue as well as what remains of her morals—all this seems deftly calculated to reinforce the national suspicion of everything French in her target London audience. *Evelina*, which champions the patriotic elements of England's more open landscape, resembles Horace Walpole's *History of the Modern Taste in Gardening* (1771), which, as Alistair Duckworth puts it, "promoted the Whig view that the natural style of the English garden was an expression of liberty, whereas the geometric formality of the French garden signified political despotism."[33] The fact that *Evelina*'s message echoes Walpole's cannot be accidental, for Walpole "had long been a friend of the Burney family" and appears under his official title, the Earl of Orford, among the subscribers to *Camilla*.[34] Frances Burney's early fiction may express a point of view familiar in her circle of acquaintances, although the novelist, whose own mother and beloved maternal grandmother were French and who would marry an émigré herself, could not have shared the typical xenophobia against the French.[35] Indeed, the grossest comments about the French in *Evelina* are spoken by Captain Mirvan, a coarse cartoonish figure whose antics pain even his wife. Still, perhaps her disavowal of her youthful writings later in life included embarrassment about French stereotypes in *Evelina*.

In possible imitation of Burney, Austen intensifies the interpretive resonances of locales and names, creating in the story entitled *Evelyn* a prototype, as it were, of the networked historical references found in *Northanger Abbey*. Although Austen departs from Burney when she critiques the contemporary vogue for "improvements" in *Mansfield Park* or hails, as I will show, John Evelyn's old-fashioned aesthetic as virtuous in *Sense and Sensibility*, in *Evelyn* she picks up on the prominence of John Evelyn in the history of landscape design, possibly in youthful imitation of an allusive style gleaned from *Evelina*. Austen's penchant for symbolic names, horticultural tie-ins, and emblematic garden scapes starts off, in other words, resembling features from *Evelina*, before settling into her own understated realism, where emblem and allusion are more deeply buried and historical names more prominent.

Significantly, while Austen ultimately finds no use for memorable names such as *Orville*, *Duval*, *Branghton*, or *Mirvan*, she prominently recycles not just one but two of *Evelina*'s major character names: *Evelyn* and *Willoughby*. These names first appear together in "A Collection of Letters" even before *Willoughby* enters *Sense and Sensibility*. While it is impossible to sort deliberate borrowings from coincidental overlaps in other shared names (plain characters named *Smith* and *Brown* unsurprisingly appear in both authors, and even *Howard* may be too common in real life to raise, by itself, much interpretive suspicion), the two standout names in Burney that find their way into Austen each carry potential historical cachet. Part of the store of associations they carry by Austen's time is, of course, their appearance in Burney. This association seems especially dominant in *Sense and Sensibility*'s rake, who echoes Sir Clement Willoughby's urban habits as well as his name.[36] Beyond Burney, however, these names invoke specific histories that Austen deploys for use in her fiction—expanding especially upon the history of John Evelyn. Whereas Burney mixes cratylic craftiness with the occasional historical allusion, Austen mixes more "real solemn history" into her recipe for invention, increasing her dependence upon historical personages for interpretive effect.

Austen's Reading of Burney

Burney was an acknowledged model and touchstone for Austen's own ambitions as a writer. In fact, the first occasion on which Jane Austen's own name appeared in print was the 1796 publication of Frances Burney's novel *Camilla*, which listed among its 1,058[37] subscribers the as-yet-unknown "Miss J. Austen, Steventon."[38] According to family legend, Mr. Austen purchased the subscription for his daughter Jane, whose youthful enthusiasm for Burney's two earlier novels was known among her family and friends. Jane Austen was but twenty then, approaching the age that Burney had been when, at twenty-five, she made her first foray into publishing with her novel *Evelina* (1778). A year later, Mr. Austen compares his daughter's own fledgling manuscript of "First Impressions" to Burney's debut novel when he tentatively approaches London publisher Thomas Cadell on her behalf: "I have in my possession a Manuscript Novel, comprised in three Vols. about the length of Miss Burney's Evelina."[39] Mr. Austen's choice of publisher seems similarly calculated to liken his daughter to Burney, for Cadell was listed in the imprint to *Camilla*. When Austen discarded the working title of her manuscript after the 1801 publication of a novel by Mrs. Holford with that same name, she may again have turned to Burney, whose *Cecilia* (1782) thrice repeats the phrase "PRIDE and PREJUDICE" in emphatic capital letters on its final pages.[40] For years, Austen proclaimed that

"Madame d'Arblay [Burney's married name] was the very best of the English novelists."[41]

Judging solely on the basis of Austen's most overt intertextual allusions to *Evelina*, the literary influence of this one Burney text visibly spans her early career. To take just some of Austen's best-known gleanings: *Sense and Sensibility* flaunts the name of Willoughby, the urban libertine in *Evelina*; *Pride and Prejudice* restages the social awkwardness of Evelina's first interactions with Lord Orville at a dancing assembly and his overheard slight about her looks; and *Emma* recasts the unwelcome proposal that takes place one evening in *Evelina* during a claustrophobic carriage ride. When the overheard exchange between Bingley and Darcy at the Netherfield ball reenacts the scene in *Evelina* in which the heroine, whose nervous silence causes her to appear sullen and proud, reports how her friend Maria listened in on Lord Orville's assessment of her at the dancing assembly, Austen does not hide her debt to Burney but parades it for a contemporary reader's redoubled enjoyment.[42] Also, Darcy is not a mere copy of Orville, whose wooden formality Austen criticizes in her letters as "not natural" in a lover.[43] Like the parallel translations so popular in the eighteenth century, *Pride and Prejudice* flaunts its imitation of *Evelina*, almost as if to claim an improvement of sorts upon the well-worn thirty-five-year-old original. As with Pope's imitations of Horace, Austen's borrowings and reworkings of *Evelina* are as much gauntlet as homage.

Unsurprisingly then, at least one volume of Austen's juvenilia was, as a biographer puts it, already "written both under and against the influence of such novels by Fanny Burney as *Evelina* (1778) and *Cecilia* (1782)."[44] This is the 1792 volume containing *Evelyn* and *Catharine; or, The Bower*, a twin set of stories spoofing landscape trends. Before turning to Austen's juvenilia, I want to acknowledge how Burney had already recycled the name of Evelyn from a much-earlier piece of juvenilia of her own—possibly dating Burney's and Austen's interests in John Evelyn to roughly the same time in their respective growings up. Interestingly, the tragic history of the Evelyn family summarized in the opening letters of *Evelina* likely constitutes the remnants of an earlier full-length manuscript known as "The History of Miss Caroline Evelyn." On her fifteenth birthday, Burney burnt her juvenilia in a large bonfire, destroying all her early poetry and plays, along with a manuscript novel known only by this title. In the absence of a surviving holograph any reflections on content constitute pure guesswork. And yet, Burney suggestively preserves the name of "Miss Caroline Evelyn" for Evelina's mother, recounting the sad history of an Evelyn family in the opening pages of her later published novel. The title of Burney's destroyed novel suggests a juvenile prequel to *Evelina*.[45] Austen could not, of course, have known about the existence of Burney's burnt early manuscript, and her own *Evelyn* responds, instead, to the published *Evelina*. Nonetheless, both young authors follow the same career path, which starts, in imitation of Virgil, with a georgic theme and a shared vocabulary of a fictionalized Evelyn.

Austen's *Evelyn*

Composed under the influence of *Evelina*, Austen's short tale *Evelyn* similarly brings into play knowledge of Restoration garden designer John Evelyn. Already *Evelyn* is, along with *Catharine; or, The Bower*, which accompanies it in the last of her three juvenilia volumes, an acknowledged Bower-of-Bliss story that comically reworks Edmund Spenser's *The Faerie Queene*.[46] In addition to the Spenser allusion, the plot of Austen's *Evelyn* responds to Burney's story of a Mr. Evelyn—trapped into an "ill-judged" marriage by an aesthetic façade—with a protagonist who similarly submits to an impulsive marriage with a pretty stranger. Written in 1792, the twenty-one pages of manuscript that constitute *Evelyn* do not, of course, allow as extensive an engagement with its titular namesake as was true for *Evelina*. And yet the story incorporates further facts about Evelyn's work and life, facts possibly learned from sources such as Hunter's "The Life of Mr. John Evelyn."[47] While *Evelyn* engages *Evelina*, it diverges from Burney's reliance upon the cratylic and symbolic, demonstrating an emphatic use of English history that becomes characteristic of Austen.

This is not to say that *Evelyn* lacks the playfulness with words shown in Burney's novel. In fact, while "a preoccupation with wordplay and hidden meaning is a recurring feature" throughout Austen's juvenilia, this story exhibits a particularly strong interest in wordplay.[48] Indeed, the plot of *Evelyn* is built around a central pun, revealed when the hero ventures into the landscape of the picturesque to retrieve, literally, a picture. Before this final disclosure, the protagonist's entrance into the apparent idyll of the village of Evelyn erases from his memory the valiant quest pursued on behalf of an ailing sister, for whom he intended to bring back a picture of her dead lover from the young man's family castle. When traveling on horseback into Evelyn, Austen's gentleman Lotus-eater is instantly struck by the village's beauty, succumbing to an irrational desire to settle there permanently. To his tearful chagrin, no vacancies exist: "Alas! Sir, replied Mrs Willis, there is *none*. Every house in this village, from the sweetness of the Situation, and the purity of the Air, in which neither Misery, Illhealth, or Vice are ever wafted, is inhabited" (*J*, 231). Like visitors to other false utopias of legend, from Circe's island to the Eagles' *Hotel California*, Evelyn's inhabitants never leave.

Many blank months later, the sight of a garden rose causes the hero to remember his now-dead sister Rose, the ill-fated "thirteenth daughter" in his family, and resume his quest on her behalf (*J*, 235). Since the rose invokes a person by that name in the story, perhaps it also obliquely recalls the famous Mr. Rose, Charles II's official gardener and John Evelyn's partner on various publications and projects. More certain, however, is that the surname of Austen's gentleman protagonist, Mr. Gower, forges a historical connection with John Evelyn, through the well-known Gower family, which Donald Greene recognized as another name Austen pulled from the peerage.[49] Genealogical accounts confirm that in the 1770s John Evelyn's descendants, the Evelyns of Godstone, married into the famous Gower family, who eventually expanded their name to Leveson-Gower.[50] Prior even to this marriage, the first Earl Gower, a Tory politician named John Leveson-Gower (1694–1754), had married an Evelyn of sorts—Lady Evelyn Pierrepont, christened after her father, Evelyn Pierrepont, Duke of Kingston upon Hull, who in turn had been named for Sir John Evelyn. As a result, the name *Evelyn* appears in Austen's time on the Gower family tree as both a first and last name—just like the name *Rose*. Austen's *Evelyn* may reward knowledge of such genealogical connections. This well-known Gower family had their seat at Trentham, Staffordshire, where the gardens were laid out in the 1690s (although not by Evelyn).[51] Originally designed by Charles Bridgeman, who initially shared much of Evelyn's formality, this garden was reconceived as a serpentine park by Capability Brown and Henry Holland after 1758. In at least one book that Jane Austen is known by this stage to have read, William Gilpin discusses the work done for Gower by Brown at Trentham, praising Brown's touches as "masterly" while also lamenting a discomfort with some residual regularities, including "the flat, newly planted area" and the "artificial squareness of the mole" forming the lake.[52] Gilpin's assessment of Trentham as insufficiently naturalized could have influenced Austen's descriptive language of the gardens in her *Evelyn*.

The comic utopia of Austen's *Evelyn* may also refer ironically to a solemn one designed by John Evelyn himself, who envisioned a "rural retreat," or countryside idyll, in a famous letter to fellow Royal Society member Robert Boyle, the architect of Boyle's Law.[53] Hunter reproduces many pages from this letter in his biography, explaining that Evelyn's love for his retired life at Sayes Court, combined with "his disgust of the world, occasioned by the violence and confusion of the times," generated a proposal for a rural retreat dedicated to like-minded men who wanted to "pass their days without care or interruption" in studying and conversing together. Evelyn proposes to Boyle the "purchasing of thirty of forty acres of land, in some healthy place, not above twenty-five miles from London" and provides the architectural specs for an ideal rural getaway "somewhat after the manner of the Carthusians": "six apartments or cells for the members of the society" and their families built around a central courtyard and fronted and backed by "a plot walled in" with several satellite buildings. He includes details about the sunk "kitchen, larders, cellars, and offices," as well as stables, servant quarters, conservatory, even a museum for "rarities," and "an aviary, dove-house, physic-garden, kitchen garden, and a plantation of orchard-fruit." With minute calculations about foods, costs, and every type of provision, Evelyn crafts an imaginary oasis separated from political strife. His precision lends the letter psychological urgency, for his blueprint for a "college" that never existed reads like the catharsis of a disenchanted intellectual. If Austen knew of this extraordinary letter, which features prominently in all of Hunter's editions of *Silva*, she might have associated Evelyn with a utopian vision shared by the most learned members of the Royal Society and perhaps reworked that association into a story about a false utopia named, therefore, *Evelyn*.

Austen's Mr. Gower soon finds a house in Evelyn through the Webb family, whose "peculiar Generosity of Disposition" causes them to instantly bestow upon this stranger both their pretty lodge and their wealthy eldest daughter in a cartoonish gesture of unbridled hospitality. His arrival generates a detailed landscape description in which "regular" plantings, meticulous symmetry, and sylvan scenery conjure up the village's namesake, author of *Silva*:

> As he approached the house, he was delighted with its situation. It was
> in the exact center of a small circular paddock, which was enclosed by a
> regular paling, and bordered with a plantation of Lombardy poplars,

and Spruce firs alternately placed in three rows. A gravel walk ran through this beautiful Shrubbery, and as the remainder of the paddock was unincumbered with any other Timber, the surface of it perfectly even and smooth, and grazed by four white Cows which were disposed at equal distances from each other, the whole appearance of the place as Mr Gower entered the Paddock was uncommonly striking. A beautifully-rounded, gravel road without any turn or interruption led immediately to the house. (*J*, 231–32)

Although this *hortus conclusus*, with its circular boundary of trees, resembles the formalist aesthetics of Evelyn's day rather than the open picturesque landscapes of Austen's, the bull's-eye-like pattern of the scene, with a house at the "exact" center of a bald enclosure surrounded by a paling and three further concentric rows of tall trees, is hideous by any standard—and there resides the humor. This passage is, as Brian Southam asserts, "a satire upon the layout of the formal garden, by then outmoded, and also upon the elaboration of inconsequential detail," betraying an early distrust of the lingua franca of landscape aesthetics generally.[54] As others point out, Austen shows her awareness of contemporary landscaping habits in the "thoroughly unpicturesque" distribution of four, not three, ridiculously equidistant bovine (*J*, 484n15).[55] While landscapers from Evelyn to Brown and beyond commonly planted poplars to delineate property boundaries, none "would have planted tall poplar trees and bushy spruce trees around a house in the middle of a 'small paddock,' blocking out the light," observes Peter Sabor (483n12). As with everything else about this seemingly perfect village, the rejection of sense betrays the incongruities of what will prove, for Mr. Gower, a false utopia. The gravel driveway, if both "beautifully-rounded" and without sharp bend or "turn," cannot lead "immediately" to the Webb house, if that means the most direct route. If curved rather than straight, it could reach a house at the center of a circular paddock only by arduous and ever-narrowing circumnavigation, much like the spider's web invoked by the owners' name.[56] In short, Austen paints an absurdist landscape of false perfection. Prominently inverting the centuries-deep allegory of the *hortus conclusus* as virginal perfection, she relies on unrelenting wordplay based upon historical associations and factual calculations.

Mr. Gower, the story tells us, originally set out from Carlisle, where the sad news about the death at sea of his sister's betrothed prompted his long journey.[57] The cold northern gloom of Carlisle, a genuine city in Cumbria, makes for a fitting contrast with the imagined village of Evelyn, loosely placed in "a retired part of the County of Sussex" and described as "perhaps one of the most beautiful Spots in the south of England" (*J*, 230). The reference to Carlisle attests to Austen's early reliance upon geography and history for interpretive effect. First, the reference elicits comical astonishment at Gower having ridden on horseback some 350 miles from Cumbria to lose his way in Sussex. Mr. Gower's failed navigation resembles that of Lindsay, that "noble Youth" of *Love and Freindship*, who mounts his horse at his Bedfordshire home with the intention of riding to his aunt's in Middlesex, but turns a journey of less than 30 miles south into a more than 100–mile ride west to the Vale of Usk: "Tho' I flatter myself with being a tolerable proficient in Geography, I know not how it happened, but I found myself entering this beautiful Vale which I find is in South Wales, when I had expected to have reached my Aunts" (108–9). Second, Austen selects her references to real-world settings with a care to what histories these places might invoke. This is as true for Carlisle in *Evelyn* as for Bath in *Northanger Abbey* (or the Wye Valley in *Love and Freindship*). Historically, Carlisle's proximity to the border with Scotland led to its being the site of numerous wars and invasions. Because it also boasts one of England's first-generation castles, with parts constructed as early as 1098, it is difficult to imagine a location more evocative of Britain's lengthy war-torn history. Part of the humor in *Evelyn* therefore derives from the fact that Mr. Gower, who as a native of Carlisle should be a well-seasoned veteran of grounds "of a very ancient date," finds "the gloomy appearance of the old Castle" at the story's end utterly horrifying (238). That a stout northerner from Carlisle, the battleground of kings, should be "always timid in the Dark and easily terrified when alone" provokes more laughter than if he had set out from one of the "many counties" that, as Emma Woodhouse knows, are called "the garden of England" (238; *E*, 295).

If the historically allusive name games continue, then perhaps the mention of Carlisle may invoke more than just a distant place with a fierce history but another person: the Earl of Carlisle. This earldom was awarded in 1661 to Charles Howard, whose sister married Sir Thomas Gower, second Baronet, the founder of the Gower family already referenced by Austen and so intertwined with the Evelyn family tree. Incidentally, the prominent role of a Lady Howard in Burney's *Evelina* may have prompted Austen's reach for the name *Carlisle* in her own Evelyn-centered story, since in elite society both *Howard* and *Carlisle*, surname and title, might be used to designate the same family at Howard Castle in Yorkshire. Provocatively, the first Earl of Carlisle, like Austen's invented Mr. Gower, had bungled a long-distance commission. Desirous to promote trade with Russia, Charles II sent Carlisle to Moscow, where he bumbled and fumbled before the czar's ministers, refusing even to take customary gifts back to the king. John Evelyn's diary comments upon Carlisle's return to Charles II's court, where he somehow explained away his problematic conduct. When Austen wrote *Evelyn*, the reigning Earl of Carlisle was Frederick Howard, fifth Earl of Carlisle (1748–1825), who lived at Castle Howard with his wife, Margaret Leveson-Gower, a representative of the same branch of the Gower family so recently coupled with the Evelyns of Godstone.[58] As a trio, therefore, the interconnected mentions of *Evelyn*, *Gower*, and *Carlisle* in the one story allow Austen's youthful wit to skip from one name to another, bringing three historically interlocking allusions into alignment.[59]

Independent of genealogy, strong historical connections existed between these Howards and the Evelyns, connections so public and prominent that they may even have colored Burney's use of the Howard name in *Evelina*. In real life, the Evelyns and the Howards were Surrey neighbors, a circumstance that led to John Evelyn designing several of the Howard family's famous gardens. Evelyn's work at Albury Park, near Guildford in Surrey, for Henry Howard, sixth Duke of Norfolk (1628–84), is "widely known." Henry Howard was, incidentally, the second son of Henry Frederick Howard and Lady Elizabeth Stuart, the same couple who partially inspired Austen's imaginary amalgam of romance, privilege, and wealth in the fictional marriage banns that feature a "Henry Frederick Howard Fitzwilliam." It would appear that, as with the Wentworths, Austen had the history of the Howards in her creative sights early on and might have been as attentive to the Howard name in *Evelina* as to that of Evelyn. In 1638, the Evelyns and the Howards became neighbors, when the then-Earl of Arundel purchased Albury Park, just a few miles away from the Evelyn family estate at Wotton in Surrey. Young John Evelyn grew particularly close to a number of the Howards when their travels through Italy converged in 1645, and he became the "lifelong confidant" of Henry Howard, who "turned to Evelyn for advice on the remodeling of the landscape" at Albury in 1665.[60] An "idealized plan" of Evelyn's designs for Albury Park, drawn up after the fact and "probably in the late 1670s," survives[61] (fig. 4.2). Evelyn's plan shows his typical fondness for symmetry, tight circular and crisscrossed plantings, and

FIGURE 4.2. John Evelyn's Plan of Albury Park, 1667. Harry Ransom Center, The University of Texas at Austin.

straight parallel walks—the stuff of Austen's parody in *Evelyn*. Although there is no definitive record of Austen having seen Albury Park in person, she "travel[ed] the Guildford road" through Surrey on numerous occasions, frequently breaking her journey there, so that her letters mention Albury Park's environs with frequency and casual familiarity (*Letters*, 179). Given her interests in gardens, manor houses, and local history, it would be strange if she had not, like Elizabeth Bennet, eventually wandered onto the grounds of such a splendid and famous park.

Of potential further significance to Austen's thematic preoccupations in *Evelyn* is that Castle Howard, the primary residence of the Earl of Carlisle, also became famous during the eighteenth century for a landscape garden conceived on such a grand scale that it rivaled Blenheim. John Dixon Hunt hails the gardens at Castle Howard "as one of the earliest, let alone one of the most striking, examples of the English landscape garden."[62] Hunt relates how "the route all visitors must take in approaching Castle Howard . . . inaugurates their response to what the place represents."[63] The visceral reaction to an old castle and its landscape experienced by Mr. Gower at the close of Austen's story resembles the one that, according to Hunt, the gardens of the Earls of Carlisle deliberately attempted to solicit: "from the very beginning, the name Castle Howard signals something medieval, something from English history."[64] The eighteenth-century landscapers exploited such fabricated historical association by making the approach from the York road emphasize "strong representations of castle-ness," forcing visitors to pass "through two sets of battlemented walls" and a gatehouse.[65]

In possible reference, then, to the staged historicism of the actual gardens belonging to the Earl of Carlisle, who married a Gower and was connected to the Evelyns, Austen closes *Evelyn* with Mr. Gower's visceral reaction to an "ancient" castle in a picturesque setting. Whatever the referent, Austen comically bookends a story named for a garden designer with two telltale landscapes: an old-fashioned, perfectionist design at the front and its modern, picturesque counterpart—ironically containing the oldest structure—at the back. Unfortunately, Austen's landscape descriptions in *Evelyn* are too brief and too cartoonishly generic to either rule out or confirm a resemblance to, say, Evelyn's designs of Albury Park or the grand-scale woods of Castle Howard. Whatever the particular models Austen used, Mr. Gower's irrational reaction to the picturesque castle and its locale, coupled with the continuing historical allusions invoked by the story's names and landscape types, suggests that even in this early work Austen was keen to mix old and new, ancient and modern, in her aesthetic judgments.

Mr. Gower leaves the "paddock of Evelyn lodge" on a fool's errand compensating for his aborted quest to bring back "a picture" of Rose's lover that might "soften her affliction" at his death at sea (*J*, 236). This, then, is where Austen finally reveals her story's core pun: Mr. Gower enters the picturesque to retrieve a picture. The destination that he belatedly reaches satisfies all picturesque expectations, with a craggy castle dramatically "situated on a woody Eminence commanding a beautiful prospect of the Sea" (238). Although Mr. Gower "did not dislike the situation," he misjudges the "profusion of old Timber" as "illsuited to the style" of the ancient building.[66] As an absurd and ahistorical witness, Mr. Gower finds the castle "certainly greatly inferior to that of his own house," reasoning that it wants a bald paddock and lodge to "enliven the structure" through "Contrast" (238). Although this refers to the Webb home, which has become Mr. Gower's "own house" in the village of Evelyn, Austen's phrase may toy with a possible reference to historic grounds owned by the real-world namesakes of her characters.

As the increasingly irrational Mr. Gower follows the castle's "winding approach," so unlike the "immediate" and curveless path to Evelyn lodge, the narrator describes how the castle "struck him with terror" (*J*, 238). Fear eventually overwhelms Mr. Gower when he leaves the "Gloomy Castle blackened by the deep shade of Walnuts and Pines" (240). Already unsettled by his emotional exchange with the unnamed lord and lady of the castle, Mr. Gower is frightened by sylvan shadows and shuts his eyes to the moon and "Stars which alarmed him by their twinkling" (240).[67] Mr. Gower rides in a "full gallop all the way" back to Evelyn with his eyes dangerously closed "to prevent his seeing either Gipsies or Ghosts" (240). If Mr. Gower's point of origin in the story, Carlisle, invokes a famous castle home—whether in the form of Castle Howard, seat of the Earls of Carlisle, who were connected to the genuine Gower and Evelyn families, or because the city of Carlisle boasts ancient Carlisle Castle—his panic at the sight of an old castle further increases the absurdity. Like Gulliver who returns home after years of absence only to be repulsed by the sight of his own family, Mr. Gower has been so altered by his stay in Evelyn that he flees from what was once intimately familiar.

Although *Evelyn* seems neatly framed by two contrasted landscapes, the old formal paddock and the modern picturesque vista, a significant gap in pagination and two separate continuations by Austen's relatives profess incompleteness.[68] *Sense and Sensibility* may extend Austen's juvenile musings on John Evelyn, developing her maturing interests in emblematic gardens and historical personages in that later story. Just as *Evelyn* seems to grow out of the use to which Burney put history in *Evelina*, so *Sense and Sensibility* shows Austen further elaborating on the memory, work, and time of John Evelyn.

Silva and Sylvan Discourse in *Sense and Sensibility*

The Godmersham Park Library Catalogue lists several works by John Evelyn, including Hunter's important edition of *Silva* in quarto ("Evelyns Silva York 1776") and "Evelyn on Medals London 1697" in folio.[69] The Godmersham catalog also lists "Memoirs of John Evelyn 2 vols London 1819," attesting to a continued family interest in Evelyn's life and work after Jane Austen's death. In addition, an earlier *Silva* from the Knight collection at Chawton has recently come to light.[70] The resurfacing of this other Knight-family copy allows for a nearby *Silva* to have been available even at Chawton, where, it is said, Austen thoroughly revised *Sense and Sensibility*. Irrespective of these specific copies, editions of *Silva* would, Simon Schama suggests, have been part of every genteel collection wherever she traveled. In other words, while I cannot pin down the specific copy of *Silva* read by Austen, the probable contents of her family's holdings only confirm her likely intimacy with this text—perhaps even in multiple editions.

Metaphorically speaking, *Silva* already functions as the *Sense and Sensibility* of horticulture. Just as trees unequivocally hold multiple and contradictory positions in our culture—mixing spiritual and aesthetic value with practicality—utility and aesthetics are, forgive the pun, at loggerheads in *Silva*. A tension between the necessary propagation of forests for "timber" and the preservation of old trees as regal "ornament" in a well-designed landscape animates a text one historian deems "one of the greatest influences on the English feeling for landscape and the place of trees in it."[71] Although Evelyn wrote his final section of *Silva*, headed "Of the Laws and Statutes for the Preservation and Improvement of Woods," expressly to help replenish England's timber supply after the devastation of the Civil War, he launched a movement in silvicultural conservation that went well beyond sustainable logging. This, in turn, led to the viewing of trees as aesthetic objects. As witnessed in Alexander Pope's *Windsor Forest* (1713), in the wake of *Silva* trees figured in eighteenth-century literature as political symbols of history and value, not just mere timber. Elizabeth Heckendorn Cook observes how "literary representations of trees from this period explore the intersections, or collision, of arboreal values, and that this collision became an increasingly compelling subject for writers."[72] A similar tension between practical and emotive valuation animates Austen's *Sense and Sensibility*. Of course, since so many contemporary authors engage with arboreal values, *Silva* is unlikely to be Austen's only silvicultural source, and indeed her fictions also gesture to Brown, Repton, Gilpin, Knight, and Price on the subject of trees. At Godmersham, the Knights owned a considerable collection of works on landscape gardening and the picturesque, including William Mason's *The English Garden* (London, 1778), several works by Gilpin previously mentioned, and the English translation of René Girardin's *Essay on Landscape* (1783). Nonetheless, Austen's early engagement with Evelyn in her juvenilia attests to a long-held fascination with this prominent figure in landscape aesthetics—upon whom she continues to draw for the sylvan imagery in her first published novel.

Already in the opening pages of *Sense and Sensibility*, Austen expresses the prevailing tension of the novel's title through differing evaluations of trees. Norland's trees first come into view through the lens of practicality, when the narrator explains how the "valuable woods" on the Norland property are legally "secured in such a way" as to prevent Henry Dashwood from selling the timber to support his family (*S&S*, 4).[73] While a practical narrator initially accounts for woods as missed income, the emotive Marianne soon laments leaving Norland's "well-known trees" because they are the aesthetic companions of her youth: "—And you, ye well-known trees!—but you will continue the same.—No leaf will decay because we are removed, nor any branch become motionless although we can observe you no longer!—No; you will continue the same; unconscious of the pleasure or the regret you occasion, and insensible of any change in those who walk under your shade!—But who will remain to enjoy you?" (32). With the first glimpse of Norland's "valuable woods" at the front and Marianne's parting soliloquy at the close, Austen frames the opening episode at Norland with a sylvan version of the tension between sense and sensibility, that is, between trees as timber and trees as aesthetic objects—just as in Evelyn's *Silva*.

In *Sense and Sensibility*, the destructive extreme of silvan utility is predictably embodied by John and Fanny Dashwood, who unfeelingly level a grove of established walnut trees to make way for a planned greenhouse. In "An Historical Account of the Sacredness and Use of Standing Groves," prominently advertised on the 1776 *Silva*'s title page as included in Hunter's edition, Evelyn insists upon the immorality of just such tree cutting. The fact that "there is not a stone laid of Fanny's greenhouse, and nothing but the plan of the flower-garden marked out" hints that the sacrifice of these majestic trees may prove in vain if Fanny's building project, which will cost money she is loathe to spend, never comes to pass (*S&S*, 257). In sharp contrast, Marianne, who "would have every book that tells her how to admire an old twisted tree," nurtures what Elinor teasingly labels a "passion for dead leaves" (107 and 101). Such sylvan extremes are, of course, tempered in the story. Barton's "fine timber" and "snug" valley arouse Edward's admiration because they balance form and function: "It exactly answers my idea of a fine country, because it unites beauty with utility" (111–12). Significantly, Edward counters Marianne's "picturesque principles" with sylvan examples: "I do not like crooked, twisted, blasted trees. I admire them much more if they are tall, straight, and flourishing" (113). As the battle between sense and sensibility is fought out in the story's many arboreal passages, Austen may spar with the author who famously combined the nation's practical view of trees with their aesthetic appreciation.

Colonel Brandon's Gardens at Delaford and Evelyn's at Deptford

In the middle of *Kenilworth*, Sir Walter Scott brings his characters to "Say's Court, near Deptfort," explaining how it was "afterwards the residence of the celebrated Mr Evelyn."[74] Although more subtly than Scott, Austen invokes this same well-known historical location in *Sense and Sensibility* when Colonel Brandon's estate at Delaford echoes Evelyn's famous home and gardens at Deptford in more than mere name.[75] The detailed description of Delaford by Mrs. Jennings, who stresses its old-fashioned comforts and itemizes its garden features, may invoke Evelyn's home best. In 1902, Austin Dobson singled out "Mrs. Jennings's description of Delaford" in Austen as "nearer a picture than we usually get from her pen," declaring it "scarcely possible" not to believe it based upon a "real" country house.[76] Although Austen sketches a generic Restoration-era garden, or as Park Honan puts it, "a typical south-county manor of Wren's period," the particulars neatly fit with Evelyn's Deptford home: a walled garden, fruit trees, one extraordinary mulberry tree, a dove-cote, canal, stew-ponds, and proximity to the road and nearby church.[77] Even in the abstract, as Duckworth remarks about all landed estates in Austen, "trees suggest organic growth and continuity" while "the nearness of church and house stresses the religious content of landed life."[78] In other words, Brandon's estate at Delaford offers a landscape of virtue, regardless of whether one recognizes there the echoes of Evelyn's historic gardens at Deptford. The existence of a particular real-world model, however, enhances a reading's poignancy and imparts specific meanings to the details in Austen's story.

Before zeroing in on the historically resonant details of Delaford, I should acknowledge its larger emblematic function. Elizabeth Bennet's visit to Pemberley under the guidance of the aptly named Gardiners is a standard talking point in any classroom discussion that would judge Mr. Darcy's moral character by means of his handsome house and extensive grounds. Likewise in *Sense and Sensibility*, Austen infuses her garden descriptions with implied moral judgments about their owners, signaling the qualities of a potential husband through evidence of husbandry. The matchmaker Mrs. Jennings, eager to offer Colonel Brandon as balm for Marianne's romantic disappointment, thus praises his garden: "Delaford is a nice place, I can tell you; exactly what I call a nice old fashioned place, full of comforts and conveniences; quite shut in with great garden walls that are covered with the best fruit-trees in the country: and such a mulberry tree in one corner! Lord! how Charlotte and I did stuff the only time we were there!" (*S&S*, 223). The "old fashioned" layout of the "great garden walls" that "shut in" Brandon's garden suggest a traditional *hortus conclusus*. Unlike Burney in *Evelina*, Austen hesitates before the modern open and unbounded landscape. An open aesthetic aligns itself with Marianne and Willoughby, whose relationship Elinor characterizes as "uniformly open and unreserved" (93). While *Emma*'s Mr. Knightley wishes for a wife with an "open temper" in claustrophobic Highbury, things left open in *Sense and Sensibility*, such as the garden gate to Barton cottage, "which had been left open by Margaret," allow dangerous libertines such as Willoughby into the imagined perfection symbolized by the *hortus conclusus* (*E*, 311; *S&S*, 50).

In the description of Delaford's garden, Austen inverts the gender of this standard metaphor, commenting on the Colonel's virility rather than, as is traditional, a bride's virginity. The presence of "the best fruit-trees in the country" therefore represent his potency as well as moral goodness, unspoiled by "the little lovechild" that Mrs. Jennings erroneously assigns to him earlier in this long, breathless paragraph (*S&S*, 223). Although Mrs. Jennings callously dismisses the child as of no consequence with "aye, I had forgot her; but she may be 'prenticed out at small cost, and then what does it signify?" the robust yield of Brandon's fruit trees attests to his moral innocence (223). Mrs. Jennings's testimonial to Brandon's extraordinary mulberry tree may also hint at the Colonel's history, eventually told to Elinor in a later scene, by means of an encoded reference to Pyramus and Thisbe, the tragic Babylonian lovers whose blood, tells Ovid, gave the fruit of the mulberry its color. Thanks to Ovid, mulberry trees became cultural symbols of tragic love.[79] Although Brandon waits to disclose his personal history, the mulberry tree in his privately walled garden evokes, along with his fragmentary hint about "unfortunate circumstances" surrounding a lady he once knew, "the most melancholy order of disastrous love" (67). Perhaps the plentiful fruit on this old tree encourages hope for Brandon's romantic future. The one-time invasion of Mrs. Jennings and her daughter, stuffing themselves on his mulberries, fails to violate the sanctity of Brandon's symbolic garden, even if the activity suggests sexual innuendo and comically reworks the prohibition in Genesis.

Emblematic trees reappear, of course, in the landscape of Austen's subsequent fictions. In *Mansfield Park*, as Kathleen Fowler observes, "Jane Austen plants for us an emblem for the entire novel" in the moor park apricot tree praised by Mrs. Norris and judged "insipid" by Dr. Grant.[80] Fowler explains how "Austen uses plants to help delineate the characters with which they are associated," citing how "the Misses Bertram make 'artificial flowers,' while the life-draining Mrs. Norris dries roses."[81] Similarly, the hickory nut gleaned in the hedgerows of *Persuasion* is glossed by the novel's own hero as symbolizing a steadfast purpose and the "happiness" enjoyed by retaining "original strength" of will (*P*, 94). The mere botanical hint of the estate name of Maple Grove in *Emma*, is similarly interpreted by Stephen Derry as a Spenserian allusion to falsity that he connects to Austen's intentional "error" of allowing an orchard to blossom in midsummer at Knightley's estate.[82] Since other critics have already harvested the significance of these individual sylvan moments, I merely align them with a rhetorical habit developed under the twin influences of Burney's *Evelina* and Evelyn's *Silva*.

Evelyn's country seat at Deptford served, I believe, as a real-world model for Brandon's imaginary estate of Delaford in *Sense and Sensibil-*

ity. It was, after all, at Sayes Court in Deptford that Evelyn first put his planting ideas into practice. Here Evelyn planted a dense forest of trees of all kinds, eight hundred in one year alone, including groves bearing abundant fruits, long walls of evergreens, and at least one long-lived mulberry tree. While today Deptford constitutes a suburb of greater London, through Austen's time it remained a more distinct part of northwestern Kent. Austen mentions Deptford twice in her letters, as if a familiar place (*Letters*, 13 and 125). Sayes Court at Deptford was hailed as Evelyn's "true masterpiece" and "the wonder and admiration of the greatest and most judicious men of his time."[83] In 1769, Rev. James Granger still praised the beauty and Edenic qualities of the Deptford gardens, describing them as "one of the finest gardens in the kingdom" and recalling Evelyn as "one of the best and happiest men in it."[84] The year Austen turned seventeen, Cadell began publishing a series of guidebooks by Daniel Lysons under the title *The Environs of London* (1792–96). Lysons, too, praises John Evelyn and "his famous gardens," explaining that Sayes Court dates back to the time of William the Conqueror, when it was called "the manor of Deptford."[85] His guidebook quotes an eyewitness during the Restoration who describes Evelyn's gardens as the embodiment of the principles of his *Silva*: "most boscaresque, being, as it were, an exemplar of his book of forest trees."[86] In stressing Evelyn's manicured and structured aesthetic, Lysons points out how Evelyn "most prided himself" upon his "hedge of holly" at Sayes Court and boasted of the massive evergreen wall as an "impregnable" barrier four hundred feet in length, nine in height, and five in thickness. Evelyn's hedge proved all too vulnerable when Czar Peter the Great famously vandalized it during a tumultuous stint at Sayes Court, amusing himself and his men by plowing through it with a wheelbarrow. Lysons laments that "there is not the least trace now" of these plantings and gardens, explaining that in 1728 or 1729 the house was pulled down.[87] Thus, although all these colorful details about Sayes Court appear in a popular guidebook published in Austen's youth, the lost gardens could never have been seen by the author herself, not even on a family excursion to Deptford from Godmersham—perhaps en route to London.

Nevertheless, while Brandon's walled garden and plantations of "the best fruit-trees in the country" reinforce Evelyn's sylvan reputation generally, the lone mulberry tree emphasized by Mrs. Jennings may clinch the presence of his memory most directly. Maggie Campbell-Culver observed in 2006 how a single "vulnerable" mulberry tree still stands on the small plot that is the local authority park at the site of the former Sayes Court, and "may be the sole remnant of the glorious garden that was once Evelyn's."[88] Although the inference of a three-hundred-year-old mulberry tree seems to defy possibility, black mulberry trees are known to bear fruit for hundreds of years.[89] The famous mulberry tree that Shakespeare supposedly planted, which in 1756 fed an impossibly large number of relics claiming to be made from its wood, had thrived a generous century and a half before being needlessly cut down, inciting nationwide lament. If Austen did visit the site in Deptford of the by-then demolished Sayes Court, she might have witnessed Evelyn's single surviving mulberry tree and worked it into her novel. The precedent of Shakespeare's mulberry may have added to the affecting significance of Evelyn's. Indeed, one anonymous historian in 1860 still describes how "an arbor vitae, successor, if not sole survivor, of the bosky shades reared by the author of the 'Sylva,' stands a mournful guardian on the spot" of the former Sayes Court. This 1860 inventory of the "scanty relics" of Sayes Court, specifically mentions "a mulberry-tree, said to have been planted by Evelyn" that "has only of late years disappeared."[90] While Evelyn's mulberry did not inspire the marketing furor of Shakespeare's, its survival was thus tracked well beyond Austen's lifetime.

Bracketing the slight possibility that Evelyn, Austen, the anonymous historian of 1860, and Campbell-Culver in 2006 all witnessed the same mulberry tree, Evelyn dedicates a generous section of *Silva* to "Morus, the Mulberry," explaining how mulberry trees have "heart-shaped" leaves and that older trees offer better-flavored and larger fruit. In 1776, Hunter emphasizes this last point with an index category under "MULBERRY" that reads, "The oldest trees the most fruitful." The implied age of Brandon's mulberry tree, with its abundant and tasty fruit, befits the maturity of the Colonel. If Evelyn's *Silva* helps decode this passage in Austen, the mulberry tree's famous resistance to disease may further signal the Colonel's strength of character, for the mulberry "suffers no kind of vermin to breed on it."[91] Since Evelyn points to the mulberry's stamina and vigor, knowledge of *Silva* may belie Marianne's hasty assessment of Brandon's presumed "infirmity" (*S&S*, 44). Incidentally, Evelyn also mentions that the fruit of the mulberry "is excellent to feed poultry," while the leaves nourish "cattle, especially young porkers"—popular uses that comically gloss the stuffing of Mrs. Jennings and her daughter.[92]

Mrs. Jennings catalogs Delaford's garden buildings and its easy proximity to the church and turnpike with, as Dobson observed, standout precision:

> Then, there is a dove-cote, some delightful stewponds, and a very pretty canal; and every thing, in short, that one could wish for: and, moreover, it is close to the church, and only a quarter of a mile from the turnpike-road, so 'tis never dull, for if you only go and sit up in an old yew arbour behind the house, you may see all the carriages that pass along. Oh! 'tis a nice place! A butcher hard by in the village, and the parsonage-house within a stone's throw. To my fancy, a thousand times prettier than Barton Park, where they are forced to send three miles for their meat, and have not a neighbour nearer than your mother. (*S&S*, 223–24)

Delaford is an outmoded Restoration-style garden. Every detail, including the "dove-cote, . . . stewponds, and . . . canal," indicates that its grounds remain untouched by modern improvers. Even the terminology is a tad old-fashioned, for Brown and Repton preferred the naturalizing vocabulary of *pools* to that of *stews*, although their comparatively camouflaged ponds still confined fish for the owner's table.[93] Mrs. Jennings's comment that "'tis never dull" because the sight of carriages nicely distract, is ironic in light of the extraordinary effort and expense lavished by the nation's contemporary improvers upon changes that would hide from view all roads and buildings, soften straight canals into curved rivers, and remove fences, replacing them with sunken ha-has—all in the cause of a more natural-seeming and unspoiled landscape. The Colonel's financial circumstances, as relayed earlier by Mrs. Jennings, partly explain why his gardens appear as if dipped in amber: "The estate at Delaford was never reckoned more than two thousand a year, and his brother left every thing sadly involved" (82). While Brandon emerges as a man of old-fashioned rather than modern tastes if judged by his gardens, he may not be entirely averse to Marianne's modern aesthetics. It is Willoughby, in fact, who rigidly rejects even the practical improvements Mrs. Dashwood hopes will ease life at the cottage: "Not a stone must be added to its walls, not an inch to its size" (84). When it comes to improvements, Austen advocates an Aristotelian mean. However, that Austen assigns the worthy Colonel Brandon an estate praised as "old-fashioned" may constitute, along with her story *Evelyn*, her most explicit indictment of the contemporary fads for "improvements."

Some further bits of Sayes Court's history—particularly its functions as a workhouse and naval provisioning station—may bear upon Austen's

PETER THE GREAT'S HOUSE AT DEPTFORD (1850).

FIGURE 4.3. "Peter the Great's House at Deptford," or Sayes Court, c. 1850.
Used as an illustration in *Old and New London* (1873-1880). Harry Ransom
Center, The University of Texas at Austin.

possible interest in reviving its memory in *Sense and Sensibility*. After
Sayes Court was pulled down in the late 1720s, a workhouse was built in
its stead, a fact given prominence in Lysons's guidebook of 1796 and even
cited in editions of Defoe's *Tour*. The Sayes Court Workhouse remained
active in Austen's day and stood until demolished in the 1930s[94] (fig. 4.3).
While Brandon's melancholy story of Eliza dying in a "spunging-house,"
unable to pay her debts, resounds with literary echoes of *Clarissa*, it
also resonates with the history of the Deptford workhouse, in place for
over a century at the time of *Sense and Sensibility*'s publication (*S&S*,
235).[95] In addition, Sayes Court had long played several strategic roles
in the navy and the building of ships, a context that Jane Austen, with
her sea-faring brothers, would be in a position to know. The proximity to
the nearby dockyards was the reason that the outlying areas of Evelyn's
extant gardens at Deptford were purchased in 1742 for the building of
the Admiralty Victualling Yard, a massive facility of warehouses, baker-
ies, and cattle yards for the processing of navy provisions (fig. 4.4). This,

FIGURE 4.4. Deptford Dockyard, c. 1869. From the supplement to the *Illustrated London News*, 24 April 1869. Private Collection.

161

then, was the function of what remained in Austen's day of the elegant gardens and meticulously tended groves planted by John Evelyn.

As a virtuous army man, Colonel Brandon conspicuously deviates from Austen's marked preference for the navy in her other novels. Perhaps the resonant history associated with Deptford and Evelyn mitigates her choice of profession for this character. Evelyn's main contribution to the navy was, of course, his *Silva*'s encouragement of the large-scale replanting of Britain's sources of timber. Both during and after the Napoleonic Wars this legacy was actively celebrated. Isaac Disraeli reasoned that the "present navy of Great Britain has been constructed with the oaks which the genius of Evelyn planted!" insisting that the name of Evelyn should excite "the gratitude of posterity" because his replanting "contributed to secure our sovereignty of the seas."[96] Indeed Evelyn's expressed aims of *Silva* included the rebuilding of England's "wooden walls," a common metaphor for the navy, by providing it with uninterrupted supplies for future ship building and repair.[97] More immediately, Evelyn also served the defensive forces of Britain as a member of the commission for the sick and wounded and prisoners of war in the Second and Third Anglo-Dutch Wars (1664–67 and 1672–74). "The commissioners were expected to be superhuman," writes Darley, and labored fiercely in their efforts to provide large-scale humanitarian relief and medical assistance under war-time chaos and the simultaneous threat of plague.[98] In 1665, Evelyn remained at his post during an outbreak of the plague in London, "apparently the only commissioner to do so."[99] Toward the end of his life, Evelyn also served for nearly a decade as treasurer to the Hospital for Seamen at nearby Greenwich, which he helped found. If Evelyn's memory is already fired in *Sense and Sensibility* by the descriptions of Colonel Brandon and his garden, his care for the sick may even illuminate Brandon's reluctance to leave Marianne during an illness that frightens away the Palmers.

Avignon, Brandon, and Willoughby

Evelyn's haunting of Delaford may explain the curious references to Colonel Brandon's sister in Avignon. With needless precision and redundancy, Austen mentions twice that Brandon has a sister who resides in France. Upon the sudden arrival of a letter that derails the planned excursion to Whitwell, Mrs. Jennings asks, "No bad news, Colonel, I hope. . . . Was it from Avignon? I hope it is not to say that your sister is worse" (*S&S*, 74). A few pages later, she repeats her concern: "May be his sister is worse at Avignon, and has sent for him over. His setting off in such a hurry seems very like it" (83). This mysterious sister never reappears or affects the remaining story. She is notably absent from the Colonel's later account of his upbringing and his brother's marriage to Eliza Williams, that more-than-sister, and thus constitutes precisely the type of gratuitous off-plot detail that encourages critics to seek a larger authorial purpose. Could this reference to France be a further clue to Evelyn's presence? Does Austen allude, like Burney, to Evelyn's association with French aesthetics? While Evelyn is not intimately associated with the town of Avignon, the Jacobites were. As Edward Copeland points out in his edition of *Sense and Sensibility*, this city in southern France was home to "a strong British presence" because all the Jacobite hopefuls, since the days of the Glorious Revolution, which began during Evelyn's lifetime, took refuge there, including the "Old Pretender" and "Bonnie Prince Charlie" (454n1). Since Avignon's political resonance reinforce Evelyn's own loyalties, it seems possible that the city is a symbol for such revolutionary politics as align the Colonel's own factious family with the unrest of the Restoration and its Jacobite aftermath. Additional references to England's history of religious strife—between Protestants and Catholics, Continental aesthetics and patriotic allegiances—further augment this historical context in *Sense and Sensibility*, as I show in the next chapter.

I want to close by briefly glossing the names of Marianne's two suitors: *Willoughby* and *Brandon*. Both names have robust, and multiple, historic associations. In light of Austen's significant debt to Burney's *Evelina*, the rake of *Sense and Sensibility* seems—first and foremost—a straightforward homage to Sir Clement Willoughby. In spite of her extensive reading of romances, Marianne cannot recognize, as any reader might, how the name of the dashing Willoughby dangerously warns her of his rakishness. In addition, the real-world dimensions of the elite Willoughby family could not have been lost on Jane Austen, whose mother, Cassandra, was named for their relative Cassandra Willoughby (1670–1735), Duchess of Chandos. Since this forbear was born at Middleton Hall, Warwickshire, where the resident Willoughbys held the Barony of Middleton, the appearance of cousin Sir John Middleton in *Sense and Sensibility* may possibly reinforce a personal intimacy with the historic Willoughby clan.

Literary sources for the name of Brandon have been put forward by others: Jocelyn Harris points to the mention of a Brandon Hall in the 1801 edition of *Pamela,* while Edward Copeland finds a Miss Brandon and a Mr. Willoughby in a story entitled "The Shipwreck," published in *Lady's Magazine* in 1794.[100] These prior occurrences in fiction, too, could have fed Austen's imagination, along with *Evelina.* One prominent historical association with the name of Brandon, however, seems worth probing in the prevailing context of John Evelyn's presence in Austen's story: Charles I is thought to have been executed by a hangman named Richard Brandon. Patrick Parrinder, who sees *Sense and Sensibility* in terms of Tory and Whig archetypes, recognizes the historical allusion in Brandon's name but finds the plot's resolution "unsatisfactory" as a result: "[If] Willoughby is a cavalier rogue, Brandon (who is named after Charles I's executioner) is manifestly a Roundhead and a prig."[101] Evelyn's lingering presence in the descriptions of Delaford should ease Parrinder's harsh disappointment. If the Colonel's name brings to mind the brute who allegedly "wielded the fateful axe" (and many claimed Brandon was coerced), that same character's strong invocation of the memory of John Evelyn, staunchest of loyalists, creates precisely the type of dramatic tension that would animate the character of Colonel Brandon from within.[102] The "version of the Cavalier-Roundhead alliance" that Parrinder seeks in Austen's ending may reside in the Colonel. The tragic conflict of allegiances that, Brandon explains to Elinor, severed the peace of his family's past may echo the psychology of a nation torn by Civil War. Austen may summon this era as an acute friction in the reader's mind between the violent Roundhead associations offered by Brandon's name and the Cavalier history conjured up by her descriptions of his estate at Delaford.

Jointly, the pairing of the names of Willoughby and Brandon—the story's competitors for Marianne's affections—point to one further historical person: the Duchess of Suffolk. Born Katherine Willoughby (1519–80), this rich noblewoman married Henry VIII's brother-in-law Charles Brandon, first Duke of Suffolk (c. 1484–1545). The couple became acquainted when, at age ten, the wealthy Katherine Willoughby was taken under Brandon's protection as his young ward. At fourteen, she became his fourth wife. In spite of an uncomfortable difference in age of thirty-five years, Katherine's marriage to Charles Brandon was judged "successful" and led to her becoming a prominent and much-celebrated Protestant patron.[103] Upon the death of her husband, she so deployed her wealth in support of the Protestant clergy in Lincolnshire that the change of regime under Queen Mary forced her into exile. After the early death of her sons, Katherine Willoughby-Brandon lost the duchy of Suffolk but married Richard Bertie (1517–82), by whom she had additional children. When she died, her maiden name passed to her son Peregrine Bertie, who was declared Lord Willoughby. Austen's own family's connections to these Berties may have offered the novelist additional reasons to interest herself in this history: in 1792, her brother James married the daughter of Lady Jane Bertie, a connection reinforced when Brownlow Bertie, fifth and last Duke Ancaster, became Anna Austen's godfather. Both Austen's personal connection to the Bertie family and their national prominence urge the significance of this bit of Protestant history to a reading of *Sense and Sensibility*, where the romantic rivalry between a Brandon and Willoughby may play with the fame of a duchess who, launched into public life as a young Willoughby, eventually married a much older Brandon.

So far, the history that I have discussed in *Northanger Abbey, Evelyn*, and *Sense and Sensibility* is a safe type of history. It is not only authentic and real but, for the most part, genuinely solemn. Of all historical episodes so far, the most risqué (I'm thinking now of the Vernon squabbles and the persecuted Lady Grosvenor) were not submitted for publication in Austen's lifetime. When daring to allude to scandal, sexual intrigue, and murder in *Northanger Abbey*, Austen keeps her references safely at a great historical remove. The celebrity estates to which she refers— from the Wentworth estates in Yorkshire to Prior Park in Bath and Sayes Court in Kent—had long been admired for setting aesthetic standards in landscape gardening. All this changes when the garden-centered history that Austen plays with concerns the nearer and notorious Dashwoods of West Wycombe Park.

CHAPTER FIVE

Hell-Fire Jane

Dashwood Celebrity and *Sense and Sensibility*

MODERN READERS OF *Sense and Sensibility* have been reluctant to acknowledge that the novel rewards detailed knowledge of one of England's most notorious families in Austen's time, namely, the Dashwoods of West Wycombe Park.[1] The best-known member of the Dashwood clan was Sir Francis Dashwood (1708–81), second Baronet and Lord Le Despencer, leader of a group of high-profile libertines whose decades of bacchanals and mock-Catholic drinking rituals earned it the label Hell-Fire Club (fig. 5.1). At West Wycombe, Sir Francis also designed an emblematic garden, infamous for the ribald features that mimicked the female form. Although Francis Dashwood died in 1781, throughout Austen's lifetime the stories about his garden and Hell-Fire shenanigans proliferated in print, while his heirs (the next two baronets were both named John Dashwood) perpetuated his rakish legacy with high-profile domestic conflicts. In short, a lively print market for gossip at the turn of the century insured that, at the time of *Sense and Sensibility*'s publication in 1811, the infamous name of Dashwood remained synonymous with diabolism, sexual lewdness, and the dubious privileges of wealth.

This chapter outlines some of the interpretive implications of this ignored historical context for the Dashwood-centered story of *Sense and Sensibility*. Along the way, it documents the manner in which Austen might have heard details about the real-world Dashwoods that appear as if woven into the fabric of her novel. The print trail of Dashwood history leads through reference works, newspapers, ephemera, a famous "it-novel," popular prints and portraits, miscellanies, and scandal sheets. Only a modicum of this material expands the current scholarly inventory of Austen's voracious reading, adding slightly to the list of texts that she may have put to use in her own writing. Whatever Austen's specific sources, she not only knew of the Wentworths of Yorkshire and the Allens of Bath but was also thoroughly familiar with the history of the baronetcy

FIGURE 5.1. Portrait of Sir Francis Dashwood, Second Baronet (1708-81), in an oriental coat and turban. Dashwood Heirloom Collection.

held by the Dashwoods of West Wycombe in Buckinghamshire. Beyond the dominant allusion in the family name chosen for the protagonists of *Sense and Sensibility*, a plethora of minor references in the novel to the Dashwood line of baronets reinforce links to the real Dashwood family. Most obviously, the name Fanny (short for Frances) Dashwood may tar her novel's most transparently invidious character with the infamy of Sir Francis Dashwood, which would occasionally focus Austen's unique brand of diffuse irony into something resembling satire. Not only does the history of West Wycombe share with Austen's fiction a Francis Dashwood of sorts, but there is also more than one John Dashwood, a Henry Dashwood, Mary Anne Dashwood, several more Fanny Dashwoods, and a Mrs. Jennings. These sharings do demand recognizing homophones and variant spellings: *Frances* for *Francis* and *Marianne* for *Mary Anne*. Over and above the echoes of mere names and their variants, the circumstances and widespread reputations of the actual Dashwoods map, with astonishing coherence, onto the thematic preoccupations of Austen's novel. This is not to say that the Dashwoods offer, to continue the mapping metaphor, a simple legend or key to specific characters. I do not argue, for example, that John Dashwood of Norland is merely a fictionalized version of a John Dashwood of West Wycombe. Austen's first published fiction is, once again, not a straightforward roman à clef. Instead of appearing as simple equivalencies, the real-world Dashwoods and their history emerge in Austen's fiction in transmuted form—just recognizable enough to generate an uneasy atmosphere of wealth, infamy, and illicit sexuality.

My argument does not rest upon biographical links between the Austens and the Dashwoods. I do *not* presume that Austen ever met a member of the well-connected Dashwood family, or indeed that she ever set foot in West Wycombe, although she may have done both.[2] Even so, the Austens of Kent did enjoy vague but suggestive historical connections to the Dashwoods of West Wycombe. Sir Robert Austen, of Kent, married the sister of the infamous Sir Francis Dashwood, second Baronet. While the relationship that David Waldron Smithers traces between Jane Austen's family and these other Austens of Kent is a distant one, the author could not have been unaware that she shared her last name with a prominent branch of the Dashwoods.[3] In fact, in the years prior to the publication of *Sense and Sensibility* specific events brought this old family connection to the fore. Between 1804 and 1811, the illegitimate daughter of Sir Francis Dashwood, then known as Mrs. Lee, involved herself after a scandalous elopement and a brief marriage in at least two public spectacles: an Oxford-based legal proceeding in which she alleged being abducted by gownsmen, as well as a prolonged and public dispute with her relatives that included minor pamphlet wars with her aunt, Lady Austen, and her brother's wife, Lady Anne Dashwood.[4] The fight between niece and aunt was over the false title of Baroness Le Despencer, which both Mrs. Lee and Lady Austen had boldly adopted.[5] This public drama would have brought the Austen-Dashwood connection to light during the final stage of the novel's composition. Since *Lee* is already a homonym of *Leigh*, the maiden name of Jane Austen's mother, any talk of Lee-Dashwood-Austen news would most likely have made young Jane's ears perk up with interest. Finally, as I will show, there is also the tantalizing fact that intimates of the Austens, the Lefroys, played a central role in the history of the West Wycombe estate. While the widespread notoriety of the Dashwoods from the mid-eighteenth century onward already allows for their encoded presence in any novel published in 1811, these biographical circumstances help explain why Jane Austen, in particular, may have had personal reasons to attend to their history.

I also eschew that favorite red herring of Austen scholarship, the assumed dates of composition for *Sense and Sensibility*. With no surviving manuscript or author's notes, we know little about the original design for *Sense and Sensibility* or the inspiration for its precursor, "Elinor and Marianne." Dates of composition remain imprecise, with no record of the nature of the transition from the epistolary manuscript read aloud to her family in 1796 to the finished novel published in 1811. Critics have accepted that *Sense and Sensibility* was intensely revised at Chawton between 1809 and 1811.[6] Cassandra, however, remained distressingly vague about the nature of these revisions, remarking only that the final novel was "something of the same story & characters" as the original manuscript.[7] Since Jane Austen occasionally renamed her characters between manuscript and print (*Susan* is a good example), Cassandra's comment about resemblance ("something of the same") does not even confirm that the story's central family was named Dashwood from its inception. Brian Southam asserts, however, that "the change affected structure rather than content" and embraces the dates of 1809–10 as the sole period of revision.[8] Expanding this window, Jocelyn Harris argues against the presumed "eclipse" of Jane Austen's creative powers between 1801 and 1809, pointing to a number of historical references and allusions in *Sense and Sensibility* that allow prolonged revision between 1802 and 1808.[9] More recently, Deirdre Le Faye leaves the window of revision deliberately unlocked by pointing to November 1797 as the month Jane Austen "starts converting 'Elinor and Marianne' into *Sense and Sensibility*."[10] Le Faye allows for the possibility that any revision started in late 1797 continued off and on until publication in 1811. Thus, the only genuinely fixed endpoints of this tempestuous timeline, from a family reading in 1796 to publication in 1811, allows an argument such as mine a generous fifteen-year period from which to offer historical circumstances that might have influenced Austen's story. In addition, the events that prompted young

Jane's original draft might well have occurred during her teenage years. Given the extraordinary notoriety of the West Wycombe Dashwoods from the 1760s onward, my argument comes nowhere near to spending all of this generous time allowance.

I argue that specific events in the history of West Wycombe, such as the renovations by Humphry Repton in the 1790s and the relationship of the Dashwoods to a King family fortune, inform a reading of the fictional Fanny Dashwood's so-called improvements to Norland and John Dashwood's annexing of the Kingham farm. More broadly, even the vague backdrop of the ribald gardens at West Wycombe heightens the sexual innuendo of the garden locales mentioned in *Sense and Sensibility*. Furthermore, the pairing of the name of Dashwood with that of Ferrars in the story invokes opposing extremes of religious practice in England's history—with the Ferrars family strongly associated with Catholic fervor and the Dashwoods with a profane mockery of just such Romish faith in the form of black masses. Finally, in her choice of the name *Dashwood*, Austen seems to court an audience for her first published novel by appealing to contemporary sensationalism. Even a general familiarity with West Wycombe's reputation, which was so widespread as to have been accessible to all of Austen's contemporary readers, would lend any story about a Dashwood family an air of libertinism. Given the title of *Sense and Sensibility*, Austen's commercial appeal to the sensational lore of West Wycombe may harbor pedagogical intention.

If *Sense and Sensibility* stirs up salacious Dashwood history, Austen risks turning Marianne's emotional self-abandon and "excess" into something dangerously approaching the actions of a Bacchante (*S&S*, 7). Admittedly, and as Roger Sales points out, it is generically true for every rake that "bacchanalia is his business," so Austen may not need the specific context of the Hell-Fire Club to conjure up images of Bacchus-like self-abandonment in her fiction.[11] Nonetheless, for over half a century the name of Dashwood embodied bacchanalia in the British popular press, fading into a mainstream reappropriation of this mythological cliché in the fashionable art of the 1780s and '90s that, through the work of Romney and Reynolds, newly deemed the figure of the Bacchante romantic.[12] Contemporary portraits of Emma Hart–turned–Lady Hamilton, for example, forged a popular aesthetic in which Austen's possible allusions to Bacchantes, even when amplified by Dashwood history, would not have appeared so entirely out of keeping with Marianne's professed Romanticism as they might do now. In addition, and although music's reputation for inciting wantonness was traditional, Marianne's musical flamboyance fans the fiery history of the Music Temple on the Dashwood estate, a site particularly associated with Sir Francis's bacchanals. In other words, the context of Dashwood history in the popular press, while it may not radically alter Austen's intent, allows us to see how her text, as Sales argues for her other critiques, "seems to be more of an open than a camouflaged one."[13]

If the story's celebrity references are so open, why have we not noticed them before? I remain somewhat incredulous that prior critics never explored the relationship between the real and fictional Dashwoods. The scholarly silence about a possible allusion implies that the Dashwoods are off-limits in a reading of *Sense and Sensibility* precisely because of their notoriety—that they are irrelevant to Austen's work, not because they were unknown, but because they were too much in public view. Only for readers today, when a Google query about "John Dashwood" is apt to yield far more Austen-related hits than references to the National Trust site for West Wycombe Park, does such a reading of the novel seem excusable.[14] Austen's fictional Dashwoods have now thoroughly displaced their real-world namesakes in the cultural zeitgeist. Even so, the raw historical material from which Austen refashions her deeply original fictions has been available to curious scholars for nearly two centuries. It is possible that our dominant scholarly view of Austen remains clouded by anachronism and residual Victorian sensibilities.[15]

Born in 1775 and dying in 1817, Austen remained a stranger to the Victorian mores that would, two decades later, extol and chaperone her work after the first reprinting in 1833—just as the gardens at West Wycombe Park were cleansed of any residual priapic statuary. Perhaps it takes a reader comfortable with eighteenth-century history and idiom to notice how the Dashwood name in *Sense and Sensibility* invokes a celebrity family known for dastardly deeds. Yet Austen was precisely that kind of reader, the public image of "Dear Aunt Jane" so painstakingly starched by her Victorian relatives notwithstanding. As Peter Sabor observes of the *Juvenilia*, as a teenager she already wrote about "murder, suicide, violence, theft, verbal abuse, gluttony, and drunkenness" and joked openly about homosexuality (*J*, lxii). Coincidentally, "Love and Friendship," the title of an epistolary story written by young Austen in June of 1790, was also the motto of Sir Francis's Hell-Fire Club.[16] Austen's letters further show that she read "gossipy articles" and "was familiar with at least some of the royal scandals of the period."[17] Although critics continue to disagree about whether Austen means to refer to sodomy in *Mansfield Park* with Mary Crawford's risqué pun ("Of *Rears*, and *Vices*"), her boast to Cassandra of her ability to spot an adulteress in a crowd stands no equivocation (*MP*, 71).[18]

Nonetheless, I admit that a contemporary reader's presumed awareness of the sensational history of the Dashwoods at West Wycombe presents interpretive challenges. As a writer who dealt with highly charged surnames, Austen would have been familiar with the problem of controlling imported meaning from the inside. Wherever *Sense and Sensibility* draws on the Buckinghamshire Dashwoods, Austen surely wrestled through the long and vexed process of composition with the difficulties of accommodating the realm of external references to her own purposes and themes. If scandals associated with the genuine Dashwoods intrude upon the novel from its very first sentence, the second deliberately delimits the historical parallel, for the narrator insists that the family at Norland lived "in so respectable a manner" as to have long won the good opinion of their neighbors (*S&S*, 3). The Norland Dashwoods are not the stuff of Wycombe legend, although the respectability of their heir is quickly undermined by mounting disclosures of the evil to which he is party, an irony perceived by the first of Austen's reviewers who noted that John Dashwood is "what the world calls, a *worthy respectable* character," but who "takes good care of the *main chance*."[19] For these reasons, Dashwood fact and Dashwood legend both undergo a sea change in Austen's story. Austen also deliberately balances the anti-Catholic revelry for which the Dashwoods were known with the contrasting legacy of Romish devotion conjured up by the name of Ferrars, endowing her references to both historic families with a moral tone that is weighted with the gravity of national history. While at times it might seem as if this chapter focuses exclusively on *Sense and Sensibility*'s historical allusions to eighteenth-century vice, Austen keeps these in equilibrium with her story's depictions of virtue.

I shall begin by offering a quick overview of the history of the genuine Dashwoods up to 1811, before exploring how Austen and her contemporaries had access to this history and how, in turn, such knowledge bears upon a reading of *Sense and Sensibility*. I would like to clarify at the outset that while all the names and events that I relate are pulled directly from the historical record, I do not challenge the possibly blasphemous rumors about the Hell-Fire Club that circulated in print during the latter half of the eighteenth century. Bruce Redford and others rightly warn that the "lurid exposés" penned by former Hell-Fire members "must be treated with extreme caution" by the historian, as these accounts were doubtless "tainted by personal and political rancor."[20] While this may be so, I do not purport to offer a carefully sifted history of the Dashwood fraternity. I merely track what Austen might have heard and read about the celebrity Dashwoods, for in *Sense and Sensibility* she seems to draw upon rumor as well as fact.

The Dashwoods of West Wycombe

THE BARONETS OF WEST WYCOMBE FROM 1707 TO 1811

Sir Francis Dashwood, 1st Bt = 1. Mary Jennings (d. 1694)
    (c. 1658–1724)   2. Lady Mary Fane (d. 1710)
                      3. Mary King (d. 1717)
                      4. Lady Eliz. Windsor-Hickman (d. 1736)

Sir Francis Dashwood, 2nd Bt and Lord Le Despencer = Lady Sarah Ellys (d. 1769)
    (1708–81)   ≈ Frances Barry

Sir John Dashwood-King, 3rd Bt = Sarah Moore (d. 1777)
    (1716–93)

Sir John Dashwood, 4th Bt = Mary Anne Broadhead (d. 1844)
    (c. 1765–1849)

The initial Baronet of West Wycombe was Sir Francis Dashwood (c. 1658–1724), who founded the family estate in 1707. His first marriage was to Mary Jennings (d. 1694), who, like the Mrs. Jennings of Austen's novel, bore him two daughters. It is by his second wife, Lady Mary Fane (d. 1710), that he had his infamous namesake and heir Francis (second Baronet and future Lord Le Despencer) as well as another daughter, Rachel. She would marry Sir Robert Austen of Hall-Place, Bexley, in Kent, a distant relation of the Austens.[21] The elder Francis Dashwood's third wife was named Mary King, niece of the resident vicar of West Wycombe. Francis had two sons with Mary King, John and Charles, as well as two daughters, Henrietta and Mary. All but the last of these four children would eventually yoke the name of King to that of Dashwood to comply for one generation with a bequest from their mother's clergyman-uncle, Dr. John King (1655–1739), who had risen to become Master of the Charterhouse.[22]

At sixteen, Sir Francis Dashwood (1708–81) became the second Baronet. After a protracted Grand Tour, Sir Francis returned to West Wy-combe permanently in 1741 and over the next decades turned an unre-markable country home into one of the most theatrical and Italianate houses in England[23] (fig. 5.2). He was a cultivated man of taste and a founding member of the learned Society of Dilettanti, which helped pro-pel the revival of classical architecture in Britain. For twenty-two years he was also a member of Parliament, where he was known as a fair-minded politician and a reformer, active in poor relief, drainage, and road building (fig. 5.3). But this Sir Francis was also an infamous liber-tine. He formed a club variously known as the Monks of Medmenham, the Order of St. Francis of Wycombe, and, somewhat later, the Hell-Fire Club[24] (fig. 5.4). A substantial number of modern book-length accounts about this Hell-Fire Club exist, essentially differing only in degrees of scholarly prurience.[25] This club allegedly "engaged in obscene parodies of religious rites and in the deflowering of local virgins."[26] While it ini-tially met in the rented ruins of Medmenham Abbey along the Thames, the club soon shifted the six miles to Dashwood's country estate of West Wycombe, where for decades it held regular meetings in the gardens

WEST WYCOMBE PARK, Buckinghamshire.

FIGURE 5.2. "West Wycombe Park, Buckinghamshire." Plate 38 from *Copper-Plate Magazine,* engraved by William Ellis, after a drawing by Richard Cor-bould and published by Harrison & Co., 1 August 1793. Private Collection.

FIGURE 5.3. Portrait of Sir Francis Dashwood, Second Baronet (1708-81), as postmaster-general, by Nathaniel Dance. Dashwood Heirloom Collection.

that Sir Francis designed to mimic the female form, creating prospects in keeping with the club's rakish deeds. The bacchanals that took place in West Wycombe's ornate garden temples and a nearby catacomb of caves became the stuff of legend, as Dashwood's legacy of vice subsumed his reputation for exquisite taste and connoisseurship. In 1745, after gaining the title of Lord Le Despencer, Sir Francis Dashwood married Lady Sarah Ellys (variously spelled Ellis) (d. 1769), with whom he had no children. He did father two illegitimate children, a son named Francis and a daughter, Rachel Fanny Antonia (1773?-1829), with his long-term companion after his wife's death, Frances Barry. Their daughter became the Mrs. Lee who gained a reputation during Austen's life as an adven-

FIGURE 5.4. Satirical print of Sir Francis Dashwood worshipping Venus, engraved by William Platt, after William Hogarth (late eighteenth century). © Trustees of the British Museum.

turer and pamphleteer. Since the infamous Sir Francis is indubitably the best-known of the Dashwoods, I will return to his story and its bearing upon Austen's fiction shortly.

Because Sir Francis died without legitimate issue in 1781, his half-brother, Sir John Dashwood-King (1716–93), inherited the title and West Wycombe estate. Dashwood-King was in his mid-sixties when he came into the property and spent little time in residence, although he

FIGURE 5.5. Portrait of Sir John Dashwood, Fourth Baronet. Dashwood Heirloom Collection.

had been an active member of Sir Francis's rakish club in his younger days.[27] In turn, his son, Sir John Dashwood (c. 1765–1849), held the title of fourth Baronet during Austen's adulthood (fig. 5.5). He inherited the title at the death of his father in 1793. As a point of reference, family tradition holds that Austen began drafting the novel's precursor, "Elinor and Marianne," around 1795. Sir John Dashwood, fourth Baronet, was chiefly known as an avid sportsman with a keen knowledge of dogs and horses, subjects on which he apparently advised the Prince of Wales. He kept a large pack of hounds at West Wycombe and consulted Repton about modifications that would make for better hunting grounds. In 1789 Sir John had married Mary Anne, variously spelled Marianne,

FIGURE 5.6. Sketch of Mary Anne (née Broadhead), Lady Dashwood, by Henry Bone (1803). © National Portrait Gallery, London.

Broadhead (d.1844) (fig. 5.6). They had three sons. Their eldest, heir to
the estate, was George Henry Dashwood (c. 1790–1862). The marriage
between Sir John and Mary Anne, already strained by some impropriety,
suffered further injury in 1800 when the husband accused his wife of
having an affair with the Prince of Wales and banished her to his hunting
lodge at Bourton, Gloucestershire. Perhaps the estate name of Barton
in *Sense and Sensibility,* to which Marianne and her mother and sisters
are effectively banished by John and Fanny Dashwood, echoes even this
historical detail.

Also in 1800, and perhaps to spite his estranged wife, Sir John Dashwood "held a five-day sale of 'household furniture' at West Wycombe" to

liquidate assets; in 1806 he tried to sell the entire estate.[28] The trustees of his eldest son, George Henry, acting on behalf of the underage heir, prevented the outright sale. The opening chapters of *Sense and Sensibility* possibly restage the conflict over the Dashwood estate when the family of a fictional Henry Dashwood, which again includes a Marianne Dashwood, is ousted from their home by a John Dashwood, just as their namesakes were in real life. Rarely does Austen's sparse manner of description allow space for "linen, plate, china, and books," yet in this novel the "furniture" of Norland features prominently as a nexus of tension (*S&S*, 30). The newly installed Mrs. John Dashwood begrudges "the handsome pianoforte of Marianne's" and witnesses "with a sigh" the departure of packages of household items bound for Barton, reasoning that the comparatively "trifling" income of the departing Dashwood women makes it hard to see them leave "with any handsome article of furniture" (30). By Fanny's cruel logic, their contemptible poverty makes them undeserving of anything that is handsome. Austen further reworks historical events by declaring that the estate is "secured" to "a child of four years old" whose name is Harry, a transparent diminutive of Henry (4). In the novel, Henry Dashwood's family is displaced by their father's young namesake, an inversion of how the father of the real George Henry Dashwood nearly sold his son's birthright out from under him. If Austen's names invoke Dashwood history, a reader's knowledge of these disputes over the assets and properties at West Wycombe would likely intensify the opening family tension of *Sense and Sensibility*. Austen can create, as it were, a synecdoche that allows the brief mention of a father's "life interest," a few begrudged articles of furniture, and the legal prohibition against the father's sale of Norland's "valuable woods" to stand in for, or hint at, escalating conflict over family finances (4). Burdened by debt, the real Sir John moved out, let West Wycombe to tenants, and retrenched to the Dashwoods' subsidiary house at Halton, ostensibly because it offered "better hunting."[29] While the marriage was eventually patched up, Mary Anne "remained an unhappy, neglected woman until her death."[30] Thus, in 1811, the choice of the name Marianne Dashwood for the emotional sister in *Sense and Sensibility* allowed Austen to surround her character with an aura of alleged impropriety, domestic tension, and sentimental tragedy. Just as the name of Frederic Vernon invoked a celebrated family dispute over a castle and the name of Allen conjured up a well-known legacy in Bath, the name of Marianne Dashwood, plucked from contemporary newspapers, predicts romantic disappointment.

Sir Francis and the Hell-Fire Club at West Wycombe

Sir Francis Dashwood's leadership of the Monks of Medmenham, or Franciscan Brotherhood, overshadows his other, more legitimate, activities as a long-term member of Parliament and an intellectual. Although initially connected with the disused abbey along the Thames that Sir Francis rented and decorated with pornographic murals for its initial meetings, the Hell-Fire Club soon retreated from increasingly prying eyes to Dashwood's private estate at West Wycombe. As a result, accounts of the club focus on West Wycombe's extensive park and garden follies, especially a temple on the lake's largest island and some nearby catacomb of caves, naming them as sites of pagan rites and blasphemous black masses performed at club gatherings. Reports of such clandestine meetings spread, in part, because its members included so many high-profile individuals. The membership of the core group of "apostles" remains somewhat hazy, although we know it included John Wilkes and Sir Thomas Stapleton, Sir Francis as reigning "Prior," and poet Paul Whitehead as secretary. Other names linked to the club include: John Montagu, fourth Earl of Sandwich; George Bubb-Dodington; Sir John Dashwood-King, who would inherit the baronetcy; Thomas Potter; Sir William Stanhope, MP; John Hall Stevenson; John Tucker, MP; and the Vansittart brothers, Arthur, Henry, and Robert.[31] Later, poet Charles Churchill, who caused a great fracas by seducing the fifteen-year-old daughter of his landlord, joined the Wycombe group. Occasional visitors may have included: Horace Walpole; Benjamin Franklin, with whom Dashwood partnered on a prayer book; the Prince of Wales; Giuseppe Borgnis; and William Hogarth, who comically painted Le Despencer in Franciscan garb. In 1815, Nathaniel Wraxall, the memoirist, recalled how the group's activities at West Wycombe "far exceeded in licentiousness of conduct anything exhibited since Charles II."[32] The club was, like the cultures it imitated, a mass of contradiction, combining the grossest of outrages with the most refined study of classical architecture in its time: "nuns" were brought in from London brothels to participate in sexual lewdnesses that took place amidst England's finest and most elaborate recreations of Ionic architecture and Italianate design. Thus Hell-Fire Club members enacted the paradox of the Libertine, a man simultaneously refined and base.

Contradiction is also part and parcel of the emblematic garden. With prominent symbolic gardens in both Genesis and the Song of Songs, even biblical garden terrains can be simultaneously pious and erotic, a duality that makes for complex representations of the female body through landscape in Western culture. While the study of eighteenth-century English landscape starts with the notion that garden terrains are aesthetically, morally, and politically engrossing, it further recognizes the strong presence of sexual symbolism, tracing a sexualized landscape aesthetic that arguably culminated in the ribald gardens of Sir Francis Dashwood.[33] Carole Fabricant, for example, observes that eighteenth-century male gardeners spoke of landscape in a dominant rhetoric suggestive of a mistress: "the landscape's feminine allurements were highlighted but also kept in check by gentlemen gardeners who felt called upon to restrain the 'careless and loose Tresses of Nature.'"[34] Thus, while garden historians routinely acknowledge what James Turner calls "an aesthetic of sexualized topography," Sir Francis Dashwood took existing metaphors to the extreme.[35] "His was clearly an X-rated garden," summarizes Stephanie Ross.[36]

Admittedly, the dominant presence of a sexualized aesthetic in most eighteenth-century discussions of landscape makes it difficult to isolate the particular influence of Dashwood history upon the gardens mentioned in *Sense and Sensibility*. Even so, Austen's initial description of Willoughby, carrying Marianne in his arms, while "passing through the garden, the gate of which had been left open by Margaret," seems a knowing reference to the *hortus conclusus*, that traditional metaphor for the female body which Dashwood's emblematic designs so famously exploited (*S&S*, 50). Moments earlier, however, the "delightful sensations" that animate Marianne and Margaret in their lively romp through the landscape of "high downs," including their ecstatic "running with all possible speed down the steep side of the hill which led immediately to their garden gate," may yet be innocent of similar innuendo (49–50). After all, the scene enacts a prelapsarian joy before the arrival of the story's libertine.

Then again, at West Wycombe a hill was never just a hill. The most famous of the garden buildings was the Temple of Venus, which perched on a belly-like mound and was rumored to house "forty-two erotic statues" in Sir Francis's time.[37] Underneath the temple, an anatomically shaped doorway in the hill opened to a small womb-like grotto, dubbed "Venus' chamber" (fig. 5.7). After a political rupture with Sir Francis in 1763 and an incident that may have involved a monkey and certainly led to his being ousted from the Hell-Fire Club, John Wilkes penned a sa-

FIGURE 5.7. Venus's Temple and the entrance to the grotto below, as it appears now. Photo by Author.

tirical tell-all description of the garden for the *Public Advertiser*. In this venomous little essay he glosses the temple's emblematic entrance: "It is the same Entrance by which we all come into the World, and the Door is what some idle Wits have called *the Door of Life*."[38] Wilkes also recounts how "Lord *Bute* particularly admired this Building, and advised the noble Owner to lay out the 500l. bequeathed to him by Lord *Melcombe's* Will *for an Erection,* in a *Paphian* Column to *stand* at the Entrance."[39] Additional accounts agree on there being a central lake in the shape of a swan, possibly intended to recall the erotic myth of Leda (fig. 5.8). On that lake's largest island stood a Temple of Music, designed by architect and club member Nicholas Revett, which the Hell-Fire Club used as a frequent meeting place (fig. 5.9). Donald Mannix, by far the most uninhibited historian of the place, describes how Sir Francis urged a local parson to hold his Sunday picnic in the gardens. During the pic-

FIGURE 5.8. "A View of Walton Bridge, Venus's Temple &c. in the Gardens of the L.^{d} Le Despencer at West Wycomb Bucks." Print by William Woollett, after William Hannan (1757). Private Collection.

nic, he invited the clergyman to climb the purpose-built church steeple for a better view. From that height, the female forms embedded in the landscape, including a triangle of dark shrubbery below two hillocks that were each topped with a small central circle of red flowers, were instantly recognizable. Standing at the top of the steeple, Sir Francis reputedly asked the clergyman what he thought of his gardens. On cue, three fountains turned on—two spouting a milky liquid from the red-flowered mounds, while the third gushed water from the area of the shrubbery below. The clergyman, rendered speechless, had to be revived with drink.[40]

Where Might Jane Austen Have Learned of Such Things?

Official Dashwood history, including detailed descriptions of each baronet and the names and backgrounds of their family, is duly recorded in dry reference works such as Debrett's *Baronetage*. The unofficial rumors about Sir Francis and his Hell-Fire Club at West Wycombe are almost as easy to track, although impossible to verify. The truth behind the outrageous legends of the ribald garden's sexual symbolism and activities remains debatable. But that such rumors circulated "for many genera-

FIGURE 5.9. Painting of the Music Temple on the lake, c. 1781, by Thomas Daniell. Dashwood Heirloom Collection.

tions" and persist even today in the discussions about West Wycombe Park is a fact.[41] Perhaps Jane Austen grew up, like Mary Delany's great-niece, Mary Hamilton, hearing the Hell-Fire Club stories from older relatives. A journal entry by Hamilton suggests she learned from her great aunt that the club "consisted of about a dozen persons of fashion of both sexes, some of ye females unmarried," all guilty of "horrid impieties." She was told that "they used to read and ridicule ye Scriptures, and their conversation was blasphemous to ye last degree; they used to act plays, some represented ye Virgin Mary."[42] Handicapped by the lack of a journal and the incomplete nature of Jane Austen's surviving letters, which Cassandra would surely have fed into the fire had they contained any references to talk of this nature, I can only track how Austen and her readers might have gleaned such information through print. "The annals of the Hell Fire Club . . . are scattered throughout all sorts of contemporary books and pamphlets emanating from all kinds of pens," one historian remarks.[43] Not all of these printed materials, however, are items we can easily imagine falling into Jane Austen's hands.

Examples from Sir Francis's most prurient print record include a piece of minor erotica, *The Fruit-Shop* (1765), and a colorful guide to brothels, *Nocturnal Revels* (1779), the latter of which provocatively claims on its title page to have been penned "By A Monk of the Order of St. Francis."[44] For all of its titular titillation, *Nocturnal Revels* normalizes the Medmenham Priory as "the seat of wit, pleasantry, anecdote and gallantry." Its author recounts how "a certain Nobleman" organized the club after a grand tour had impressed upon him the "absurdity of . . . sequestered societies" such as he'd witnessed in the Continent's religious seminaries.[45] The anecdotes in *Nocturnal Revels* confirm the identity of Sir Francis Dashwood and his set, even if exact names are avoided, ensuring that Sir Francis's role in his self-styled "Order of St. Francis" did not remain a secret long. Indeed, this book explicitly asserts that the club's secrecy was semitransparent from the outset, when it cheekily declares that all visitors "are required to take an oath of secrecy, which, however is rather a matter of form that is frequently dispensed with." It further insists that only "reciprocal interest" among lady visitors keeps the women silent and thus safe from scandal.[46] Although Austen was a voracious reader, it is hard to imagine these works among the open shelves of the lending libraries she frequented.

In addition to such coarse full-length histories, however, many shorter pieces in popular magazines reported on the doings at West Wycombe, including *Town and Country Magazine*,[47] the *Morning Post*, and the *Public Advertiser*, where Wilkes's piece appeared in 1763. Such seeming ephemera often enjoyed surprising longevity. For example, Wilkes's 1763 newspaper report, the one with his racy descriptions of the garden, was reprinted in at least half a dozen different books, in whole or in part, over the next decade alone, greatly increasing its readership.[48] In May 1773, a letter signed "W——" lamented in *Town and Country Magazine* that the Medmenham-Abbey fraternity, "phoenix like, is arisen out of its flames" once more.[49] As late as 1776, the *Morning Post* continued to report on active Hell-Fire Club meetings, half-hearted recruitment, and even a doomed effort to restore the deteriorating original Abbey six miles from Wycombe. On 22 August of 1776, it ran the following notice: "The Order of the Franciscan Society at Medmenham being nearly demolished, J——y Twitcher, who is almost the only surviving member of that club (formerly called the Hell-Fire Club), is determined to restore it to its original glory; in consequence of which intention we hear he has taken down the Circumnavigator and W. Salamander in order to initiate them into that infernal society."[50] I introduce this newspaper notice into evidence as much for its relatively late date, which demonstrates the club's cultural longevity, as for its cloaking of identities with semitransparent nicknames and encoded clues. During the age into which Austen was born, even the newspaper encouraged the kind of clue-based reading that her fiction rewards.

The same habit of cautiously cloaking names governed the printing of many poems and satires about Sir Francis, although such disguises wore off with time. Poet Charles Churchill, a core club member, portrays Dashwood in "The Candidate," published in 1764 as a forty-page poem and subsequently reprinted in various collections.[51] In Churchill's original, the name of Dashwood does not appear. However, a 1784 edition of a multivolume miscellany, *The New Foundling Hospital for Wit*, evidences the manner in which, after his death in 1781, Sir Francis's name and perfidy may, ironically, have become more, rather than less, overt in print. This is because publishers apparently felt freer to name names. For example, in a spot-checking of editions of Churchill's "The Candidate" from 1764, 1765, 1772, and 1774, Dashwood's name had only been marked by a telltale dash, or aposiopesis:

> ————, shall pour, from a Communion Cup,
> Libations to the Goddess without eyes,
> And *Hob* or *Nob* in Cyder and Excise.

However, the 1784 edition of *The New Foundling Hospital for Wit*, while quoting these same three lines as a footnote to another poem about Dashwood, inserts his name outright into the blank. The poem is coyly titled "Ode, Addressed to the Earl of S——nd——ch," but the edition removes even that mask in the volume's table of contents, which lists it as "Ode to Lord Sandwich."[52] Not only does *The New Foundling Hospital for Wit* straightforwardly fill in names and identify the lines as Churchill's, but on a nearby page it directs the reader to the reprinting of Wilkes's 1763 newspaper report on West Wycombe, included in the set's third volume: "See Wilkes's letters, with an account of Medmenham abbey in Buckinghamshire."[53] This evidence suggests that a reader in 1784, although the Hell-Fires were now quite out, might actually have had *better* access to the full fury of West Wycombe's perfidy than original readers of Churchill's 1764 poem or Wilkes's 1763 newspaper piece—precisely because materials that had been scattered by print culture across two decades were now clustered together and more forthcoming. Certainly the well-known associations of Churchill, Sandwich, and Wilkes with Dashwood's club are made clear from the cross-referencing of the texts in the 1784 multivolume miscellany. Although Austen's biographers do not index her knowing anyone by the name of Churchill, Jane Austen does use the name prominently in *Emma* for the rakish Frank Churchill, and might have known at least a smattering of the controversial poet's works. Suggestively, the *Godmersham Park Library Catalogue* lists a copy of "Churchills Poems London 1763" in quarto. Stronger still, and as Jill Heydt-Stevenson points out, Mr. Woodhouse in *Emma* quotes a ribald poem included in *The New Foundling Hospital for Wit*, namely, David Garrick's "A Riddle" (which begins "Kitty, a fair, but frozen maid"), increasing the odds of Austen having encountered a collection "already remarkable for the number of contributors known to be members of the Hell-Fire fraternity.[54]

The illustriousness of his acquaintances also fueled the lasting notoriety of Sir Francis. The histories of a number of great politicians and thinkers intersect with the Dashwood estate at West Wycombe: not only the core members of the so-called Medmenham Brotherhood but also the Society of Dilettanti, various high-ranking members of Parliament, well-known politicians, literati, and artists—even the Prince of Wales. Eminent individuals, even if they were not members themselves, recorded the club's doings for posterity, lending their own fame to the infamy of the club. Horace Walpole and Nathaniel Wraxall, for example, both muse on the club in their memoirs. Artists of the period provided another type of high-profile public record. Donald McCormick writes that certain painters, "notably Knapton and Hogarth, are largely responsible for Dashwood's portrayal as a debauched, crazy figure."[55] Although originally executed as canvasses, their cartoonish portraits also circulated as prints.[56] Lord Byron, whom McCormick claims "was also guilty of perpetuating the 'Hell-Fire' legend," insisted that Sir Francis's Brotherhood were "worshippers of satan" and in 1809 held a mock recreation at Newstead Abbey, where he and other revelers drank burgundy from a human skull in supposed imitation of Sir Francis.[57]

Still, the most widely known account of Sir Francis's Hell-Fire Club came from the pen of Charles Johnstone, whose popular novel *Chrysal; or, The Adventures of a Guinea* (1760–65) is the print vehicle through which the Hell-Fire Club lore could well have reached Austen, an unabashed novel reader.[58] With a guinea that passes from hand to hand narrating the story, the episodic *Chrysal* ostensibly offered to expose the profligacy of well-known public figures of its day. Because of this novel's social bite, Sir Walter Scott would praise its author as a "caustic satirist" and a virtual prose Juvenal.[59] The third volume of *Chrysal*, expanded from two volumes to four by 1765, includes what Scott brashly refers to as "the orgies of Medenham Abbey."[60] Johnstone's own prose is slightly more guarded, though not at all discreet, describing "a society, formed of a number of persons of the first distinction, in burlesque imitation of the religious societies which are instituted in other countries" and led by "a person of a flighty imagination, and who possessed a fortune that enabled him to pursue those flights."[61] Johnstone recounts the society's meeting, led by the thinly disguised Sir Francis Dashwood, as taking place in a recognizable version of the Music Temple that stood on the island at West Wycombe: "In the middle of a large lake upon his estate there was an island, the natural beauties of whose situation had been heightened by every improvement of art. On this island he erected a building exactly on the model of the monasteries, which he had seen in other countries; and to make the resemblance complete, there was not a vice, that he had ever heard imputed to the inhabitants of them, for practicing which he did not make provision in his."[62] The National Trust's modern guidebook to West Wycombe now describes this same building as "a chaste Doric temple."[63] Johnstone's narrative demonstrates how this locale became notorious as the site of wanton summertime revelry by the Hell-Fire Club.

Johnstone's novel, although it fell into relative obscurity in the twentieth century and is only now regaining its foothold in the history of the genre, was immensely popular during Austen's lifetime. Having already enjoyed roughly twenty British editions by 1794, *Chrysal* was selected for inclusion in Charles Cooke's popular series of pocket editions in 1797, where, in accordance with Cooke's hallmark strategy of illustrating lavishly, it was "Superbly Embellished."[64] In this manner *Chrysal* received its first illustrations, designed by none other than novelist Frances Burney's favorite cousin, Edward Burney.[65] By 1801, *Chrysal* had virtually become the go-to-guide for information on Sir Francis and his Hell-Fire Club. This can be seen in the most complete travel resource of the age, Britton and Brayley's multivolume *Beauties of England and Wales* (1801–16), where a footnote in the early entry on "Medmenham" directs a reader to "Chrysal, or the Adventures of a Guinea."[66] As a novel, *Chrysal* would again make a strong appearance in James Ballantyne's well-known *Novelists' Library* (1821–24), where it enjoyed the distinction of being edited by Sir Walter Scott in 1822. In the context of the canonizing force of the *Novelist's Library*, Johnstone's *Chrysal* was apparently regarded as a "great novel," along with select works by Richardson, Fielding, Smollett, and Le Sage.[67] *Chrysal*, Scott notes, warranted attention as "the Scandalous Chronicle of the time."[68] Because time had eroded the novel's immediacy and satiric purpose, an official key to the identity of *Chrysal*'s personages was eventually published by William Davis as *Olio of Bibliographical and Literary Anecdotes and Memoranda* (1814), a quirky collection of annotations and commentary on, mostly, eighteenth-century works. This key identifies all the *Chrysal* characters by name, confirming the significant presence of Sir Francis Dashwood and his Hell-Fire Club members in the novel.[69] Before 1814, the print market had deemed such a key unnecessary, presumably because knowledge of these tales and individuals had not yet faded. The earthy *Chrysal*, with its suggestive tangential genetics to other major novelists, may well have passed through Jane Austen's hands, too, to be kneaded into the clay of her first novel.

Taken in all, the prominent recordings of Sir Francis Dashwood's notorious deeds straddle the late-eighteenth and early-nineteenth centuries, extending the reach of Dashwood's perfidy over the entirety of *Sense and Sensibility*'s possible years of composition and revision. To sum up, before Jane Austen was born, accounts by estranged club members John Wilkes and Charles Churchill first raised contemporary consciousness in the newspapers and satires of the 1760s, which saw decades of reprintings. A steady stream of editions of Johnstone's novel *Chrysal* continued to feed the appetite for West Wycombe scandal through the 1790s—twenty by the time Austen drafted "Elinor and Marianne." In 1801, the definitive travel guide to Buckinghamshire prominently footnotes *Chrysal*, incorporating legend into local history. Apparently word of the Sir Francis Dashwood's bacchanals had reached Lord Byron by 1809. *Chrysal*'s continued currency, now illustrated by Burney's cousin, would generate a published "key" to its personages in 1814 and cause it to be again reprinted under Sir Walter Scott's supervision in 1822. The publication in 1815 of Nathaniel Wraxall's *Historical Memoirs of My Own Time, from 1772 to 1784* threw more fuel on the embers of Sir Francis's Hell-Fire Club, causing the history of decades past to reflame with another controversial tell-all book in the wake of Austen's novel.[70]

Meanwhile, specific events in the Dashwood family periodically stirred up public interest in the old family lore. First, Sir Francis's death in 1781 rereleased many of the old stories. Next, other Dashwood events made the papers: the marriage of Sir John and Mary Anne in 1789; the transition of the land and title in 1793, with the death of Sir Dashwood-King; and the public accusations of Mary Anne Dashwood's alleged infidelity in 1800. Throughout it all, the high-profile shenanigans of the latest Sir John Dashwood—who was racked with debt, maintained at least one mistress, and ran with a fast set that, yet again, included the Prince of Wales—would have reminded the current generation of the Dashwoods' uncanny ability to perpetuate rakish family tradition. Although the essays by Jane's brothers James and Henry in the *Loiterer*, a publishing venture that started on 31 January 1789 and lasted sixty weeks, do not directly narrate scandal, the family involvement with periodicals stimulated Jane Austen's reading in that genre. According to Park Honan, she "read popular histories and many a periodical that James and Henry brought home."[71] In short, during the years Jane Austen composed *Sense and Sensibility*, anyone aware of current events would have been bombarded with mentions of high-profile Dashwoods.

West Wycombe's proximity to Oxford might further have enhanced Jane Austen's awareness of the Dashwoods through either her brothers, who attended university there, or her mother's Oxford connections. West Wycombe Park lies less than thirty miles from the town of Oxford and was so visible to travelers en route to the university that Repton described it as "a place generally known from its vicinity to the road to Oxford."[72] Since the Hell-Fire Club had boasted of so many members from the university community, it is hard to imagine the Austen boys at university being unaware of this site of juicy local history and gossip. At least one popular guidebook in 1801 pronounced on West Wycombe Park's "fascinating scenery" and "the harmonious intermixture and disposition of its woods and waters."[73] By 1813, Austen writes of indulging in the pastime of touring gardens herself, including a visit to Painshill Park, another mid-eighteenth-century landscape garden.[74] Glimpses of the famous grounds, even if only from the Oxford road, might have made the Austens more receptive to its stories.

One further story that drew Georgian travelers from Oxford and beyond to West Wycombe concerned a memorial to the heart of a celebrated poet. Because the human heart is regarded as the symbolic seat of affections, a curious tradition of heart bequests developed in England starting around the time of the First Crusade, when legacies began to direct a deceased's heart, carefully embalmed in rich urns or silver vessels, to their best friend, spouse, parent, or even a church or abbey, as a sign of devotion.[75] Both romantic love and religious fervor could motivate such a gesture. In accordance with Paul Whitehead's final wishes and as a sign of his friendship with Sir Francis, this old practice was revived and the writer's disembodied heart brought with much ceremony to West Wycombe Park in 1774. It was housed in a "very elegant urn of curious and variegate marble" and engraved with an epitaph, thought to be penned by Sir Francis, that declared it "a heart that knew no guile."[76] Whitehead's heart remained on view in a dedicated niche inside the Dashwood mausoleum until it was stolen in 1829. Although the gift of Whitehead's heart approaches the macabre and "drew many invidious squibs," it also constitutes the type of enthusiastic material proof of friendship that might be romanticized and admired by someone such as Marianne Dashwood, whose illness after Willoughby's rejection testifies to her tendency to take metaphors of broken and gifted hearts literally.[77]

The Lefroys and the Dashwoods

The links between West Wycombe Park during Sir Francis's time and the Lefroy family, close friends and neighbors of the Austens during their years in Steventon, suggest further reasons for thinking that young Jane Austen would have been thoroughly aware of Dashwood history. As a teenager, she became the "special friend" of Mrs. Lefroy, born Anne Brydges, a "dramatic, impassioned woman" whose personal inoculation of "upwards of 800" neighboring poor against the smallpox conjures up the bravery and audacity of Lady Mary Wortley Montagu.[78] Austen's friendship with the forthright Mrs. Lefroy, twenty-six years her senior, may have made the young Jane even more likely to develop a genuine and detailed interest in the Dashwood estate, because, as Deirdre Le Faye notes, all of the Lefroy families whom the Austen's knew "had a common ancestor in Anthony Lefroy (1703–79)" (*Letters*, 544). Anthony was, in fact, the father-in-law of Mrs. Lefroy as well as the paternal grandfather of Tom Lefroy, Jane Austen's would-be amour. Biographers of Austen describe Anthony Lefroy as "a banker, in partnership with Peter Langlois of Leghorn, Italy."[79] With modern banking still in its infancy, the profession of "banker" involved all manner of trading schemes and mercantile investment opportunities. Lefroy's financial partnerships at Leghorn (Livorno) included taking advantage of the strong antiquities market fed by the Grand Tour tradition—the bulk shipping, in other words, of suitably antique collectables to English estates for a profit. It was on the

Florence leg of his own Grand Tour that Sir Francis Dashwood, who re-turned to England in 1741, met "the merchants Anthony Lefroy and Peter Charron, who became his agents and were later to ship from the nearby port of Leghorn consignments of pictures and Antique statuary for the embellishment of West Wycombe."[80] Biographers of the Dashwoods thus give the name of Anthony Lefroy's partner in Leghorn as Peter Charron, rather than Peter Langlois, whose daughter Lefroy married,[81] but the broad outline of the Lefroy family antiquities business emerges clearly in spite of any confusion about whether there were two or more partners in the double-pronged business of banking and shipping from Leghorn.

As one of Dashwood's designated agents, Anthony Lefroy supplied the West Wycombe estate with regular consignments of Italian sculpture, antique statuary, paintings, and other trimmings—possibly even plants—ferried to England in a ship owned partly by Sir Francis.[82] Since the am-bitious remodeling of the main house extended over three decades, the length of Lefroy's relationship with Sir Francis suggests years of ship-ments of similar relics and antiquities. Remarkably, this means that Anthony Lefroy, "who concentrated on supplying statuary," was largely responsible for the mischievous ornamentation of Sir Francis's ribald garden, providing the accoutrements for West Wycombe's bacchanalian Italianate landscape.[83] In her biography of Sir Francis Dashwood, Betty Kemp describes how part of the estate was transformed to resemble the classical temple of Bacchus at Teos: "The park was landscaped, given a lake by blocking the waters of the tiny river Wye, and embellished with statues, busts, urns, and trees sent from Italy, many by the dealers Le-froy and Charron of Leghorn."[84] As the daughter-in-law and grandson of Anthony Lefroy, the "worldly-wise" Mrs. Lefroy and her "philandering" nephew Tom must have been able to supply some juicy details of the West Wycombe gardens.[85] Perhaps the Dashwoods had already been the subject of "a *tête-à-tête* with Mrs. Lefroy" by the time that Jane Austen met the nephew.[86] Suggestively, Austen wrote "Elinor and Marianne," the manuscript beginnings of her own story about a Dashwood family, around the same time that she first "danced and flirted" with the grand-son of Sir Francis Dashwood's agent.[87]

The Names Fanny Dashwood and Mrs. John Dashwood

Like the well-known naughty pun realized across the opening pages of Swift's *Travels*, the implications of "Fanny" Dashwood's nickname may be slightly postponed to increase the interpretive impact upon the reader. She is initially introduced into the text only as "Mrs. John Dashwood," a moniker that the text repeats four more times in the two opening chapters before revealing that her first name is Fanny, the traditional nickname for *Frances*. Importantly, we do not learn her full Christian name until we have grasped her character. The text's first mention of "Mrs. John Dashwood" already reveals how she is the cause of her husband's blinkered soul: "Had he married a more amiable woman, he might have been made still more respectable than he was:—he might even have been made amiable himself; for he was very young when he married, and very fond of his wife. But Mrs. John Dashwood was a strong caricature of himself;—more narrow-minded and selfish" (*S&S*, 6). Her name remains hidden as we learn of her "indelicacy" and disregard for the feelings of others: "No sooner was his father's funeral over, than Mrs. John Dashwood, without sending any notice of her intention to her mother-in-law, arrived with her child and their attendants. . . . Mrs. John Dashwood had never been a favourite with any of her husband's family; but she had had no opportunity, till the present, of shewing them with how little attention to the comfort of other people she could act when occasion required it" (6–7). Having "degraded to the condition of visitors" the four Dashwood women in their own home, Fanny's character is thoroughly tarred by the time that we learn, through Austen's use of free indirect discourse, of her miserly intent to block even the little that remains of her husband's residual generosity toward his sisters: "Mrs. John Dashwood did not at all approve of what her husband intended to do for his sisters. To take three thousand pounds from the fortune of their dear little boy, would be impoverishing him to the most dreadful degree" (9). Elsewhere, Austen usually trusts her reader to judge character. In this case, she repeatedly hammers home a definitive moral assessment before providing even a Christian name. Only after the book's irrefutable blackening of his wife's character does John address her as "my dear Fanny," revealing that her full name is, fittingly, Frances Dashwood (12). The revelation seems, in light of the notorious Francis Dashwood, uncharacteristically lacking in irony, a historical coincidence intended to clinch her moral character.

With multiple Frances and Francis Dashwoods milling about at the turn of the century, Jane Austen gets a lot of mileage out of Fanny Dashwood's name. In *Sense and Sensibility*, for all of Fanny's transparent ambitions and pretensions to gentility, her first name may, coupled with that of Dashwood, convey a certain amount of illegitimacy. Although at its most straightforward the implied Christian name of Frances is simply the female form of Francis, offering up a comic resemblance between the two Francis/Frances Dashwoods that could point to a common depravity, the nickname Fanny could also invoke other real persons in the Dashwood line. In particular, the name Fanny belonged to two women with illegitimate, yet strong, claims on the Dashwood name. One long-term resident of West Wycombe, Frances Barry, was dubbed "Fanny" by her friends; she lived at West Wycombe as Sir Francis's companion after the death of his wife in 1769, bearing the Hell-Fire Club leader two children—a boy also named Francis and a girl named Rachel "Fanny" Antonia. Although Fanny Barry never officially took the name of Mrs. Dashwood, her daughter, the other real-world "Fanny" at West Wycombe, dared to adopt her father's title. Refusing to accept her illegitimacy and, as if to offer proof that she was every inch her flamboyant father's daughter, she styled herself Baroness Le Despencer and boldly lived the life of a declared atheist and adventuress. As previously mentioned, in the years leading up to the publication of *Sense and Sensibility*, she carried on the shameless public dispute with her relations, in particular with her aunt Lady Austen.

While the name of Fanny Dashwood invokes Sir Francis's acknowledged mistress, and possibly their illegitimate daughter, another unlawful Mrs. Dashwood was the mistress of Sir John Dashwood, fourth Baronet, who held the title from 1793 onward. Thus, even Fanny's official moniker of Mrs. John Dashwood, which appears so often in Austen's text (twenty-five times in all), resonated at the turn of the nineteenth century with scandal and illegitimacy. For example, a typical rumor-mongering text of the time, *The Fashionable Cypriad* (1798), publicized gossip about a woman calling herself Mrs. John Dashwood. As its title suggests, *The Fashionable Cypriad*, which enjoyed multiple editions and was followed by a Part 2, was essentially a published rumor mill about fallen women—that is to say, it offered a miscellany of Eliza stories. One of the text's many "letters," a transparent euphemism for tittle-tattle dressed up as a would-be journalism, gets the header "*Mrs. DASHWOOD*" and tells the following tale:

> Mrs. *Dashwood* is the daughter of a respectable farmer, in the county of *Sussex*, of the name of B——*tt*. When very young, she was seduced from her family by the then Mr. —— now Sir *John D——w——d*, with

whom she cohabited for some years, and from whom she continues her present name.

Upon Mr. *D*——'s marriage with Miss B——*dh*——*d*, he settled £100. a year upon his *faithful* and forsaken *chere amie*, though his father, Sir *John*, was known to have declared, on the occasion, that he would rather have seen his son, by a thousand degrees, *married* to his *mistress*, than to his *elected wife.*[88]

The identities of these thinly veiled characters perfectly match the Dashwood family of West Wycombe: young Sir John Dashwood, fourth Baronet; his new wife, Mary Anne Broadhead; and his elderly father, Sir John Dashwood-King (the marriage took place in 1789; old Sir John died in '93). Given the letter's header, the aposiopesis of the names in this passage is a crude tease rather than a genuine effort to hide the identities of West Wycombe personages. *The Fashionable Cypriad* records in print the detailed rumors in public circulation about an abandoned mistress of John Dashwood's who defiantly took the name of her seducer.

The sentence that begins Austen's novel ("The family of Dashwood had been long settled in Sussex") not only calls prominent attention to the name of Dashwood but provocatively matches the Sussex origins of *The Fashionable Cypriad*'s yellow journalism, which insisted that the illegitimate "Mrs. John Dashwood" hailed from a Sussex farm (*S&S*, 3). Of all the locales in which to place her fictional Dashwoods, Austen selects the one linked by rumor. Perhaps this is why her next sentence insists that her Dashwoods "had lived in so respectable a manner, as to engage the general good opinion" of their neighbors (3). Austen's appropriation of the family history of the genuine Dashwoods needs careful finessing from the start—a yin and yang of similarity and difference. In the novel's opening clash between Mrs. John Dashwood and Mrs. Dashwood, Austen comically reconfigures the battle between an *"elected wife"* and a rejected one. Austen's characterization of Fanny as "narrow-minded and selfish" possibly comments on why a father might have preferred his son to marry the mistress. Remarkably, the novel's initial discussion about annuities for the cast-out Mrs. Dashwood zeroes in on the amount cited in *The Fashionable Cypriad*. When John Dashwood contemplates that "a hundred a year would make them all perfectly comfortable," he names the very sum that was said to have bought off his namesake's mistress (12). His wife, in turn, insists: "I have known a great deal of the trouble of annuities" and slowly causes him to abandon the idea of giving the other Mrs. Dashwood any monetary assistance (12).

While the fictional Fanny's tightfisted cruelty toward the Mrs. Dashwood of the novel is transparent, irrespective of any knowledge of real-world gossip, *The Fashionable Cypriad* does offer a displaced jealousy as the additional motivation behind the fictional Fanny's vengeful foiling of her husband's good intentions. Austen essentially replays the actual rivalry between a wife and a mistress who vied for the same name as a competition between a wife and her youngish mother-in-law. In so doing, she endows the contest of wills between her own two fictional Mrs. Dashwoods with latent sexual tension borrowed from the tabloids, adding a wry comedic dimension to her opening scenes. Edward Copeland, editor of *Sense and Sensibility* for the new Cambridge edition, describes Austen's "intertextual debts" in this particular novel as "cloaked and unacknowledged" compared to the more open style of references in later works. He suggests that in this novel Austen shares with her sister Cassandra "a private code" in which "the in-jokes and literary allusions buried deep in family reading practices only occasionally break surface for positive identification" (*S&S*, liv). If the things to which Austen refers include, like *The Fashionable Cypriad*, tabloid gossip about one of the most notorious families of the age, such canny concealment about her source material seems understandable. And yet her "in-jokes" are precisely the opposite of "a private code," a phrase that limits the audience for Austen's wit to a small coterie of family members. Known to have nurtured long-standing ambitions to publish, Austen creates a very public code instead, one that is accessible to any reader of contemporary newspapers and tabloids. Characteristically, however, Austen's wit stings, since it betrays those who get her joke as lowly tabloid readers— like herself, to be sure. Given the lessons of moderation taught by both the title and story of *Sense and Sensibility*, Austen's sly appeal to the arm of print culture that embraced the sensational surely also harbors pedagogical intention, warning and rewarding simultaneously.

John Dashwood and the Improvements to West Wycombe and Norland

Sir John Dashwood (c. 1765–1849), the reigning Dashwood baronet at the time of *Sense and Sensibility*'s publication, is "chiefly remembered as a keen huntsman."[89] As an active politician who served as MP for West

Wycombe representing Tory interests from 1796 to 1831, Sir John Dashwood and his hunting mania were much in the public eye. Because he enjoyed "keeping up with the fast set surrounding the Prince of Wales, whom he advised on horseflesh and beagling," his identity as a fast liver and hunter was, like that of many rakes, one and the same.[90] While all this was common knowledge, Austen may even have known of Dashwood's hiring Humphry Repton to alter West Wycombe Park to improve his hunting with dogs. In fact, these alterations resemble those described by the fictional John Dashwood in *Sense and Sensibility*.

Repton reported on his work at West Wycombe in *Observations on the Theory and Practice of Landscape Gardening* (1803). Jane Austen, who was familiar enough with Repton's reputation to mention him directly in *Mansfield Park*, must have known this famous work, which incidentally also details his improvements at Wentworth Woodhouse and Blaise Castle. Another family connection makes this more than likely. In 1802, a cousin of Mrs. Austen, the Rev. Thomas Leigh, had hired Repton to consult on improvements at Adlestrop, where the rectory housed his family and the main house his nephew, Mr. James Henry Leigh. It is not difficult to imagine, either during her visits to the Leighs at Adlestrop (one recorded visit was in 1806) or any time after learning of Repton's prominent publication, Jane Austen poring over a copy of *Observations* for an account of changes she herself had seen. Because Repton reports on Adlestrop in the same chapter that recounts the changes brought about at West Wycombe, even if Jane Austen selected the volume only to read the Adlestrop reportage, she would also have seen the write-up on West Wycombe.

In his descriptions of West Wycombe, even Repton, a highly stylized writer with a keen eye for metaphor, must wrestle with its infamous history. The chapter that deploys both West Wycombe and Adlestrop as illustrative examples focuses on Repton's aesthetic preferences for artificial lakes and the ideal placement of driveways. Already its prominent header unwittingly invokes a garden metaphor that risks uneasy associations in the context of Dashwood history: "Water—it may be too naked or too much clothed—Example from West Wycombe."[91] Although Repton's metaphor of wood as clothing for the landscape is part of the standard lingua franca of contemporary landscape architecture, the expression tacitly acknowledges this garden's vernacular status and ribald reputation. But Repton's reputation rests upon discretion, so he judiciously casts his role at West Wycombe in terms of an effort to bring the

FIGURE 5.10. View of "West Wycombe, Buckinghamshire" before alterations, as illustrated in Humphry Repton's *Observations on the Theory and Practice of Landscape Gardening* (1803). Harry Ransom Center, The University of Texas at Austin.

landscape back into balance. Repton argues that the by-then-overgrown plantings (of Sir Francis, whom he never mentions by name) project such "gloom and melancholy" upon the lake and house in the form of excessive shade and damp that it excuses his "boldly advising the use of the axe." He deems this a fortunate example of improvements that, unlike plantings that need time to mature, can be "instantly produced."[92] In truth, what he did at West Wycombe was to cut down a great many trees, at the request of Sir John Dashwood, fourth Baronet, who was keen to create vistas that might allow him better to follow his dogs in the hunt.

Repton, by no means a mere woodcutter and aware that removing so many trees invites criticism, offers a hinged plate with a "before" and "after" view of the scene to "justify the sacrifice of those large trees which have been cut down upon the island"[93] (figs. 5.10 and 5.11). Repton's eye

FIGURE 5.11. View of "West Wycombe, Buckinghamshire" after alterations, as illustrated in Humphry Repton's *Observations on the Theory and Practice of Landscape Gardening* (1803). Harry Ransom Center, The University of Texas at Austin.

for landscape composition is unrivaled, and his "after" picture certainly shows the aesthetically superior view across the lake's island. However, for anyone who, like Austen, is aware of the estate's history, Repton ensnares himself in his own metaphors when he reasons that, as West Wycombe remains in many other places "richly clothed with wood," he might be justified in having stripped this central island of many of its trees. Irrespective of intention, what began at the chapter's start as a gentle nod at the designs of Sir Francis escalates, in the context of de-nuding his landscape, into an assault upon the female body that this emblematic garden was known to represent. It is difficult to maintain an innocent reading when one knows that the partially denuded island pictured in Repton's plate was a favored locale of the Hell-Fire Club, as emphatically recorded in *Chrysal*. Of all places to denude, the stripping bare of West Wycombe's large island sets loose uncomfortable historical associations.

Whereas Repton, I believe, struggles vainly against West Wycombe's history in even the bland and generic metaphors of his *Observations*, Austen encourages such associations with Dashwood's infamous landscape in *Sense and Sensibility*, deploying her reader's knowledge for her own ends. The event in the novel that most closely recalls Sir John Dashwood's recent denuding of the West Wycombe estate with Repton's assistance is Fanny's preparation for a greenhouse at Norland.[94] John Dashwood reports on "Fanny's green-house," planned to be erected upon "the knoll behind the house," during a chance meeting with his sister Elinor: "The old walnut trees are all come down to make room for it. It will be a very fine object from many parts of the park, and the flower-garden will slope down just before it, and be exceedingly pretty. We have cleared away all the old thorns that grew in patches over the brow" (*S&S*, 257). Even the sober Elinor, relieved that Marianne is not present to "share the provocation," is aggrieved by the cutting down of majestic "old walnut trees" in order to build an outmoded structure whose sole purpose is to cultivate that which has no business growing at Norland. Edward Copeland notes the manner in which Elinor shares the contemporary sentiment voiced by Gilpin in *Forest Scenery* (1791): "Every graceless hand can fell a tree."[95]

Through the changes wrought at Norland, however, Austen conveys far more than commonplace picturesque sentiment. Austen's particular language when alluding to these events at the Dashwood estate may illuminate larger religious and historical patterns in her story. In addition to Repton's recent tree-cutting, Fanny's felling emblematically recalls Dashwood's diabolism. Leveling a whole grove of "old walnut trees" constituted an assault upon the sacred, as John Evelyn urged in *An Historical Account of the Sacredness and Use of Standing Groves*.[96] In addition, the walnut tree was, specifically, a symbol of Christ since medieval times.[97] The removal of the thorn bushes from the "brow" of the hill further augments Austen's choice of this symbolic species of tree with a detail that may even invoke the crown of thorns upon Christ's brow. Fanny is lavishing great expenditures on an aesthetic blunder tantamount, Austen's emphatic symbolism insists, to the sacrilegious. With West Wycombe Park and its history of black masses as the novel's primary touchstone, Fanny Dashwood's arboreal sacrilege neatly echoes the doings of her moral twin and namesake, Francis Dashwood. This resonant scene of provocative sacrilege may also gloss the presence of other religious allusions that run through *Sense and Sensibility*. For example, not only does Fanny play Satan (and Sir Francis) when her garden plan, metaphorically, attacks Christ, but later, and with the requisite number of denials from her betrayer, Marianne rises from the third day of her near-fatal illness while in the netherworld below stairs the fork-tongued Willoughby speaks to Elinor of "the devil" in one breath and "God" in the next (*S&S*, 359–60). In this sequence, which Patrick Parrinder characterizes as "heavily contrived," Austen may also draw upon the Hell-Fire Club's mock-Catholic ceremonies, which so famously emphasized sacrilegious role-play.[98] Although these historical allusions to West Wycombe lore may not free Austen from the implied charge of artificiality, it does infuse *Sense and Sensibility* with a heightened religious purpose.

I wish to gloss one final detail from John Dashwood's report before pursuing the novel's religious undercurrent further. As Elinor politely continues to endure her brother's tiresome account of his recent expenses, she learns of at least one other change wrought at Norland that could, again, point to West Wycombe. With, possibly, a soft reference to the actual King family, the fictional John Dashwood relates his annexing of the East Kingham Farm: "And then I have made a little purchase within this half year; East Kingham Farm, you must remember the place. . . . The land was so very desirable for me in every respect, so immediately adjoining my own property, that I felt it my duty to buy it. I could not have answered it to my conscience to let it fall into any other hands" (*S&S*, 256). As mentioned earlier, the first of the real John Dashwoods, namely, the third Baronet, took on the name of Dashwood-King to comply with a bequest from his maternal uncle, John King, whose estate the Dashwoods at West Wycombe had absorbed. In changing his name, Sir John Dashwood-King publicly declared his annexing of the King property. Thus the pious John King's fortune poured into the rakish coffers of his grandnephew John Dashwood, a key member of the Hell-Fire fraternity.[99]

Religious Conflict, the Ferrars Family, and *The Rape of the Lock*

Since Austen selects so many of her prominent surnames for their evocative family histories, what then of the uncommon and aristocratic name of Ferrars for the mean family of flashy social climbers into which the admirable Edward is marooned? Here too, Austen plays against type by inverting a reader's contemporary associations. While the Dashwood name invokes an estate known for its sacrilegious antics and anti-Catholic rituals, the historical family of Ferrars (variously spelled Ferrers) was known for its "steadfast adherence to the Catholic faith" and pious Romish devotion.[100] By pairing the names of Dashwood and Ferrars in her plot, Austen may play about with the contrasting religious, and sacrilegious, histories of these two well-known families, since their stances toward Roman Catholicism could not have been further apart. From Jane Austen's perspective as an Anglican clergyman's daughter, the disparate attitudes to Catholicism displayed by the Dashwood and Ferrars/Ferrers families may, in fact, have appeared equally perverse.

Baddesley Clinton, a medieval manor in Warwickshire, remains the ancestral home of the Ferrers family (and I shall keep to this spelling only to better differentiate the historic family from its fictional namesake). It lies eight miles West of Kenilworth and thirteen miles from Stoneleigh, less than a two-hour ride in a decent carriage from places, therefore, that Austen is known to have toured in Warwickshire during her time with the Leighs.[101] By then this branch of the Ferrers family "was in decline," as "the estate had become quite run down" and for lack of funds may have sat unoccupied from the end of the eighteenth century until 1813, two years after *Sense and Sensibility's* publication[102] (fig. 5.12). In 1811, therefore, the name of Ferrars/Ferrers dredges up, like the names of Tilney and Drummond in *Northanger Abbey*, England's Reformation and distant past—and in terms of Austen's own religious views, the outdated. By contrast, the Dashwood name, with a baronetcy dating to only 1707 and a reputation for high living and radical ideas, seems comparatively agleam with tawdry modernity. The two names offer, parallel to the title of Austen's novel, a study in historical opposites and contrasting religious sensibilities. If Austen's story advocates moderation between sense and sensibility, the Ferrars and Dashwood pairing confront the reader with diametrically opposed, and indeed equally radical, spiritual attitudes.

Logistically, Austen could easily have visited the derelict Ferrers manor to see some of its Jesuit relics. Even today, visitors can still view the preserved chapel and the priest holes in which the Ferrers family hid Catholic clergy during the Reformation. Even if she only saw the "run down" Baddesley Clinton from the outside, what impression might have lingered in her mind? Architecturally, the differences between the

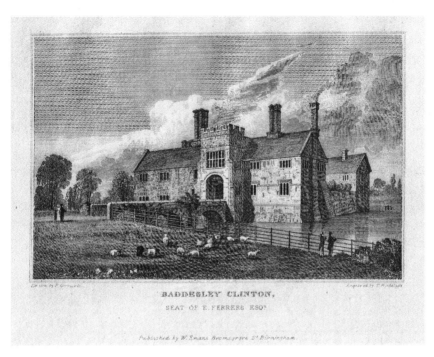

BADDESLEY CLINTON,
SEAT OF E. FERRERS ESQ.ʳ

Published by W. Emans Bromsgrove Sʳ Birmingham

FIGURE 5.12. "Baddesley Clinton, Seat of E. Ferrers Esq.ʳ" Engraved by T. Radclyffe, after a drawing by P. Cormouls. Plate from *A New and Complete History of the County of Warwick*, published by W. Emans (1829). Private Collection.

Ferrers's medieval manor and the Italianate villa of the Dashwood estate could not be greater. Baddesley Clinton is described as "remarkable" for surviving as a rare example of the "medieval manor house."[103] Indeed, the perfectly preserved manor—with its crenellated gatehouse, moat, bridge, narrow rooms, and stained-glass windows—appears as if frozen in time. Like Prior Park and West Wycombe, Baddesley Clinton is now under the care of the National Trust. Aesthetically speaking, the sturdy, square, and grey brick house of Baddesley Clinton is the antithesis of the airy eighteenth-century villa at West Wycombe, with its colonnade and bright yellow façade looking out over the open green landscape. While both locales are, to paraphrase P. G. Wodehouse, positively soggy with British atmosphere, at Baddesley Clinton one can smell the old damp.

The continued Catholic faith of the Ferrers family at Baddesley Clinton was bolstered throughout the centuries with marriages into other aristocratic and well-placed Roman Catholic families. In this manner, the Ferrers family became connected with the prominent Fermor fam-

FIGURE 5.13. Heraldic glass in window at Baddesley Clinton. Photo by Author.

ily, whose breach with yet another family of Catholics famously inspired Alexander Pope's mock-epic poem *The Rape of the Lock* (1712–14).[104] Because the real Arabella Fermor served as the acknowledged model for Belinda, it is possible that the connection between the Ferrers and Fermor families further heightens the strong literary allusion to *The Rape of the Lock* that other scholars have already recognized as at work in *Sense and Sensibility*, even without knowing of such a historical link. Edward Copeland, for example, notes how Willoughby's scissoring of a lock of hair from Marianne suggests "the rich erotic subtext of Alexander Pope's poem."[105] Jocelyn Harris also attends to the ring made from Lucy's hair that veritably ensnares Edward, arguing that when Marianne mistakes it for Elinor's, "Edward is pushed towards rake rather than saint by a brief association with the Baron from *The Rape of the Lock*."[106] Perhaps the real-world connection between the Ferrers and Fermor families will result in a reassessment of how Austen's allusions to Pope might shape interpretation through shared referents to genuine families and their history—using literary allusion to align history and vice versa.

The tidy juxtaposition of the names of Dashwood and Ferrars, placed as they are within other historical references to the Restoration and the career of John Evelyn in this text, makes a soft allusion to the real-world Ferrers family increasingly likely in *Sense and Sensibility*. The original builder of the manor and founder of the Ferrers family was, like Austen's character, named Edward Ferrers (c. 1468–1535). As a result, the official Ferrers family tree is veritably weighed down by men named Edward—at least half a dozen before 1811. In fact, a father, son, and grandson who were each named Edward lived in quick succession prior to the publication of Austen's book: Edward Ferrers (1740–94), Edward Ferrers (1765–95), and Edward Ferrers (1790–1830). It is this same full name that remains emblazoned in the heraldic patterns on the stained-glass windows of Baddesley Clinton[107] (fig. 5.13). Of course, Austen's own Ferrars family is, apart from the saintly Edward, an ungodly lot, and the vicarage for which he is destined decidedly Anglican. If, from *Sense and Sensibility*'s fractious start to its happy finish, Austen pairs her Dashwoods with members of the Ferrars family in ways that invoke the dubious excesses of both historic families for interpretive effect, this may be part of her ironic game.

If Austen did see this estate or hear of the Ferrers family history during her visit to nearby Stoneleigh, the contrast of their pious Popery with the reputation of the Dashwoods at West Wycombe, where Sir Francis's brotherhood made a mockery of Catholic rites, must have struck her as worth exploiting for just such ironic juxtaposition. Reestablishing the historical context of these names, in turn, not only confirms the strong religious and historical undercurrents at work in *Sense and Sensibility* but also reinfuses the realism of Austen's art with its original scope, daring, and humor. In *Persuasion*, Austen draws the battle lines of historical conflict differently. Nonetheless, Austen's method of creatively reworking the histories of some of England's most famous estates for interpretive effect continues in her final novel, arguably reaching its zenith.

CHAPTER SIX

Persuasion's Battle of the Books

Baronetage versus *Navy List*

I N *PERSUASION*, TWO VERY different history books engage in symbolic battle: "the Baronetage," which chronicles the history of the Elliots at Kellynch Hall, and the "navy-list," which tracks the career of Captain Frederick Wentworth (*P*, 3 and 70). Because the novel opens with Admiral Croft's displacement of Sir Walter Elliot at Kellynch, it seems as if the established social system of rank represented by the *Baronetage* gives way in Austen's story to the entrepreneurialism and meritocracy of the navy. With a navy admiral's dislodgment of a baronet at the start and the marriage of that same baronet's daughter to a valiant navy captain at its close, *Persuasion* has suggested to critics the revolutionary advent of a new order. The notion that Austen deviates in her last novel from her prior investment in the landed gentry, celebrating instead her strong "enthusiasm for the Navy," is now a standard reading.[1]

But *Persuasion*'s seemingly radical modernity is challenged, rather than supported, by the *Baronetage* and the navy list, the two important historical inventories that Austen holds up to her reader's gaze. These two books show how the vast majority of the names in *Persuasion* operate *contra factum*, boldly against the grain of worldly facts. For example, Austen selects names from the most ancient families of England's landed aristocracy, notably Wentworth and Croft, to give to her heroic new sailor class. Conversely, the names she assigns to her landed gentry, including Dalrymple, Carteret, and Elliot, belong to navy greats recorded in the lists. Austen's choice of names for her fictional characters thus complicates the novel's opposition between old and new, land and sea. Provocatively, Austen's own publisher, John Murray, had a hand in the latest editions of both the *Baronetage* and the navy list, giving her yet another set of reasons to reference these particular publications. While the inevitable temptation in *Persuasion* is to read the plot as advocating great, almost rebellious, social change, Austen's own uncertainties express themselves in the detailed historical clues embedded in plain view inside those books explicitly read within her own. *Persuasion's* balanced social message may reflect the Austen family's own precarious financial situation between August 1815 and August 1816, the year that Jane Austen wrote the novel. In the fiction's symbolic competition between land and sea, between an old and a new order, Austen may invert real-world associations with the key surnames from both publications to balance her loyalties and hedge, as it were, her family's financial future.

Baronetage versus *Navy List*

Austen opens her novel with a sustained look at "the Baronetage," the only book Sir Walter reads for pleasure and where he finds "occupation for an idle hour, and consolation in a distressed one" (*P*, 3). Sir Walter obsessively reads and rereads "with an interest that never failed" the entry for his own family (3). Although, when Austen began writing on 8 August 1815, a number of publications called "the Baronetage" existed in multiple editions and by various hands, critics usually point to the 1808 edition of John Debrett's elegant two-volume *Baronetage of England* as the most likely referent.[2] Since, when Austen commences her novel, a new, much-touted, and "considerably enlarged," third edition of Debrett's book had just appeared, its preface dated "March 25, 1815," it seems probable that she was gesturing to the latest version of this *Baronetage*, advertised on its title page as available from a consortium of booksellers that included John Murray, her own publisher.[3] In his 1815 preface, Debrett explains that "the great increase in the number of Baronets" since 1808 rendered an updated edition "necessary." With so many recent additions to that rank, Sir Walter was not the only baronet in England basking in the social glitter of his family entry.

Austen sets an alternative system of rank against Sir Walter's "book of books" when the Misses Musgrove "pore over" a copy of the "navy-list" with "the professed view of finding out the ships which Captain Wentworth had commanded" (*P*, 7 and 70). As Roger Sales first pointed out, this equally ubiquitous title also existed in many versions, including *The Naval Chronicle*, Pepys's *List of the Royal Navy*, and Steel's *Original and Correct List of the Royal Navy*.[4] Advertised as "The Original Navy List," Steel's was the most dominant brand, for it had appeared regularly from 1782 to 1814 and sporadically thereafter through at least 1816. In February of 1814, however, it was supplanted by a "new" and "official" *Navy List*, with an imprint that read "Published by John Murray, Bookseller of the Admiralty and Board of Longtitude." Thus Austen's own publisher was also behind the latest edition of the navy list. Perhaps the coincidence of Murray's involvement in both publications gave Austen an idea upon which to build. Incidentally, the references in *Persuasion* to Scott and Byron, both authors in Murray's stable, suggest further significance to Murray's involvement in the publications that Austen mentions by name in this novel. Although Austen was never part of an official literary circle, she routinely responded to contemporary cultural events and publications. It is possible that *Persuasion* reacts to John Murray's role as the publisher of a specific set of authors and works in greater measure than previously acknowledged.

Wentworth's remark that the Musgrove sisters will not find the *Asp*, the ship he commanded in 1806, in their copy, confirms that the navy list they peruse is relatively current, given the novel's temporal setting of "the summer of 1814" (*P*, 9). "You will not find her there.—Quite worn out and broken up. I was the last man who commanded her.—Hardly fit for service then.—Reported fit for home service for a year or two,— and so I was sent off to the West Indies" (70). This comment, along with the fact that the fetched list constitutes "the first that had ever been at Uppercross," increases the likelihood that Austen refers to Murray's official post-February 1814 publication (70). Because Murray boasted in his advertisements that this new navy list was "sold by every Bookseller and Newsman throughout the British Empire," the Musgroves would not have sent away for an out-of-date copy of Steel's list but purchased Murray's latest version nearby.[5] Navy lists, which came out monthly in wartime and quarterly during a time of peace, cataloged the names of officers in the royal fleet and their ships. Like a baronetage, which is organized by the year in which a particular baronetcy was patented, a navy list records the date a commission was first granted, along with the names of ships, designated officers, and vital statistics such as classification and number of guns. It might also give the stations of ships in commission and the names of man-of-war vessels taken by or from the enemy. By 1814, navy lists contained catalogs of flag officers, captains, commanders, lieutenants, masters, surgeons, and officers of the Royal Marines. Although both the baronetage and the navy lists are, in essence, organized indexes of names and dates, they "represent radically different definitions of honor and rank."[6] Because of *Persuasion*'s dates of composition and Austen's link to Murray, I will draw on the third edition of Debrett's *Baronetage* (1815) and also on assorted navy lists published by Murray after his license commenced in February 1814. But whatever the edition Austen used, she deliberately juxtaposes the official lists of two separate and distinct systems of rank.

Such juxtaposition invites comparison of two value systems. Jocelyn Harris sees the difference in terms of active versus passive virtue, "with the navy list's proud record of names and deeds everywhere challenging the Baronetage's parade of inherited but not always deserved privilege."[7] Admiral Nelson, the third son of a Norfolk clergyman, famously proved that the navy offered a unique meritocracy—a place where a young man might make, rather than inherit, a large fortune. Although good connections often hastened promotion, which is why Mr. Austen tirelessly wrote letters to acquaintances on behalf of his sons at sea, the advancement to the rank of captain was strictly by merit. After reaching captain, time spent in rank as well as luck at sea (precisely the events tracked by a navy list) determined one's further advancement. Wentworth, like many captains in the navy, makes his fortune from the "prize-money" awarded in the capture of enemy vessels, either warships or privateers, for which there were fixed formulas of distribution among the ranks (*P*, 104). The Captain's prize money impresses Charles Musgrove almost as much as Mr. Bingley's "four or five thousand a year" affects Mrs. Bennet: "Charles 'had never seen a pleasanter man in his life; and from what he had once heard Captain Wentworth himself say, was very sure that he had not made less than twenty thousand pounds by the war. Here was a fortune at once; besides which, there would be the chance of what might be done in any future war; and he was sure Captain Wentworth was as likely a man to distinguish himself as any officer in the navy. Oh! it would be a capital match for either of his sisters.'" (81). The navy gave younger sons such as Wentworth a chance to earn a place in society, even to consider marriages otherwise inaccessible to them.

These two value systems appear not merely in the abstract, but as physical objects held and read by the characters in *Persuasion*, setting up a tangible material opposition between inherited aristocratic privilege and recent naval achievement. As Barbara Hardy has shown for the objects in *Mansfield Park*, Austen routinely invests interpretive significance in the material components of her imagined world.[8] Although the cited entry for "Elliot of Kellynch-Hall" is obviously invented, Austen insists upon the materiality of Sir Walter's "favourite volume" when she adds that "precisely such had the paragraph originally stood from the printer's hand" (*P*, 3). Just as Sir Walter "turned over" each "leaf" of the *Baronetage* "with an interest which never failed," Captain Wentworth is similarly so captivated by the physical reality of the "navy list" perused by the Musgroves that he "could not deny himself the pleasure of taking the precious volume into his own hands" (3 and 72). While the navy list may be sentimentally and psychologically "precious" to Wentworth, as a material object it looked modest and plain. By 1810, *Steel's Navy List* came out as small cheap booklets, unbound volumes wrapped only in a printed blue cover and roughly stitched and glued at the spine. A *Steel's* was about 15 cm tall, offered the portability of a slim paperback, sold for a shilling (raised from sixpence around 1800), and usually amounted to fewer than a hundred closely printed pages on thin paper. It allowed for little margins, and in some editions virtually none at all, to save on paper cost. In late January 1814, John Murray announced in the *Morning Chronicle* that he, as the newly designated "bookseller of the Admiralty and Board of Longtitude," would start to print the new navy lists from "original and authentic Documents": "By Authority—a Navy List. On Tuesday the 1st of February will be published, price 1s. 6p. to be continued Monthly."[9] Although Murray capitalized on his new relationship with the Admiralty by raising the price, his navy lists differed only superficially in format, being squarish and thus somewhat bigger, but with their production quality at best only slightly better than *Steel's*. The printing of Murray's lists remained cramped and the paper cheap, although the layout gained some uniformity. Since they continued to be replaced with new ones, few owners bothered to bind their copies. Thus, the production values of all navy lists, whether Steel's or Murray's, reflected expectations of transience.

In sharp contrast, the volume studied so obsessively by Sir Walter is probably one of two in a leather-bound set of Debrett's, for both the editions in 1808 and 1815 appeared in two volumes. While the novel's temporal setting precludes Sir Walter from owning a fictional copy of the specific edition of 1815 in which Murray took part, it did not preclude Austen, as I shall show, from referencing the baronetage's latest print iteration in her choices of character names. While Murray priced his sturdy pamphlet of a navy list at one shilling and sixpence, he advertised "The New Baronetage of England" as available "in two large volumes, price, in boards, 1/.8s."[10] In other words, for the price of a new *Baronetage*, a consumer could buy eighteen navy lists, or a year and a half of updated naval news during wartime. Most genteel households kept their *Baronetage* on hand, perhaps along with Debrett's *Peerage*, which followed in a new edition in February 1816, so that they could quickly look up social callers and their backgrounds. The fact that the advertisement shows the 1815 edition of the *Baronetage* being sold in a rudimentary binding of mere "boards" does not, therefore, imply the book's low cultural status. In fact, a trade binding was probably thought unnecessary for the type of durable reference work that customers would want leather bound to individual specifications, so as to match the rest of the volumes in their library. The baronetage did not add members to its ranks as speedily as the navy, and so even older editions retained their usefulness in tracing a family's history. Like Sir Walter, many readers added subsequent births, deaths, and marriages to entries in their own venerable copies.[11] Whereas wartime sped up naval promotion and a new navy list made the last one obsolete every few months, editions of the *Baronetage* were spaced years apart—seven in the case of Debrett's, which had last appeared in 1808.

William Playfair's *British Baronetage* of 1811 perhaps best illustrates how production values reflect the cultural status of the Baronetage. Published in four massive folio volumes, each rivaling Johnson's *Dictionary* (1755) in girth and heft, Playfair prioritizes status over utility, making his reference work difficult to operate but impossible to miss. Sir Walter's copy of the *Baronetage* is not, however, a giant folio, for he admires how his family's entry fills "two handsome duodecimo pages," a detail that matches the bibliographical reality of Debrett's in the second and third editions—which both stand at about 15 cm tall—even as it allows Sir Walter to exaggerate about a mere duodecimo (*P*, 4). While *Persuasion's* physical descriptions of Sir Walter's *Baronetage* and the Musgroves' navy list thus allow them to be roughly equal in height, their material reality suggests an uneven combat between an old and a new order: print culture records the long-held rankings of Britain's baronets in durable, expensive, multivolume works, while it lists the changeable achievements of the navy in diminutive throwaway publications that, while not strictly qualifying as bibliographical ephemera, lack permanence. Rather than invert this insuperable cultural inequality, Austen swaps names from within book and booklet for her seafaring and landed gentry, hinting at a parity that is, in and of itself, already fairly radical.

Yet scholars have read the novel as championing the heroism of the navy against the outmoded virtues of the landed gentry. If Edward Copeland observes that *Persuasion* has "the distinction of celebrating the professional ranks frankly and openly, of placing them above the aristocracy and the gentry as responsible economists," Gillian Beer celebrates the triumph of things new: "The new world of the professions is taking over from the old landed gentry."[12] Harris views Austen's celebration as a "revolution" of outward thinking about a society founded on merit. All these critics agree that in *Persuasion* the landed gentry represented by the vain Sir Walter Elliot is literally and symbolically unseated by a new class of men, represented by the worthy Crofts and Wentworths—men who have risen through ranks based upon merit rather than birth and whose money is acquired at sea through active deeds in war. Captain Wentworth, a younger son, is cut out of even a modest inheritance by the accident of birth. His prize money, a legitimate profit miraculously derived from capturing an enemy's floating goods, therefore offers a modern, that is, landless wealth. For Austen, who typically rewards a heroine's virtue with a suitable place among the landed gentry—through marriage to what Juliet McMaster terms "as close to a prince" as Austen allows— the union of Anne Elliot and Captain Frederick Wentworth dares to strike a new note.[13] Captain Wentworth's self-made social position and ocean-born wealth certainly looks as if it departs from the landlocked world of Austen's prior fiction. As the last of Austen's completed works, *Persuasion* suggests a rethinking of her previous approach to landed virtue, an embrace of a new worldview. Her last novel appears as if written by a changed Austen.

But was it? Once opened, the two books reveal the patent facts of "real solemn history" that complicate such a view. Austen chooses names for her fictional characters that upset *Persuasion's* seeming radicalism, mixing associations between old and new, land and sea. It is simply not true to claim categorically that Austen "never presents . . . any of the great aristocrats who still owned great tracts of the country, and were prominent in its government," for the names of great families are all over *Persuasion* and, indeed, all over her works.[14] The names of Wentworth and Croft, which Austen assigns to her sailor class, belong to two of the oldest and best-connected landholding families in the kingdom. Conversely, the elite families and title-holders to whom the toadying Sir Walter defers, particularly Dalrymple, Carteret, and Elliot, share their names with navy greats. The names in these two systems of rank are, of course, not mutually exclusive, as many of the landed gentry sent sons, although usually not their primary heirs, into the navy, making its lists a heady mixture of knowns and unknowns. Also, as in science, not every gene expresses when it comes to the thousands of names in the tightly printed lists of the navy's genetic code. As I will show, Austen nonetheless assigns her characters high-profile names that are easily decoded using the very same books that she mentions.

Austen mixes values of all kinds in *Persuasion*, starting with an opening chapter that problematically ignores distinctions between moral and monetary evaluation. The vocabulary of "credit," "value," and "economy" is deployed as if ethical and economic meanings operate simultaneously and interchangeably (*P*, 7, 5, and 10). From the start, then, the free indirect discourse of the narrative evidences that Sir Walter, in his blind attachment to the *Baronetage*, misapplies its hierarchy of rank: "His two other children were of very inferior value" (5). The man who "considered the blessing of beauty as inferior only to the blessing of a baronetcy" is a slave to brand (4). Austen upends the signals of value that Sir Walter prizes—beauty, name, money, and inherited rank—with pedagogical intent throughout *Persuasion*. Her plain-looking heroine is past her "bloom," while her hero lacks the credentials of birth (6). She presents the most dominant and recognizable brands of Sir Walter's worldview, the illustrious names of the nobility, in a contrarian manner. Just as the disarrangement of Belinda's dressing table suggests a lack of moral order in Pope's *Rape of the Lock*, Austen plays about with the names "from A to Z" in Sir Walter's most revered book (9). Thus Austen hails a new sailor class that she names for Britain's oldest landowning families, while indicting as languid, vain, and wasteful caricatures of the landed gentry named for naval leaders. Poised between two equally strong allegiances, Austen balances her loyalties in *Persuasion*'s surnames. In point of fact, the Austen family's own economic situation, precariously dependent upon incomes from both land and sea, may have prompted Jane to show sympathies for two differing value systems.

At first glance, the contrast between Sir Walter and Captain Wentworth sets the failures of conservative economic strategy against successful modern entrepreneurialism, represented by Captain Wentworth, who began with "nothing but himself to recommend him" (*P*, 29). His profession, which Charles Musgrove estimates has netted him £20,000 in profit over eight years, resembles that of the modern venture capitalist, a speculator who banks upon a small chance at a huge reward. Wentworth's wealth grows continuously, for at the close of the book we learn that his finances now amount to £25,000. While this striking difference in Wentworth's pre- and post-summer wealth is more likely due to an earlier underestimate than a massive rate of return on an off-page high-risk venture, Austen's numbers are never casual throwaways, for they neatly hint at Wentworth's further gains. In terms of economic production, a man such as Sir Walter, who inherits an established property, lives secure in a steady income from land that by law he usually cannot sell outright and by moral law should always venture to improve. Unless a new event results in a sudden increase in revenue, such as the discovery of minerals or coal, his prosperity depends upon managing existing holdings and living conservatively within his steady income.[15] Austen makes clear that Sir Walter is a spendthrift who manages his affairs poorly. Habitual overspending has outstretched even his substantial line of credit. Lady Russell calculates that only a biblical "seven years" of prudence and retrenchment will set him right (13). The Austen family, who mixed conservative spending with radical risk-taking, relied in equal measure upon both approaches: upon the landed income and essential prudence associated with Sir Walter's type of wealth, as well as the naval entrepreneurialism and comfort with risk represented by Wentworth. Before returning to the larger historical associations attached to the names from both land and sea sources found in *Persuasion*, I shall outline the economic context of the Austens, since the battle between the baronetage and navy list is fought in pounds and pence.

Money from Land and Sea

Brian Southam urges us "to read *Persuasion* biographically" when it comes to "Austen's gallery of naval characters."[16] Austen, whose two brothers proudly held captaincies in the Royal Navy in 1815, is obviously sympathetic toward the navy. Yet, Southam's own impeccably detailed account of the harsh fiscal realities of naval captains suggests that *Persuasion*'s depiction of the prize-wining Wentworth is at best a generous wish-fulfillment fantasy, what he terms a "re-writing of history" that allows Jane to "set right in the realm of imagination" the wealth denied to Charles and Francis during the war.[17] Even Southam allows "that Jane Austen skates over a good deal" in *Persuasion*, where "the gap . . . between fiction and fact is wide."[18] In truth, the Austen family relied in equal measure upon Sir Walter's and Captain Wentworth's mechanisms of wealth creation, upon land as well as sea. By 1815 both fiscal approaches had proven equally tenuous for the Austens. Jane Austen, the realist, cannot help but reflect in *Persuasion*'s names her family's fragile quasi-gentility and its two-pronged dependence upon the old landed gentry and the modern entrepreneur. Everyone in her immediate family, including Edward, the heir to Chawton, was experiencing financial doubts and difficulties. If Austen prevaricates in *Persuasion*'s economic battle between land and sea, perhaps her hesitation reflects how her family's economic future remained undecided when she wrote *Persuasion*.

Throughout her life Austen depended not upon the trickle of funds occasionally generated by her pen but upon the income stream of her immediate family. Research by many fine biographers and scholars, most notably Edward Copeland, into the economics of the Austens reveals the fiscal context for Austen's own life and work. For the early years, Robert Clark and Gerry Dutton have demonstrated the Austen family's dependence upon farming and the agricultural scene.[19] They explore how the economics of enclosures, crop rotation, and farming of the so-called sheep-corn type in Hampshire had an impact on the Cheesedown farm leased by George Austen during his tenure as rector of Steventon. Since "tithes as rector comprised 10 per cent by value of agricultural production in the parish and varied with prices" for the community's crops, Clark and Dutton point out that "*all* of George Austen's revenue, whether from farming or tithes, was derived from the land and related to the market for agricultural products."[20] At a time "when even the King was affectionately known as 'Farmer George' and espoused the merits of the farming life," the surviving letters by Austen's parents show how "farming is a constant concern."[21]

Jane Austen's own correspondence similarly teems with farming references, with specific mentions of day-to-day farming activities worded in the vernacular of one who is agriculturally savvy and knows the difference between "Bantam-Cocks & Galinies" or "Beech, Ash, & Larch" (*Letters*, 73 and 51). When the family moved to Bath, they sold their livestock and possessions: "We have heard the price of nothing but the Cows, Bacon, Hay, Hops, Tables, & my father's Chest of Drawers & Study Table." Jane Austen takes solace from livestock prices: "Sixty one Guineas & a half for the three Cows gives one some support under the blow of only Eleven Guineas for the Tables" (84). The advertisement for the sale of Reverend Austen's farm implements and stock in the *Reading Mercury* of 14 September 1801 offers an inventory of the sizeable enterprise at Cheesedown farm: "Comprising five capital cart horses, three sows, 22 pigs, and seven stores, three market wagons, two four-inch wheel dung-carts, two narrow wheel ditto, one grass cart, four ploughs, eight harrows, two drags, two rollers, troughs, timber bob, shovels, prongs, useful plough timber and iron, &c." The bulk sale of these farming implements at "Auction, by Mr. Stroud" suggests that the Austens leave farming behind when they set out for Bath.[22]

Even after the move to Bath, however, Austen continues to "walk round the Farm" and tally crops, even though these activities now take place at Godmersham: "Edward began cutting St foin on saturday & I hope is likely to have favourable weather;—the crop is good (*Letters*, 107 and 130–31). Jane judges the harvest of Sainfoin, an herb fed as hay to horses, with the easy confidence of an experienced farmer. After her father's death in 1805, the family finances continued to depend upon farmland, this time Edward's. The evolving "plan" to move into the cottage at Chawton not only generated enquiries from Jane to Cassandra about their independent ability to grow vegetables ("What sort of a kitchen garden is there?") but also some assessment of the neighboring farm run by the Digweed family: "We had formed the same views on H. Digweed's farm" (150 and 152). Whatever those views were, the Austens considered farmers noteworthy neighbors.

Jane Austen's agricultural idiom alters somewhat as the wealth and security of her brother Edward grows. After Edward officially inherits the Chawton estate from the Knights and the Austen women move into the cottage, the detailed references to crops and agriculture diminish in frequency and detail. Over time, even the remarks about gardening found in the letters change from the early minutiae of cucumbers, hens, and baskets of food to slightly loftier mentions of elegant visits to Painshill and increasingly ambitious improvements to the landscapes of Edward's estates, such as the planting of "64 Trees" (260). As Jane's farming talk transforms into a discourse of gardening, her youthful exactitude about the price of cows blurs into the occasional, perhaps affected, mention of a person doing "something in the Cow Line" (263). While talk of harvests and greens persists in the letters post-Chawton ("Apples are scarce in this Country; £1–5–a sack."), Jane becomes increasingly uneasy about such obsessions with market prices (127). In a letter from Godmersham, dated 25 September 1813, to Frank, then serving on the *Elephant* in the Baltic, she attempts to shake off her old idiom: "But I have no occasion to think of the price of Bread or of Meat where I am now;—let me shake off vulgar cares & conform to the happy Indifference of East Kent Wealth" (229). Austen was indeed eager to "shake off" the agriculturally determined minutiae that had occupied daily life, especially when writing to a brother at sea. Yet, such "happy Indifference," whether at Godmersham or Chawton, still depended upon farming the land and knowing the price of grain and beef. As it proved, the period in which she composed *Persuasion* remained plagued by inescapable "vulgar cares" for all the members of her family.

The Austens' financial situation in August of 1815 was, quite simply, precarious. Although both Edward and James had seemed destined for significant portions of landed wealth, an inheritance had only materialized for one of them. Edward, adopted by the Knights at "fifteen or sixteen," took his much-anticipated place among the landed gentry in 1812, allowing him to offer a home to his mother and sisters at Chawton cottage.[23] Eldest brother James, disappointed in his hopes for anything similar from the long-lived Leigh-Perrots, had turned the modest living he took over from his father at Steventon into a prudent way of life—a life where strict fiscal vigilance occasionally permitted luxuries such as a clock bought on credit. Copeland, who meticulously tracks James's expenditures at the local merchant, reckons that James's marriage to Anne Mathew had spurred his wife's father to add £100 per year to his clergyman's income of about £200.[24] After Anne's death in 1795, James married Mary Lloyd, a cousin of the Earl of Craven. While this marriage inched James closer to the aristocracy, it did not add to his modest income.

Frank and Charles, meanwhile, were building careers in the navy. While it is true that they would eventually rise to the positions of admiral and rear-admiral, respectively, their fiscal prospects in a time of peace were uncertain. In 1815, Frank remained a mere captain of Nelson's former flagship the *Elephant*, a nearly thirty-year-old ship about to be downgraded from a 74–gun third-rate ship of the line to a 58–gun fourth-rate. Frank missed out on all prizes during his captaincy and, as father of five, he doubtless felt conflicted about spending most of the previous year on half-pay safely on shore in Hampshire. Even after the Admiralty's pay hike of June 1814, Frank was earning only £230 per annum after the peace.[25] Meanwhile, a recently widowed Charles had left behind his three motherless children to patrol the final phase of the war on the *Phoenix*, returning to an annual salary of £192. As a captain, Charles only managed "a small prize" in 1808, "a French schooner laden with Sugar" captured near Bermuda and nearly lost to bad weather.[26] The Hubbacks and Southam agree that the economics of captaincy as experienced by Frank and Charles proved far closer to the life of the

Harvilles and Benwick, who share a "small house" and narrow incomes at Lyme, than that of Wentworth (*P*, 103). In sum, when Austen wrote *Persuasion*, neither of her sailor brothers could boast secure or large fortunes.

Moreover, in August 1815 their jobs were in peril from the peace. With the army and navy vying for dominance and strategic importance toward the end of the Napoleonic War, these institutions struggled for support on the political and cultural battlefields. Like all government agencies, the navy and the army competed for the public purse, and a navy is notoriously more expensive to maintain than an army. *Persuasion*'s symbolic battle between land and sea, between the landed gentry of the baronetage and the men of the navy list, may thus also reflect a contemporary political struggle between army and navy. In *Persuasion*, Austen aligns her Elliot baronets symbolically with the army, first through Sir Walter's early approval of Colonel Wallis ("not an ill-looking man") and then through the would-be-baronet Mr. Elliot's friendship with this same army man (*P*, 150). The story's temporal setting of the summer of 1814, when Admiral Croft and Captain Wentworth return home, marked a brief hiatus in rather than an end to the Napoleonic wars. It also saw the first dismantlings of England's wooden walls, for a navy's power wanes quickly in peacetime. Because so-called man-of-war vessels were fitted with seventy to one hundred guns, each floating platform held firepower greater than an entire army might maneuver on land. In peacetime, these expensive ships were quickly decommissioned, crews beached at half pay, and guns and rigging sold. Although Napoleon was exiled to Elba in April 1814, he would escape and resume the war in March 1815. The novel is set inside a temporary window of false and fragile security.

The decisive battle of Waterloo, which ended the war permanently on 19 June 1815, was also not a naval victory. While the navy had been the key to the victory at Trafalgar in October of 1805—and earlier naval victories included the Glorious First of June (1794), the Battle of the Nile (1798), and the Battle of Copenhagen (1801)—it was the army that clinched the definitive victory over Napoleon at Waterloo. A "shift of loyalties" took place at Waterloo, where "Wellington had taken over as the nation's hero."[27] This means that on 8 August 1815, when Austen began *Persuasion*, the close of the war signaled, as Southam remarks, "the turning of the tide in favour of the Army, at the Navy's expense."[28] Political discourse about what parts of the fleet to maintain in a time of peace predictably resumed, which was why a thirty-year-old ship, such as Frank's *Elephant,* was on the block. Although by the time she drafts *Sanditon* Austen manages a wry joke when Mr. Parker wishes he had not named his house Trafalgar, "for Waterloo is more the thing now," the entire Austen family on behalf of Frank, at home on half-pay, and Charles, just returning from the war, must have experienced in July and August the mixed feelings shared by all naval families who celebrated a victory that also brought an end to hopes for steady promotion or prizes (*LM,* 156). Worse still, the peace increased the threat of decommissioning and life on perpetual half-pay. With two brothers as captains of ships, doubtless Austen shared the instinct to defend the navy and, like Louisa, to "burst forth into raptures of admiration and delight on the character of the navy—their friendliness, their brotherliness, their openness, their uprightness; protesting that she was convinced of sailors having more worth and warmth than any other set of men in England; that they only knew how to live, and they only deserved to be respected and loved" (*P,* 106–7). While some read this passage as a definitive exaltation, Austen tempers these raptures by not assigning them to Anne, placing them instead in the mouth of the all-too-exuberant Louisa.

Even as genteel squalor and uncertainty distressed his naval brothers, Henry Austen's sophisticated London bank was sinking. Jane, having previously nursed Henry through a prolonged and grave illness, finished *Persuasion* while her favorite brother faced bankruptcy, a threat that jeopardized all her siblings by depriving them of precious savings invested in his bank. Henry's bank in Henrietta Street partook of those developments in the national economy that saw modes of production evolve. The landed wealth dominating the eighteenth century was being supplanted by moneyed wealth, which would dominate the nineteenth century (think "the funds"). Rich people were growing richer, apparently by harvesting money itself. Henry's business rode this wave of the future, promoting investments that promised another source of landless wealth. During Jane's London visit, however, the Henrietta Street bank was in crisis. "Jane may not have known all the particulars of Henry's business affairs, but she was well aware that they remained in a precarious state."[29] When Henry's bank failed on 15 March 1816, he was officially declared bankrupt, a fact he could not keep from his family since his brothers were his primary investors. In his fall, Henry pulled his entire family with him. Edward and his uncle Leigh-Perrot suffered the greatest losses, amounting to thousands of pounds, but since James was the presumed heir to the Leigh-Perrot fortune, this affected him too.

"James and Frank and even Charles lost money calculated in hundreds of pounds, considerable sums to them."[30] Even Jane lost some of the hard-earned pounds she had made from her writing. Thus, the failure of Henry's investment schemes must have proved to all the Austens the instability of an economy based on credit and speculation, an economy divorced from the tangible harvests they knew so well how to assess and predict.

Austen portrays Wentworth's dangerous comfort with economic risk cautiously, as Anne Kostelanetz Mellor notices. For that reason, Mellor regards Wentworth as an unsuitable model for English heroism. Seizing upon the very qualities of risk-taking illustrated by Henry Austen's banking venture, she declares Wentworth "too enthusiastic, too rash, too self-confident, too proud."[31] In what Mellor neatly terms "the parable of the hard nut," she reads Wentworth's advice to Louisa to remain steadfast as a dangerous recipe for economic prosperity: "Wentworth's affirmation of decisiveness for its own sake, beyond prudence or rational calculation, in effect offers a rationale for laissez-faire mercantile capitalism: for high-risk investments, aggressive entrepreneurship, and uninsured stock speculation."[32] Although Wentworth's wealth vindicates his unwavering course of action, his initial success turned confidence into gambling: "He had always been lucky; he knew he should be so still" (P, 29). Wentworth's name, selected by Austen for her entrepreneurial sailor, may mitigate his economic risk at sea with the hint of landed wealth, almost as if the name of one of the largest landholders in England stands guarantor for her most entrepreneurial risk-taker.

Finally, another development in the economics of Austen's life proved that landed wealth, like moneyed wealth, can be lost—even when there is "method, moderation, and economy" rather than mismanagement or recklessness (P, 9-10). In the fall of 1814, distant relatives of Thomas Knight, who had officially adopted Edward as his son and heir, threatened to challenge his ownership and take Edward to court for the rights to the Chawton and Steventon estates. Jon Spence terms this news "potentially even more devastating to Jane's own life" than the failure of Henry's banking business. "That such a catastrophe was pending rather than actual must have made it all the worse by creating a constant, wearing sense of uncertainty."[33] Austen wrote *Persuasion* then, in the context of economic threats to all her brothers, on land and sea, threats that directly affected her own way of life. In such a financially insecure world, it would be folly to look to only one mechanism of wealth creation.

Time in Rank

Although it might appear that the competing systems of rank represented in the novel by the baronetage and the navy list contrast old with new, respectively, this is not historically accurate. Austen would have known that in Britain's history the rank of "baronet" was a relatively recent invention, technically slightly younger even than the structures of promotion within the Royal Navy, expanded to their modern complexity during the reign of Henry VIII. In 1611, James I created the rank of baronet to raise money for a war against Ireland, selling this hereditary title between knight and baron for £1,000 to anyone whose annual income from landed estates was at least that sum and whose paternal grandfather had been entitled to display a coat of arms. Although birth and land were thus part of the qualifications, even the baronets given patents in 1611 held a rank that was relatively new, as well as modest, compared to the loftier and more ancient hierarchy of the peerage. Subsequent regimes sold further baronetcies as warranted by political events: James I created 205 new baronets; Charles I created 253; Charles II nearly doubled that number with 426; James II added only 20; William III 37; Anne 29; George I a modest 41; George II another 49; and George III a whopping 469. These tallies are listed at the front of most baronetage publications and confirmed by the patent dates beside the names of each baronet on the list. As any tally shows, and the opening of *Persuasion* acknowledges, William Pitt had expanded the existing ranks of the baronets by more than 40 percent in order to raise money for his various policies during the reign of George III. This explains why Sir Walter feels "pity and contempt" for "the almost endless creations of the last century" (*P*, 3). In the entry invented by Austen for her Elliots, she calculates the commencement of their baronetcy to, roughly, the final years of the seventeenth century (Mr. Elliot, "Heir presumptive," is listed as "great grandson of the second Sir Walter"), so that Sir Walter might sneer at eighteenth-century patents separated by a historical hair's breadth from his own (4).

The plethora of fresh baronets created after 1760 challenged the old aristocracy from within, just as the power and wealth of naval entrepreneurs challenged it from without. As noted by Greene, Sir Samuel Egerton Brydges, Austen's would-be relative and the brother of her close friend Mrs. Lloyd, was particularly critical of this diluting of the honors system, attacking those who purchased promotion: "Men who have been advanced from nothing in the last fifty years—they are a miserable set."[34] Brydges, whom Austen disliked, may thus have served as a model for Sir Walter Elliot as well as for Lady Catherine de Bourgh. As Harris observes, Sir Walter echoes the resentful Brydges when he complains that the navy is "the means of bringing persons of obscure birth into undue distinction, and raising men to honours which their fathers and grandfathers never dreamt of" (P, 21).[35] Nevertheless, Brydges lobbied loud and hard for his own elevation to the peerage, based upon arguments about reestablishing his birthright to an inherited title, the extinct barony of Chandos, which he claimed to trace back generations. Publicly humiliated for these claims, Brydges had to make due with the knighthood of the Swedish order of St. Joachim, a "bogus distinction," which he nonetheless "accepted with considerable delight" in 1808.[36] In the third edition, Debrett records how on 27 December 1814, after years of further self-promotion and pleading, Brydges was also awarded the lesser rank of baronet.[37] In other words, these recent family events must have reanimated Austen's awareness of the baronetage's place within the peerage itself. With the ink on the entry for the sycophantic Brydges barely dry in the latest 1815 *Baronetage* co-published by Murray, she began writing *Persuasion*.

As she therefore constructs the ironic opposition between old and new orders in *Persuasion*, Austen takes the relative age of a patent into account, since the length of time a baronetcy had been held constituted part of its pedigree and social legitimacy. The entries for each family in any *Baronetage*, whether Debrett's in 1815 or Wotton's in 1741, are arranged not in alphabetical order but "according to the Dates of their Patents," or "Precedence." Only the Appendix, which indexes Irish and Scottish baronets, lists names alphabetically, as if to dismiss precedence as insignificant among these lesser baronetcies. In the central text of Debrett's, names appear in the order of their establishment, with older patents listed first—relegating relative newcomers to the end. Neighbors within the list, therefore, did not much alter from edition to edition.

Austen's selection of names for her fiction reveals her acute awareness of their location and tenure in these published lists. For example, Wentworth, the name assigned to her hero, takes its predictable place among the first set of baronets created in 1611, as does the more modest-seeming name Musgrave, the closest match with Musgrove (at times a variant). This means that the Wentworths and the Musgraves, whose namesakes befriend each other in the novel, were near-neighbors in any early edition of the *Baronetage*, having both received their patents in 1611. The Crofts were never far behind, with a patent dated 1671. As all three families were historically significant in much earlier centuries and could boast far-loftier titles in the peerage, the purchase of a mere baronet's rank in 1611 and 1671 must have been a mere obligatory show of political support for the fundraising schemes of James or Charles. Precedence similarly determines seniority among the officers in the Royal Navy. For example, in 1814 Frank stood 139th on the Captains' list, while Charles ranked toward the bottom, at 369th. A significant difference in salary reflected the gap in their seniority.[38] So-called extinct baronetcies are listed separately in a *Baronetage*, their names removed from their established position in the central catalog and shifted to an appendix of lapsed titles (due to the lack of a male heir). In Debrett's edition of 1815, a graphic marker distinguishes those in the Appendix who had left the rank of baronet for loftier heights: "Those marked thus *, have been advanced to the Peerage."[39] Austen also plays about with such information, taking everything that may be gleaned from the physical artifact mentioned at the start of *Persuasion* and reassigning the names in the *Baronetage* for maximum contradiction, irony, and wit.

Conversely, she seems to pluck from naval records names for those characters in *Persuasion* who represent the landed gentry. Critics such as Southam and Harris document Austen's extensive knowledge of the navy, shattering the myth of "Dear Aunt Jane" that held her innocent of war and naval matters. Harris notices a particularly significant clustering of naval names around Captain Wentworth:

> Austen may therefore by thinking of Cook when she bestows upon her characters a quartet of names closely associated with him—Wallis, Carteret, Elliot, and Dalrymple. Captain Samuel Wallis, the fist European to find Tahiti, wrote journals of his circumnavigation that John Hawkesworth drew on in 1773 for *An Account of the Voyages Undertaken . . . for Making Discoveries in the Southern Hemisphere . . . by Commodore Byron, Captain Wallis, Captain Carteret, and Captain Cook*. Captain Philip Carteret circumnavigated the world in 1767–69, John Elliott accompanied Cook on the *Resolution* during his second voyage, and Alexander Dalrymple was a notable hydrographer and cartographer for the East India Company and the Admiralty. Cook often referred to him.[40]

Bracketing Harris's argument about resemblances between Captains Wentworth and Cook, the names grouped by Sir Walter's prejudices reinforce, as a company of men, an ironic allusion to the sea. Suggestively, The *Godmersham Park Library Catalogue*, which lists dozens of famous sea voyages, confirms Austen's access to these naval greats through, for example, "Cooks Voyages 2 vols London 1784," "Cooks Voyage 3 vols London 1785," and "Byrons Voyage London 1767."[41] Names in *Persuasion* such as Wallis or Elliot, too commonplace to resist interpretive pressure, cannot invoke the navy by themselves, even though they appeared routinely in navy lists. As a distinctive "quartet," however, the names Wallis, Carteret, Elliot, and Dalrymple—although assigned by Austen to her landed gentry and nobility—harmonize into a resonant reference to the sea. As shown in my earlier chapters, patterns formed by the groupings of Austen's names, rather than the individual names themselves, often reveal historical contexts and allusions in her fictions.

Not all pertinent contexts are so precise in *Persuasion*. A *Baronetage* in Austen's day provides only the briefest of histories for each family, and a navy list, squeezing thousands of bare names and dates into a small booklet, has no room even for skeletal summary. Neither list therefore always offers interpretive exactitude. A hit for even the uncommon *Carteret* or *Dalrymple* among the thousands of entries in any of the published navy lists, even one boasting, say, the name of a sailor brother of Austen's on another page, would be statistically inconclusive. In order to confirm, therefore, a strong naval association with a particular family name, I occasionally reach, like Harris, beyond the navy lists to additional proof of relative fame, to a relationship with other names found nearby in *Persuasion*, or to published evidence of cultural recognition. That said, Austen does not encourage, in *Persuasion*, historical associations much beyond the two books to which she points. Many print sources might have supplemented a reader's association with her high-profile names, some of which conjure up far loftier positions in the peerage than that of a mere baronet. The name of Wentworth, for instance, was associated with prime ministers, marquesses, and earls. But even though these names appear elsewhere, it is the *Baronetage* and navy list that Austen sets up in symbolic opposition in *Persuasion*—as if proffering them as special keys to her restructured code of value. In the rest of this chapter, I turn to these two books for the historical associations invoked by the surnames in *Persuasion*. Since the *Baronetage* situates its families in specific locations, I also look to the history of their estates for further clues to Austen's purpose. I start with the names of her fictional sailors in order of historical precedence, finding that their original ranking in the

Baronetage matches roughly their prominence in *Persuasion*. She may not, after all, be debunking the *Baronetage* but dispersing its authority to her naval men. Conversely, her evident fondness for the story's sailors casts sympathy back upon their original namesakes among England's baronets.

Wentworth, 1611 (extinct) and 1795

Austen, who grew up in counties where "baronets are as thick as blackberries," must have observed how the great Wentworth legacy—which she so assiduously tracked—had thinned in the latest edition of the *Baronetage* to a single active entry for an American surveyor.[42] The illustrious Wentworths, at their grandest in the eighteenth century for wealth, land, elevations to the peerage, high political office, and honors, were starting anew in America. The long-standing entry for the 1611 patent for "Wentworth, of Wentworth Woodhouse" was now relegated to the back of the *Baronetage*, where it languished with other great families lamenting an heir.[43] Debrett's tracks the extinction of the original 1611 patent right up to 1799, the year the last Earl of Strafford died (named Frederick Wentworth). Only a modest new Wentworth baronetcy "Of Parlut, Lincolnshire," acquired in 1795 for a "Surveyor-General of his Majesty's Woods in British North America," kept the old name of Wentworth among the list of active entries.[44] As told in that entry, this new Wentworth was descended from a branch of the famous Yorkshire family that had moved to the New World in 1628.[45] In other words, a new breed of Wentworths thriving in America now superseded the old Wentworths of Yorkshire in the *Baronetage*. What would Sir Walter say?

As previously discussed, when Austen introduces the celebrated name of Wentworth into her novel, she is quick to deny a connection between her fictional Wentworths and their real-world namesakes. Sir Walter categorically dismisses the Wentworths as unrelated to the wealthy family in the peerage: "Mr. Wentworth was nobody, I remember . . . nothing to do with the Strafford family" (*P*, 26). As a devotee of the *Baronetage*, Sir Walter may lament how the old Wentworth legacy is no more. Like many literary disclaimers, this denial, as I explained in Chapter 1, proves double-edged. Here the shelving of the name is transparently disingenuous, being placed in the mouth of an unreliable snob. But, by working in reverse, Sir Walter's sneer does draw attention to the dominant associations with the Wentworth surname.

Austen's landless sailor and supposed harbinger of the new money-based economy is named for a family synonymous with the long-standing privileges and political activities of one of the oldest and most prominent landed families in England. As previously explained, the well-known Yorkshire estates of the genuine Wentworths offer the antithesis of her captain's new landless wealth. Rumor and fact contributed to the enormity of both Wentworth Woodhouse and Wentworth Castle in the popular imagination, as images of these great estates circulated widely as prints and illustrations in books and magazines. Wentworth Woodhouse remained the biggest stately home in all England, boasting a 600-foot Palladian façade that made it the longest in Europe, at twice the length of Buckingham Palace. Eighteenth-century expansions had resulted in an architectural giant of 365 rooms, one for every day of the year, and 1,000 windows, with which the owners thumbed their nose at the window tax mentioned in *Mansfield Park*. With a reputed "five miles of underground passageways" trafficked by servants and a steady flow of goods, "the place is so big," one historian recounts, "that guests were given confetti of different colours to strew so they could find their way back to their rooms."[46] The dual fronts of Wentworth Castle, although more compact, made their own statements of grandeur, preferred by Arthur Young and Horace Walpole as more dignified.[47] By 1815, both estates fed the nation's growing hunger for coal and timber. The grounds of Wentworth Woodhouse would continue to be mined for coal (scarring the landscape) by thousands of miners through all of the industrial revolution.[48] In the last decade of the Napoleonic wars, newspaper advertisements touted the sale of Wentworth Castle's "excellent OAK, TIMBER, & POLES."[49] Planted by Thomas Wentworth, these now-mature woods sustained a decade and a half of steady logging, testifying in yet another way to the sheer size of the Wentworth estates.

Such contemporary land-based associations with this "well-sounding name" compound the irony of Austen's choice for her landless hero. While the name brings Captain Wentworth eventually, as Southam puts is, "up to the mark as a son-in-law" for Sir Walter, Austen's use of Wentworth family history complicates and expands this irony.[50] Significantly, Sir Walter links the name of Wentworth directly to the lapsed earldom of Strafford. That is, Sir Walter readily leaps over a century and a half of Wentworth history to reach back to Thomas Wentworth (1593–1641), the original "first Earl of Strafford," whose heroic death on the scaffold made him the principal martyr of the Royalist cause. Sir Walter's implied admiration of this earl is not in and of itself ironic, since Austen herself had praised Strafford as one of the "noble five" in her early *History of England* (*J*, 187). But, while Sir Walter's Whiggish thoughts reach far back into English history, Austen knew of more recent Earls of Strafford in the Wentworth line—who all happened to be Tories. Although the initial Strafford title died out in 1695, the Tory side of his family at Wentworth Castle regained the earldom in 1711, when the politician Thomas Wentworth (1672–1739) was appointed first Earl of Strafford "of the second creation." The resurrection of the title, balm to his wounded family pride, prompted Wentworth to remodel his property as a rejoinder to his usurping cousins at nearby Wentworth Woodhouse. As I detailed in my first chapter, the renowned building projects at Wentworth Castle became part taunt, part vindication. I did not yet, however, reveal this new Strafford's financial connections to the sea. Thomas Wentworth made much of his fortune serving as First Lord of the Admiralty under Queen Anne.[51] In addition, he married ocean wealth: heiress Anne Johnson (d. 1754), the daughter of Sir Henry Johnson of Bradenham, who had amassed his vast fortune in shipbuilding. Thus, it was the combined watery fortunes of husband and wife that financed the grandeurs of Wentworth Castle. The latest Earl of Strafford's family had everything, rather than nothing, to do with the navy and ocean wealth.

In my earlier reading of *Lady Susan*, I suggested how turn-of-the-century events at Wentworth Castle were closely observed by Jane Austen. When she wrote *Persuasion* in 1815, the family residing there were a relatively new set of Wentworths, headed by the youthful Frederick Vernon-Wentworth, who inherited the eighteenth-century Strafford fortune from his uncle.[52] That uncle, Frederick Wentworth, the third Earl of Strafford, who died in 1799, had hailed from Dorset—from the dilapidated estate of Henbury, near the town of Sturminster-Marshall, about forty miles east of Lyme Regis. If the full name of *Persuasion*'s hero acknowledges the full history of the genuine Wentworths, so might the names of the women paraded before him as potential marriage choices: Anne, Louisa, and Henrietta.[53] With Sir Walter's lamentations about primogeniture and William Elliot's impending inheritance of Kellynch, the promise of a new Anne Wentworth may bring the history of the Wentworths into further relief. This is because Wentworth women named Anne had played a key role in channeling wealth.

While many Wentworth titles had died out with the death or lack of sons, the landed properties of both Wentworth Woodhouse and Wentworth Castle had passed to male descendants through the female line. In two cases, including that of Frederick Vernon-Wentworth, immense estates passed via the sisters of prior owners, rather than reverting with the title to the nearest male cousin, as with the fictional Mr. Collins and Mr. Elliot. Twice, the Wentworth Woodhouse estate passed through a woman named Anne Wentworth, the first time insuring that the Wentworth coffers remained Whig and did not finance the Tory politics of Thomas Wentworth. At the close of *Persuasion*, a jealous Mary takes solace in the idea that Anne, while a rich captain's wife, is landless and still childless at twenty-seven: "Anne had no Uppercross-hall before her, no landed estate, no headship of a family; and if they could but keep Captain Wentworth from being made a baronet, she would not change situations with Anne" (*P*, 272). The change in the heroine's name to Anne Wentworth allows—along with that of a husband whose name invokes Wentworth Castle's most recent heirs—for the vision of as wealthy and landed a future for Anne and Frederick Wentworth as had been enjoyed by their historical counterparts.

Conversely, if Captain Wentworth were to select a wife from among the Musgrove girls, which possibility Charles enthusiastically endorses as "a capital match for either of his sisters," his choice would risk creating another Henrietta Wentworth (*P*, 81). In a novel alive with naval history and politics, the name Henrietta Wentworth offers a dangerous, if romantic, future. Several historical Henrietta Wentworths existed, both Whig and Tory, but when Austen turns toward the setting of Lyme Regis, she hints at a specific event in the Wentworth past to illustrate just how dangerous another Henrietta Wentworth might prove. As Jocelyn Harris shows, the fishing village of Lyme Regis remained known almost exclusively for its role as the landing site of the Duke of Monmouth's failed rebellion of 1685.[54] *Persuasion* itself dislodged this dominant association with Lyme as early as 1867, when Alfred Tennyson exclaimed during his visit, "Don't talk to me of the Duke of Monmouth—show me the spot where Louisa Musgrove fell."[55] The Duke of Monmouth's mistress was Henrietta Wentworth, *suo jure* Baroness Wentworth (1660–86), who, with her share of the Wentworth family jewels, "guaranteed the loan which enabled him to launch his ill-fated rebellion in 1685."[56] In Lyme, the specter of a Henrietta Wentworth conjures up the woman who financed a brief but bloody British rebellion.

Austen toys with Henrietta as an ill-fated and foolhardy choice for Frederick Wentworth, and as fiction meets fact during the walk along the Cobb, Louisa's fall confirms the dangers of this historic place. Even so, Henrietta Wentworth's active role in the rebellion radiated romance. On the scaffold, Monmouth famously "renewed his pledges of devotion to Henrietta," calling her a "religious, godly lady" who had redeemed him from a licentious and empty life, and his virtual "last act was to ask an attendant to convey a memento of him to her."[57] She died, some said, of a broken heart the following year. As Harris, the first to spot the double echo of the name and place, observes: "In her 'History of England,' the young Jane always supported lost causes, especially Stuart ones, and Lyme was the site of a particularly romantic doomed Stuart landing."[58] Henrietta Wentworth's name does indeed project both romance and doom. As such, she represents the wrong choice for Austen's hero, even if his ambitions and fierce personal loyalties are almost a match for the woman who pawned the Wentworth jewels to fund an invasion of England in an attempt to place her lover on the throne.

In picking the exact location for Louisa's climactic fall, Austen may take advantage of another, and somewhat quirky, historical coincidence in Lyme's setting—the type of physical marker that only an author's personal knowledge of a place could turn into a deliberate gesture. In addition to the Wentworth association with Lyme generally, Austen's particular choice of spot along the Cobb for her most dramatic scene again points to the Wentworth family tree—and not merely because the Cobb extends outward from Monmouth Beach. Austen locates her characters specifically along "the high part of the new Cobb": "There was too much wind to make the high part of the new Cobb pleasant for the ladies, and they agreed to get down the steps to the lower, and all were contented to pass quietly and carefully down the steep flight, excepting Louisa; she must be jumped down them by Captain Wentworth" (P, 117–18). Louisa Musgrove falls from the "steps" where "the high part of the new Cobb" connects to "the lower" by a steep flight. Anyone who has been to Lyme, like Tennyson, eager to see "the spot where Louisa Musgrove fell," discovers that there are three sets of steep stairs spaced at almost equal intervals along the Cobb's snakelike structure that allow for passing to and fro between its levels. The first set of steps form a roof over a small recess known as the Gin (meaning crane) Shop. These steps are wider and less dangerous than the second set, the so-called Granny's Teeth. Only the third set of steps, however, the narrow stone set farthest from shore, was part of what might be considered "the new Cobb" in 1814. This is because the part of the Cobb that extends farthest into the sea was repaired after a severe storm in January 1792. Marked by a commemorative inscription into the new stone, these repairs were completed in 1795, making only this last section "the new Cobb" in the summer of 1814.[59] With this careful detail, Austen thus takes pains to point out that it is the Cobb's outermost steps that her characters descend.[60]

Remarkably, beside these particular steps a commemorative stone extols the accomplishments of a captain D'Arcy. In 1834, a historian of Lyme describes the extensive repairs, transcribing the commemorative "inscription on a stone in the parapet wall": "The work extending 273 feet west of this stone was erected by James Hamilton, builder and contractor with the honourable Board of Ordnance, to repair the breaches made in the Cobb in January, 1792, under the direction of captain D'Arcy, engineer, 1795."[61] Today, although worn by sea spray and weather, this commemorative stone remains readable beside the Cobb's farthest steps (fig. 6.1).

Thus the name of D'Arcy is literally cut into the parapet wall at the exact spot along the Cobb where Austen stages *Persuasion*'s most dramatic scene. Given her steady interest in all things Wentworth, and the connection that, Greene showed, she already exploited in *Pride and Prejudice* between the historical D'Arcy family and the Fitzwilliams of Wentworth Woodhouse, the inscription must have struck Austen during her own walks along the Cobb in August of 1804, the same month that, after much warring about Wentworth pedigrees, boy-heir Frederick Vernon officially took on the surname of Wentworth.[62] Of all the seaside locations to which she might have led her characters, even within sight of Monmouth Beach at Lyme, and with three sets of Cobb stairs to choose from, she places them in crisis beside the Wentworth-family name of D'Arcy, a name that she had already made her own. As noted in Chapter 1, another author who aligns these two surnames in 1815 is Lord Byron, stepson of a D'Arcy and recently married to a Wentworth.[63] Provocatively, in the very paragraph that precedes the account of Louisa's fall, Austen mentions him by name: "Lord Byron's 'dark blue seas' could not fail of being brought forward by their present view" (*P*, 117). Although her characters ostensibly speak of *Childe Harold* (1812), the dark seas in which Byron found himself during the composition of *Persuasion* consisted of a sinister public scandal that triangulated his name with that of Wentworth and D'Arcy. "Rumours of Byron's sexual relations with his sister Augusta grew louder" precisely while Austen composed *Persuasion* (366n7).

FIGURE 6.1. Commemorative 1795 stone by the final steps along the Cobb, Lyme Regis. Photo by Author.

Of course, the uncanny juxtaposition of Wentworth and D'Arcy in this scene remains veiled and encoded—unlike the bold combo of "Fitzwilliam Darcy" in *Pride and Prejudice*—for no Cobb plinth memorializing a D'Arcy is mentioned in the novel.[64] Only for those who know Lyme's history and architecture does Austen's scene align these names into a virtual crumb-trail of historical allusion. The interpretive significance of unspoken details of setting in her other texts, such as the proximity of Ralph Allen's Sham Castle to Catherine's residence in *Northanger Abbey*, increases the likelihood that Austen would not overlook the Wentworth resonance of this prominent inscription. Did Tennyson recognize Austen's wry choice of location when he stood in front of those stairs, to the right of which was, then as now, carved the name of another of her heroes? In 1867, the stone was presumably less weathered. Even if he did notice the inscription, would he have considered it part of Austen's wit or shrugged it off as a coincidence?

If intentional, the crisis point on the Cobb is an inside joke, rewarding only a Lyme-savvy reader in the same way that *Northanger Abbey* rewards intimate knowledge of Bath's sights. But any informed contemporary would know of Lyme's historical association with a Wentworth-funded rebellion without consulting a copy of the *Baronetage*. And such a reader need not have nurtured, like Austen herself, a lifetime infatuation with the Wentworth family tree. Given the many gestures in *Persuasion* toward the Wentworths and their venerable place in history, it seems significant that this legendary family held only a single remaining active baronetcy in 1815. Reviving and reworking different aspects of Wentworth history throughout *Persuasion*, Austen breathes new life into this old family name—just as the latest *Baronetage* promised a renewal of their legacy in distant foreign parts. Since several key names from her own family tree also appear among those in the appendix of "extinct" patents, including Leigh, Perrot, and the variant Austin, perhaps the gesture also betrays personal hopes for nearer family renewals.

Musgrave, 1611

While the *Baronetage* does not include an English family by the name of Musgrove, it does list the ancient family of Musgrave that "came into England with the Conqueror" and to which the Austens could, again, claim distant connections.[65] One of Jane Austen's godmothers was named Musgrave, Mrs. Jane Musgrave, "wife of James Musgrave, a Vicar of Chinnor in Oxfordshire, whose mother was Mrs Austen's great-aunt and a rich Perrot."[66] Although the Austen connection to the Musgraves listed in the *Baronetage* is therefore slight and distant, and Mrs. Jane Musgrave died in 1788, it must have been fragile if it involved that aging, grim, and changeable aunt from whom James Austen continued to nurture wilted hopes of an inheritance. By 1815, Austen may have decided to mute any reference in that dangerous direction, although a decade earlier she had been less cautious when introducing Tom Musgrave as "a great flirt" in her unpublished manuscript of *The Watsons* (*LM*, 80).[67] Possibly constrained by biography and certainly licensed by variations in spelling across centuries, Austen may have intended the name of Musgrove to veil but not conceal her reference to Musgrave in the *Baronetage*. For the moment then, I treat them as close variants, although Austen's change in the vowel may simultaneously point to a location in Somerset, as I shall show.

Lingering in the background of the Musgrove dinner party scene, with all its talk of luck and good fortune, may be a fairy story about a legendary glass goblet called "The Luck." The seat of the Musgrave bar-

FIGURE 6.2. "Eden Hall." Chromolithograph published in Morris's *Country Seats* (c. 1880). Private Collection.

onets, listed in the 1815 edition of the *Baronetage* as "Eden-Hall, Cumberland," was associated in popular culture with the story of a magical cup that came into the family's possession after being accidentally left behind in the Gardens of Eden Hall by fairies, disturbed while drinking of the well[68] (fig. 6.2). If this glass, known as "The Luck of Eden Hall," were ever to break, so would the fortunes of the family. Longfellow famously reworked this popular myth into a poem in the 1840s. Meanwhile, "The Luck" itself stayed safely in the possession of the Musgraves until acquired by the Victoria and Albert Museum in the 1950s, where it remains on display. Austen's emphasis in *Persuasion* on the role played by "luck" in the careers of navy men may reflect upon the well-known Musgrave myth, endorsing with her allusion how chance remains a great equalizer between the landed gentry and the navy. While "luck" naturally gets mentioned in Austen's other stories too, as in the opening sentence of *Mansfield Park*, its role seems particularly emphasized in *Persuasion*, where it appears sixteen times in discussions of Wentworth's career while he dines with the Musgroves. Incidentally, tradition has it that the

Musgraves only showed "The Luck" to dinner guests, when they would pass the cup around the table. Even in the absence of the myth, all talk of Captain Wentworth's having been a "lucky fellow, to get any thing so soon" and his own acknowledgment—"I felt my luck, admiral, I assure you"—emphasizes the risks and fragility associated with his naval entrepreneurialism (*P*, 70). In spite of such acknowledgments, Wentworth presents himself as a gambler flush with recent winnings, dangerously certain that he will win again: "He had always been lucky; he knew he should be so still" (29). Jane Austen, as the daughter of a man who advised her brother Frank "on no account whatever be persuaded to risk by gaming" and who had himself lost a significant amount of money on government lottery tickets, seems suspicious of Wentworth's certainty and fearful that his "Luck," like that of the famed Musgraves, might one day shatter.[69]

Although the Musgraves officially held to a maxim never to change—their ancient family motto being *Sans Changer*—the *Baronetage* also records their extraordinary capacity for adjustments to modern living.[70] The Musgraves had for centuries made their home in a medieval fortress at Hartley Castle, Cumberland, which they abandoned in 1677 for more comfortable accommodation. The castle was eventually demolished in the early decades of the eighteenth century, its stone recycled in the building of Eden Hall. Ever practical in marriage too, the *Baronetage* documents how the Musgraves incorporated clerks, "a storekeeper of the Dock," and heiresses with apparently equal enthusiasm into their midst.[71] In *Persuasion*, Austen's own treatment of the unassuming family at Uppercross may hint at their namesakes' established pattern of turning old into new: "The Musgroves, like their houses, were in a state of alteration, perhaps of improvement. The father and mother were in the old English style, and the young people in the new" (*P*, 43). Austen represents her Uppercross Musgroves as a family that, while never wholly abandoning the past, embraces change. When Anne enters the "Great House," she finds within the austere space of an "old-fashioned square parlour" a striking hodgepodge of purchases arranged with the careful nonchalance of the latest fashion, with "flower-stands and little tables placed in every direction" (43). Whereas the Musgrove ancestors experience the shock of the new from the vantage point of "the portraits against the wainscot," which seem "to be staring in astonishment" at "such an overthrow of all order and neatness," Austen approvingly juxtaposes old and new in her own remaking of the Musgroves in *Persuasion* (43). Her fictional family embodies a historical irony, precisely because their adaptable namesakes in the *Baronetage* officially vowed never to change.

The name of Uppercross may hint of a further and far newer Musgrave baronetcy in Ireland, for Upper Cross is an actual "barony" south of Dublin, an Irish geographical territory. The fictional name for the estate is thus Austen's bad pun; while her Sir Walter is a *baronet*, nearby Uppercross is a *barony*. In Ireland, Sir Richard Musgrave (c. 1755–1818), first Baronet, held strong views, made more extreme by the events of the French Revolution, about the dangers of "papist aggression against protestants." He staunchly "insisted that vigorous law enforcement was the only practical remedy" to Irish rebellion and "personally flogged convicted rioters when no one else could be found to do so."[72] Austen's own views on Catholics may have been more moderate, for her Richard Musgrove is a troublesome son, whose early death at nineteen is the only thing that endows him with sympathy: "He had, in fact, though his sisters were now doing all they could for him, by calling him 'poor Richard,' been nothing better than a thick-headed, unfeeling, unprofitable Dick Musgrove, who had never done any thing to entitle himself to more than the abbreviation of his name, living or dead" (*P*, 54). With a long-standing antipathy to the name Richard and its abbreviation, Austen possibly indicts the "unfeeling" politics of his living Irish namesake. This ulterior purpose would help explain the crude comedy of a passage that others recognize as incongruous with the tragedy of a young boy's death at sea.[73] In the novel Dick Musgrove is the only family member of Uppercross sent to sea, an event connecting the Musgroves to Wentworth, his captain on the *Laconia* for six challenging months. While the coincidence of Wentworth's visit to their new neighbors sparks a friendship, in truth these two names had neighbored each other in the *English Baronetage* since 1611. Nothing, however, in the primary entry under "Musgrave" suggests a strong allegiance to the sea, although a sixteenth-century Philip Musgrave married the daughter of the "admiral of the fleet" and a Simon Musgrave "drowned."[74]

Austen may have changed *Musgrave* to *Musgrove* in order to point obliquely to a small village in Somersetshire called Charlton-Musgrove as the real-world setting for her imaginary Uppercross, a name already suggestive of a geographical source. As in *Northanger Abbey*, Austen maps the distances and names mentioned in *Persuasion* obliquely onto real-world locations in Somersetshire, where she knew her way. Specifically, the fictional home of Charles Musgrove, where Mary is said to be "fixed only three miles off" from Kellynch, may recall the genuine village of Charlton-Musgrove, which lay about three miles from a fine manor called Redlynch (*P*, 33). These two real-world locations, the hall at Redlynch and the nearby farming village of Charlton-Musgrove, sit roughly midway between Bath and Lyme, thirty miles from Bath and forty from Lyme, along precisely the main thoroughfare traced by *Persuasion*'s characters in their journeys.[75] As in the mapping of *Northanger Abbey*, such geographical hints of genuine Somersetshire locales may amount to more than mere realism or mild puns—providing resonant histories that unlock interpretive possibilities.

Not only are the resemblances between fictional names and real-world locations temptingly suggestive in and of themselves, but Redlynch was—like Kellynch—also an aristocratic seat for rent in Somersetshire. The very advertisement in the *Bath Chronicle and Weekly Gazette*, 6 April 1797, quoted by Harris as a model for the typically "grandiloquent language of advertising" used by Austen in her descriptions of Kellynch, concerns Redlynch.[76] This advertisement, which in its early form offered the "Noble Seat and Estates called Redlynch" for sale in its entirety but was eventually amended so "that any part of the estate may be treated for separately," ran for at least two and a half years in the London and Bath papers.[77] The surprising longevity of the advertisement, in addition to suggesting that Redlynch's "Capital" splendor proved a white elephant, increases the chance that Austen saw or heard of the advert. In *Persuasion*, the Elliots decline advertising in print: "Mr. Shepherd had once mentioned the word, 'advertise;'—but never dared approach it again" (*P*, 16). The brassy advertising of Redlynch proved, in the end, unsuccessful, for no buyers responded to the long-running notice. Redlynch, by then turned into a farmhouse, was not sold until 1912.[78]

Not only does the opening of *Persuasion* match the outlines of Redlynch history at the turn of the century, but Redlynch's contemporary politics had lately set itself up in opposition to the Wentworths—particularly over and against the political views of William Wentworth Fitzwilliam (1748–1833), heir to the Wentworth Woodhouse estate in 1782. Redlynch, begun by Sir Stephen Fox (1627–1716), financier and government official, and completed by his younger son Henry (1705–74), first Baron Holland of Foxley, proudly symbolized a family's eighteenth-century wealth and status. In 1762, Horace Walpole remarked about the recently completed Redlynch that it was "a comely dwelling, a new stone house with good rooms and convenient." His catalog of its pictures, damask curtains, ebony and glass tables, gilt furniture, and "chimney-piece from one of Inigo Jones" would have satisfied even Mr. Collins's need for material evidence of pedigree.[79] Due to the prominence of Redlynch and the extended network of Fox family members in government, George III paid a visit in 1789.[80] Henry's older brother, Stephen Fox Strangways, first Earl of Ilchester (1704–76), had inherited Redlynch, which then became the home of his eldest son, Henry Thomas Fox Strangways, the second Earl of Ilchester (1747–1802). The Fox family was a close-knit group, and politician Charles James Fox (1749–1806) "took great trouble with the upbringing of his nephew, the heir to the family's name and reputation."[81] Charles James Fox had gone to school with Fitzwilliam and initially took a prominent role in the Rockingham government until the close friends fell out over the French Revolution, pitting the family at Redlynch against the house of Wentworth in an emotionally fraught series of "public disputes" with which, as one contemporary put it, "every one is acquainted."[82] Fox, who had famously eulogized the fall of the Bastille as "the greatest" and "best" event in world politics, dismissed as alarmist Burke's dark vision that the French Revolution posed dangers to English government. Fitzwilliam sided with Burke, in defiance of his long friendship with Fox.[83]

Whether or not repercussion from this political fracturing of the Whig party had anything to do with the decision of the Fox Strangways family to downsize is unclear. But in 1793, "eight months after the dowager Countess's death," the family moved out, to the nearby family estate at Melbury.[84] An auction of household items at Redlynch took place in July 1801, just as the Austens took tenancy at No. 4 Sydney Place, a residence they had found through advertisements in the same papers announcing the Redlynch auction of goods.[85] When Susan O'Brien visited the park of Redlynch in 1804, she reflected on the manor's visible deterioration in a letter to her niece Elizabeth Talbot: "It affected my spirits a good deal . . . So would [it] you, to find poor Redlynch, the seat of your former glorys, look so abandoned and forsaken, the house unfurnished and the shrubbery quite overgrown and ruinous, and though the time of my glorys is more remote, yet I assure you I could hardly stand it."[86] Austen, who crisscrossed Somersetshire several times and visited the cities mentioned in *Persuasion*, may have seen the derelict Redlynch property—a memento mori of Whig glory.[87]

Austen could not, however, have grieved long for Redlynch's lonely state, for she and her family had reason to dislike the famous Mr. Fox and, by extension, his family and Whig politics. That dislike may best gloss her choice of Redlynch as a model for Kellynch Hall. If Fox's dismissal of the violence of the French Revolution, in which cousin Eliza's husband lost his life, and his fight with the Earl Fitzwilliam were not enough to make him a villain, his involvement in the trial of Warren Hastings would have made him persona non grata to the Austens. It was Fox who in 1788 opened the charge that Hastings had gravely misused his powers, "in a speech that was widely recognized as an oratorical *tour de force*."[88] Jane was then only a child, but Henry's letter congratulating Hastings after his vindication shows that the Austens closely watched these events. With Hastings's "several connections of enduring friendship with the Austens," family loyalty might make Austen resent the Foxes on principle. [89]

In 1815, a letter from her sailor brother Charles, then "chasing after French and Neapolitan squadrons in the Mediterranean," may have triggered a memory of Redlynch.[90] In this letter, written on 6 May 1815 and probably arriving in Chawton many weeks later, just before Austen started *Persuasion* on 8 August, Charles reported how "books became the conversation" among the officers: "a young man present observed that nothing had come out for years to be compared with 'Pride and Prejudice', 'Sense and Sensibility', &c. As I am sure you must be anxious to know the name of a person of so much taste, I should tell you it is Fox, a nephew of the late Charles James Fox."[91] Perhaps Austen rewards this young man's exquisite discrimination, even if he was a Fox, by echoing his old family home in the name and location of the fictional Kellynch. With her heroine's obvious attachment to the place, Austen softens the Foxite opprobrium that might attach itself to Kellynch Hall through any resemblance to Redlynch. Although the allusion cannot be pinned down, the coincidence of her place names follows the same pattern witnessed in earlier novels, where Austen works imaginatively with stately homes evocative of a history simultaneously national and personal. Even if Charles's letter did not prompt a veiled allusion to Redlynch, his mention of yet another son of the landed gentry mingling with navy men in the Mediterranean offers further proof of the fluidity between the worlds mixed in Austen's novel.

Carteret, 1645 (Extinct) and 1668 (Extinct)

It seems, at first, that the early dates on the entries for "Carteret" in the *Baronetage* of 1815 run counter to the contrarian chronology elsewhere maintained by Austen. The name affects the status-loving Sir Walter like a Pavlovian bell. The seventeenth-century patents for Carteret would therefore confirm rather than deny Sir Walter's prejudiced approval. But the *Baronetage* not only reveals these old Carteret patents to be extinct but also shows how this family earned its relatively early place there, in 1645, for the nautical accomplishment of a naval officer born a farmer's son on the Isle of Jersey. Subsequent Carterets from Jersey also pursued splendid seafaring careers. By 1815, with the old Carteret baronetcies appearing only among extinct patents in the *Baronetage*, their maritime legacy was so extensive that even someone who had never read a navy list might associate their name with exploits at sea.

In *Persuasion*, Austen gives the name of Carteret to a fictional daughter of a viscountess, a distant cousin of her Elliots. For Sir Walter Elliot and his favorite daughter Elizabeth, the mere mention in the newspaper of this name, along with that of Dalrymple, thrills: "The Bath paper one morning announced the arrival of the Dowager Viscountess Dalrymple, and her daughter, the Honourable Miss Carteret; and all the comfort of No.——, Camden-place, was swept away for many days; for the Dalrymples (in Anne's opinion, most unfortunately) were cousins of the Elliots; and the agony was, how to introduce themselves properly. . . . 'our cousins Lady Dalrymple and Miss Carteret;' 'our cousins, the Dalrymples,' sounded in her ears all day long" (*P*, 160–61). In truth, and as Harris showed, if the names of Carteret and Dalrymple had appeared together in print, it would have been in a naval publication, since Dalrymple was a famous hydrographer and Carteret the explorer who traveled with Cook.

Sir George Carteret (1610?–80), naval officer turned first baronet, is believed to have had only "rudimentary schooling," perhaps near his father's farm, since he continued to be mocked for a "defective education and provincial accent."[92] Still, as Mr. Elliot warns, good company "is not very nice" "with regard to education," and even Lady Fanshawe, who sneers in her *Memoirs* that Carteret was "bred a sea-boy," gratefully partook of his hospitality on Jersey after escaping a storm at sea (*P*, 162).[93] Carteret's evident lack of "breeding and education" did not prevent his promotion to officer or his mixing in society, for he quickly rose through the ranks of lieutenant, captain, and, in 1637, vice-admiral.[94] At the time of his death, the king was about to raise Carteret to the rank of earl and consequently granted his widow precedence (by a warrant dated 11 February 1680), as if the creation had already taken place. Carteret's rare posthumous elevation allowed the king to bestow further privileges of rank on his widow and children. This same family from Jersey would produce a number of other naval greats, two of whom must have been well-known to Austen, by reputation at least.

Rear-Admiral Philip Carteret (1733–96) was a famous explorer and circumnavigator. In 1747, he set out from Jersey to begin a naval career starting, like his forbear, at the very bottom of the ranks. By 1815, however, Philip Carteret's name in naval history was associated with those of famous captains Wallis and Byron, whom he followed from ship to ship. Although the death of an elder brother led to his inheriting Trinity Manor, he abandoned neither his naval career nor Byron, whom he served as lieutenant on the frigate *Dolphin* during his circumnavigation through the Pacific. Soon a follow-up expedition was dispatched "to search for the great southern continent in whose existence Byron now firmly believed," offering Carteret his first command.[95] The party consisted of the *Dolphin*, captained by Samuel Wallis, and the *Swallow*, by Carteret. Like Wentworth, who protests the fitness of the *Asp*, "Carteret knew the *Swallow* was old, decrepit, poorly fitted out, and incompletely manned, and lost no opportunity of telling the Admiralty so."[96] Although his protests were resented, his luck held and he eventually rose to the post of rear-admiral. Carteret's companions Byron and Wallis may or may not make cameo appearances in *Persuasion* through Benwick's passion for that other famous Byron and, as Harris notes, the liminal presence of a Colonel Wallis. The ease with which Austen slips in and out of the lingua franca of naval history—where *the* Byron of note is a captain and not a poet—makes it impossible to pin down the allusion.

Name recognition may have assisted the career of the rear-admiral's son, also named Philip Carteret (1777–1828). Philip Carteret junior, who entered the navy in 1792, was promoted to lieutenant by 1795, serving on ships such as the *Impérieuse, Greyhound, Britannia*, and *Cambrian* in the English Channel and along the French coast.[97] Commander by 1802 of the sloop *Bonne Citoyenne* and "paid off" in 1803, he next served in the North Sea on the brig *Scorpion*. The admiralty selected him in 1805 for intelligence duties in the West Indies, where he shadowed the movements of French squadrons, sending home reports until 1807. He served on and commanded so many other ships during the Napoleonic war years that by the time Austen started on *Persuasion*, the younger Carteret was renowned for his own achievements rather than his father's. Indeed, on 4 June 1815, just two months earlier, he had been made a Companion of the Order of the Bath, the third-highest order in the British Honors system, awarded for exemplary levels of service to one's country. In January 1822, he would add the name Silvester to Carteret and succeed to a baronetcy, by a special clause in the patent of his uncle. Austen did not live to see this aspect of his success, but even in the *Baronetage* of 1815 she could track the Carterets of Jersey, who earned there an early place by naval achievements. Allusions to this Carteret legacy take aim at Sir Walter's disdain for the navy.

Croft, 1671

While Anne finds Admiral Croft's "goodness of heart and simplicity of character" simply "irresistible," his name alone may already predispose Austen's reader in favor of the admiral (*P*, 137). Debrett records that the baronetcy for "Croft, of Croft Castle, Herefordshire" was created on 18 November 1671.[98] As a prominent Herefordshire family of Norman descent, the Crofts enjoyed a long-standing reputation for good works: "In almost every generation from the commencement of the fourteenth century, records exist of the public services of its representatives."[99] In *Persuasion*, the integrity of the kindly Crofts befits their ancient name. When Anne reflects upon their tenancy, she "felt the parish to be so sure of a good example, and the poor of the best attention and relief," that her "conscience" allows "that Kellynch-hall had passed into better hands than its owners" (*P*, 136). As was the case for the Wentworth and Musgrave families, the Austens could also claim a distant connection to the Crofts of Croft Castle, possibly reinforcing Jane Austen's interest in their history and pedigree with a personal connection.[100] Whatever the catalyst, all such borrowing from the baronetage for the navy complicates what Southam calls "the distance between the cold Elliot world of polite society and the naval world of warmth and good fellowship," because Austen bridges this supposed gap by means of her choice of names.[101]

The history of the baronetage may also gloss why Austen's Crofts are "without children" (*P*, 24). Childlessness had once been rare among the Crofts, for this family "presents one of the very few instances in which property has descended from father to son for more than seven hundred years."[102] No noble family in England seemed less prone to the lack of an heir than the Crofts. And yet, in 1792 the third baronet passed away "without issue male" after his infant son died "by the accidental application of an improper medicine."[103] A mere five years later, in 1797, his brother John Croft, now fourth baronet, also died "without issue." To these unprecedented personal losses in the Croft baronetcy was now added the absence of an heir, for the then-current baronet, age sixty-four, had three daughters but no son by his first marriage, and no additional children with his second wife. These recent turns in Croft family history may further enhance the quiet tragedy of the childlessness of the Crofts in *Persuasion*, a fact already treated unfeelingly by the Elliots as a practical boon: "A lady, without a family, was the very best preserver of furniture in the world" (25). When Austen bestows upon her own Sophia Croft, aged "eight and thirty," the Christian name of the reigning baronet's first lady, she adds further poignancy to a loss shared by Crofts of fiction and fact (52).

The actual Crofts had also recently lost their family home, Croft Castle, which had "always" been their seat since "Saxon times" and was located a hundred miles directly north of Bath.[104] Begun in the fourteenth century and remodeled and expanded over generations, this estate remained the proud home of the Croft Baronets until 1746, when Sir Archer, third baronet, "cut off the entail, and sold Croft Castle, to Thomas Johnes, esq."[105] In *Persuasion*, even the cash-poor Sir Walter balks at a sale of one's ancestral home: "No; he would never disgrace his name so far. The Kellynch estate should be transmitted whole and entire, as he had received it" (*P*, 10). Great financial pressures provoked the outright sale of Croft Castle, in violation of tradition and family honor, which left the baronetcy officially and permanently homeless. In Debrett's 1815 *Baronetage* the family remains listed as the Crofts of Croft Castle but is on record as having squandered away the family seat. Although no evidence suggests that genuine Crofts were forced to rent a fellow-baronet's country house in nearby Somerset, that Admiral Croft rents Kellynch may slyly nod to the relatively recent homelessness of the famous Crofts. Pecuniary pressure continued to plague the Croft baronetcy, the difficulties of the current and fifth Baronet in 1815 being "increased by his volatile character, which prevented him from settling into a profession, or dealing responsibly with his finances."[106]

As the entry in Debrett's explains, the reigning baronet Herbert Croft (1751–1816) was a fellow author: "The public have been indebted to Sir

Herbert, for many useful and entertaining works, though many of them are anonymous." In fact, "Sir Herbert Croft, bart. in holy orders" was a popular humorist and a veritable Laurence Sterne, although his ambitions as a lexicographer suggest he may have preferred being likened to Johnson.[107] For years, Sir Herbert devoted himself to an English dictionary that never came to fruition as well as to other misjudged projects, all the while relying upon the mere £100 per annum from the living at the small vicarage of Prittlewell, in Essex. Debts forced him to the Continent for long periods. His numerous publications include genuine works of scholarship, such as a "Life" of Edward Young, pieces in periodicals, and topical book-length satires with transparently humorous titles. He lampooned contemporaries in the futuristic *Abbey of Kilkhampton; or, Monumental Records for The Year 1980* (1780), which proved so popular it "ran to fourteen editions" before prompting a sequel in 1822.[108] If Austen gives Sir Herbert a taste of his own satirical medicine in the gout-riddled and plain-speaking Admiral Croft, she does so without malice. In spite of possible references to a legacy of mismanagement that rendered a baronetcy homeless, her portrait of the endearing Crofts remains deeply sympathetic.

Russell, 1629 (Extinct), 1660 (Extinct), and 1812

Patrick Parrinder surmises how "Sir Walter's snobbish observation that Frederick Wentworth was not one of the Strafford family implies strongly that his friend Lady Russell must be one of the Whig Russells."[109] This is indeed the impression with which Austen's story begins. The name of Russell, Sir Walter's "book of books" confirms, was an esteemed old feature of the *Baronetage* (*P*, 7). But a closer look reveals that all the old Russell patents for Whig families were now extinct.[110] Like the childless Lady Russell of *Persuasion*, who resides in the subsidiary residence of Kellynch Lodge, the position of her venerable namesakes in the *Baronetage* had diminished through a lack of heirs. A new race of self-made Russells, however, had risen to the rank of baronet in 1812. Duly entered into the latest edition of Debrett's *Baronetage*, these new Russells, like the new American line of Wentworth baronets, thrived in distant parts of the empire. The only Russell baronetcy active in 1815 belonged to a judge in India with sons in the East India Company's service. The *Baronetage* again deflates Sir Walter's pride. As the plot of *Persuasion* moves toward a reconciliation between Captain Wentworth and Lady Russell, additional historical associations with the name of Russell may cumulatively help soften the starting Whiggish connotations of her surname.

Henry Russell (1751–1836), the newest Russell baronet, was a merchant's son who studied law and rose to become the chief justice of Bengal. Russell's legal work in India "attracted great attention" in 1808, when he sentenced to death John Grant, a company cadet, for maliciously setting fire to a poor Indian's hut.[111] Russell explained his decision in the logic of the colonial protectorate: "The natives are entitled to have their characters, property, and lives protected; and as long as they enjoy that privilege from us, they give their affection and allegiance in return."[112] After being awarded a baronetcy on 10 December 1812, Russell retired, returning to England to live upon a pension from the East India Company. By all accounts, he was a remarkably modern and moral man: "After his retirement he declined his brother-in-law Lord Whitworth's offer of a seat in parliament, as member for East Grinstead, a pocket borough of the Sackville family, "on the ground that he 'did not choose to be any gentleman's gentleman.'"[113] Since Deirdre Le Faye records several events that link the Austens with Lord Whitworth starting in 1813, it is possible that Austen heard how this Russell had refused a pocket borough but had been elevated to baronet entirely upon his own merit. His entry in the *Baronetage* may have demonstrated that the baronetage, too, had a future as a meritocracy. When, at the end of the novel, a green-eyed Mary contemplates whether Captain Wentworth might be kept "from being made a baronet," Austen implies that virtuous men may enter the peerage through hard work (*P*, 272). For all of its past abuses, the rank of baronet may be the site where Austen sees the nobility evolving with changing times.

In any navy list of around 1814, "Thomas M. Russell, Esq." is listed on the preliminary pages, before thousands of lesser-ranked officers, as an "Admiral of the Blue." When Sir Walter suspiciously asks "And who is Admiral Croft?" Anne responds with the type of headlines-only summary of a career that may be gleaned from the pages of consecutive navy lists: "He is rear admiral of the white. He was in the Trafalgar action, and has been in the East Indies since; he has been stationed there, I believe, several years" (*P*, 24). Thomas Macnamara Russell (c. 1740, d. 1824), son of an English settler in County Clare, started out as a mere "able seaman," rising through the ranks for his quick-thinking and daring in his skirmishes with the enemy. In the late 1780s, "Russell modestly declined a knighthood, which his small fortune could not support."[114] In 1805 he was promoted to vice-admiral, and in 1807 to commander-in-chief of the squadron in the North Sea, where he led a strategic victory. On 12 August 1812, Russell became an admiral. Russell's career, even if only tracked by his name ever-ascending toward the top of the navy lists, exemplifies the promotion-by-merit permitted by the navy, which, Sir Walter protests, is "the means of bringing persons of obscure birth into undue distinction, and raising men to honours which their fathers and grandfathers never dreamt of" (21).

An entry for "Russell" in any contemporary navy list also takes the form of the 74–gun frigate, third class, the *Russell*. Austen's emphasis on the navy list allows how the name of Russell eventually attached itself to a famous ship. Launched on 10 November 1764, the *Russell* was commanded by Captain Saumarez at the Battle of the Saintes and was part of Admiral Howe's fleet at the Glorious First of June in 1794.[115] In 1795, though thirty years old, she was still considered among "the best sailing ships" in the fleet when Admiral Lord Bridport called upon her to give chase to enemy ships in an action with the French on 22 June.[116] Captained by Sir Henry Trollope in the glorious battle off Camperdown on 11 October 1797, she remained with the Channel Fleet for some years, served in Nelson's fleet during the Battle of Copenhagen in 1801, and took part in the Battle of Trafalgar on 21 October 1805. When "sold out of the service" in 1811, the ship was an astonishing forty-seven years old, having survived some of the greatest battles of the wars. As late as December 1814, she still appeared on a navy list ("Russell, 74.") along with other inactive ships like the *Elephant*, Nelson's former flagship and Frank's one-time command.[117] Although these ships continued to appear alphabetically among the list of ships in the royal fleet, they were no longer assigned a crew of officers. Thus, like entries for extinct titles in the *Baronetage*, these well-known ships, whether sold, captured, damaged, or decommissioned, became bare names only. Austen would know that navy lists record dead legacies just as faithfully as the *Baronetage*. Lacking a captain, lieutenant, or purser, the entry for *Russell* reads, as do the extinct Russell baronetcies in that other book, like a veritable epitaph. Descriptions of the tough-minded Lady Russell, a widow "of steady age and character" whose signs of aging, such as "the rapid increase of the crow's foot about Lady Russell's temples," so distressingly challenges

Sir Walter's powers of denial, and for whom the heroine continues her steady regard, may comically invoke the longevity and noble spirit of even a man-of-war (*P*, 5 and 7).

In the context of Austen's established interest in the history of the Civil War, as well as the cameo in *Persuasion* of a haughty and despicable Dalrymple (discussed more below), the name Lady Russell may also conjure up the romanticized figure of Rachel Wriothesley (c. 1636–1723), know colloquially as "Lady Russell" and remembered for her role as her husband's devoted secretary during his trial for treason as a conspirator in the Rye House Plot of 1683. Her *Letters*, first published in 1773, challenged accounts by historian Sir John Dalrymple (more about him below). Most importantly, perhaps, Lady Russell's letters continued to be valued and quoted at the turn of the nineteenth century for their expressions of affection between husband and wife.[118] Like her contemporary Henrietta Wentworth, the Duke of Monmouth's mistress, Lady Russell was remembered as a tragic romantic figure of the late seventeenth century. Wentworth reconciles himself to Lady Russell in the end, for "Lady Russell, in spite of all her former transgressions, he could now value from his heart" (*P*, 274). Historical associations, within Wentworth's naval profession as well as romantic sentimentalism writ large, possibly advance the hero's radical change of heart about Lady Russell.

Dalrymple, 1814

Austen's Englishness may show in her sardonic use of the name Dalrymple for the highest ranking and least-developed character in *Persuasion*, a Dowager Viscountess with a "broad back" whose only recorded speech belittles Captain Wentworth as "Irish, I dare say" (*P*, 201, 204). Lady Dalrymple's disparaging insistence upon Wentworth's foreignness is ironic in the context of the *Baronetage*, since her name may be identified with Scottish rather than English baronets. When Sir Walter urges his daughter Anne to visit Lady Dalrymple and honor their "family connections among the nobility of England and Ireland!" Austen plays with the decidedly Scottish ring of *Dalyrmple*, with four entries in the appendix of "Baronets of Nova Scotia, or Scotland" in the 1815 edition of *The Baronetage of England* (*P*, 171). The Scottish appendix, a bare list of names, includes one extinct Dalrymple baronetcy dated to 1664 and two active patents dated to 1697, with another following in 1701. Only in December 1814, less than a year before Austen wrote *Persuasion*, did the name Dalrymple enter the *Baronetage of England* with the elevation of Sir Hew Whiteford Dalrymple (1750–1830). With the entry of Sir Hew, the 1815 edition became the first to print the name of Dalrymple in Debrett's among the English patents.

To make matters worse, this new Dalrymple baronet was an army rather than a navy man. Sir Hew was the lieutenant governor of Gibraltar who, as Jocelyn Harris notes, was "nicknamed 'Dowager Dalrymple' for his pusillanimous role in the hugely unpopular Treaty of Cintra (1808)."[119] Harris reasons that because Austen twice refers in her correspondence to the death of Sir John Moore at Corunna in the same campaigns, her scornful portrayal of a "Dowager Dalrymple" may point to the army general as a referent.[120] If the portrait of Lady Dowager Dalrymple lampoons a much-disliked army general only recently elevated to the baronetcy, the implied criticism of the army fits the text's general sympathy for the navy. *Persuasion's* only army officer, Colonel Wallis, is already disparaged through his close association with Mr. William Elliot, whose rakish schemes he promotes. Austen sides unequivocally with her brothers in any army-navy rivalry.

A copy of "Dalrymple's Memoirs 3 vols London 1771" is listed under the quarto books in the *Godmersham Park Library Catalogue*, suggesting that someone in the Austen family circle read a Scottish baronet turned Whig historian. A minor member of the Edinburgh literati, Sir John Dalrymple, fourth baronet (1726–1810), was best known for his *Memoirs of Great Britain and Ireland from the Dissolution of the Last Parliament of Charles II until the Sea Battle of La Hogue* (1771), which appeared in quarto in 3 volumes. As "a traditional whig attempt to unlock the hidden secrets of the revolution of 1688 with new documentation," the *Memoirs* irritated some, including the descendants of Lady Russell, who published her *Letters* in 1773 with an "Introduction Vindicating the Character of Lord Russell against Sir John Dalrymple."[121] Dalrymple was dismissed as "a damp squib" by Hume, and he amused Boswell: "One cannot help smiling sometimes at his affected *grandiloquence*, there is in his writing a pointed vivacity, and much of a gentlemanly spirit."[122] With her interests in historiography, Austen may fold in this Dalrymple baronet also. His resonant presence, especially in tandem with the name of Lady Russell, would conjure up a Whiggish pomposity—an irritant that soon slides into comic relief—that suits Austen's vacuous viscountess and agrees with the novel's other challenges to Whig history.

Austen might still, however, play with a strong naval connection to

Dalrymple, even though these further associations are not redemptive and so do not soften her fictional sketch of the viscountess. The Dalrymple name had cachet in the Royal Navy, where Alexander Dalrymple (1737–1808) transformed navigation as head of the Hydrographic Office. The eleventh of fifteen children, this Dalrymple joined the East India Company, developing a reputation as an explorer and a maker of charts.[123] After publishing *An Historical Collection of the Several Voyages and Discoveries in the South Pacific Ocean* in 1769–71, he became the Royal Society's candidate to lead the transit of Venus expedition. A misunderstanding between the Royal Society and the Admiralty resulted in James Cook being appointed instead.[124] After various navigational projects, including a scheme for coastal charts from the Mozambique Channel to China, Dalrymple was appointed hydrographer to the Admiralty in 1795. The post was expressly created for him "to give official status to the geographical and navigational information he was increasingly asked to provide." Under Dalrymple, the Hydrographic Office transformed navigational information systems, coalescing existing data to engrave hundreds of new charts for the Admiralty "from materials supplied by ships' officers, supplemented by manuscripts in the hydrographical office and by foreign printed charts."[125] When Captain Frank Austen commanded his men to take those painstaking soundings off Simon's Bay and the northwest side of the island of St. Helena in 1808, he—like countless other captains—took on the risky close-to-shore navigation upon instruction from the Hydrographic Office.[126] Although Dalrymple's leadership proved a watershed moment in the publishing of geographical information for the navy, he was nevertheless dismissed by the Admiralty in 1808, for refusing to share "security copies made in 1795" of yet-unpublished material belonging to the French. After hastily compiling a pamphlet in his defense, entitled the *Case of Alexander Dalrymple*, he died of a heart attack brought on, it was said, by the stress of his dismissal. Significantly, Austen selects a name for her supercilious viscountess that not even naval associations might render fully sympathetic.

Elliot, 1778 (Extinct)

The many possible spellings of *Elliot*, including *Eliot* and *Elliott*, add to the ubiquity of this name. It is therefore surprising that, while Elliots of all sorts appear in contemporary navy lists, there is no active main entry in the 1815 edition of Debrett's *Baronetage of England*. This makes the name of Elliot a smart choice for the vain Sir Walter and his vain-glorious heir, the future Sir William Elliot. No citation for the "Elliots of Kellynch-Hall" can offend any baronets by that name, at least not in England. Several Elliot baronets lived in Scotland, however, including one fashionable baronet by the name of Sir William Eliot, of Stobshouse, who might well take issue with the portrait of the story's "heir presumptive" sharing his complete name (*P*, 7). Roger Sales shows how Austen openly depicts the Regency dandy in *Persuasion*'s two Elliot baronets, present and future. Perhaps Austen points brazenly to a specific society dandy, for Sir William Elliott's appearance in London circles was newsworthy among the fashionable set. On Wednesday, 13 April 1814, the social column of the *Morning Chronicle* announced, under the banner "The Mirror of Fashion," the arrival in London of "Sir William Elliott, Bart. at Caulson's Hotel, Lower Brookstreet, from his seat Stobs Castle, Roxburghshire." Because this William Eliot/Elliott was Scottish, he entered Debrett's *Baronetage of England* only through its skeletal Appendix. Playfair's massive *British Baronetage* (1811), on the other hand, provides further information about the chic baronet from Scotland. Playfair, who spells the name *Eliot*, explains that the "present Sir William Eliot of Stobs, Bart.," had "married in 1790 the daughter of John Russell, Esq. of Roseburn," with whom he had many children. The fact that the real-world heir to an extant Elliot baronetcy married a Russell might give a reader pause at several points in *Persuasion*, particularly when Lady Russell expresses her strong preference for William Elliot as a partner for Anne. Whether by accident or design, Austen's combination of names give her final novel an edgy currency.

Another Scottish baronetcy, patented in 1699 according to Debrett's, belonged to the Elliots of Minto. Unsurprisingly, given Austen's ironic pattern of inversion, this family included many prominent navy men. John Elliot (1732–1808), the younger son of Sir Gilbert Elliot (bap. 1693, d. 1766), second baronet and Lord Minto, moved through naval ranks to retire as admiral in 1795, just as Austen's brothers were setting out in the navy.[127] In 1800, Nelson was still praising John Elliot for heroic deeds committed at sea forty years earlier, which he proclaimed "will stand the test with any of our modern victories."[128] The young Austen boys at sea surely knew about Admiral Elliot. John Elliot's older brother, the third baronet, Sir Gilbert Elliot of Minto (1722–77), in turn held the post of Lord of the Admiralty from 1756 to 57 and became Treasurer of the Navy in 1770. His son, the fourth baronet, Gilbert Elliot (1751–1814), became governor-general of Bengal from 1807 to 1813, having apparently begun his career in Calcutta under the tutelage of an Austen relation, Tysoe Saul Hancock, husband of Philadelphia and father of Eliza.[129] In 1813, Gilbert Elliot was exalted in the peerage as first Earl Minto. That is to say, just before Austen began writing *Persuasion*, she was in a position to know how a naval set of Elliots had just abandoned mere baronetage status for a far loftier position in the peerage.

Even before his father's elevation to earl, however, George Elliot (1784–1863), a young naval officer also singled out for praise by Nelson, could hardly have gone unnoticed by the Austens, especially since he served on the same ships and with some of the same officers as Frank Austen. From Calcutta to the Mediterranean and across several generations, the Austen family lived at only a one- or two-degree remove from the naval Elliots: the young George Elliot "entered the navy in 1794 on the St. George with Captain Foley, whom he followed to the *Britannia*, *Goliath*, and *Elephant*," a ship that Frank Austen would command from 9 July 1811 to 7 May 1814.[130] Elliot served under Nelson in the *San Josef* and *St. George* and volunteered for him in the *Victory*: "Nelson then wrote that he was one of the best officers in the navy." After Nelson's death, "Elliot continued actively employed on the home station, in the Mediterranean, and in the East Indies; he was at the capture of Java in August 1811, and the suppression of Borneo pirates in June 1813."[131] Elliot's career at sea, like Wentworth's in the novel, is marked by valor and risk-taking. Like Wentworth, he is the younger son of the landed gentry. And in the summer of 1814, the dapper thirty-one-year-old Elliot commanded his own ship, just like Austen's leading man. Although only the younger son of a newly promoted earl, naval Commander George Elliot would have taken precedence at any social function over a mere baronet like Sir Walter. If Austen has a real-world navy man named Elliot in mind, one who defies Sir Walter's prejudices at every turn, this too may be part of the fun.

The *Baronetage* of 1815 records one short-lived English baronetcy for *Elliot/Eliot*, which appears only in the appendix of extinct baronetcies.[132] In 1778, the physician John Eliot (1733/36–86) was made a baronet by a reluctant George III, who feared the promotion would mean the loss of Eliot as his personal physician. In this manner, the Eliot name did briefly enter the *Baronetage*, exiting a mere eight years later when, in 1786, Eliot died without an heir.[133] In the context of the *Baronetage of England* then, an entry for the name of Elliot invokes an ephemeral baronetcy, a dead end. Austen adds poignancy to historical accident when she dates the loss of her Elliot heir to "5 Nov. 1789," fusing the foiled plot of Guy Fawkes with the terrors of the French Revolution (*P*, 3). Like the real Eliot baronet, whose only legal child died "soon after birth," Sir Walter Elliot, whose only son is "still-born," suffers the lack of an heir most keenly.[134] To his chagrin, Kellynch Hall and the baronetcy will pass to his nephew, who—although an undeserving rake—saves the Elliot line from extinction (4). Austen does not bestow upon her Elliots the fate that befell the real-world Eliot baronetcy. If Austen invokes the historical baronetcy of Eliot, she may do so to stress the continuation of her fictional line and the possibility of its redemption in future generations.

That Austen knew about this one and only English baronet named Eliot is suggested by her linking her own Elliots to the Dalrymples. When Sir Walter Elliot adamantly maintains "family connection" with his "cousins" the Dalrymples, Austen's project of ironic inversion becomes increasingly risqué, for the real Sir John Eliot, physician turned baronet, married Grace Dalrymple (1754?–1823), a woman who became nationally known as a high-society courtesan. Austen's historical allusion to "Mrs. Grace Dalrymple Elliot . . . a fashionable demi-rep" has not gone entirely unnoticed.[135] In fact, the exploits of Dalrymple-Eliot were as notorious as they were numerous. Soon after her marriage in 1771 to John Eliot, professed boredom drove the young Mrs. Eliot to an affair with a known libertine, prompting the husband to sue his wife for divorce and ridicule her in open court, turning Grace Dalrymple Eliot into a "celebrity" who was "much talked about in society."[136] She then began another high-profile affair with a Whig peer who commissioned a full-length portrait from Thomas Gainsborough that circulated as a popular print (fig. 6.3). The press fed avidly upon her affairs, and "month after month the newspapers chronicled her movements." After a brief stay in France prompted reports of further dalliances, she "began her reign as Dally the Tall, among the most notorious of London's courtesans."[137]

The Dalrymple-Eliot history suggests that Austen's careful use of famous names in *Persuasion* may also—as was true for *Sense and Sensibility* and *Lady Susan*—cautiously fold in high-society scandal. Dalrymple-Eliot "pursued her vocation at the highest level, eventually counting George, Prince of Wales, among her lovers." Rumors of a royal connection led the *Morning Herald* to report "The Dalrymple has declared herself pregnant." When she subsequently gave birth to a daughter, she insisted upon royal paternity by baptizing her "with the feminine

FIGURE 6.3. "Mrs. Elliot." Print by John Dean of Grace Dalrymple Elliot, after a portrait by Thomas Gainsborough (4 June 1779). © Trustees of the British Museum.

forms of the prince's names: Georgina Augusta Frederica Elliott."[138] In 1786, Dalrymple-Eliot settled down with the duc de Chartres, by now d'Orléans, in Paris, where she caught even Napoleon's eye, giving him the cold shoulder when he professed to hate the British. During the terror, her connection with d'Orléans led to her imprisonment. After her release she came back to England, where her niece Lady Shelley describes her around 1802 as "the most beautiful woman" she had ever beheld, even though dressed in the "indecent style of the French republican period."[139] While it remains merely conceivable that Austen's cousin Eliza, also known as Madame La Comtesse de Feuillide, had likewise met Dalrymple-Eliot, it seems impossible that Eliza did not know about her. In turn, Jane Austen, who jokingly boasted that she could spot an adulteress in a crowded room, would surely not let the scandalous pairing of Dalrymple and Elliot enter her story unchecked: "I am proud to say that I have a very good eye at an Adultress, for tho' repeatedly assured that another in the same party was the *She*, I fixed upon the right one from the first" (*Letters*, 85). Moreover, a letter to Anna Austen suggests that as an author Jane Austen so routinely researched the surnames of her fictional characters for connections with titled families that she had become a family resource on that topic by 1814: "There is no such title as Desborough," she assures her niece, "either among the Dukes, Marquisses, Earls, Viscounts or Barons.—These were your enquiries" (267–68). Before Austen chose names for her characters, she did her homework.

Stalemate

The edition of Debrett's *Baronetage of England* published in 1815 by a consortium that included John Murray showed proof of the navy and the baronetage merging in ever-increasing ways. Its preface acknowledges the meritorious actions of the army and navy men who had newly joined its ranks. Prejudices against the army aside, judging from *Persuasion*'s balanced worldview, Austen considered such new entries, unlike Sir Walter or her cousin Sir Samuel Egerton Brydges, as legitimate as any of the others, and just as "precious" as Wentworth deems the navy list. Austen's choice of names in *Persuasion* may thus suggest a stalemate between hostilities in the novel: land versus sea; baronetage versus navy list; old versus new. Although she never warms to the army, in her crisscrossing of *Persuasion*'s names from two competing systems of value, Austen shows mixed sympathies. By focusing on names that have risen, through merit and controversy, to high positions in both the *Baronetage* and the *Navy List*, Austen may point out that both systems of rank allow for promotion and change. Both systems are equally meritorious and sometimes corrupt. Theoretically, both systems allow for merit to rise, however slowly, to the top: Horatio Nelson became not only an admiral but also a duke and a viscount. Some of the most ancient families in the *Baronetage*, most notably the homeless Crofts, and "extinct" Russells and Wentworths, need renewal. Their legacies may be coming to an end, or they may yet rally—possibly in foreign parts. Just as these lists are not mutually exclusive, so Austen's modernity is compatible with her respect for rank and tradition. At a time of great change, Austen took the past into account.

Jane Austen's Fictive Network

I HAVE ARGUED THAT Austen consistently references historic families, events, and locations in her work. While I have sketched some of the local interpretive implications of these references to "real solemn history" for a reading of Austen's fictions, I have not speculated about an overarching organizing principle behind her selections from England's past. A backward glance over the families that I have discussed suggests surprising connections. For example, "A Collection of Letters," the earliest piece of juvenilia to use the names of Evelyn, Willoughby, and Dashwood, also includes prominent mention of Grevilles. On 14 July 1776, Lord Greville, having just inherited an earldom, married Henrietta Vernon, daughter of Richard Vernon and Lady Evelyn Leveson-Gower, whose father was the first Earl Gower mentioned in my discussion of *Evelyn*. In other words, the Vernons, those cousins of the Yorkshire Wentworths who would inherit Wentworth Castle in 1802 and likely served as the inspiration for *Lady Susan*, were related to the Gowers, Evelyns, and Grevilles, whose names already appear in Austen's earlier stories.

The close weave of the emerging social network among Austen's names may simply be a historical consequence, given that many families in the stratum of society from which she pulls them (often to bestow them on fictional characters less grand and less wealthy) are related to other families in the peerage. If Austen references in her novels the histories of elite families, such references cannot remain hermetically sealed from story to story. Since Austen's allusions draw upon hundreds of years of England's past, from the medieval to her present, historical accident might also place members of one family in unwitting proximity to those of another. John Evelyn, for example, was a horrified witness to the beheading of Thomas Wentworth, the first Earl of Strafford, by the axe of Richard Brandon. Likewise, the Wentworths of Wentworth Woodhouse, the estate inherited during Austen's youth by the Earl Fitzwilliam, briefly held the title of Lord Le Despencer, which was later bestowed upon Sir Francis Dashwood. In turn, the real Dashwoods married into the Knightleys, after they had already married into the Ferrars family.[1] Given Austen's mimetic realism, it may be inevitable that the *Oxford Dictionary of National Biography* entry for the medieval branch of the "Vernon family (*per.* 1411–1515), gentry" details that family's brief connections with persons who share names found elsewhere in Austen's work, in this case Lord Ferrars and Sir Henry Willoughby. Wouldn't Austen have known that the half-brother of Cassandra Willoughby, the supposed ancestor of her mother, became the Earl Tylney/Tilney in 1731? Yielding to healthy skepticism, I did not think it worth stressing that the rich Allens of Bath married into a respectable family of Bennets.[2] Should I have mentioned that Evelyn's mentor, the Earl of Arlington, was, similarly, born Henry Bennet, or that his daughter, Izzy Bennet, was subject to an "engagement" of such "a peculiar kind" that Evelyn saw her married, at the age of five, to a Fitzroy (*P&P*, 393)? All these tantalizing coincidences and near overlaps may be nothing more than inevitable historical coincidence. And yet, as I have shown, Austen is capable of playfully exploiting some of history's coincidences for interpretive effect.

Any vague sharing of ancestry or coincidental overlaps in titles and pedigree between many of the high-society names in Austen's fiction need not suggest that her selection criteria for a name in a new story included its proximity to other family histories already deployed elsewhere. Even so, I must acknowledge that patterns emerge across Austen's history-infused fiction that cannot be accounted for from within individual novels and stories. As Nikolaus Pevsner remarks of the tightly clustered geography of the London addresses in the novels, "Jane Austen's upper-class characters are all within walking distance from one another."[3] In her choices of leading historical names across her writings, Austen might track a cluster of *related* families, whose complex social network is familiar to her. By means of a judicious clustering of names, she might occasionally signal that familiarity to her reader, who presumably also knows that the earldoms of Gower and Carlisle are related through marriage to Howards and Evelyns, that the Knightleys and the Ferrars families are connected by blood, or that a few Willoughbys grew up in the house of a famous Tilney. For such a genealogically aware reader, the historical names in multiple works might line up in still a different formation than the configurations of names that impinge, as I have shown for some Austen novels, upon an interpretation of any individual text. Just as Austen's fascination with the Wentworths, first noticed by Donald Greene, grows increasingly overt from text to text, linking Darcys and Woodhouses to Watsons and Vernons to Bertrams and Wentworths, perhaps other networks of historic families also connect the characters of her novels across her writings.

I hope, therefore, that the arguments of my preceding chapters will be taken up by others, not only to test my approach against novels that I leave relatively unexplored, such as *Emma, Pride and Prejudice,* and *Mansfield Park,* but to reach a deeper level of historical engagement, one that might expose networks of historic references across Austen's oeuvre. Much fine genealogical detective work, most notably by Deirdre Le Faye, has parsed the expansive history of Austen's own family. Perhaps this same expertise can unearth patterns in the potentially related genealogies and social networks of the historic families to which Austen alludes so creatively in her fictions. At present, I dare not guess at Austen's selection criteria or the connections that possibly exist between her historical borrowings across all the novels. All that I hope to have established is the persistent historicist impulse behind her choices of names and settings. Much work remains to be done, for Austen's historicism surely extends far deeper than can be measured in the pages of a single book.

NOTES

INTRODUCTION. "History, real solemn history" in Austen

1. Henry Austen's "Biographical Notice of the Author," dated December 1817, is reprinted in *P*, 326–32, quoted at 330.

2. R. W. Chapman, *Facts and Problems*, The Clark Lectures (1948; Oxford: Clarendon Press, 1970), 121.

3. Ibid.

4. Ibid., 122.

5. Statement by Wordsworth reported by Sara Coleridge (1802–52), the poet's daughter. Quoted in B[rian] C. Southam, *The Critical Heritage* (London: Routledge & Kegan Paul; New York: Barnes & Noble, 1968), 117.

6. John Aikin, *General Biography; or, Lives, Critical and Historical, of the Most Eminent Persons of All Ages, Countries, Conditions, and Professions*, 10 vols. (London, 1799–1815), 10:61.

7. *DNB*, s.v. "Wentworth, Charles Watson, second marquess of Rockingham (1730–1782), prime minister."

8. D[onald] J. Greene, "Jane Austen and the Peerage," *PMLA* 68.5 (1953): 1017–31, at 1017. Hereafter cited parenthetically as Greene.

9. See Mary Luckhurst and Jane Moody, eds., *Theatre and Celebrity in Britain, 1660–2000* (London: Palgrave, 2005), esp. Felicity Nussbaum, "Actresses and the Economics of Celebrity, 1700–1800," 148–68.

10. Tom Mole, ed., *Romanticism and Celebrity Culture, 1750–1850* (Cambridge: Cambridge Univ. Press, 2009), 2.

11. Joseph Roach, *It* (Ann Arbor: Univ. of Michigan Press, 2007), 3.

12. Ibid., 1.

13. Journal entry by Sir Walter Scott dated 14 March 1826. Quoted in B[rian] C. Southam, *Jane Austen: The Critical Heritage*, vol. 2, *1870–1940* (London: Routledge & Kegan Paul, 1987), 6.

14. Quoted in William Galperin, "The Uses and Abuses of Austen's 'Absolute Historical Pictures,'" *European Romantic Review* 14 (June 2003), 225–31, at 225.

15. Southam, *Critical Heritage*, 2:249 and 250.

16. For a few standout examples of such recent historical approaches to Austen, see Paula Byrne, *Jane Austen and the Theatre* (London: Hambledon & Lon-

don, 2002); Penny Gay, *Jane Austen and the Theatre* (Cambridge: Cambridge Univ. Press, 2002); Jocelyn Harris, *A Revolution Almost beyond Expression: Jane Austen's Persuasion* (Newark: Univ. of Delaware Press, 2007); and Brian Southam, *Jane Austen and the Navy* (London: Hambledon & London, 2000).

17. See Janet Todd, ed., *Jane Austen in Context* (Cambridge: Cambridge Univ. Press, 2005), and Claudia L. Johnson and Clara Tuite, eds., *A Companion to Jane Austen* (Chichester, UK: Wiley-Blackwell, 2009).

18. Daniel Pool, *What Jane Austen Ate and Charles Dickens Knew: From Fox Hunting to Whist; The Facts of Daily Life in Nineteenth-Century England* (New York: Touchstone, 1993).

19. Jane Austen, *Pride and Prejudice*, ed. Vivien Jones (London: Penguin Books, 1996), "Notes," 412.

20. The original Penguin Classics introduction from 1972 by Tony Tanner is reprinted as an appendix to Jones's 1996 edition (see 368–408). Quoted in Jones, 412 and 369.

21. Ibid., 431; *P&P*, 274.

22. Byrne observes that "Austen's use of the names Yates and Crawford in the context of her private theatre may well have been noted with amusement by readers familiar with the famous eighteenth-century theatrical dynasties" that consisted, first, of the tragedienne Mary Anne Yates (1728–87), often compared to Siddons, whose husband, Richard Yates (1706–96), was a popular comedian at Drury Lane, and, second, Mrs. Ann Crawford (1734–1801), known as the "lover of the stage," and her handsome husband, Thomas "Billy" Crawford (1750–94) (204).

23. John Wiltshire, ed., *MP*, 652n5.

24. Deirdre Le Faye, *Jane Austen: A Family Record*, 2nd ed. (Cambridge: Cambridge Univ. Press, 2004), 233.

25. See, for example, Clive Caplan, "The Source for Emma's William Larkins," *Persuasions On-Line* 21.2 (2000); Douglas Murray, "Jane Austen's 'passion for taking likenesses': Portraits of the Prince Regent in *Emma*," *Persuasions* 29 (2007): 132–44; Laurie Kaplan, "Emma and 'the children in Brunswick Square,'" *Persuasions* 31 (2009): 236–47; Christine Kenyon Jones, "Ambiguous Cousinship: *Mansfield Park* and the Mansfield Family," *Persuasions On-Line* 31.1 (2010); and Jocelyn Harris, "Jane Austen and Celebrity Culture: Shakespeare, Dorothy Jordan, and Elizabeth Bennet," *Shakespeare* 6.4 (2010): 410–30.

26. G. D. Boyle to James Edward Austen-Leigh, 7 October 1869, in J. E. Austen-Leigh, *A Memoir of Jane Austen and Other Family Recollections*, ed. Kathryn Sutherland (Oxford: Oxford Univ. Press, 2002), 196.

27. See Devoney Looser, "Reading Jane Austen and Rewriting 'Herstory,'" in *Critical Essays on Jane Austen*, ed. Laura Mooneyham White (London: G. K. Hall & Co., 1998), 34–66.

28. Ibid., 34 and 35.

29. Ibid., 35.

30. William H. Galperin, *The Historical Austen* (Philadelphia: Univ. of Pennsylvania Press, 2003), 2 and 32.

31. Devoney Looser, "Dealing in Notions and Facts: Jane Austen and History Writing," in Johnson and Tuite, *A Companion to Jane Austen*, 216–25, at 216.

32. Claire Lamont, "Jane Austen and the Old," *Review of English Studies* 54 (2003): 661–74, at 661; Daniel Woolf, "Jane Austen and History Revisited: The Past, Gender, and Memory from the Restoration to *Persuasion*," *Persuasions* 26 (2004): 217–37, at 221; and Terry F. Robinson, "'A mere skeleton of history': Reading Relics in Jane Austen's *Northanger Abbey*," *European Romantic Review* 17.2 (2006): 215–27.

33. Woolf, "Austen and History Revisited," 231.

34. Ibid., 232.

35. Looser, "Herstory," 36.

36. Franco Moretti, *Graphs, Maps, Trees: Abstract Models for Literary History* (London: Verso, 2005), 54.

37. Ibid., 53–54.

38. Kathryn Sutherland, *Jane Austen's Textual Lives: From Aeschylus to Bollywood* (Oxford: Oxford Univ. Press, 2005), 31.

39. Ibid., 31–32. Chapman's notes survive in the Bodleian Library, Oxford, among his "Jane Austen Files." R. Brimley Johnson displays a similar impulse in his biography *Jane Austen: Her Life, Her Work, Her Family, and Her Critics* (London: Dent; New York: Dutton, 1930), where he includes quirky maps for *Northanger Abbey, Sense and Sensibility*, and *Pride and Prejudice* that amalgamate fictional and real-world locations.

40. Vladimir Nabokov, *Lectures on Literature*, ed. Fredson Bowers (New York: Harcourt Brace, 1981). Bowers includes facsimiles of the dense annotations found on the teaching copy's first page as well as some of the maps and charts drawn on separate sheets. The remainder of Nabokov's marginalia—a storehouse of copious local observations scrawled throughout the text—is part of the Henry W. and Albert A. Berg Collection of English and American Literature at the New York Public Library.

41. Ibid., 12.

42. Only the folders of lecture typescript and a few notes became part of the text of Bowers's edition of the *Lectures*. Perhaps a future edition of *Mansfield Park* will draw more fully upon Nabokov's annotated copy and sheaf of notes.

43. In addition to Sutherland's *Textual Lives*, see Deidre Lynch, ed., *Janeites: Austen's Disciples and Devotees* (Princeton, NJ: Princeton Univ. Press, 2000); Emily Auerbach, *Searching for Jane Austen* (Madison: Univ. of Wisconsin Press, 2004); Claire Harman, *Jane's Fame: How Jane Austen Conquered the World*

(Edinburgh: Canongate, 2009); and Susannah Carson, ed., *A Truth Universally Acknowledged: 33 Great Writers on Why We Read Jane Austen* (New York: Random House, 2009).

44. The source of Austen's amusement is unclear. The ship's name is a variant of Ponsbourne, a district in London that, in turn, derives its name from the Hertfordshire manor that once belonged to Thomas Seymour and Catherine Parr (widow of Henry VIII). Like people, ships with difficult names often received nicknames from those closest to them. The best-known example may be the famous frigate the *Bellerophon*, eventually captained by Austen's brother Charles, which was dubbed "The Billy Ruffian" by her crew. See David Cordingly, *The Billy Ruffian: The* Bellerophon *and the Downfall of Napoleon; The Biography of a Ship of the Line, 1782-1836* (New York: Bloomsbury, 2003).

45. The Piermont Morgan Library, for example, holds a puzzle-letter from Austen to her young niece, Cassandra, in which all the words are spelled backwards. It is signed "Enaj Netsua" (Manuscript 1034).

46. The name De Courcy, deployed in *Lady Susan*, is another prominent overlap between *Self-Control* and Austen's cache of character names.

47. Although a *claw* is a nail, a *clew* can refer to various knots and ball-shaped yarns (it is even a naval term concerning the knotting of sails), according to the *OED*.

48. Deirdre Le Faye, *Jane Austen's Outlandish Cousin* (London: British Library, 2002), 108.

49. Austen had, of course, already used the family name of Lesley herself in the juvenilia fragment "Lesley Castle."

50. See Maggie Lane, *Jane Austen and Names* (Bristol: Blaise Books, 2002).

51. John Wiltshire, "The Importance of Being Edmund: On Names in *Mansfield Park*," in *New Windows on a Woman's World: Essays for Jocelyn Harris*, ed. Colin Gibson and Lisa Marr, Otago Studies in English 9 (Dunedin, NZ: Univ. of Otago, 2005), 138–47, at 138.

52. Lane, *Names*, 11.

53. Wiltshire, "Importance," 138.

54. Annette Upfal, "Introduction," in Jane Austen's "The History of England," ed. Annette Upfal and Christine Alexander (Sydney, AU: Juvenilia Press, 2009), xiv.

55. Ibid., xxxix and xli.

56. Park Honan, *Jane Austen: Her Life* (London: Phoenix Giant, 1997), 179.

57. Ibid., 225.

58. Ibid., 227.

59. Ibid., 225.

60. Ibid., 224.

61. Arthur Collins, *The Peerage of England*, 3rd ed., 6 vols. (London, 1756), 1:675.

62. Quoted in Greene, 1028.

63. Samuel Johnson, *Mr. Johnson's Preface to His Edition of Shakespear's Plays* (London, 1765), xxiii.

64. Stuart Gilbert, *Reflections on James Joyce: Stuart Gilbert's Paris Journal*, ed. Thomas Staley and Randolph Lewis (Austin: Univ. of Texas Press, 1993), 20–21.

65. "I am more anxious to know the amount of my books, especially as they are said to have sold well" (*Letters*, 84).

66. See Chapman, *Facts and Problems*, 37, and the list of "Books Owned by Jane Austen," in David Gilson, *A Bibliography of Jane Austen* (Winchester: St Paul's Bibliographies; New Castle, DE: Oak Knoll Press, 1997), 429–46.

67. Peter Sabor suggests that the more than one hundred marginal comments strewn throughout Goldsmith were made just before she wrote her own "History of England" in 1791 (*Juvenilia*, 316–51). Sabor includes her marginal comments as Appendix B.

68. Jane Austen to Cassandra Austen, 14–16 January 1801 (*Letters*, 74). No inventory of these books has yet come to light.

69. Robin Vick, "The Sale at Steventon Parsonage," *Jane Austen Society Report* (1993), 14.

70. Jane Stabler, "Literary Influences," in Todd, *Jane Austen in Context*, 41–50, at 42.

71. Jocelyn Harris notices traces of Lockean philosophy in *Northanger Abbey*, to which Peter Knox-Shaw adds proof of David Hume and other "liberal historians." See the chapter called "*Northanger Abbey*" in Jocelyn Harris, *Jane Austen's Art of Memory* (Cambridge: Cambridge Univ. Press, 1989), and also Peter Knox-Shaw's chapter, "*Northanger Abbey* and the Liberal Historians," in his *Jane Austen and the Enlightenment* (Cambridge: Cambridge Univ. Press, 2004).

72. For a fuller discussion of this manuscript catalogue, see Alice Marie Villaseñor, "Edward Austen Knight's Godmersham Library and Jane Austen's *Emma*," in *Persuasions* 29 (2007): 79–88. I am immensely grateful to Katherine Hysmith for sharing with me a preliminary transcript of the catalogue, which she, in turn, received from Jacqui Grainger, the Chawton House Librarian, who reports that a searchable database of the manuscript catalogue is under way.

73. Jane Austen to Cassandra Austen, 14–15 October 1813 (*Letters*, 239).

74. See Jane Austen, *Later Manuscripts*, ed. Janet Todd and Linda Bree (Cambridge: Cambridge Univ. Press, 2008), esp. 245–46 and notes.

75. See John Cary, *Cary's New Itinerary; or, An Accurate Delineation of the Great Roads, Both Direct and Cross, throughout England and Wales* (London, 1798).

76. The *Godmersham Park Library Catalogue* lists "Cary's Atlas London 1787" in folio.

77. *The Treble Almanack for the Year MDCCLXXXVI* (Dublin, [1786]), 5.

78. The growing tourist industry fed a demand for maps of all sorts to aid would-be travelers. From Sandy Lerner I learned of the existence of so-called toll scarves, pieces of cloth printed with tables of distances, tolls, and coach rates, presumably to substitute for paper charts that might not withstand rain and wear as well as those on cloth. The Victoria & Albert Museum owns just such a handkerchief or scarf, plate-printed in red and inscribed "Peele and Simpson, Inv." in one corner and "L. Barwick and Co. Ex March 1769" in another. See Ada K. Longfield, "More Eighteenth-Century Advertisements and English Calico-Printers," *Burlington Magazine* 102.684 (1960): 110–15.

79. From Jane Austen to Cassandra Austen, 29 January 1813 (*Letters*, 202).

80. James Joyce to Mrs. William Murray, 2 November 1921. *Letters of James Joyce*, ed. Stuart Gilbert (New York: Viking, 1957), 175.

81. David Lodge, *The Language of Fiction: Essays in Criticism and Verbal Analysis of the English Novel* (London: Routledge; New York: Columbia Univ. Press, 1966), 45.

82. Southam, *Critical Heritage*, 22.

CHAPTER ONE. "Quite unconnected": The Wentworths and *Lady Susan*

1. Patrick Parrinder, *Nation and Novel: The English Novel from Its Origins to the Present Day* (Oxford: Oxford Univ. Press, 2006), 188.

2. Horace Walpole, *Anecdotes of Painting in England*, 4 vols. (Strawberry Hill, 1765–71), 4:151.

3. See Joseph Wilkinson, "Wentworth Castle," in *Old Yorkshire*, ed. William Smith, 5 vols. (London: Longmans, Green & Co., 1884), 5:208–14.

4. D[onald] J. Greene, "Jane Austen and the Peerage," *PMLA* 68.5 (1953): 1017–31, at 1026. Hereafter cited parenthetically as Greene.

5. Joseph Roach, *It* (Ann Arbor: Univ. of Michigan Press, 2007), 1.

6. To witness the full force of Wentworth acclaim, a reader had to recognize that an item about an Earl of Strafford or about someone styled Rockingham concerned the same Wentworth family. Substitutions of exalted titles for humbler surnames were, however, frequent in British public life. When in doubt, one reached for *Debrett's* or Collins's *Peerage*.

7. Park Honan, *Jane Austen: Her Life* (London: Phoenix Giant, 1997), 162.

8. See *DNB*, s.v. "Dillon, Wentworth, fourth earl of Roscommon (1637–1685), poet." Wentworth Dillon married Elizabeth, daughter of Sir William Wentworth of Wentworth Woodhouse.

9. Austen began *Persuasion* on 8 August 1815. Incidentally, the Wentworth-centered story of *Persuasion* not only mentions Byron by name but also shares his publisher, John Murray, a fact of possible importance that I discuss in Chapter 6.

10. See the frontispiece of the *Juvenilia* volume edited by Peter Sabor for a partial facsimile and transcription of the register entries.

11. See Elizabeth Jenkins, "The Marriage Registers at Steventon," *Collected Reports of the Jane Austen Society* (1965), 294–95. A number of scholars have reiterated Jenkins's speculations, including John Halperin, in "Jane Austen's Lovers," *Studies in English Literature* 25 (1985): 719–36, at 723, and Donald Greene, in "The Original of Pemberley," *Eighteenth-Century Fiction* 1.1 (1988): 1–23, at 20.

12. See the *DNB*, s.v. "Howard, Henry Frederick, fifteenth earl of Arundel, fifth earl of Surrey, and second earl of Norfolk (1608–1652), nobleman."

13. For example, Austen flares up at Goldsmith's bias in a description of the Duke of Ormonde: "Unworthy because he was a Stuart I suppose. Unhappy family" (App. B, *J*, 340). See also Brigid Brophy, "Jane Austen and the Stuarts," in *Critical Essays on Jane Austen*, ed. B. C. Southam (London: Routledge, 1968), 21–38. Brophy points to long-standing family loyalties for the Stuarts, including how Austen's maternal ancestors at Stoneleigh Abbey sheltered Charles I. For a reading of Austen's "History of England" as an engagement with the politics of the 1790s, see Mary Spongberg, "Jane Austen and the History of England," *Journal of Women's History* 23.1 (2011): 56–80.

14. Joseph Edmondson, *The Present Peerages: With Plates of Arms, and an Introduction to Heraldry* (London: Printed for J. Dodsley, 1785), 63.

15. See the full entry for "Wentworth, Earl of Strafford" in Arthur Collins, *The Peerage of England*, 5th ed., 8 vols. (1779), 4:279–93

16. See *Jane Austen: A Collection of Critical Essays*, ed. Ian Watt, Twentieth Century Views (Englewood Cliffs, NJ: Prentice-Hall, 1963), at 154–65. Although reprinted under the same title, the text of Greene's essay differs slightly from the one in *PMLA* ten years earlier.

17. Greene, 1020, and Susannah Fullerton, "'We . . . Call it Waterloo Crescent': Jane Austen's Art of Naming," *Persuasions* 19 (1997): 103–16, at 113.

18. Barbara Benedict suggests Vicesimus Knox's *Elegant Epistles* (1789–90) as the original from which Austen "may have borrowed some of the names she uses in *Persuasion*" in "A Source for the Names in *Persuasion*," *Persuasions* 14 (1992): 68–69, quoted at 68. See also Leslie F. Chard II, "Jane Austen and the Obituaries: The Names of *Northanger Abbey*," *Studies in the Novel* 7 (1975): 133–36, and Elaine Bander, "A Possible Source for Jane Austen's Names," *Notes and Queries* 29.3 (1982): 206.

19. Sir Walter Scott, *Ivanhoe*, ed. Graham Tulloch (London: Penguin, 2000), 15.

20. John Halperin, *The Life of Jane Austen*, 2nd ed. (Baltimore: Johns Hopkins Univ. Press, 1984; repr. 1996), [ix]. For Greene's pedigree of Austen's family, see ibid., [xviii–ixx]. It was also reproduced as a stand-alone piece: see Donald Greene, "A Partial Pedigree of Jane Austen," *Persuasions* 6 (1984): 31–33.

21. Halperin, *Life*, [ixx].

22. Jon Spence, *Becoming Jane Austen* (London: Hambledon, 2003), 90.

23. See the following articles by Michael Charlesworth: "Thomas Wentworth's Monument: the Achievement of Peace," *New Arcadian Journal* 57/58 (2005): 31–64; "The Imaginative Dimension of an Early Eighteenth-Century Garden: Wentworth Castle," *Art History* 28.5 (2005): 626–47, quoted at 629; "The Wentworths: Family and Political Rivalry in the English Landscape Garden," *Garden History* 14.2 (1986): 120–37; and "Elevation and Succession: The Representation of Jacobite and Hanoverian Politics in the Landscape Gardens of Wentworth Castle and Wentworth Woodhouse," *New Arcadian Journal* 31/32 (1991): 7–65.

24. Charlesworth, "Imaginative Dimension," 629.

25. *DNB*, s.v. "Wentworth, Thomas, first earl of Strafford (1672–1739), diplomatist and army officer."

26. Nicolas Tindal, *The Continuation of Mr. Rapin's History of England; from the Revolution to the Present Times*, 4th ed., 7 vols. (London, 1758), 5:398.

27. Charlesworth, "Imaginative Dimensions," 637.

28. Charlesworth, "The Wentworths," 126.

29. Geoffrey Howse, *The Wentworths of Wentworth: The Fitzwilliam (Wentworth) Estates & the Wentworth Monuments* (Wentworth: Trustees of the Fitzwilliam Wentworth Amenity Trust, 2002), 21.

30. Patrick Eyres, "The Rivalry between Wentworth Castle and Wentworth Woodhouse, 1695–1750," *New Arcadian Journal* 63/64, 2nd ed. (2008): 15–47, at 25.

31. Ibid., 25.

32. Tim Richardson, "The Politics of the Garden," *Country Life*, 10 December 2008, 43–47, at 47.

33. See Alistair M. Duckworth, *The Improvement of the Estate: A Study of Jane Austen's Novels* (Baltimore: Johns Hopkins Univ. Press, 1971; pbk., 1994).

34. Wentworth Castle apparently promoted publicity by welcoming tourists and travelers warmly. This led one guidebook to praise "the easy access which strangers have to examine every beauty of the place" (William Mavor, *The British Tourists; or, Traveller's Pocket Companion, through England, Wales, Scotland, and Ireland*, 6 vols. (London: Printed for E. Newbery, 1798–1800), 2:344.

35. Walpole, *Anecdotes of Painting*, 4:151. Although the Godmersham *Catalogue* lists a copy of "Walpole of Painting 4 vols London 1762," its early date suggests that it lacked this closing praise of Wentworth Castle. The 1762 edition did not yet include *The History of the Modern Taste in Gardening*, which was added to the text subsequently, singling out Wentworth Castle as a model. Since the *Catalogue* only records dates for first volumes, a slim possibility remains that Gosmersham's was a mixed set.

36. Horace Walpole to Richard Bentley, written from Wentworth Castle and dated August 1756, in *Correspondence of Horace Walpole*, 3 vols. (London: Henry Colburn, 1837), 1:342.

37. The *Godmersham Park Library Catalogue* lists "Gilpins Observations 2 vols London 1786" as well as "Gilpins Forest Scenery 2 vols London 1791."

38. William Gilpin, *Observations, Relative Chiefly to Picturesque Beauty, Made in the Year 1772, on Several Parts of England*, 2 vols. (London, 1786), 2:208 and 209.

39. Ibid., 2:207–8. Built between 1727 and 1730, Strafford's hilltop castle was a first-generation garden folly. Not built as a ruin, the miniature castle was not to Gilpin's taste; the decayed remnants would probably meet with his approval now.

40. Henry Skrine, *Three Successive Tours in the North of England and Great Part of Scotland* (London, 1795), vi.

41. Ibid., vii and viii.

42. Richard Warner, *A Tour through the Northern Counties of England, and the Borders of Scotland*, 2 vols. (Bath: Printed by R. Cruttwell, 1802), 1:220.

43. Ibid., *Tour*, 1:221 and 1:225.

44. Ibid., 1:234 and 1:225.

45. Brian Southam, *Jane Austen and the Navy* (London: Hambledon & London, 2000), 273; *P*, 271.

46. I'm grateful to Michael Charlesworth for nudging me toward the real Frederick Wentworth, third Earl of Strafford.

47. *Evening Mail* (London), 30 March 1791, and *Diary of Woodfall's Register* (London), 4 April 1791.

48. For the text of Frederick Wentworth's obituary, see *The Historical, Biographical, Literary and Scientific Magazine*, 3 vols. (London, 1800), 1:69.

49. For a detailed discussion of the legal contest over Wentworth Castle between 1799 and 1803, see A. P. W. Malcomson, "The Fall of the House of Conolly, 1758–1803," in *Politics and Political Culture in Britain and Ireland, 1750–1850*, ed. Allan Blackstock and Eoin Magennis (Ulster: Historical Foundation with the Bookshop at Queen's, 2007), 107–65, quoted at 128.

50. Ibid., 127.

51. The Vernons did not maintain the rivalry with Wentworth Woodhouse. In 1807, a newspaper account of the "Grand Fete at Wentworth" mentions how "The Hon. Mrs. Vernon" lost a diamond earring during the festivities at Wentworth Woodhouse, which "was not only found, but uninjured" (*Morning Chronicle* [London], 3 November 1807). Their presence at the annual fête confirms how these Vernons, at least, were on friendly terms with their Wentworth Woodhouse relations.

52. This is why Britton and Brayley's multivolume *Beauties of England and*

Wales (1801–16) inscribes its plate of Wentworth Castle in the 1812 volume dedicated to Yorkshire as "The seat of Henry Vernon, Esq.," even though it was known to belong to Henry's teenage son, Frederick. By the time that Austen composes *Persuasion*, however, Wentworth Castle had become "the seat of Frederick Vernon Wentworth, Esq.," which is how John Neale's famous *Jones's Views of the Seats* still records its ownership in 1829.

53. R. W. Chapman, *Facts and Problems*, The Clark Lectures (1948; Oxford: Clarendon Press, 1970), 49.

54. Deidre Le Faye, *A Chronology of Jane Austen and Her Family* (Cambridge: Cambridge Univ. Press, 2006), 159.

55. Brian Southam, *Jane Austen: A Students' Guide to the Later Manuscript Works* (London: Concord Books, 2007), 27.

56. Christine Alexander and David Owen, eds., "Introduction" to *Lady Susan* by Jane Austen (Sydney, AU: Juvenilia Press, 2005), xi.

57. See, Marilyn Butler, "Simplicity," a review of David Nokes's *Jane Austen: A Life*, and Claire Tomalin's *Jane Austen: A Life*, in *London Review of Books*, 5 March 1998), available online. See also the responding letters by Brian Southam (*LRB*, 2 April 1998) and Trevor Fawcett (*LRB*, 4 June 1998), protesting the lateness of Butler's dating. The constantly updated online version of the *Oxford Dictionary of National Biography* entry for Jane Austen, authored by Butler, currently dates the composition of *Lady Susan* to "about 1795," a radical change from the dates given in the published paper version in 2004, presumably in response to scholarly resistance to her thesis.

58. See *DNB* print edition (2004), s.v. "Austen, Jane (1775–1817), novelist."

59. Although the deceased Frederic Vernon is not named directly in the story, Lady Susan describes his nephew as her husband's namesake: "a young Frederic, whom I take on my lap and sigh over for his dear uncle's sake" (*LM*, 10). The name of her daughter, Frederica Vernon, reinforces this logic, borne out by contemporary naming habits.

60. Alexander and Owen, "Introduction," xiv; *LM*, 8; and Honan, *Jane Austen*, 102.

61. Malcomson, "House of Conolly," 128.

62. Ibid., 127.

63. Alexander and Owen, "Introduction," xiv.

64. Austen's choice of surname possibly plays on the fate of John de Courcy (d. 1219), the princely conqueror of Ulster, who was eventually ousted from his rightful lands by King John and forced to live in exile from his Irish estate.

65. In 1920, Mary Augusta Austen-Leigh (1838–1922) declared Lady Susan to be a "Study from Life" and pointed to the "cruel" Mrs. Craven, maternal grandmother of Martha and Mary Lloyd, as a model for the woman who tyrannizes

her daughter (*Personal Aspects of Jane Austen* [New York: Dutton, 1920], 104). Austen's recent editors, Linda Bree and Janet Todd, instead follow Q. D. Leavis and Brian Southam in seeing a resemblance with "Eliza de Feuillide, a flirtatious widow with a dazzling personality and an eye to the main chance" ("Jane Austen's Unfinished Business," *Persuasions* 30 [2008]: 222–34, at 225). For the original Eliza / Lady Susan identification, see Q. D. Leavis, "A Critical Theory of Jane Austen's Writings," first published in *Scrutiny* (1941/42) and reprinted in *Collected Essays* (Cambridge: Cambridge Univ. Press, 1983). See also Brian Southam, *Jane Austen's Literary Manuscripts: A Study of the Novelist's Development through the Surviving Papers* (London: Oxford Univ. Press, 1964), 145–46.

66. See also *DNB*, s.v. "Vernon family (*per.* 1411–1515), gentry."

67. A good Grubstreet example is *The Genuine Copies of Letters Which Passed between His Royal Highness the Duke of Cumberland and Lady Grosvenor; Her Ladyship's Letters to the Hon. Miss Vernon, Maid of Honor to the Queen* (London: Printed for J. Wheble, 1770), which advertised itself as the "seventh edition."

68. See, for examples, Civilian, *Free Thoughts on Seduction, Adultery, and Divorce: With Reflections on the Gallantry of Princes, Particularly Those of the Blood-Royal of England. Occasioned by the Late Intrigue between his Royal Highness the Duke of Cumberland, and Henrietta, Wife of the Right Honourable Richard Lord Grosvenor* (London, 1771); and *The Adulterer: A Poem* (London: Printed for W. Bingley, 1769).

69. *DNB*, s.v. "Grosvenor, Richard, first Earl Grosvenor (1731–1802), politician and landowner."

70. For a discussion of Mary Robinson's high-profile affair with the prince regent and how it, too, remained connected in the popular imagination with the sordid affair of Lady Grosvenor and the Duke of Cumberland, see Laura L. Runge, "Mary Robinson's *Memoirs* and the Anti-Adultery Campaign of the Late Eighteenth Century," *Modern Philology* 101.4 (2004): 563–86.

71. Deirdre Le Faye states that Warren Hastings had "several connections of enduring friendship with the Austens" (*Letters*, 534). Hastings virtually grew up with Jane Austen's mother as neighbor of the Leigh family in Gloucestershire. On the strength of this connection, he placed his own young son under the care of the Austens at Deane, as "foster-child and pupil," during his time in India (534). He was also godfather to Eliza de Feuillide. Like the Austens, Henrietta Vernon was distantly connected to the famous trial, since the prosecution was fronted by Edmund Burke, member of Parliament for the Yorkshire constituency of Malton, a so-called pocket borough of Rockingham's, and known for his allegiance to the Whig politics of Wentworth Woodhouse.

72. *Star*, Friday, 15 June 1792.

73. Honan, *Jane Austen*, 101.

74. John Rushworth, *Historical Collections of Private Passages of State, Weighty Matters in Law, Remarkable Proceedings in Five Parliaments*, 8 vols. (London, 1721). The whole of the final volume is devoted to the "Tryal of Thomas Earl of Strafford." A partisan historian, Rushworth was an embedded journalist of sorts, serving as secretary to General Fairfax.

75. See Woolf, "Austen and History Revisited," esp. 231, and Jocelyn Harris, "Jane Austen, Jane Fairfax, and Jane Eyre," *Persuasions* 29 (2007): 99–109.

76. The Bingley name connects to that of Wentworth along multiple axes, since a Thomas Bingley (1757–1832), a landowner with a deep family history in the region, was an early partner in the Swinton Pottery soon known as Rockingham Works, the manufacturer of fine ware that operated under the aegis of the family at Wentworth Woodhouse. Early incarnations of the Rockingham Pottery traded under the banners of "Bingley, Wood, & Co." as well "Greens, Bingley and Company." The "Bingley" mark may have been used on Rockingham pottery from 1778–1806, the years that Bingley was a co-partner. See Alwyn Cox and Angela Cox, *Rockingham, 1745-1842* (Woodbridge, UK: Antique Collector's Club, 2001), 384.

77. Greene, 1021. Edward Gower (d. 1662) married Dorothy Wentworth, daughter of Thomas Wentworth of Elmshall; Evelyn Leveson-Gower (1725–63) married Richard Vernon of Hilton, Staffordshire.

78. *The Court Miscellany; or, Ladies New Magazine Containing a . . . Variety of Original Pieces in Prose and Verse . . . By Matilda Wentworth* (London: Printed for Richardson and Urquhart, 1765). One advertisement appeared in the *London Chronicle*, 27 July 1765.

79. Edward Bancroft, *The History of Charles Wentworth, Esq. in a Series of Letters*, 3 vols. (London: Printed for T. Becket, 1770).

80. *The New Eloisa; or, The History of Mr. Sedley and Miss Wentworth. In a Series of Letters. By a Lady*, 2 vols. (Dublin: Printed for C. Jackson, 1781), 2 and 3.

81. Kathryn Sutherland, "Jane Austen and the Invention of the Serious Modern Novel," in *The Cambridge Companion to English Literature, 1740-1830*, ed. Thomas Keymer and Jon Mee (Cambridge: Cambridge Univ. Press, 2004), 244–62, at 257.

82. *Letters*, 186. See Mary Brunton, *Self-Control: A Novel* (Edinburgh: Printed by G. Ramsay & Co. for Manners & Miller, 1811). Over the next five years, Austen periodically criticized (and reread) Brunton's novel, leaving Kathryn Sutherland to conclude that "Mary Brunton's success clearly worried Austen" (Sutherland, "Invention of the Serious," 256).

83. The wife of the second Earl of Strafford was born Anne Campbell, daughter of the Duke of Argyll. A family of Campbells, of course, already featured in Austen's *Emma*—where the related surnames of Woodhouse and Fairfax may reinforce the common name of Campbell against historical coincidence.

84. Woolf, "Austen and History Revisited," 232.

CHAPTER TWO. Mapping *Northanger Abbey* to Find "Old Allen" of
Prior Park

1. The epithet was widely known outside of Bath and apparently stems from a poem by Nathaniel Cotton. Cotton's praise of Ralph Allen ("Rise muse, and sing the Man of Bath!") appeared during Austen's youth in a number of poetry collections, especially those intended for children and ladies.

2. In actuality there were two women by the name of Mrs. Ralph Allen. Allen's first wife was Elizabeth Buckeridge (d. 1736), after whose death he married Elizabeth Holder (d. 1766). Ralph Allen left no issue, an only child from his first marriage, named George, having died as a toddler.

3. For a thorough discussion of Bath's economic rise and fall, see R. S. Neale, *Bath, 1680–1850, A Social History; or, A Valley of Pleasure, Yet a Sink of Iniquity* (London: Routledge, 1981).

4. Quoted from the full transcription of the memorandums by Kathryn Sutherland, "Chronology of Composition and Publication," in *Jane Austen in Context*, ed. Janet Todd (Cambridge: Cambridge Univ. Press, 2005), 12–22, at 16. Deirdre Le Faye, *Jane Austen: A Family Record*, 2nd ed. (Cambridge: Cambridge Univ. Press, 2004), xxii–xxiii.

5. See Benedict and Le Faye's "Introduction" to their edition of *Northanger Abbey*, xxiii–xxiv, and Emma Austen-Leigh, *Jane Austen and Bath* (London: Spottiswoode, 1939; repr. Folcroft, PA: Folcroft Library Editions, 1976), 1. These early visits are presumed to have been short stays with relatives in Bath. For the minority argument that Austen began her novel in 1794, see C. S. Emden, "The Composition of *Northanger Abbey*," *Review of English Studies* 19.75 (1968): 279–87. For further discussions of Austen in Bath, see also Maggie Lane, *A Charming Place: Bath in the Life and Novels of Jane Austen* (Bath: Millstream, 1988), and Jean Freeman, *Jane Austen in Bath*, rev. ed. (Chawton: Jane Austen Society, 2002).

6. See Neale, *Bath, 1680–1850*, 116–50, and Benjamin Boyce, *The Benevolent Man: A Life of Ralph Allen of Bath* (Cambridge, MA: Harvard Univ. Press, 1967), esp. 30, where he identifies a powerful quartet—Humphrey Thayer, Robert Gay, Lord Chandos, and Ralph Allen—as the driving force behind Wood's Italianate vision for Bath. Hereafter cited parenthetically as Boyce.

7. For a detailed discussion of these circumstances, see A. A. Mandal, "Making Austen Mad: Benjamin Crosby and the Non-Publication of *Susan*," *Review of English Studies* 57.231 (2006): 507–25.

8. Jane Austen, *Northanger Abbey*, ed. Marilyn Butler (London: Penguin Classics, 1995; repr. 2003), "Introduction," xi–l, at xiv.

9. J. E. Austen Leigh, *A Memoir of Jane Austen* (London: Macmillan, 1906), 129. In 1897, Austin Dobson had also insisted upon a Bath sale, testifying to the

long-standing nature of the assumption that *Susan* was first sold there. Dobson's introduction to the 1897 edition of *Northanger Abbey* and *Persuasion* steadfastly assumes that Jane Austen sold her manuscript to "a Boeotian bookseller of Bath." He proclaims "Mr. Bull of the Circulating Library at Bath (if Mr. Bull it were) was constitutionally insensible to the charms" of Austen's style (*Northanger Abbey and Persuasion*, ed. Austin Dobson, illus. Hugh Thomson [London: Macmillan, 1897], "Introduction," vii–xiv, at vii).

10. David Gilson cites an advertisement for a pamphlet account by William Legge in the *Bath Chronicle* (vol. 43, no. 2001) for Thursday, 24 April 1800: "This day published, price Eighteen-pence, with marginal notes, sold by Crosby, Stationer's Court, Pater-noster-Row, London; and Mr. Cruttwell, Bath" (*A Bibliography of Jane Austen* [Winchester: St Paul's Bibliographies; New Castle, DE: Oak Knoll Press, 1997], 454).

11. Ibid., 83.

12. Mandal, "Making Austen Mad," 511.

13. See *DNB*, s.v. "Cruttwell, William (*bap.* 1741, *d.* 1804), printer and bookseller."

14. Ibid.

15. See Benedict and Le Faye's "Introduction" to *NA*, xxvi.

16. J. C. Trewin, *The Story of Bath* (London: Staples Press, 1951), 78.

17. Frances Burney, *Evelina; or, A Young Lady's Entrance into the World*, 2nd ed., 3 vols. (London: Printed for T. Lowndes, 1779), 3:237–38.

18. Jocelyn Harris, *A Revolution Almost beyond Expression: Jane Austen's Persuasion* (Newark: Univ. of Delaware Press, 2007), 161.

19. George Saville Carey, *The Balnea; or, An Impartial Description of all the Popular Watering Places in England* (London, 1799), 123.

20. "Let low-born ALLEN, with an aukward Shame,/Do good by stealth, and blush to find it Fame" (*One Thousand Seven Hundred and Thirty Eight: A Dialogue Something Like Horace; By Mr. Pope.* [London: Printed for T. Cooper, 1738], 8, lines 127–28). Pope subsequently changed "low-born" to "humble."

21. *DNB*, s.v. "Allen, Ralph (*bap.* 1693, *d.* 1764), postal entrepreneur and philanthropist."

22. See Neale, *Bath, 1680–1850*, 56, and *DNB*.

23. V. C. Chamberlain, *The City of Bath* (Bristol: Rankin Bros., 1951), 51.

24. General Tilney's pointed remarks to Catherine about his garden and "pinery," which led him to inquire specifically into Mr. Allen's "succession-houses" and gardening efforts, may further nod to Prior Park's extensive reputation for gardening (*NA*, 182 and 183).

25. *DNB* entry for "Allen, Ralph."

26. Boyce, 120 and 257. Richardson's editions of Defoe's *Tour through the Is-*

land of Great Britain, as least as early as the fourth edition of 1748, also mention Mr. Allen and his estate at Prior Park prominently.

27. Boyce, 219. "As Allen's house became better known, so did his face," which sold as a mezzotint by J. Faber Jr.

28. The friendship between Fielding and Allen was of long duration. Named executor in Fielding's will, Allen (as was doubtless Fielding's hope) provided for the impoverished author's widow and children. Allen even extended financial assistance to Henry's sister, Sarah.

29. The eponymous foundling of *Tom Jones* is, admittedly, discovered in Allworthy's bed and not on his doorstep.

30. The imprint reads "W. Williams Del. Pub. By R.E. Peach 8 Bridge St. Bath. J. Shury Sc[ulpsit]" (Bath Central Library, Box A S16).

31. I am grateful to Anne Buchanan, Local Studies Librarian at Bath Central Library, for her help in dating the features shown in these maps.

32. Around the time of the canal's completion it was moved about thirty yards or so south, as already shown in the 1808 map.

33. The real Allen household was also no stranger to the gout, for a "gouty chair" is listed among items sold at the auction on August 1769, in which his niece disposed of many of Ralph Allen's personal effects (Boyce, 296).

34. *The New Bath Guide; or, Useful Pocket Companion for All Persons Residing at Or Resorting to this Antient City* (Bath: Printed by R. Cruttwell, 1795), 49.

35. See J. H. Hubback and Edith C. Hubback, *Jane Austen's Sailor Brothers: Being the Adventures of Sir Francis Austen, G.C.B., Admiral of the Fleet and Rear-Admiral Charles Austen* (London: John Lane, 1906). These soundings were apparently so precise that, as late as 1906, two of Captain Austen's charts remained in use at the Admiralty (194).

36. See Park Honan, *Jane Austen: Her Life* (London: Phoenix Giant, 1997), 179.

37. *The Strangers' Assistant and Guide to Bath* (Bath: Printed by R. Cruttwell, 1773), 100. The same advertisement (with no change in price) may be found in the back matter to Cruttwell's *New Bath Guide* for the years 1775, 1777, and 1780.

38. *The Original Bath Guide, Containing an Essay on the Bath Waters; with A Description of the City; And a Variety of Miscellaneous Information* (Bath: Printed by and for M. Meyler, [1828?]), between 122 and 123. Although guidebook maps were often torn out for use, the Huntington Library owns two copies, bound together, which survive with their Thorpe-based plans intact (DA690 B3 O7 1828).

39. Mowbray A. Green, *The Eighteenth Century Architecture of Bath* (Bath: Gregory, 1904), 128. Copies of Thorpe's original map remain available for viewing at Bath Reference Library (LS/OS B912.423 THO and LS B912.423 THO).

40. Richard Gough, *Anecdotes of British Topography* (London: Printed by W. Richardson & S. Clarke, 1768), 471.

41. *A Catalogue of the Maps and Charts in the Library of Harvard University in Cambridge, Massachusetts* (Cambridge: E. M. Melcalf & Co., 1831), 102.

42. For further details about the history of the Widcombe parish to which Catherine and Thorpe travel in their carriage, see Maurice Scott, *Discovering Widcombe and Lyncombe, Bath: A Short History*, 2nd ed. (Widcombe, UK: Widcombe Association, 1993). Scott mentions also a "large ink-drawing" by Thorpe entitled "Survey of the Manours of Hampton, Claverton, and Widcombe Belonging to Ralph Allen" (c. 1755) (12).

43. Marilyn Butler, endnotes to her edition of *Northanger Abbey* (London: Penguin Classics, 1995; repr. 2003), 249.

44. Edith Sitwell, *Bath* (London: Faber & Faber, 1932), 190.

45. James Tunstall, *Rambles about Bath and Its Neighbourhood*, 6th ed. (London: Simpkin, Marshall & Co.; Bath: R. E. Peach, 1876), 77.

46. David Nokes, *Jane Austen: A Life* (New York: Farrar, Straus & Giroux, 1997), 82.

47. Catherine has driven by the Sham Castle before. During the "several minutes" of silence that begins her first carriage ride with Thorpe, they had an unobstructed view of Bathwick Hill on their left.

48. *New Bath Guide* (1795), 49.

49. Much of the information that follows is corroborated in Boyce, esp. 296–98.

50. See *DNB*, s.v. "Warburton, William (1698–1779), bishop of Gloucester and religious controversialist."

51. Richard Warner in *Bath Characters* (1807) lampoons Stafford Smith as "Gaffer Smut."

52. Ralph Allen's brother, Philip Allen, married a Jane Bennet, with whom he had three children: Ralph, Philip, and Mary. These are, in 1796, Mrs. Smith's deceased cousins. On 10 June 1766, Mary Allen had married a widower named Conwallis Maude, who was subsequently awarded the title of Viscount Hawarden.

53. Again Austen clocks the heroine's progress: Catherine leaves the abbey at "seven o'clock" and, "stopping only to change horses," travels "for about eleven hours without accident or alarm, and between six and seven o'clock in the evening found herself entering Fullerton" (*NA*, 232 and 240).

54. Harris, *Revolution*, 165. See also Keiko Parker, "'What part of Bath do you think they will settle in?' Jane Austen's Use of Bath in *Persuasion*," *Persuasions* 23 (2001): 166–76.

55. Harris, *Revolution*, 165.

56. Ibid., 166.

57. Jane Austen to Fanny Knight, 13 March 1817 (*Letters*, 333).

58. Dobson, "Introduction," x–xi.

59. Ibid., vii and viii.

CHAPTER THREE. Touring Farleigh Hungerford Castle and Remembering Miss Tilney-Long

1. William H. Galperin, *The Historical Austen* (Philadelphia: Univ. of Pennsylvania Press, 2003), 139.

2. A. Walton Litz, *Jane Austen: A Study of Her Artistic Development* (London: Chatto & Windus, 1967), 68.

3. Jane Austen, *Northanger Abbey*, ed. Marilyn Butler (London: Penguin Classics, 1995; repr. 2003), "Introduction," xv.

4. In the Cambridge edition, editors Benedict and Le Faye calculate that the Vale of Berkeley marks the spot where the imagined Northanger Abbey should lie. Because there was "no country house in this part of Gloucestershire which in any way resembled Northanger Abbey as described by Austen," they argue that she "could feel safe in placing it there, without being afraid that some local landowner might take offence in the belief he was being pilloried in the character of General Tilney" (xxiv). A historical resemblance between events at Northanger and the inhabitants of a castle near Bath during the reign of Henry VIII would not compromise Austen's relative safety in this regard.

5. Richard Warner, *Excursions from Bath* (Bath: Printed by R. Cruttwell, 1674–1744), 279.

6. Mrs. Austen was related to James Brydges, first Duke of Chandos (1674–1744).

7. From above, this small eighteenth-century folly looks like the ace of clubs, a shape which led to rumors that playing cards had inspired its design. Unlike the open-air follies of Allen's Sham Castle and Blaise, Midford Castle was built in 1775 as a habitable, if small, residence. In 2007, it was purchased by film-star Nicholas Cage.

8. J. F. Meehan, *More Famous Houses of Bath & District* (Bath: Meehan, 1906), 165, and *A Picturesque Guide to Bath, Bristol Hot-Wells, The River Avon, and the Adjacent Country. Illustrated with a Set of Views By . . . Mess. Ibbetson, Laporte, and J. Hassell* (London: Printed for Hookham & Carpenter, 1793), 112.

9. Meehan, *More Famous Houses*, 165, and James Tunstall, *Rambles about Bath and Its Neighbourhood*, 6th ed. (London and Bath, 1876), 405. Bath guides differ only slightly in their assessment of the distance between Bath and the castle, with a few estimating the castle to lie six miles from Bath. Meehan allows that the walk over Brass Knocker Hill "considerably" shortens a journey, while "even shorter cuts are known to the initiated" (165).

10. John Collinson, *The History and Antiquities of the County of Somerset*, 3 vols. (Bath: Printed by R. Cruttwell, 1791), 3:351.

11. See *DNB*, s.v. "Hungerford, Sir Edward (1632–1711), politician, merchant, and spendthrift."

12. See Charles Kightly, "Farleigh Hungerford Castle," English Heritage Guide-books (London: English Heritage, 2006), 29. Although Kightly describes Baynton's wife as the poet's "daughter," J. E. Jackson identifies her as Lady Anne Wilmot, the earl's sister, in *A Guide to Farleigh Hungerford, Co. Somerset, Illustrated with Ground Plans*, 3rd ed. (London: Houlston, 1879), 15. In the 1690s, the Bayntons may, in truth, have occupied, not the deteriorating ruins of Farleigh Castle, but nearby Farleigh House, which "in the time of the Hungerfords . . . was occupied by their principal tenant" and was reinforced and expanded with stone pilfered from the castle's remains (Jackson, *Guide*, 71).

13. Kightly, "Farleigh Hungerford Castle," 29.

14. Ibid., 29–30.

15. Warner, *Excursions*, 22–23.

16. Ibid., 27.

17. Ibid., 29.

18. For locals during the late 1790s, Farleigh Castle's associations with all things gothic may even have included the recent death of a madman. The *Courier and Evening Gazette* of 10 November 1795 reported: "On Saturday se'nnight Henry Kandall, a poor lunatic, was found dead in the Park of J. Houlton, Esq. at Farleigh Castle. He had broke out of a mad-house in Wiltshire, and had strayed to the above spot, where, lying concealed under hedges for two days and nights, his death was occasioned."

19. Kightly, "Farleigh Hungerford Castle," 23.

20. Ibid.

21. The phrase was in circulation by 1797, as part of Rumford's advertising campaign. James Gillray's caricature, published as "The Comforts of a Rumford Stove" on 12 June 1800, puns in part on Rumford as a location famous for leather breeches (see "Rumford" in Francis Gross, *A Classical Dictionary of the Vulgar Tongue*, 3rd ed. [London, 1796]).

22. Meehan, *More Famous Houses*, 164.

23. Tunstall, *Rambles about Bath*, 403.

24. Kightly, "Farleigh Hungerford Castle," 23.

25. Ibid., 24.

26. Ibid.

27. See *DNB*, s.v. "Hungerford, Walter, Baron Hungerford of Heytesbury (1503–1540), alleged traitor."

28. See Maggie Lane, *Jane Austen and Names* (Bristol: Blaise Books, 2002 and John Wiltshire, "The Importance of Being Edmund: On Names in *Mansfield Park*," in *New Windows on a Woman's World: Essays for Jocelyn Harris*, ed. Colin Gibson and Lisa Marr, Otago Studies in English 9 (Dunedin, NZ: Univ. of Otago, 2005), 138–47.

29. In the novel, Mrs. Allen tells Catherine how she learned the maiden name of Mrs. Tilney from a Mrs. Hughes: "Mrs. Tilney was a Miss Drummond . . . and Miss Drummond had a very large fortune; and, when she married, her father gave her twenty thousand pounds, and five hundred to buy wedding-clothes" (*NA*, 65). After a few more details about clothes and jewelry, "Catherine inquired no further" and dismissed Mrs. Allen's intelligence as insignificant: "She had heard enough to feel that Mrs. Allen had no real intelligence to give" (66). Catherine's dismissal of these facts as empty information may well be ironic.

30. Such conjuring also occurs in Mrs. Crawford's "Autobiographical Sketches," published in the 1830s, when the name of Drummond focuses a gossiper's attention: "'Drummond, did you say?' with somewhat more both of attention and curiosity . . . on learning for the first time the patronymic, as ancient and honourable as any in Scotland, which the claimant bore. 'Did you say the man's name was Drummond?'" (*Metropolitan Magazine* 8 [July–December 1839] [American ed., New York: Jemima M. Mason, 1839], 58–62, at 58).

31. See *DNB*, s.v. "Drummond family (*per.* 1363–1518), nobility."

32. *DNB*, s.v. "Tilney, Edmund (1535/6–1610), courtier."

33. The Drummonds became high-profile leaders in the Jacobite cause. The most "formidable" Drummond was arguably the dowager Duchess of Perth (1683–1773), widow of James Drummond, who played "hostess" to the Jacobites at Drummond Castle. Although allegedly fierce in her Catholic sympathies, the elderly duchess became a curiously empathetic national figure after being imprisoned for entertaining Bonny Prince Charlie and collecting funds on behalf of his cause. See *DNB*, s.v. "Drummond, James, styled sixth earl of Perth and Jacobite third duke of Perth (1713–1746)."

34. By 1769, a modern set of Drummonds had founded a successful private bank with annual profits of "over £10,000," rising to £30,000 by 1795. This banking family, with its "colony of Drummonds round Charing Cross," thrived so that the founder's son, John Drummond (1723–74), married aristocracy. The new wealth of this banking House of Drummond makes a Drummond daughter with "a very large fortune" a potential celebrity reference in 1803, which, like the allusions to the self-made Allen fortune, might also bring this famous name up into the present during the novel's first volume (*DNB*, s.v. "Drummond, Andrew (1688–1769), goldsmith and banker").

35. Patrick Parrinder, *Nation and Novel: The English Novel from Its Origins to the Present Day* (Oxford: Oxford Univ. Press, 2006), 188.

36. Kathryn Sutherland, "Chronology of Composition and Publication," in *Jane Austen in Context*, ed. Janet Todd (Cambridge: Cambridge Univ. Press, 2005), 16.

37. See Tunstall, *Rambles about Bath*, 143, and Warner, *Excursions*, 24.

38. Tunstall, *Rambles about Bath*, 144.

39. Nikolaus Pevsner, "The Architectural Settings of Jane Austen's Novels," *Journal of the Warburg and Courtauld Institutes* 31 (1968), 404–22, at 404.

40. Ibid., 407.

41. Warner, *Excursions*, 24. The Cambridge editors of *Northanger Abbey* attribute Northanger's "cells" to outright error, speculating that Austen meant to refer to study "carrels" instead, which would then imply that "Northanger Abbey was originally a Benedictine foundation" (*NA*, 344n3). Still, Austen uses the term *cells* four times in describing features at Northanger.

42. B[rian] C. Southam, *The Critical Heritage* (London: Routledge & Kegan Paul; New York: Barnes & Noble, 1968), 20.

43. The *DNB* gives seven entries for famous British women known simply as *Isabella* and eight for *Eleanor*: all are famous medieval historical figures born before the turn of the fifteenth century, including seven queens of England and four princesses. See also Lane's discussion of the "Eleanor crosses" (*Names*, 59).

44. Gillian Dow also calls for an expanded view of Austen's influences in "Northanger Abbey, French Fiction, and the Affecting History of the Duchess of C***," *Persuasions* 32 (2010): 28–45.

45. Peter Knox-Shaw, *Jane Austen and the Enlightenment* (Cambridge: Cambridge Univ. Press, 2004), 113 and 112; A. Walton Litz, *Jane Austen: A Study of Her Artistic Development* (London: Chatto & Windus, 1967), 63.

46. *A Picturesque Guide to Bath*, 113. See also John Collinson, *The History and Antiquities of the County of Somerset, Collected from Authentick Records, and an Actual Survey Made by the Late Mr. Edmund Rack*, 3 vols. (Bath: Printed by R. Cruttwell, 1791).

47. *Weekly Entertainer; or, Agreeable and Instructive Repository, Containing A Collection of Select Pieces, Both in Prose and Verse*, 59 vols. (Sherbourne: Printed by J. Langdon & Son, 1783–1819), issue for 11 March 1816 in vol. 56:219–20, quoted at 219. Farleigh Castle's popularity as a tourist destination continued into the Victorian period. In 1846, "Prince Louis Napoleon . . . being at Bath, visited the ruins of Farleigh Castle," where he "made a sketch of the picturesque tower" (*Historical Associations of Farleigh Castle* [Westbury: Printed by W. Michael, 1869], at [3]).

48. Archibald Robertson, *A Topographical Survey of the Great Road from London to Bath and Bristol. With historical and descriptive accounts of the country, towns, villages, and gentlemen's seats on and adjacent to it; illustrated by perspective views of the most select and picturesque scenery*, 2 vols. (London: Printed for the author and W. Faden, 1792), 2:151 and 153.

49. *The New Bath Guide; or, Useful Pocket Companion for All Persons Residing at Or Resorting to this Antient City . . . Embellished with Six Copper-Plate Engravings* (Bath: Printed by R. Cruttwell, 1798), 55.

50. Tunstall, *Rambles about Bath*, 402.

51. See also *A Picturesque Guide to Bath* (1793), 117.

52. *New Bath Guide* (1798), 56.

53. Meehan, *More Famous Houses*, 165.

54. See Deirdre Le Faye, *A Chronology of Jane Austen and Her Family* (Cambridge: Cambridge Univ. Press, 2006), 202 and 225–28, for mentions of shopping, visits, long walks by the "family party" through Bath's countryside and nearby villages, and even a performance attended on 22 June 1799 of a pantomime called *Blue Beard*, which, if seen in the wake of a Farleigh Castle visit, must have nicely reinforced its lore.

55. Yet, as Austen would remind Cassandra in 1805, the two of them did go to the "Ridinghouse" and see Miss Lefroy on horseback (*Letters*, 99). Their own presence at an indoor practice ring also allows the slim possibility that they entertained ideas of exploring Bath's countryside on horseback, or, more likely, of hiring a horse and plain vehicle from such an establishment, perhaps the simple one-horse gig variety that transports characters in the novel.

56. Warner, *Excursions*, 22 and 33.

57. See R. W. Chapman, *Facts and Problems*, The Clark Lectures (1948; Oxford: Clarendon Press, 1970), 38n1.

58. Chapman reports: "On p. 332, at a mention of a woolen works 'called New-Mill belongs to Messrs. Austin,' is a note (I believe) in J.A.'s hand: 'A haunt of the Austens—"the Gray Coats of Kent."'" Gilson includes the book in his own list of "Books Owned by Jane Austen," although he tempers Chapman's enthusiasm by allowing that this marginal note (and one more such) might have been penned by either Jane Austen or her father (*A Bibliography of Jane Austen* [Winchester: St Paul's Bibliographies; New Castle, DE: Oak Knoll Press, 1997], 445–46, item K20).

59. Warner judges Midford Castle, "as it is called," an utter misnomer and architectural folly—"an anomaly in building, equally at war with taste and comfort." "This edifice," he continues, "without back or front, beginning or end, would form a triangle, were not the corners rounded off into towers, which, with its embattled top, Gothic windows, and bastion on the lower side, suggested, with sufficient impropriety, the proud name which it at present bears" (*Excursions*, 20).

60. Ibid., 23.

61. Ibid., 33.

62. Ibid., 34.

63. *Weekly Entertainer*, 56:220.

64. Warner, *Excursions*, 34–35. A Victorian pamphlet about Farleigh Castle elaborates upon, and warns against, Warner's suggestion: "Experimentalists had been known actually to insert a stick, and taste the embalming liquor. In order to prevent further mischief, an iron-barred gate (originally there) has been re-

stored, through which all that is within can be seen perfectly well" (*Historical Associations*, [8]).

65. Ann Radcliffe, *The Mysteries of Udolpho*, 4 vols. (1794), 4:400.

66. Coincidentally, Jocelyn Harris hears in Henry's words an echo from yet another Richard Warner guidebook, namely, his *New Guide through Bath*, a Cruttwell production of 1811: "As Bath has little trade, and no manufactures, the higher classes of people and their dependents constitute the chief part of the population; and the number of the lower classes being but small, there are consequently few whose avocations are not known, and whose persons and characters are not familiar; a notoriety that necessarily operates with them as a powerful check upon all attempts at open fraud, violence, or breaches of the peace" (*A New Guide through Bath* [Bath: Printed and Sold by Richard Cruttwell, 1811], 109). See Jocelyn Harris, *A Revolution Almost beyond Expression: Jane Austen's Persuasion* (Newark: Univ. of Delaware Press, 2007), 182–83.

67. Knox-Shaw, *Enlightenment*, 111.

68. Galperin, *Historical Austen*, 150.

69. Knox-Shaw, *Enlightenment*, 110–11.

70. Butler, "Introduction," xix.

71. See Knox-Shaw, *Enlightenment*, 118. David Hume, "Of the Study of History," in *Essays Moral, Political, and Literary*, ed. Eugene F. Miller, rev. ed. (Indianapolis, IN: Liberty Classics, 1987), 563.

72. James Boswell, *The Life of Samuel Johnson*, 3rd ed., 4 vols. (London: Printed by H. Baldwin & Son, 1799), 2:371. For a discussion of Austen's familiarity with Boswell's *Life*, see Peter L. De Rose, *Jane Austen and Samuel Johnson* (Washington, DC: Univ. Press of America, 1980), 17. The edition recorded in the *Godmersham Park Library Catalogue* ("Boswells Life of Johnson 2 vols London 1791") does not yet include the exchange with Gibbon; the Godmersham catalog also lists "Anecdotes of Johnson London 1786," by Hester Lynch Piozzi.

73. Boswell, *Life*, 2:371.

74. See also Knox-Shaw, "Jane Austen and *Modern Europe*," *Notes and Queries* 55.1 (2008): 23–25, and "Jane Austen and *Modern Europe* Revisited," *Notes and Queries* 56.3 (2009): 381–83.

75. A friar in the book's opening pages declares that "a solemn history belongs to this castle," pointing the narrator to a manuscript in the Mazzini library. Ann Radcliffe, *A Sicilian Romance*, 2 vols. (London, 1790), 1:3.

76. Jocelyn Harris has suggested that "Jane Austen's defense of fiction" in chapter 5 of *Northanger Abbey* may have been inserted in 1816, after several publications in the "ferocious contemporary debate about the status and value of fiction" had spurred Austen to defend the female novelist (Harris, *Revolution*, 20). On the basis of the advertisement alone, Claire Harman confidently asserts

that "Austen was making extensive changes to the manuscript of *Susan*" in the wake of Henry's having rescued it from "Benjamin Crosby's slush pile" (*Jane's Fame: How Jane Austen Conquered the World* [Edinburgh: Canongate, 2009], 77). Even so, no changes other than the title can be unequivocally dated to 1816.

77. Jane Austen to Fanny Knight, 13 March 1817 (*Letters*, 333).

78. The author of *Susan* (1809) was John Booth (Deidre Le Faye, *A Chronology of Jane Austen and Her Family* [Cambridge: Cambridge Univ. Press, 2006, 369]). There has been one further speculation about Austen's change of title. Butler suggests that "Austen seems to acknowledge the emergence of a new style" by alluding in her title to "Simple Susan" (1800), the longest of Edgeworth's tales for children ("Introduction," xxi). But since Butler deftly reasons elsewhere that Austen wrote the manuscript in the 1790s, this connection seems a bit of a stretch. Edgeworth's story concerns a girl who learns to value her pet lamb as a commodity to be sold in hard times. It therefore seems more plausible that Austen later *abandoned* the title of *Susan* in light of Edgeworth's publication, since the coincidence of a shared title with an existing children's story may have pointed too far away from the gothic.

79. Mrs. Crawford, "Autobiographical Sketches Connected with Lacock Abbey," *Metropolitan Magazine* 14 (September–December 1835): 306–18, at 311.

80. William Gilpin, *Observations, Relative Chiefly to Picturesque Beauty, Made in the Year 1772, on Several Parts of England*, 2 vols. (London, 1786), 2:208. The 1786 edition of Gilpin's *Observations*, which contains this passage (already discussed in Chapter 1, in the context of Wentworth Castle), appears in the *Godmersham Park Library Catalogue*. In 1969, Darrel Mansell Jr. observed that a description by Gilpin of Wanstead House in 1809 bears a slight resemblance to the description of Northanger, suggesting a possible late-date revision. In 1973, F. B. Pinion countered that the resemblances are so slight and generic that they must be accidental. While I concur with Pinion that Austen did not need Gilpin to know of regal Wanstead, Mansell was on the right track.

81. John Burke and John Bernard Burke, *Genealogical and Heraldic History of the Extinct and Dormant Baronetcies of England, Ireland, and Scotland*, 2nd ed. (London, 1844), 322.

82. Crawford, "Sketches," 311.

83. A popular poem by Peter Pindar (pseudonym of John Wolcot) also references the duke's failed courtship of the rich heiress, further confirming that the event was common knowledge and much-mocked: *Three Royal Bloods; or, A Lame Regent, A Darling Commander and a Love-Sick Admiral. A Poem*, 5th ed. (London, 1812), esp. 5–6.

84. The wooing was of some duration, since the duke complains in his private letters of the cruelty of being "kept six months on the rack" by "the bewitch-

ing Catherine" (A. Aspinall, ed., *Mrs. Jordan and Her Family: Being the Unpublished Correspondence of Mrs. Jordan and the Duke of Clarence, Later William IV* [London: Arthur Barker, 1951], 209 and 210).

85. Roger Sales remarks that "the Duke of Clarence stayed at Nelson's Crescent at Ramsgate when he was trying to captivate an heiress," presumably Catherine Tilney-Long (*Jane Austen and Representations of Regency England* [London: Routledge, 1994], 205). See also Jocelyn Harris, "Jane Austen and Celebrity Culture: Shakespeare, Dorothy Jordan, and Elizabeth Bennet," *Shakespeare* 6.4 (2010): 410–30.

86. See Rosemary O'Day, ed., *Cassandra Brydges (1670-1735), First Duchess of Chandos: Life and Letters* (Woodbridge, UK: Boydell Press, 2007), 2.

87. See *DNB*, s.v. "Child, Sir Josiah, first baronet (*bap.* 1631, *d.* 1699), economic writer and merchant."

88. Jane Austen may have known more about the larger Tilney family through a possible familiarity with Tilney Hall, in Rotherwick, Hampshire, just fourteen miles from her home in Steventon. Through the Cravens, who married into that family, the Austens could claim another distant social connection.

89. *DNB*, s.v. "Pole William Wellesley- [*formerly* Wesley-], third earl of Mornington (1763-1845), politician." Although this entry is ostensibly devoted to the father, William Pole-Tylney-Long-Wellesley (1788-1857) gets considerable mention.

90. Crawford, "Sketches" (1835), 311.

91. Ibid.

92. Linda Bree and Janet Todd, "Jane Austen's Unfinished Business," *Persuasions* 30 (2008): 227–29.

93. Ibid., 229.

94. Brian Southam, *Jane Austen's Literary Manuscripts: A Study of the Novelist's Development through the Surviving Papers* (London: Oxford Univ. Press, 1964), 86.

95. Bree and Todd, "Unfinished Business," 231.

96. Ibid.

97. Elizabeth Scala, "Editing Chaucer," in *Chaucer: An Oxford Guide*, ed. Steve Ellis (Oxford: Oxford Univ. Press, 2005), 481–96, at 490.

98. Eleanor Prescott Hammond, *Chaucer: A Bibliographical Manual* (New York: Macmillan, 1908), 177. Thomas W. Ross, "Thomas Wright," in *Editing Chaucer: The Great Tradition*, ed. Paul Ruggiers (Norman, OK: Pilgrim Books, 1984), 148; quoted in Scala, "Editing Chaucer," 490.

99. W. W. Skeat, *The Chaucer Canon* (Oxford: Clarendon Press, 1900), 28; quoted in Scala, "Editing Chaucer," 488.

100. Bree and Todd, "Unfinished Business," 231.

101. Le Faye, *Chronology*, 291 and 555.

102. Pevsner, "Architectural Settings," 418.

103. Southam, *Critical Heritage*, 125 and 124.

104. David Masson, *British Novelists and Their Styles* (Cambridge, MA: Macmillan, 1859), 189.

105. Max J. Friedländer, *On Art and Connoisseurship* (Boston: Beacon Hill Press, 2008), 261.

CHAPTER FOUR. "The celebrated Mr. Evelyn" of the *Silva* in Burney and Austen

1. See Duncan Wu, *Wordsworth's Reading, 1770-1799* (Cambridge: Cambridge Univ. Press, 1993), 56, entry 99.

2. See William H. Galperin, *The Historical Austen* (Philadelphia: Univ. of Pennsylvania Press, 2003), 82-105. This chapter is entitled "Why Jane Austen Is Not Frances Burney: Probability, Possibility, and Romantic Counterhegemony."

3. *Silva's* companion piece, *A Philosophical Discourse of Earth* (1676), or *Terra*, was the lesser known, although often bundled with it in later republications.

4. John Evelyn, *Silva; or, A Discourse of Forest-Trees, and the Propagation of Timber in His Majesty's Dominions: As It Was Delivered in the Royal Society*, ed. A[lexander] Hunter (York: Printed by A. Ward for J. Dodsley, 1776). Quoted from the unpaginated "Advertisement," essentially an explanatory list of terminology, at the front. Although the preliminaries lack page numbers, I continue to refer to Hunter's 1776 edition of the *Silva*, thus keeping to information available to Burney and Austen.

5. Robert Southey, "Evelyn's Memoirs," *Quarterly Review* 19 (April 1818): 1-54.

6. John Evelyn, *Sylva; or, A Discourse of Forest-Trees, and the Propagation of Timber in His Majesty's Dominions . . . Second Edition Much Inlarged and Improved*, 2nd ed. (London: Printed by Jo. Martyn and Ja. Allestry, 1670). The dedication lacks page numbers.

7. From the preliminaries to Hunter's 1776 edition, which cites many celebrity encomiums.

8. Abraham Cowley, *Cowley's History of Plants, a Poem in Six Books: with Rapin's Disposition of Gardens, a Poem in Four Books: Translated from the Latin* (London: Printed and sold by J. Smeeton, 1795), ccxvi-ccvii. The old notice by Bernard Lintot remained attached in 1795.

9. Few degrees of separation exist between Cowley and either Burney or Austen. Two editions of the poet's works were published in the 1770s by Thomas Cadell, the publisher of Burney whom Mr. Austen approached about *First Impressions*. Cadell's 1772 edition is listed among the books at Godmersham.

10. Sir Walter Scott, *Kenilworth*, 3 vols. (Edinburgh: Printed for Archibald Constable & Co., 1821), 2:18-19.

11. Michael Hunter and Frances Harris, eds., *John Evelyn and His Milieu* (London: British Library, 2003), 2.

12. *DNB*, s.v. "Evelyn, John (1620–1706), diarist and writer."

13. Simon Schama, *Landscape and Memory* (New York: Alfred A. Knopf, 1995), 162.

14. Ibid., 172.

15. Ibid., 169.

16. For confirmation that this sense was "introduced by Evelyn," see the *OED*, s.v. "avenue."

17. *Sylva* (1670), 70.

18. Jane Austen to Cassandra Austen, 31 May 1811 (*Letters*, 192).

19. By 1785, a "sixth edition" of "The Silva of Mr. Evelyn, one of the best books upon planting ever published," was already being advertised.

20. Mary Browne was twelve or thirteen when she married Evelyn, who was then twenty-six. They did not cohabit for another three years, but their age difference may inflect Marianne's marriage to Colonel Brandon in *Sense and Sensibility*. See *DNB*, s.v. "Evelyn, John (1620–1706), diarist and writer" and "Evelyn [née Browne], Mary (*c*.1635–1709), correspondent."

21. A horrified witness to the executions of members of Charles I's court, Evelyn published a few Royalist tracts prior even to the Restoration: *A Character of England* (1659), *An Apology for the Royal Party* (1659), and *The Late Newes from Brussels Unmasked* (1660).

22. See *DNB*, s.v. "Rose, John (1619–1677), gardener and nurseryman." Evelyn and Rose collaborated on a number of projects, including *The English Vineyard Vindicated* (1666) and *A Treasure Upon Fruit Trees* (1688).

23. In *Fumifugium* Evelyn suggests combating London's increasingly dense and foul-smelling smoke by planting aromatic trees and shrubs.

24. In 1774, the Burney family moved into Isaac Newton's former house in St. Martin's Street on Leicester Square. Although Newton's relationship with the Royal Society was tumultuous, he was elected president in 1703. Burney's new surroundings were therefore coincidentally steeped in Royal Society history.

25. Although the original text of *Evelina* never reveals the Christian name of the heroine's grandfather, instead referring to him only as "Mr. Evelyn," at least one modern editor has assumed that his first name was John. See Susan Kubica Howard's edition of *Evelina* by Frances Burney (Peterborough, ON: Broadview Press, 2000), 36.

26. Frances Burney, *Evelina; or, A Young Lady's Entrance into the World*, 3 vols. (London: Printed for T. Lowndes, 1778), 1:6 and 1:3. This first edition hereafter cited parenthetically.

27. See Michael McKeon, *The Origins of the English Novel, 1600–1740* (Baltimore: Johns Hopkins Univ. Press, 1988).

28. In her biography *Frances Burney: The Life in the Works* (New Brunswick, NJ: Rutgers Univ. Press, 1988), Margaret Anne Doody takes up the inviting near-anagram in the name of Evelina Anville to tease out a number of thematic suggestions (see 40–41, quoted at 40).

29. Throughout the eighteenth and nineteenth centuries, the symbol of the smithy's anvil invoked clandestine marriage, particularly those performed at Gretna Green, Scotland. From the 1750s onward, generations of couples were legally united over Gretna Green's famous anvil (in *Pride and Prejudice*, Lydia and Wickham are initially presumed to have flown there). Perhaps the names of Dame Green and Mr. Macartney, who relates an explicitly Scottish childhood, provide reinforcements for this hovering emblem, as does the clandestine marriage of Evelina's parents with which the text opens.

30. St. James's Park would be significantly remodeled in the 1820s, when landscaper John Nash was commissioned by the prince regent to endow the straight canal and lake with more natural-seeming shapes and reroute the formal avenues into romantic winding paths. In 1778, Evelina's assessment of the park as aesthetically outdated suggests the lateness of these adjustments.

31. Guy Williams, *The Royal Parks of London* (Chicago: Academy Chicago Publishers, 1985), 33. Williams quotes here a newspaper report from 1766.

32. The royal Kensington Gardens gradually became public over the course of the eighteenth century, initially opening only on Saturdays to anyone "respectably dressed." By the 1790s, the popularity of the Broad Walk of Kensington Gardens would outpace that of St. James's Park in the reign of Charles II.

33. Alistair M. Duckworth, "Landscape," in Todd, *Jane Austen in Context*, 278–88, at 278. It is in *History of the Modern Taste in Gardening* that Walpole so praises the aesthetics of Wentworth Castle, as discussed in Chapter 1.

34. Peter Sabor, "'A kind of Tax on the Public': The Subscription List to Frances Burney's *Camilla,*" in *New Windows on a Woman's World: Essays for Jocelyn Harris*, ed. Colin Gibson and Lisa Marr, Otago Studies in English 9 (Dunedin: Univ. of Otago, 2005), 299–315, at 302. Repton's name also appears among the subscribers to *Camilla*, confirming perhaps the intellectual proximity of landscape design to fiction writing at that time.

35. Fifteen years later, Burney wrote what Margaret Anne Doody terms her "only direct and non-fictional political intervention," a pamphlet entitled *Brief Reflections Relative to the Emigrant French Clergy* (1793), which "bravely" defends the status of those presumed to be enemies to national identity and religion ("Burney and Politics," in *The Cambridge Companion to Frances Burney* [Cambridge: Cambridge Univ. Press, 2007]: 93–110, at 94).

36. Far earlier in the formation of the novel, of course, Aphra Behn deployed contemporary associations with the name of Lord Willoughby in *Oroonoko* (1688), for Surinam was colloquially known as "Willoughby Land." *Oroonoko* also fea-

tures other "real" names, such as Byam, Trefry, and Colonel Martin. Behn's use of contemporary names is not yet masked, partaking brazenly of the roman à clef tradition. My point is not that Burney or Austen were the first authors to use names with contemporary celebrity in their fictions, but that they do so with a difference. See *DNB*, s.v. "Willoughby, Francis, fifth Baron Willoughby of Parham (*bap.* 1614, *d.* 1666)."

37. Sabor gives this count in "A kind of Tax," esp. note 2. See also Sabor's small facsimile edition of "The Subscription List to Frances Burney's *Camilla*" (Montreal: Burney Centre and the Burney Society, 2003).

38. Since Austen published anonymously, it constitutes a rare instance of her name in print during her lifetime. See Sabor, "A kind of Tax," 300 and 312.

39. Deirdre Le Faye, *Jane Austen: A Family Record*, 2nd ed. (Cambridge: Cambridge Univ. Press, 2004), 104.

40. See Frances Burney, *Cecilia; or, Memoirs of an Heiress*, 5 vols. (London: Printed for T. Payne & Son and T. Cadell, 1782), 5:379–80. Critics regularly assume that Austen gleaned her title from Burney. See, for example, Halperin, *Life*, 65, and Pat Rogers, "Sposi in Surrey: Links between Jane Austen and Fanny Burney," *Times Literary Supplement*, 23 August 1996, 14–15.

41. Le Faye, *Family Record*, 104.

42. The enthusiastic praise of Austen's novels by Sarah Harriet Burney (1772–1844) may reflect an appreciative recognition of Austen's imitation of the fiction of her older half-sister, Frances. Sarah Burney's repeated declarations of Austen's work as "charming" and pleasurable seem genuine, even if her musings on the "careless originality" of *Pride and Prejudice* allow for a touch of irony. For a brief discussion of the letters by Sarah Burney in praise of Austen, see Lorna J. Clark, "A Contemporary's View of Jane Austen," *Notes and Queries* 43.4 (1996): 418–20.

43. "And I do not like a Lover's speaking in the 3d person;—it is too much like the formal part of Lord Orville, & I think is not natural" (*Letters*, 267).

44. Halperin, *Life*, 44.

45. Betty Rizzo assumes that the opening text of *Evelina* summarizes the plotline of the burnt manuscript. See Rizzo, "Burney and Society," in *The Cambridge Companion to Frances Burney* (Cambridge: Cambridge Univ. Press, 2007), 131–46, esp. 132.

46. For a discussion of the intertextual role that *The Faerie Queene* plays in *Catharine; or, The Bower*, see Clara Tuite, *Romantic Austen: Sexual Politics and the Literary Canon* (Cambridge: Cambridge Univ. Press, 2002), 40–49.

47. Many sources for information about John Evelyn's career existed during Austen's lifetime, including, for example, James Granger's popular *Biographical History of England* (1769), which saw regular reprintings, addendums, and even portrait volumes.

48. Annette Upfal, "Introduction," in *Jane Austen's "The History of England*

& *Cassandra's Portraits*," ed. Annette Upfal and Christine Alexander (Sydney, AU: Juvenilia Press, 2009), xiv.

49. D[onald] J. Greene, "Jane Austen and the Peerage," *PMLA* 68.5 (1953), 1021.

50. See the entry for "Evelyn, of Godstone" in John Burke and John Bernard Burke, *Genealogical and Heraldic History of the Extinct and Dormant Baronetcies of England, Ireland, and Scotland*, 2nd ed. (London, 1844), 188–89. Frances Boscawen (granddaughter of William Evelyn, of St. Clere, in Kent, who had assumed the surname of Glanville after being made heir to a Glanville fortune) married Admiral John Leveson Gower in 1773.

51. The original house does not survive, having been demolished in 1911.

52. William Gilpin, *Observations Relative Chiefly to Picturesque Beauty, Made in the Year 1776 on Several Parts of Great Britain; Particularly the High-Lands of Scotland*, 2 vols. (London, 1789), 2:183 and 184. The *Godmersham Park Library Catalogue* lists "Gilpins Observations 2 vols London 1786" and "Gilpins Forest Scenery 2 vols London 1791." The earlier *Observations* of 1786 gives Trentham only "a hasty glance" (1:69).

53. "The Life of Mr. John Evelyn" by Alexander Hunter, which prefaces his 1776 edition of the *Silva*, does not contain page numbers. The excerpts that follow therefore also lack numbers.

54. Brian Southam, *Jane Austen's Literary Manuscripts: A Study of the Novelist's Development through the Surviving Papers* (London: Oxford Univ. Press, 1964), 37.

55. Gilpin declares in his 1786 *Observations*, the edition at Godmersham, in favor of cows clustered in groups of three.

56. On a detailed map of his own gardens at Sayes Court, Evelyn labeled the paths radiating out from a central point "Spiders Clawes." See Prudence Leith-Ross, "The Garden of John Evelyn at Deptford," *Garden History* 25.2 (1997): 138–52, at 143 and 151. Perhaps this term was conventional.

57. Austen reinforces her story's comedy with ludicrous geographical details about this death, for Rose's lover perishes en route to the Isle of Wight in "a storm . . . which baffled the arts of the Seamen" and wrecked their ship "on the coast of Calshot" (*J*, 236). As Sabor notes, the narrow channel between the mainland location of Calshot Castle and the nearby Isle of Wight is "very narrow, and not known for storms of any kind" (487n32).

58. The first name given to Austen's Mr. Gower is Frederic, a lucky coincidence that may or may not enhance a reference to the then-current Earl of Carlisle, Frederick Howard, a high-profile politician during the 1790s.

59. A glance in a *Peerage* volume at the entry for the Duke of Sutherland, the loftiest title held by the Leveson-Gowers, will confirm the multiple points of intersection between the Earls of Carlisle, the Gowers, and the various branches of the Evelyn family.

60. Harris and Hunter, *John Evelyn*, 40; and Gillian Darley, "John Evelyn's Norwich Garden," *Garden History* 34.2 (2006): 249–53, at 249.

61. Darley, "Norwich," 249. "Evelyn's Plan of Albury" is included in the Pforzheimer Collection at the Harry Ransom Research Center (MS35c).

62. John Dixon Hunt, *Gardens and the Picturesque: Studies in the History of Landscape Architecture* (Cambridge, MA: MIT Press, 1994), 21.

63. Ibid., 22.

64. Ibid.

65. Ibid.

66. Part of the densely wooded landscape at Castle Howard was, incidentally, called Pretty Wood—a name that wished to leave nothing to chance.

67. With "Lord ——" and "Lady——," Austen uncharacteristically resorts to the aposiopesis commonly found in eighteenth-century fiction. With so many resonant surnames already in play, perhaps she does not wish to encumber the final scene, which features stubborn parents distressed over a lost son, with further historical associations.

68. There are nine numbered blank pages between the end of the fair copy of *Evelyn* and the start of *Catharine; or, The Bower* in the third volume of juvenilia, presumably the space Austen anticipated would be needed to complete it. For a discussion of the continuations by James Edward Austen and Anna Lefroy, see "Appendix E" in Sabor's edition of the *Juvenilia*.

69. The version of *Silva* edited by Hunter in 1776 (and again in 1786) was published in York "in two volumes royal quarto." The other Evelyn text is probably a copy of *Numismata: A Discourse of Medals, Ancient and Modern Together with Some Account of Heads and Effigies of Illustrious, and Famous Persons* (London, 1697).

70. In December 2007, Donald A. Heald Rare Books advertised a copy of the second edition of Evelyn's *Sylva* (1670) as "from the library of Chawton Manor, the country estate owned by Jane Austen's brother."

71. Maggie Campbell-Culver, *A Passion for Trees: The Legacy of John Evelyn* (London: Eden Project Books, 2006), 6.

72. Quoted from a conference paper by Elizabeth Heckendorn Cook, entitled "Arboreal Values: Dead Trees in Seward, Smith, and Austen" given at the American Society for Eighteenth-Century Studies in Portland, OR, March 2008.

73. Alistair Duckworth interprets this detail as a sign of security ("safeguards have been taken") against just the type of short-sighted ravaging of the property that Norland's new owners will engage in when they cut down the walnut trees (*The Improvement of the Estate: A Study of Jane Austen's Novels* [Baltimore: Johns Hopkins Univ. Press, 1971; pbk., 1994], 54). These legal "safeguards" prove misguided because they shackled the wrong generation of Dashwoods.

74. Scott, *Kenilworth*, 2:18.

75. The implied etymology of the fictional Delaford ("of the ford") echoes the old manor of Deptfort, which Lysons explains was "anciently written Depeford."

76. Jane Austen, *Sense and Sensibility*, ed. Austin Dobson, illus. Hugh Thomson (London: Macmillan, 1902), "Introduction," vii–xiv, at xiii. At the same time, Dobson observes that "there is actually a Barton Place to the north of Exeter."

77. Park Honan, *Jane Austen: Her Life* (London: Phoenix Giant, 1997), 113.

78. Duckworth, *Improvement*, 54.

79. See Ernst and Johanna Lehner, *Folklore and Symbolism of Flowers, Plants and Trees* (1960; New York: Dover Publications, 2003).

80. Kathleen L. Fowler, "Apricots, Raspberries, and Susan Price! Susan Price! *Mansfield Park* and Maria Edgeworth," *Persuasions* 13 (1991): 28–32, at 28.

81. Ibid., 29.

82. Stephen Derry, "Emma, the Maple, and Spenser's Garden of Adonis," *Notes and Queries* 40.4 (1993): 467. For a botanist's perspective on the blossoming trees in *Emma*, see Shannon E. Campbell, "Apples and Apple-blossom Time (Wherein Jane Austen's Reputation for Meticulous Observation Is Vindicated)," *Persuasions* 29 (2007): 89–98.

83. Gillian Darley, *John Evelyn: Living for Ingenuity* (London: Yale Univ. Press, 2006), 148, and Daniel Lysons, *The Environs of London*, 4 vols. (New Haven, CT, and London: Printed for T. Cadell, 1792–96), 4:363.

84. James Granger, *A Biographical History of England: From Egbert the Great to the Revolution*, 4 vols. (London: Printed for T. Davies, 1769), 4:368.

85. Lysons, *Environs of London*, 4:360.

86. Ibid., 4:364.

87. Ibid.

88. Campbell-Culver, *Passion for Trees*, 31.

89. The Austen family's own mulberry trees at Chawton seem not to have fared as well. Jane breaks the news to Cassandra on 31 May 1811: "I will not say that your Mulberry trees are dead, but I am afraid they are not alive" (*Letters*, 190).

90. *The Home Life of English Ladies in the XVIIth Century* (London: Bell & Daldy, 1860), 70.

91. *Silva* (1776), 306.

92. Ibid.

93. Stew ponds, or holding tanks for fish, dated to Chaucer's time, but became increasingly visible and ornamental in the Restoration. Evelyn's diary entry for 22 March 1652 recalls him making one such pond in honor of his father at the Wotton estate: "After my father's death I made a triangular pond, or little stew, with an artificial rock, after my coming out of Flanders" (William Bray, ed., *The Diary and Correspondence of John Evelyn* [London: H. G. Bohn, 1859], 290).

94. See Campbell-Culver, *Passion for Trees*, 31.

95. While a spunging house, a private holding facility for debtors, is not equivalent to a workhouse, where the poor are forced to labor, these eighteenth-century institutions are related.

96. Isaac Disraeli, *Curiosities of Literature*, 4 vols. (Cambridge, MA: Riverside Press, 1864), 2:326.

97. "Wooden walls" appear in the first sentence of Evelyn's *Introduction*, where he establishes the rationale for the Royal Society's interest in publishing *Silva*: "Since there is nothing which seems more fatally to threaten a weakening, if not a dissolution, of the strength of this famous and flourishing nation, than the sensible and notorious decay of her wooden walls, when either through time, negligence, or other accident, the present navy shall be worn out and impaired."

98. Darley, *Ingenuity*, 193.

99. Campbell-Culver, *Passion for Trees*, 23.

100. See Jocelyn Harris, *Jane Austen's Art of Memory* (Cambridge: Cambridge Univ. Press, 1989), 37, and *S&S*, 449.

101. Patrick Parrinder, *Nation and Novel: The English Novel from Its Origins to the Present Day* (Oxford: Oxford Univ. Press, 2006), 191.

102. *DNB*, s.v. "Brandon, Richard (*d.* 1649), common hangman and probable executioner of Charles I."

103. *DNB*, s.v. "Bertie [née Willoughby; other married name Brandon], Katherine, duchess of Suffolk (1519–1580), noblewoman and protestant patron." She "became the subject of a popular Elizabethan ballad that continued to be sung into the eighteenth century." Her story also appears in Foxe's *Acts and Monuments* as well as inventories such as Collins's *Peerage*.

CHAPTER FIVE. Hell-Fire Jane: Dashwood Celebrity and *Sense and Sensibility*

1. Among modern critics, only Jocelyn Harris observes a connection, noting parenthetically that "Marianne is named, as if by association, for a rake famous for diabolism, Dashwood" (*Jane Austen's Art of Memory* [Cambridge: Cambridge Univ. Press, 1989], 72).

2. Jane Austen's brother Frank attended school at Portsmouth with a "Mr. Dashwood" (Park Honan, *Jane Austen: Her Life* [London: Phoenix Giant, 1997], 2).

3. For detailed family trees of the related ancestry of the various Austen families from Kent, see "Appendix II" in David Waldron Smithers, *Jane Austen in Kent* (Westerham, UK: Hurtwood Publications, 1981), 109–24.

4. See *DNB*, s.v. "Lee [née Dashwood], Rachel Fanny Antonia (1773?–1829)," as well as Ronald Fuller, *Hell-Fire Francis* (London: Chatto & Windus, 1939), esp. 252–68.

5. See Fuller, *Hell-Fire*, 258, and Tim Knox for the National Trust, *West Wycombe Park* (London: National Trust, 2001), 56.

6. See *S&S*, xxiii, and David Gilson, *A Bibliography of Jane Austen* (Winchester: St Paul's Bibliographies; New Castle, DE: Oak Knoll Press, 1997), 7–8.

7. Deirdre Le Faye, *Jane Austen: A Family Record*, 2nd ed. (Cambridge: Cambridge Univ. Press, 2004), 259; or Brian Southam, *Jane Austen's Literary Manuscripts: A Study of the Novelist's Development through the Surviving Papers* (London: Oxford Univ. Press, 1964), 53.

8. Southam, *Literary Manuscripts*, 55.

9. Harris, *Art of Memory*, 35. Harris stresses that Laetitia Barbauld's 1804 edition of Richardson's correspondence precipitated substantive revisions to *S&S* (see 34–37).

10. Deidre Le Faye, *A Chronology of Jane Austen and Her Family* (Cambridge: Cambridge Univ. Press, 2006), 201. This remark may also be found in the *Cambridge Edition of the Works of Jane Austen*, where a summary chronology by Le Faye is included in each volume.

11. Roger Sales, *Jane Austen and Representations of Regency England* (London: Routledge, 1994), 109.

12. For shared Dilettanti connections between Dashwood's association with Bacchus and the popular images of Lady Hamilton as a Bacchante, see Bruce Redford, *Dilettanti: The Antic and the Antique in Eighteenth-Century England* (Los Angeles: J. Paul Getty Museum, 2008), esp. 135.

13. Sales, *Regency*, 193.

14. The restored house and gardens of West Wycombe Park (edited from Sir Francis's day) remain open to the public, under the supervision of the National Trust.

15. A radical minority has treated *Sense and Sensibility* as surprisingly frank about the body and sexuality, including Eve Kosofsky Sedgwick, "Jane Austen and the Masturbating Girl," *Critical Inquiry* 17.4 (1991): 818–37; Jill Heydt-Stevenson, *Austen's Unbecoming Conjunctions: Subversive Laughter, Embodied History* (New York: Palgrave Macmillan, 2005); and Marie E. McAllister, "'Only to Sink Deeper': Venereal Disease in *Sense and Sensibility*," *Eighteenth-Century Fiction* 17.1 (2004): 87–110.

16. For mentions of this as the club motto, see *DNB*, s.v. "Sir Francis Dashwood (1708–81)" and "Franciscans [Monks of Medmenham] (*act. c.*1750–*c.*1776)." The club also used other slogans, including "Fay Ce Que Voudras." Although Sabor lists many "possible sources" for Austen's choice of title, he convincingly offers an earlier comedy by Garrick, entitled *Bon Ton; or, High Life Above Stairs* (1775), as the "most likely source" to testify to a shared vocabulary between brother and sister (*J*, 427–28). Suggestively, the strong connections between Garrick and Dashwood reinforce the possibility that Austen, like her brother, recognized in Garrick's line the rakish creed of West Wycombe: Garrick was a close friend of John Wilkes as well as John Montagu, fourth Earl of Sandwich, both of whom

were members of Sir Francis's Hell-Fire Club. Certainly by 1775, the cognoscenti in Garrick's circle would have recognized the club's rakish motto, which Hogarth had placed in members' portraits.

17. Sales, *Regency*, 66 and 68.

18. "I am proud to say that I have a very good eye at an Adultress, for tho' repeatedly assured that another in the same party was the *She*, I fixed upon the right one from the first" (*Letters*, 85).

19. Southam, *Critical Heritage*, 36.

20. Redford, *Dilettanti*, 33. See also the family history written by a modern descendant, namesake, and eleventh Baronet, Sir Francis Dashwood, *The Dashwoods of West Wycombe* (London: Aurum Press, 1987), who claims that Wilkes's writings "sought to blacken [Le Despencer's] reputation" (222).

21. For some years Sir Robert Austen represented the constituency of New Romney in Parliament, a responsibility he passed on to his brother-in-law, Sir Francis, second Baronet, in 1741. In 1761 this same New Romney seat was held by Thomas Knight of Godmersham, who adopted Austen's brother Edward. Le Faye takes data from R. A. Austen-Leigh's *Pedigrees of Austen* to document "one line" of Austens, referring also to "many families by the name of Austen/Austin in Kent" less or more connected to the Steventon Austens, who date their family back to the sixteenth century (*Letters*, 484). See also, Smithers, *Austen in Kent*, 109–24.

22. Mary King, mother of the reigning baronet during Austen's youth, possibly makes a cameo appearance in *Pride and Prejudice*, along with her uncle. In that novel Mr. Wickham, a perfect homophone for Wycombe, pursues a rich heiress named Mary King but finds her uncle too quick-witted for his schemes. The real Mary King's famous uncle rose from the lowly post of country vicar at West Wycombe to that of archdeacon of Colchester and master of the Charterhouse of London. The genuine King fortune thus exemplifies the rewards of the churchly career path that George Wickham rejects, ironically, as insufficiently ambitious.

23. By 1755 Sir Francis Dashwood needed the full-time assistance of John Donowell, who had a hand in a few garden buildings but dedicated himself to the remodeling of the main house, a project that only reached completion in 1771. The final plans of his completed north and south façades at West Wycombe were included in updated editions of Colin Campbell's *Vitruvius Britannicus; or, The British Architect*, an elegant multivolume collection of Britain's architectural landmarks listed in the *Godmersham Park Library Catalogue*.

24. The phrase "Hell-Fire Club," while now definitively associated with Sir Francis Dashwood, was first coined in the 1720s to denote earlier clubs of rakes.

25. In addition to Fuller, see E. Beresford Chancellor, *The Hell Fire Club* (London: Philip Allan & Co., 1925); Donald McCormick, *The Hell-Fire Club:*

The Story of the Amorous Knights of Wycombe (London: Jarrolds, 1958); and Daniel P. Mannix, *The Hell Fire Club* (New York: Ballantine Books, 1959). Proving that the Dashwoods continue to fascinate are Fergus Linnane, *The Lives of the English Rakes* (London: Portrait, 2006), and Tony Perrottet, *The Sinner's Grand Tour: A Journey through the Historical Underbelly of Europe* (New York: Broadway Paperbacks, 2011).

26. Stephanie Ross, *What Gardens Mean* (Chicago: Univ. of Chicago Press, 1998), 66.

27. His wife, Sarah Moore, was a direct descendant of the sister of poet John Milton.

28. Knox, *West Wycombe Park*, 57.

29. Ibid.

30. Ibid. In all fairness, the real Sir John Dashwood eventually repented and reformed. But Jane Austen would not live to see Sir John, transformed by loss and old age, turn pious teetotaler.

31. For information on club membership, see *DNB* entry for "Franciscans."

32. See Sir Nathaniel William Wraxall, *The Historical and the Posthumous Memoirs of my Own Time, from 1772 to 1784*, 2 vols. (London, 1815); I quote from Henry B. Wheatley's 1884 edition (2:18). The *Godmersham Park Library Catalogue* lists the earlier "Wraxalls Memoirs 2 vols London 1777."

33. See Michael Charlesworth, ed., *The English Garden: Literary Sources and Documents*, 3 vols. (Robertsbridge, UK: Helm, 1993).

34. Carole Fabricant, "Binding and Dressing Nature's Loose Tresses: The Ideology of Augustan Landscape Design," in *Studies in Eighteenth-Century Culture*, vol. 8, ed. Roseann Runte (Madison: Univ. of Wisconsin Press, 1979): 109–35, at 111.

35. James Turner, "The Sexual Politics of Landscape: Images of Venus in Eighteenth-Century English Poetry and Landscape Gardening," in *Studies in Eighteenth-Century Culture*, vol. 11, ed. Harry C. Payne (Madison: Univ. of Wisconsin Press, 1982): 343–66, at 351.

36. Ross, *Gardens*, 66.

37. Ibid., 68. This temple was destroyed in 1819, "its statuary having been sold off years before" (Knox, *West Wycombe Park*, 42). Reconstructed in 1982, the temple currently shelters a cast of the Venus de Milo.

38. *Public Advertiser*, 2 June 1763, 2.

39. Ibid.

40. Mannix, *Hell Fire Club*, 5. Admittedly, Mannix's 1959 account constitutes unabashed sensationalism packaged as a thirty-five-cent paperback, complete with lurid cover. And yet Mannix best captures the visceral quality of West Wycombe rumor, which is—after all—what is at issue here.

41. Ross, *Gardens*, 70.

42. Lady Llanover, ed., *The Autobiography and Correspondence of Mary Granville, Mrs. Delany; with Interesting Reminiscences of King George the Third and Queen Charlotte*, 2nd ser., 3 vols. (London: R. Bentley, 1861), 3:162. I learned of this journal entry from Lisa Moore, "Queer Gardens: Mary Delany's Flowers and Friendships," *Eighteenth-Century Studies* 39.1 (2005): 49–70, at 57. Moore then kindly tracked down the full entry for me.

43. Chancellor, *Hell Fire Club*, 7.

44. *The Fruit-Shop: A Tale* (London: Printed for C. Moran, 1765) and *Nocturnal Revels; or, The History of the King's Place, and other Modern Nunneries. Containing their Mysteries . . . with the Portraits of the most Celebrated Demireps and Courtezans of this Period. By a Monk of the Order of St. Francis*, 2nd ed., 2 vols. (London: Printed for M. Goadby, 1779).

45. *Nocturnal Revels*, [vii–viii].

46. Ibid., [xi] and [xii].

47. "Intercourse between monks and nuns (unidentified mistresses or, more probably, prostitutes) was the subject of conjectural articles in the *Town and Country Magazine* in 1769, 1771, and 1773" (*DNB* entry for "Franciscans").

48. See, for example, *A Select Collection of the Most Interesting Letters on the Government, Liberty, and Constitution of England*, 3 vols. (London : Printed for J. Almon, 1763); *A New and Impartial Collection of Interesting Letters, from the Public Papers . . . Written by Persons of Eminence*, 2 vols. (London: Printed for J. Almon, 1767); *The New Foundling Hospital for Wit. Being a Collection of Several Curious Pieces, in Verse and Prose* (London, 1768); Augustus Henry Fitzroy Grafton, *Letters between the Duke of Grafton, the Earls of Halifax, Egremont, Chatham, Temple, and Talbot, Baron Bottetourt, Rt. Hon. Henry Bilson Legge* (London, 1769); *The Humours of the Times, Being a Collection of Several Curious Pieces, in Verse and Prose. By the Most Celebrated Geniusses* (London, 1771); or *The North Briton, XLVI. Numbers Complete. By John Wilkes, Esq. C. Churchill, and Others*, 4 vols. (London, 1772).

49. "Particular Account of the Monastery of St. Francis," in *Town and Country Magazine*, May 1773, 245–46, at 245. This piece elliptically refers to Sir Francis Dashwood only as "Sir Francis Wronghead"—the name of a country squire in *The Provoked Husband*.

50. Quoted in McCormick, *Hell-Fire Club*, 183. Jemmy Twitcher, a character from *The Beggar's Opera*, was by then the well-known nickname of Lord Sandwich. *The Life, Adventures, Intrigues and Amours of the Celebrated Jemmy Twicher*, by J. Brough, for example, had been published in 1770. McCormick identifies the "Circumnavigator" as Sir Joseph Banks and suggests "W. Salamander" may refer to Joseph Salvador, F.R.S.

51. Charles Churchill, *The Candidate: A Poem* (London: Printed for the Author, 1764).

52. The anonymous ode even opens with a line about the removal of secrecy: "The midnight orgies you reveal,/Nor Dashwood's cloister'd rites conceal." Quoted from *The New Foundling Hospital for Wit. Being a Collection of Fugitive Pieces, in Prose and Verse, Not in Any Other Collection*, 6 vols. (London: Printed for J. Debrett, 1784), 2:97.

53. Ibid., 2:97–100; Wilkes's essay can be found in this 1784 edition, at 3:75–80.

54. Ibid., 2:182–83, and Heydt-Stevenson, *Unbecoming Conjunctions*, 160; she notes that Garrick's poem first appeared in the 1771 edition of *The New Foundling Hospital for Wit*.

55. McCormick, *Hell-Fire Club*, 35.

56. Both Hogarth and Knapton painted Sir Francis in a friar's habit at his so-called devotions. Knapton's Dashwood, wine glass in hand and tonsured, worships a miniature Venus. Hogarth's portrait adds a cameo of Lord Sandwich to Sir Francis's halo. Nathaniel Dance painted him as an anti-saint, too, complete with demonic paraphernalia and skull. The French artist Carpentier shows a "round-faced, rather pensive" Dashwood, perhaps in mock-cherubic fashion (ibid., 35–36). Hogarth also painted all three Vansittart brothers in the recognizable costume of the club in the 1750s. The *Godmersham Park Library Catalogue* does not, of course, inventory loose prints, although it does list "Hogarth 2 vols London 1808" in quarto.

57. McCormick, *Hell-Fire Club*, 190.

58. In a letter dated 18–19 December 1798, Austen describes her family as "great Novel-readers & not ashamed of being so" (*Letters*, 26).

59. Sir Walter Scott, "Charles Johnstone," in *Lives of the Novelists* (Paris: A. & W. Galignani, 1825), 157–72, at 162.

60. Ibid., 163.

61. Charles Johnstone, *Chrysal; or, The Adventures of a Guinea*, 4 vols. (London: Printed for T. Cadell, 1794), 3:189. I quote this edition because of its relative proximity to *Sense and Sensibility*'s manuscript beginnings.

62. Ibid., 3:190–91.

63. Knox, *West Wycombe Park*, 37.

64. See *DNB* entry for "Charles Cooke (1759/60–1816), publisher" found s.v. "Cooke, John (1730/31–1810), publisher."

65. *Chrysal; or, The Adventures of a Guinea . . . Embellished with Superb Engravings*, 3 vols. (London: Printed for C. Cooke, 1797). Some of the plates in Cooke's small-format edition are signed "E. F. Burney" and "J. Burney." Edward Burney, who launched his career with watercolor illustrations for his cousin's novel *Evelina* in 1778, also illustrated *Arabian Nights, Humphry Clinker*, and *Pamela*. I cannot locate a "J. Burney" among the known clan of Burney artists. Edward did have a brother, James Adolphus, who died in 1798, allowing the 1797

date to just work for him—yet he is not known to have been an artist. Hans Hammelmann's entry for Edward Burney in *Book Illustrators in Eighteenth-Century England*, ed. T. S. R. Boase (New Haven: Paul Mellon Centre for Studies in British Art, 1975), judges the "J. Burney" signature as "probably a misprint" (23).

66. John Britton and Edward Wedlake Brayley, *The Beauties of England and Wales*, 18 vols. (London: Printed by T. Maiden for Vernor & Hook, 1801–16), 1:375. The volume on Bedfordshire, Berkshire, and Buckinghamshire, which contains the entry on Medmenham (as well as on West Wycombe), was published in 1801.

67. For a discussion of this canonizing quality, see Richard C. Taylor, "James Harrison, The Novelist's Magazine, and the Early Canonizing of the English Novel," *Studies in English Literature, 1500–1900*, 33.3 (1993): 629–43. When the short "lives" that Scott wrote as prefaces for each of Ballantyne's volumes were gathered together in 1825, in imitation of Samuel Johnson's *Lives of the Poets*, Charles Johnstone took an enviable seat on the contents page between Smollett and Sterne.

68. Scott, "Johnstone," 160.

69. William Davis, *Olio of Bibliographical and Literary Anecdotes and Memoranda* (London: Printed for W. Davis, Bookseller, 1817), 13–21.

70. Although "Wraxalls Memoirs 2 vols London 1777" is listed in the *Godmersham Park Library Catalogue*, this was the earlier of his memoirs—which did not yet mention the Dashwood club.

71. Honan, *Jane Austen*, 71.

72. Humphry Repton, *Observations on the Theory and Practice of Landscape Gardening. Including some Remarks on Grecian and Gothic Architecture* (London: Printed by T. Bensley for J. Taylor, 1803), 4.

73. Britton and Brayley, *Beauties*, 1:360.

74. See Jane Austen to Cassandra Austen, Thursday, 20 May 1813 (*Letters*, 210).

75. See the entry for "October 5th" in R. Chambers, *The Book of Days, a Miscellany of Popular Antiquities* (London and Edinburgh: Chambers, 1869). Chambers records famous examples of this practice among the British court, including Isabella, the wife of Richard, brother of Henry III, who, dying in 1239, ordered her heart to be sent in a cup to her own brother, an abbot at Tewkesbury. Eventually the heart of her murdered son was similarly sent in a golden vase to Westminster Abbey, where it was placed in the tomb of Edward the Confessor with an inscription announcing: "I bequeath to my father my heart pierced with the dagger."

76. Capt. Edward Thompson, ed., *The Poems and Miscellaneous Compositions of Paul Whitehead* (London: Printed for G. Kearsley, in Fleet Street, and J. Ridley, in St. James's Street, 1777), lvii. See also *DNB*, s.v. "Whitehead, Paul (1710–1774), satirist."

77. Thompson, *Paul Whitehead*, lv. The more than one-hundred references to *hearts* in *Sense and Sensibility* need not, of course, be explained by this contemporary Dashwood association, even if they do outnumber those in any other Austen novel.

78. Honan, *Jane Austen*, 40.

79. *Letters*, 544. See also Honan, *Jane Austen*, 105.

80. Knox, *West Wycombe Park*, 50.

81. Anthony Lefroy married Elizabeth Langlois (1720–82), the daughter of his partner Peter Langlois—for whom they named both their sons, Anthony Peter (Tom Lefroy's father) and Isaac Peter George (who married Anne Brydges, making her the "Mrs. Lefroy" who befriended Jane Austen). Tom was officially Thomas Langlois Lefroy, a name that reflects this heritage. The fact that the Lefroys closest to Jane Austen descended from both sides of an antiquities partnership begun in Livorno increases the likelihood that they served as the conduit for stories about the West Wycombe dealings of Anthony Lefroy. See also the family tree of the Lefroys in Le Faye, *Family Record* (pedigree no. x).

82. Betty Kemp, *Sir Francis Dashwood: An Eighteenth-Century Independent* (New York: St. Martins, 1967), 117; Knox, *West Wycombe Park*, 50. Knox traces specific objects back to the Leghorn suppliers: the "small, richly carved sarcophagus is perhaps the 'Sarcophage of Volterra,' supplied by the antiquaries Lefroy and Charron of Leghorn (Livorno) for £11 10s in 1755" (7). Quoting family papers, the most recent Sir Francis Dashwood, eleventh Baronet, describes how "pictures as well as busts, figures and marble slabs" were shipped from Italy in the *Fortune*, part-owned by Sir Francis for the purpose. Regular shipments from Italy held "lemons and oranges, Arteminia wine and 'an olive tree for your garden.'" On the return journeys, "the *Fortune* was loaded with crates of red herrings" (*The Dashwoods of West Wycombe* [London: Aurum Press, 1987], 217).

83. Dashwood, *Dashwoods*, 217.

84. Kemp, *Sir Francis Dashwood*, 117.

85. Claire Tomalin, *Jane Austen: A Life* (New York: Vintage, 1999), 121.

86. Honan, *Jane Austen*, 63.

87. Le Faye, *Family Record*, 92.

88. *The Fashionable Cypriad: In a Series of Elegant and Interesting Letters, with Correlative Anecdotes of the Most Distinguished Characters in Great Britain and Ireland. Part I* (London, 1798), 127–28. In the second edition, the name of the "respectable farmer" appears as "P——tt."

89. Knox, *West Wycombe Park*, 56. Knox adds only that he "was described in the *New Sporting Magazine* as 'certainly the best Master of Harriers England ever saw and one of the best judges of horses.'"

90. Ibid.

91. Repton, *Observations*, 30.

92. Ibid., 32.

93. Ibid., 35. To be fair, in *An Enquiry into the Changes of Taste in Landscape Gardening* (London: Printed for J. Taylor, 1806), Repton joined the call against short-sighted tree cutting: "The change of fashion in Gardening destroys the work of ages, when lofty avenues are cut down for no other reason but because they were planted in straight rows, according to the fashion of former times" (27).

94. For a fuller discussion of Austen's complicated relationship to Repton, see Alistair M. Duckworth, *The Improvement of the Estate: A Study of Jane Austen's Novels* (Baltimore: Johns Hopkins Univ. Press, 1971; pbk., 1994). By contrast, John Dixon Hunt argues for affinities between Austen and Repton in *Gardens and the Picturesque: Studies in the History of Landscape Architecture* (Cambridge, MA: MIT Press, 1994).

95. William Gilpin, *Remarks on Forest Scenery, And Other Woodland Views*, 2 vols. (London: Printed for R. Blamire, 1791), 2:305. See also Copeland's note (*S&S*, 483n12). In 1800 Austen herself had grieved for fallen trees, although these were damaged by a natural storm: "What I regret more than all the rest, is that all the three Elms which grew in Hall's meadow & gave such ornament to it, are gone" (*Letters*, 58)

96. According to Simon Schama, "Evelyn established the tree-priest as a royalist and patriot" (*Landscape and Memory* [New York: Alfred A. Knopf, 1995], 161).

97. For an explanation of the medieval symbolism behind the walnut tree, see Margaret B. Freeman, *The Unicorn Tapestries* (New York: E. P. Dutton, 1976).

98. Patrick Parrinder, *Nation and Novel: The English Novel from Its Origins to the Present Day* (Oxford: Oxford Univ. Press, 2006), 190.

99. Austen may have seen John King's full-length portrait in the Bodleian Picture Gallery in Oxford. Formerly attributed to Kneller, the portrait was bequeathed to Oxford University at his death in 1739 and hung in the Bodleian until 1929. As a child, Jane spent several months in Oxford with her sister under the care of Mrs. Ann Cawley, a widow of a Principal of Brasenose College. During this childhood visit to Oxford, "James, who was still in residence at St John's and full of intellectual enthusiasm on their behalf, took his sisters sight-seeing" through "dismal chapels, dusty libraries, and greasy halls" (Le Faye, *Family Record*, 47–48). A visit to the Bodleian's gallery of worthies would have been a probable part of any such tour.

100. Clare Norman, *Baddesley Clinton, Warwickshire* (Swindon, UK: National Trust, 1998), 4.

101. See Le Faye, *Chronology*, 331. Under the entry for 13 August 1806, Le Faye reports that the Austens, then staying at Stoneleigh Abbey, "have seen Kenilworth Castle and are going to Warwick Castle today." Warwick Castle also lies but eight miles from Battesley Clinton, although in a southerly direction.

102. Norman, *Baddesley Clinton*, 43.

103. Ibid., 4.

104. See the entry for "Knightley" in Sir Bernard Burke, *Genealogical and Heraldic Dictionary of the Peerage and Baronetage*, 42nd ed. (London, 1880). According to Burke, a seventeenth-century Knightley of Fawsley Park married Anne Ferrers of Badesley Clinton, the daughter of Sir Edward Ferrers. Their eldest son, in turn, married Mary Fermor, daughter of Richard Fermor. That the connection between the Ferrers and Fermor families is forged through a family named Knightley is a historical coincidence that I will leave for exploration by others.

105. *S&S*, 454n6. For similar observations about the allusion to Pope, also Jean Hagstrum, *Sex and Sensibility: Ideal and Erotic Love from Milton to Mozart* (Chicago: Univ. of Chicago Press, 1980), 269; and Juliet McMaster, *Jane Austen on Love* (Victoria, BC: Univ. of Victoria Press, 1978), 69.

106. Harris, *Art of Memory*, 63.

107. In the context of historiography, the most significant member of the Ferrers family was the designer of these windows, Henry Ferrers (1549–1633), a historian who witnessed the reigns of five monarchs and devoted his long lifetime to antiquarian collecting. Ferrers's vast historical archive is repeatedly cited by Sir William Dugdale in his *Antiquities of Warwickshire* (1656), a history that continued to be reprinted, anthologized, or extracted during Austen's lifetime. The *Godmersham Park Library Catalogue* lists a 1730 folio copy of "Dugdale's Antiq. Of Warwickshire 2 vols."

CHAPTER SIX. *Persuasion's* Battle of the Books: *Baronetage* versus *Navy List*

1. Brian Southam, *Jane Austen and the Navy* (London: Hambledon & London, 2000), 304.

2. See, for example, Thomas Wotton, *The English Baronetage*, 4 vols. (London: Printed for Tho. Wotton, 1741); *A New Baronetage of England*, 3 vols. (London: Printed for J. Almon, 1769); Edward Kimber, *The Baronetage of England*, 3 vols. (London: Printed for G. Woodfall, 1771); John Debrett, *The Baronetage of England*, 2nd ed., 2 vols. (London, 1808); William Playfair, *British Baronetage*, 4 vols. (London: T. Reynolds and H. Grace, 1811). For a typical identification of the 1808 edition of Debrett's, see *P*, 334n2.

3. John Debrett, *The Baronetage of England*, 3rd ed., 2 vols. (London: Printed for F. C. and J. Rivington et al., 1815). The consortium in the imprint also includes: "Clarke and Sons; J. Cuthell; Lackington and Co.; J. and A. Arch; R. Ryan; Longman and Co.; Cadell and Davies; J. Richardson; J. Bell; J. Booth; E. Lloyd; J. Booker; Black and Co.; J. Murray; Baldwin and Co.; S. Bagster; J. Hatchard; J. Harding; J. Mawman; Gale and Co.; J. Walker and Co.; and J. Rodwell."

4. See Roger Sales, *Jane Austen and Representations of Regency England* (London: Routledge, 1994), 182.

5. *Morning Chronicle* (London), Monday, 28 February 1814.

6. Jocelyn Harris, *A Revolution Almost beyond Expression: Jane Austen's Persuasion* (Newark: Univ. of Delaware Press, 2007), 107.

7. Ibid.

8. See Barbara Hardy, "The Objects in *Mansfield Park*," in *Jane Austen: Bicentenary Essays*, ed. John Halperin (Cambridge: Cambridge Univ. Press, 1975), 180–96.

9. *Morning Chronicle* (London), Wednesday, 26 January 1814.

10. Ibid., 7 February 1816. This was part of a new ad for Debrett's follow-up project of the *New Peerage*.

11. For example, the Evelyn Waugh Collection at the Harry Ransom Research Center includes a copy of *A New Baronetage of England* (1769) with numerous handwritten additions that span many decades, through to at least 1801. These annotations intrude upon the margins and virtually fill all available space from flyleaf to endpaper, tracking families of specific interest to the book's owners (call no. CS 424 A2 N48 1769 WAU).

12. Edward Copeland, "The Austens and the Elliots: A Consumer's Guide to *Persuasion*," in *Jane Austen's Business*, ed. Juliet McMaster and Bruce Stovel (New York: St. Martin's; London: Macmillan, 1996), 136–53, at 150; and *Persuasion*, ed. Gillian Beer (London: Penguin, 2003), "Introduction," xi–xxxiv, at xxv.

13. Juliet McMaster, "Class," in *The Cambridge Companion to Jane Austen*, ed. Edward Copeland and Juliet McMaster (Cambridge: Cambridge Univ. Press, 1997), 115–30, at 117.

14. Ibid., 116.

15. The Yorkshire Wentworths, incidentally, sat on the largest coal seam in England, which they mined profitably from the 1750s onward. For an account of the long-lived mining industry on the Wentworth Woodhouse estate, see Catherine Bailey, *Black Diamonds: The Rise and Fall of an English Dynasty* (London: Viking, 2007). In view of Sir Walter's dire finances, the name of Wentworth in the story may even conjure up a new industry on ancient lands.

16. Southam, *Navy*, 304 and 298.

17. Ibid., 305.

18. Ibid., 284.

19. See Robert Clark and Gerry Dutton, "Agriculture," in *Jane Austen in Context*, ed. Janet Todd (Cambridge: Cambridge Univ. Press, 2005), 185–93.

20. Ibid., 187.

21. Ibid., 185.

22. Quoted in Robin Vick, "The Sale at Steventon Parsonage," *Jane Austen Society Report* (1993): 14.

23. Park Honan, *Jane Austen: Her Life* (London: Phoenix Giant, 1997), 25.

24. Copeland, "The Austens and the Elliots," 143.

25. See Southam, *Navy*, 302 and 292.

26. Ibid., 136; J. H. Hubback and Edith C. Hubback, *Jane Austen's Sailor Brothers: Being the Adventures of Sir Francis Austen, G.C.B., Admiral of the Fleet and Rear-Admiral Charles Austen* (London: John Lane, 1906), 209.

27. Southam, *Navy*, 263.

28. Ibid.

29. Jon Spence, *Becoming Jane Austen* (London: Hambledon, 2003), 221.

30. Ibid., 222.

31. Kostelanetz Mellor, *Mothers of the Nation: Women's Political Writing in England, 1780–1830* (Bloomington: Indiana Univ. Press, 2000), 126.

32. Ibid.

33. Spence, *Becoming Jane Austen*, 221.

34. Sir Samuel Egerton Brydges, *The Autobiography, Times, Opinions, and Contemporaries of Sir Egerton Brydges*, 2 vols. (London: Cochrane and M'Crone, 1834), 2:49.

35. See Harris, *Revolution*, 186.

36. *DNB*, s.v. "Brydges, Sir (Samuel) Egerton, first baronet, styled thirteenth Baron Chandos (1762–1837), writer and genealogist."

37. Debrett, 1815 ed., 2:1361.

38. See Southam, *Navy*, 292.

39. Debrett, 1815 ed., 2:1371.

40. Harris, *Revolution*, 106–7.

41. While the first two titles are easily identifiable, the third is probably *A Voyage Round the World, in His Majesty's Ship the Dolphin, Commanded by the Honourable Commodore Byron . . . By an Officer on Board the Said Ship* (London, 1767).

42. R. W. Chapman, *Facts and Problems*, The Clark Lectures (1948; Oxford: Clarendon Press, 1970), 26.

43. Debrett, 1815 ed., 2:1373. The appendix even includes an extinct 1692 patent for "Wentworth, of North Amsall, co. York" (at 2:1394).

44. Ibid., 2:999.

45. See also *DNB*, s.v. "Wentworth, Sir John, first baronet (1737–1820), colonial governor."

46. *Sunday Times* (London) *Magazine*, 11 February 2007.

47. See William Bray, *Sketch of a Tour into Derbyshire and Yorkshire*, 2nd ed. (London: Printed for B. White, at Horace's Head, in Fleet-Street, 1783), 249. Bray quotes extensively from Young's by then famous account, which summed up the front of Wentworth Castle as "one of the most beautiful in the world."

48. In addition to coal, the land was also mined for clay. The Rockingham

Pottery, named for the marquess, had been making utilitarian earthenware on the Wentworth estate for half a century. By 1815, although not yet the refined rival to Wedgwood that it would eventually become, the Swinton Pottery produced a range of earthen goods under the patronage of the Earls Fitzwilliam. See Alwyn Cox and Angela Cox, *Rockingham, 1745-1842* (Woodbridge, UK: Antique Collector's Club, 2001). It is possible, I suppose, that the evocative name of Mrs. Clay puns obliquely on even this aspect of the Wentworths' landed history.

49. *Hull Packet*, 26 May 1801.

50. Southam, *Navy*, 273.

51. Michael Charlesworth, "The Imaginative Dimension of an Early Eighteenth-Century Garden: Wentworth Castle," *Art History* 28.5 (2005): 644. Hence the prominent ship in the background of his portrait in figure 1.3.

52. One newspaper reported that "Frederick Thomas William Vernon may assume and take the surname of Wentworth," having inherited the estate of Wentworth Castle through "his kinswoman, Augusta Anne Hatfield Kaye," the sister of the third Earl of Strafford ("from *The London Gazette*" in the *Hull Packet*, Tuesday, 23 October 1804).

53. It could be coincidence that Wentworth Castle's first Earl of Strafford had four children, whose names are used in *Persuasion*: three daughters—Anne, Lucy, and Henrietta—and one son and heir, William. Although Maggie Lane in *Jane Austen and Names* gives separate historical accounts of *Louisa* and *Lucy*, the latter is often considered a nickname of the former.

54. See Harris, *Revolution*, 146 and 154. For an illustrated distillation of Lyme's tumultuous history, see the pamphlet by novelist John Fowles, *A Short History of Lyme Regis* (Lyme Regis: Dovecote Press, 1991).

55. Emma Austen-Leigh, *Jane Austen and Lyme Regis* (London: Spottiswoode, Ballantyne & Co., 1941), 55; see also Fowles, *Short History*, 43. Various accounts have Tennyson demanding the "exact" spot "at once."

56. *DNB*, s.v. "Wentworth, Henrietta Maria, *suo jure* Baroness Wentworth (1660–1686), royal mistress."

57. Ibid.

58. Harris, *Revolution*, 154.

59. Another major storm on 20 January 1817 would necessitate further repairs to the Cobb by an engineer named Edward Fanshawe, whose reinforcements of its structure took nearly ten years to complete. See the entry for "Fanshaw(e), Edward, Lieutenant-General (fl. 1801–1850), military engineer," in A. W. Skempton, *A Biographical Dictionary of Civil Engineers in Great Britain and Ireland* (London: Thomas Telford, 2002).

60. Although Maggie Lane rightly warns that "we must not be too literal about the imaginative process" in locating Louisa's fall on the Cobb, the specific-

ity of Austen's own language points to the third set of steps (Lane, *Jane Austen and Lyme Regis* [Winchester: Jane Austen Society, 2003], 52).

61. I am grateful to K. C. Hysmith, who, during a memorable class fieldtrip to Lyme Regis in 2008, pointed out the name of D'Arcy in the inscription by the steps. My transcription of the much-weathered stone is taken from George Roberts, *The History and Antiquities of the Borough of Lyme Regis* (London and Lyme Regis, 1834), 235. In 1823, Roberts also gave the inscription in *History of Lyme-Regis, Dorset, from the Earliest Periods to the Present Day* (Sherborne and London, 1823), 171. Later storms, including a major blow in January of 1817, led to further repairs along other sections of the Cobb.

62. Le Faye, *Chronology*, 300. The *London Gazette* reported with a byline of "Whitehall, August 18" that Frederick Thomas William Vernon would "assume and take the surname of Wentworth." This announcement was picked up by various papers over the course of several months, including the *Hull Packet*, on 23 October 1804.

63. As previously mentioned, Byron married Annabella Milbanke (1792–1860), *suo jure* Baroness Wentworth, in January of 1815. The marriage was followed within the year by scandal involving his half-sister, Augusta Mary (1783–1851), daughter of his father's second wife, Amelia D'Arcy.

64. I have been unable to locate information about the Captain D'Arcy who engineered the 1790s repairs to the Cobb to discover how (or if) he was genuinely connected to the Wentworths. Several publications, however, confirm the information on the stone, including a newspaper report on the "extraordinary labour" of the reconstructions, which "will, when finished, do infinite honour to the able engineer employed by the Government, Mr. D'Arcy" (*Morning Post and Fashionable World*, Wednesday, 20 August 20, 1794). See also the Parliamentary Papers from the House of Commons for 1817, especially the volume entitled "Reports from Committees" for the session of 28 January–12 July 1817.

65. Debrett, 1815 ed., 1:24.

66. Honan, *Jane Austen*, 22.

67. Even earlier, in "A Collection of Letters," Austen used the variant *Musgrove* for someone in love with a Henrietta (*J*, 206–7). As previously noted, this same story contains many names, including Evelyn, Dashwood, and Willoughby, that Austen recycles elsewhere in her later fictions.

68. Debrett, 1815 ed., 1:24. In 1791 the *Gentleman's Magazine* reprinted the legendary story.

69. David Nokes, *Jane Austen: A Life* (New York: Farrar, Straus & Giroux, 1997), 123.

70. Debrett, 1815 ed., 1:28.

71. Ibid., 1:26.

72. *DNB*, s.v. "Musgrave, Sir Richard, first baronet (*c.*1755–1818), political writer and politician."

73. See Sales, *Regency*, 187. Austen recycles *Persuasion's* joke on the diminutive "Dick" from the opening of *Northanger Abbey*, where the heroine's father was "a very respectable man—though his name was Richard" (*NA*, 5). For an account by Benedict and Le Faye of this name as a long-standing joke in the Austen family, see *NA*, 291n2.

74. Debrett, 1815 ed., 1:25 and 1:26.

75. Place names ending in *lynch* or *linch* (from the OE *hlinc*, "hillside") are by no means rare in the West County—with, for example, Lydlinch, Charlinch, and Stocklinch falling within the possible ambit of the novel. None of these, however, offers the geographical proximity to Charlton-Musgrove that, combined with the celebrity history of Redlynch, suggestively narrows interpretive possibilities to this location.

76. See Harris, *Revolution*, 225n16.

77. Versions of the advertisement appear in various papers between June 1796 and December 1798; it may have run longer. For the initial notice, see *St. James' Chronicle or the British Evening Post* (London), Saturday, 18 June 1796, and for one of the latest see the *Morning Herald* (London), 10 December 1798.

78. See Joanna Martin, *Wives and Daughters: Women and Children in the Georgian Country House* (London: Hambledon Continuum, 2004), 91.

79. Quoted in Ibid., 89.

80. See Ibid., 91.

81. *DNB*, s.v. "Fox, Charles James (1749–1806), politician."

82. "With the public disputes between Mr. Burke and Mr. Fox, and with the poignant distress of mind it occasioned the latter, every one is acquainted. The defection of Lord Fitzwilliam, the friend of his childhood, and the man of whose political principles he is said to have formed the highest opinion, was however to Mr. Fox a still more severe affliction" (*Public Characters of 1799-1800* [London: Printed by J. Adlard . . . for R. Phillips, 1799], 356).

83. 30 July 1789, *Memorials and Correspondence*, 2.361; quoted in *DNB* entry for "Fox."

84. Martin, *Wives and Daughters*, 90.

85. See ibid., 91.

86. Ibid.

87. The eighteenth-century manor house at Redlynch would not survive. In 1914, a fire, rumored to have been started by suffragettes, so damaged the former service block that the house was demolished soon afterward.

88. *DNB* entry for "Fox."

89. *Letters*, 534. I discussed these connections in Chapter 1.

90. Deirdre Le Faye, *Jane Austen: A Family Record*, 2nd ed. (Cambridge: Cambridge Univ. Press, 2004), 222.

91. Ibid.

92. *DNB*, s.v. "Carteret, Sir George, first baronet (1610?–1680), naval officer and administrator."

93. Lady Fanshawe, *Memoirs of Lady Fanshawe, Wife of the Right Hon. Sir Richard Fanshawe, Bart. Written by Herself* (London: Henry Colburn, 1829), 60.

94. *DNB* entry for "Carteret, Sir George."

95. *DNB*, s.v. "Carteret, Philip (1733–1796), explorer."

96. Ibid.

97. See *DNB*, s.v. "Silvester, Sir Philip Carteret, second baronet (1777–1828), naval officer." As the *DNB* recounts, Carteret took on the surname Silvester, which belonged to an uncle, only after inheriting his title in 1822.

98. Debrett, 1815 ed., 1:428. In Debrett's appendix, an additional baronetcy of 1661 for "Crofts, of Stow, co. Suffolk" is listed as extinct (Debrett, 1815 ed., 2:1388).

99. *Debrett's Baronetage of England*, 6th ed. (London: Printed for C. and J. Rivington et al., 1828), 250.

100. Ronald Dunning, in a notice labeled "a princely Welsh ancestor for Jane Austen," remarks upon Austen's distant connections to James Croft of Croft Castle via John Scudamore of Holm Lacy, Herefordshire (d. 1571) and the Leighs in the Brydges line (*Jane Austen Society Newsletter*, October 2009, 11).

101. Southam, *Navy*, 292.

102. Debrett, 1828 ed., 250.

103. Debrett, 1815 ed., 1:430.

104. Ibid., 1:429.

105. Ibid., 1:430.

106. *DNB*, s.v. "Croft, Sir Herbert, fifth baronet (1751–1816), writer and lexicographer."

107. Debrett, 1815 ed., 1:428; see also *DNB* entry for "Croft."

108. Another popular work by Croft ran to at least seven editions and bears a title that conveys his own fondness for sensation and name play: *Love and Madness, A Story Too True, in A Series of Letters between Parties Whose Names Could Perhaps Be Mentioned Were They Less Known or Less Lamented* (1780). It tells of "the clandestine love of James Hackman, a one-time army officer and Norfolk clergyman, for Martha Ray, the mistress of Lord Sandwich, who was shot by Hackman as she was leaving Covent Garden Theatre on 7 April 1779" (*DNB* entry for "Croft").

109. Patrick Parrinder, *Nation and Novel: The English Novel from Its Origins to the Present Day* (Oxford: Oxford Univ. Press, 2006), 188.

110. See the entries for "Russell" in the appendix of Debrett, 1815 ed., 2:1380 and 1387.

111. *DNB*, s.v. "Russell, Sir Henry, first baronet (1751–1836), judge in India."

112. *Asiatic Annual Register*, 1808, 24–27; quoted in *DNB* entry for "Russell, Sir Henry."

113. *DNB* entry for "Russell, Sir Henry."

114. *DNB*, s.v. "Russell, Thomas Macnamara (*b.* before 1740, *d.* 1824), naval officer."

115. Brian Lavery, *The Ship of the Line*, vol. 1, *The Development of the Battle-fleet, 1650–1850* (London: Conway Maritime Press, 2003). See also Robert Gardiner and Brian Lavery, eds., *The Line of Battle: The Sailing Warship, 1650–1840* (London: Conway Maritime Press, 1992).

116. Edward Pelham Brenton, *Naval History of Great Britain: from the year 1783–1836*, 2 vols. (London: Henry Colburn, 1837), 1:233.

117. The *Elephant*, like the *Russell*, was a 74-gun, third-rate ship of the line. Built in 1786, she was chosen in 1801 to be Nelson's flagship in the Battle of Copenhagen. From her deck Nelson allegedly put a telescope to his blind eye and claimed that he did not see the signal ordering withdrawal. In 1814, the *Elephant* appears to have been in limbo or under repairs, before being downgraded to a 58-gun, fourth-rate in 1818 and, eventually, broken up in 1830.

118. For example, Susan E. Whyman, in *The Pen and the People: English Letter Writers, 1660–1800* (Oxford: Oxford Univ. Press, 2009), refers to a manuscript memoir by merchant Thomas Wilson (1764–1843) in which Wilson not only copied out passages from Lady Russell's published letters but also "once compared his wife's 'tender affection' to that of Lady Rachel Russell" (141).

119. Harris, *Revolution*, 224n88.

120. See Austen's letters dated 24 and 30 January 1809, in *Letters*, 171–73. A few critics have offered other models and sources for the name. For example, Margaret Kirkham finds a Carteret and a Dalrymple among announcements of new arrivals to Bath (*Jane Austen: Feminism and Fiction* [Brighton: Harvester Press, 1983], 140), while Elaine Bander locates a "Gen. Dalrymple" of Dublin in *Camilla*'s star-studded subscription list, which also included an entry for "Miss J. Austen, Steventon" ("A Possible Source for Jane Austen's Names," *Notes and Queries* 29.3 [1982]: 206).

121. See *DNB*, s.v. "Dalrymple, Sir John, of Cousland [later Sir John Hamilton-Macgill-Dalrymple], fourth baronet (1726–1810), lawyer and historian." At least five editions of Lady Rachel Russell's *Letters* appeared between 1773 and 1800, all containing her introductory challenge to Dalrymple.

122. Ibid.

123. See *DNB*, s.v. "Dalrymple, Alexander (1737–1808), hydrographer."

124. In 1773 Dalrymple wrote two pamphlets uncompromisingly critical of John Hawkesworth's literary account of the voyage.

125. *DNB* entry for "Dalrymple, Alexander."

126. See Hubback and Hubback, *Sailor Brothers*, 194.

127. See *DNB*, s.v. "Elliot, John (1732–1808), naval officer."

128. Nicolas, *Nelson Despatches*, 5.366; quoted in *DNB* entry for "Elliott, John."

129. Le Faye notes that Tysoe Saul Hancock, in August 1775, writes "a letter of introduction for Mr Elliot, son of Sir Gilbert Elliot" (*Chronology*, 65).

130. *DNB*, s.v. "Elliot, Sir George (1784–1863), naval officer and politician." Jane Austen, proud of the history of her brother's famous ship, wrote Frank on 3 July 1813, to ask whether he would allow her mention of it "& two or three other of your old Ships" to stand in *Mansfield Park* (*Letters*, 219).

131. Ibid.

132. It is listed only among the "extinct" patents, as "1776 Elliot, knt. M.D. of Peebles, co. Peebles," which is why Harris cannot find any Elliots in Debrett. See Harris, *Revolution*, 121.

133. Austen may not have known that this first and only Eliot baronet of England drew on prize money earned at sea to set up as a physician. See *DNB*, s.v. "Eliot, Sir John, baronet (1733x6?–1786), physician."

134. *DNB* entry for "Eliot, Sir John," and *P*, 3. Eliot's illegitimate offspring included three daughters (Ann, Mary, Marianne), a son (John), and another daughter (Elizabeth). Only the first four shared his last name.

135. Harris, *Revolution*, 224n88.

136. *DNB*, s.v. "Elliott [Eliot; née Dalrymple], Grace [nicknamed Dally the Tall] (1754?–1823), courtesan and writer."

137. Ibid.

138. Ibid.

139. Lady Shelley, *Diary*, 1.42; quoted in *DNB* entry for "Elliott, Grace."

AFTERWORD. Jane Austen's Fictive Network

1. See, the entry for "Knightley" in Sir Bernard Burke, *Genealogical and Heraldic Dictionary of the Peerage and Baronetage*, 42nd ed. (London, 1880).

2. Ralph Allen's brother, Philip Allen, married a Jane Bennet.

3. Nikolaus Pevsner, "The Architectural Settings of Jane Austen's Novels," *Journal of the Warburg and Courtauld Institutes* 31 (1968): 412.

Barrett, Ann, 8
Barry, Frances, 175, 194
Bath, England: maps of, 73–78; as setting for Austen's fiction, 18, 26, 63–64, 68–84, 89–91. *See also* Allen, Ralph; Farleigh Hungerford Castle; *Northanger Abbey*; *Persuasion*
Baynton, Henry, 98
Beckford, William, 91
Beer, Gillian, 212
Behn, Aphra, 285–86n36
Bellerophon (ship), 262n44
Benedict, Barbara, 265n18, 275n4
Bennet family, 256
Bentley, Richard, 2, 6–7, 43
Bertie, Brownlow, 165
Bertie, Peregrine, 165
Bertie, Richard, 165
Bingley, Baron 53
Bingley, Thomas, 270n76
Blaise Castle (Bath, England), 78, 80–81, 84, 96–97, 100, 197
Blount, Martha, 66
Borgnis, Giuseppe, 180
Boswell, James, 115, 247
Bowers, Fredson, 261n40
Boyce, Benjamin, 66, 79–80
Boyle, Robert, 145
Brandon, Charles, 164
Brandon, Richard, 164, 255
Braudy, Leo, 4–5
Bray, William, 301n47
Brayley, Edward Wedlake, 42, 188
Bree, Linda, 24, 46, 121–22, 123, 269n65
Bridgeman, Charles, 137, 144
British Baronetage (Playfair), 211, 249
Britton, John, 42, 188
Broadhead, Mary Anne, 177–78, 195
Brontë, Charlotte, 125
Brophy, Brigid, 265n13
Brown, Capability, 144
Browne, Mary, 132
Browne, Sir Richard, 132
Brunton, Mary, 15, 54
Brydges, James, Duke of Chandos, 18, 20, 61
Brydges, Sir Samuel Egerton, 20–21, 221–22
Bubb-Dodington, George, 180

Burke, Edmund, 38, 237, 269n71
Burney, Edward, 188, 189, 295–96n65
Burney, Frances, 63, 67, 285n35; John Evelyn as source for, 127–28, 129, 132, 135–36, 139; as influence on Jane Austen, 141–43. See also *Evelina*
Burney, Sarah Harriet, 286n42
Butler, Marilyn, 12, 46, 61, 78, 93, 114, 268n57, 281n78
Byrne, Paula, 8, 260n22
Byron, Augusta Mary, 32, 230, 303n63
Byron, George Gordon, Lord, 31–32, 187, 189, 230, 264n9, 303n63

Cadell, Thomas, 62, 141
Camden, William, 42
Camilla (Burney), 141
Campbell-Culver, Maggie, 157–58
Carlisle, England, 147–48
Carlisle, Frederick Howard, fifth Earl of, 147–48, 150
Caroline, Queen, 137
Cary, John, 24
Carteret, Sir George, 239–40
Carteret, Philip, 240
Carteret, Philip (son), 240–41
Carteret family, 239–41
Castle Howard, 148, 150, 151
Catharine; or, The Bower (Austen), 142, 143
Cecilia (Burney), 141
Chambers, R., 296n75
Chapman, R. W., 2–3, 11, 46, 116
Charles II, King, 5, 136, 148
Charlesworth, Michael, 38, 41
Charlton-Musgrove (Somerset, England), 235–36
Charron, Peter, 192
Chaucer, Geoffrey, 86, 123
Chawton, England, 7–8
Child, Sir Josiah, 118
Chrysal (Johnstone), 187–89, 199
Churchill, Charles, 180, 186, 189
Clark, Robert, 215
Collins, Arthur, 20, 21, 33, 35, 49
Collinson, John, 106
Cook, Elizabeth Heckendorn, 153
Cook, James, 248
Cooke, Charles, 188
Cooper, Edward, 17

Hancock, Eliza, 250
Hancock, Philadelphia, 250
Hancock, Tysoe Saul, 250
Hardy, Barbara, 209
Harford, John, 97
Harman, Claire, 280–81n76
Harris, Jocelyn, 35, 89, 118, 164, 169,
    204, 209, 212, 222, 223–24, 228,
    229, 236, 247, 280n66, 280n76
Hart, Emma, 170
Hastings, Warren, 52, 238, 269n71
Hawarden, Lord, 86
Hell-Fire Club, 166, 170, 172, 180–83,
    199, 201, 292n24; membership of,
    180; motto of, 171, 291–92n16; notori-
    ety of, 183–90
Hemingway, Ernest, 123
Henry VIII, King, 102, 103, 104, 105,
    107, 118
Heydt-Stevenson, Jill, 187
Hinton Abbey, 105, 106
Hoare, William, 66
Hogarth, William, 180, 187, 292n16,
    295n56
Holford, Mrs., 141
Holland, Henry, 144
Honan, Park, 18, 19, 31, 52–53, 73, 154,
    190
Howard, Charles, 147
Howard, Henry, 148
Howard, Henry Frederick, 32, 148
Howard family, 148
Hume, David, 10, 114, 247
Hungerford, Lady Agnes, 100–101
Hungerford, Lady Elizabeth, 102
Hungerford, Lady Margaret, 109
Hungerford, Lady Susan, 102
Hungerford, Sir Edward, 98, 100–101,
    109
Hungerford, Sir Walter, 101–2, 107
Hungerford family, 99–100. *See also*
    Farleigh Hungerford Castle
Hunt, John Dixon, 150
Hunter, Alexander, 130–33, 143, 145,
    152, 158
Hussey, Lord, 102
Hyde Park, 137
Hysmith, K. C., 303n61

Ivanhoe (Scott), 36, 54–55

Jackson, J. E., 276n12
James I, King, 136
Jenkins, Elizabeth, 32
Jennings, Mary, 173
Johnson, Anne, 227
Johnson, Sir Henry, 227
Johnson, Samuel, 21, 114–15
Johnstone, Charles, 187–89, 296n67
Jones, Inigo, 237
Jones, Vivien, 8
Jordan, Dorothy, 117–18
Joyce, James: geographic accuracy in
    works of, 24–25, 26, 91–92; wordplay
    as used by, 21–22

Kaye, Augusta Ann Hatfield, 45, 47
Kelly, Hugh, 54
Kemp, Betty, 191
Kenilworth (Scott), 130, 154
Kensington Gardens, 137–38, 139,
    285n32
Kent, William, 65
Keynsham, England, 97
Kightly, Charles, 276n12
King, John, 173, 201, 298n99
King, Mary, 173, 292n22
Kirkham, Margaret, 306n20
Knapton, George, 187, 295n56
Knight, Thomas, 220
Knox, Tim, 297n82
Knox-Shaw, Peter, 6, 35, 106, 113, 114

Lady Susan (Austen), 19, 102, 227;
    dating of, 26, 45–47; and the Vernon
    family, 45–49, 52–53, 255
—characters in, 268–69n65; Catherine
    Vernon, 48; Charles Vernon, 48;
    Frederic Vernon, 29, 45, 47, 48, 52;
    Lady Susan Vernon, 47–48, 49
Lane, Maggie, 16–17, 102–3, 302–3n60
Langlois, Peter, 191, 297n81
Leavis, Q. D., 46, 269n65
Le Despencer, Baron (or Lord), 166, 173,
    255. *See also* Dashwood, Sir Francis,
    second Baronet
Le Despencer, Baroness, 168–69, 194
Lee, Mrs., 168–69, 175–76
Le Faye, Deirdre, 46, 60, 108, 123, 169,
    191, 244, 257, 269n71, 275n4, 279n54,
    298n101

Tilney, 87, 112–13; Mrs. Tilney, 94, 109, 110

O'Brien, Susan, 237
Order of St. Francis of Wycombe, 174, 185. *See also* Hell-Fire Club
original intention, doctrine of, 123–24

Pamela (Richardson), 66, 164
Parker, Keiko, 89
Parrinder, Patrick, 28, 104, 164, 201, 243
peerage, Austen's fascination with, 33–38. See also *Baronetage of England*; *Peerage of England*
Peerage (Debrett), 211
Peerage of England, The (Collins), 20, 21, 33–34, 35
Pembroke, Henry Herbert, ninth Earl of, 65
Pepys, Samuel, 130, 139
Persuasion (Austen): *Baronetage* versus navy list in, 206–14; dating of, 89, 264n9; geography of, 89, 235–36; Kellynch Hall in, 206, 236, 238, 242, 251; Musgrove family in, 234–35; social commentary in, 206–7, 211–14; sources for names in, 206–14, 222–25, 232, 246–47, 248–51, 302n53
—characters in, 10, 32; Admiral Croft, 206, 218, 244; Sophia Croft, 242; Lady Dalrymple, 246; Anne Elliot, 4, 37, 212, 241, 244, 246, 249; Elizabeth Elliot, 239; Sir Walter Elliot, 27, 37, 44, 89, 206, 209–11, 212, 213, 214, 218, 221, 222, 225, 226–27, 235, 239, 242, 244, 246, 249, 251; William Elliot, 227, 247, 249; Charles Musgrove, 209, 213, 236; Henrietta Musgrove, 207, 208, 233–34; Louisa Musgrove, 207, 208, 229, 233–34; Mary Musgrove, 37; Richard Musgrove, 235; Lady Russell, 214, 243–44, 245–46, 249; Mrs. Smith, 86; Colonel Wallis, 218, 247; Captain Frederick Wentworth, 27, 54, 207, 208, 209, 212, 213–14, 218, 220, 225, 233–34, 244, 246
Pevsner, Nikolaus, 105, 124, 256
Pierrepont, Lady Evelyn, 144

Pindar, Peter, 281n83
Pinion, F. B., 281n80
Pitt, William the Elder, 66, 79, 221
Plato, 135
Platt, Arthur, 11
Playfair, William, 211
Pole-Tilney-Long-Wellesley, William, 120
Pope, Alexander, 64, 65, 66, 152–53, 204, 213
Potter, Thomas, 180
Pride and Prejudice (Austen), 230
—characters in, 32, 37–38, 142; Elizabeth Bennet, 37, 155; Mr. Bingley, 53, 142; Lady Catherine de Bourgh, 20–21, 37, 222; Mr. Collins, 20; Lady Anne Darcy, 37; Georgiana Darcy, 38; Fitzwilliam Darcy, 4, 27, 37, 142, 155; Mrs. Reynolds, 8; George Wickham, 38, 292n22
Prior Park (Bath, England), 59, 60, 63–66, 68, 69, 85–87

Quin, James, 66

Radcliffe, Ann, 94, 105–6, 111, 115
Ranelagh Gardens, 138
Rape of the Lock, The (Pope), 204, 213
Redford, Bruce, 172–73
Redlynch, 304n87; as source for *Persuasion*, 236–38
Repton, Humphry, 8, 42, 170, 190, 197–200, 298n93
Revett, Nicholas, 182
Reynolds, Sir Joshua, 8
Richardson, Samuel, 25, 66
Roach, Joseph, 5
Roberts, George, 303n61
Robertson, William, 10
Robinson, Mary, 269n70
Rochester, John Wilmot, second Earl of, 98, 137
Rockingham Pottery, 270n76, 301–2n48
Roman Catholicism: attitudes toward, 166, 170, 202, 235; and the Ferrers family, 170, 172, 202–5
Rose, John, 132, 136, 144
Ross, Stephanie, 181
Royal Society, 133, 248, 284n24
Rushworth, John, 270n74
Rushworth Papers, 53

Russell (ship), 245
Russell, Henry, 244
Russell, Lady. See Wriothesley, Rachel
Russell, Thomas Macnamara, 244–45
Russell family, 243–46

Sabor, Peter, 14, 146, 171, 263n67, 291n16
St. James's Park, 136–37, 139, 285n30
Sales, Roger, 12–13, 118, 170, 171, 207, 282n85
Sanditon (Austen), 123
Sayes Court, 132, 145, 157, 158, 159–60
Schama, Simon, 131, 152, 298n96
Scott, Sir Walter, 5–6, 36, 54–55, 115, 116, 130, 154, 188, 189
Sense and Sensibility (Austen), 126, 142; dating of, 169–70; and John Evelyn's Deptford estate, 154–55, 156–62; John Evelyn's Silva as influence on, 128–29, 140, 152–54, 164; family conflict in, 179; historical allusions in, 141, 164–65; historical context of, 166–69; literary allusions in, 204; precursor to, 169, 177, 189, 192; religious allusions in, 200–201; role of Delaford estate in, 155–56; sources for names in, 163–64, 168–69, 179, 194–96, 204–5
—characters in, 18, 140–41; Colonel Brandon, 154–56, 157–63, 164; Elinor Dashwood, 154, 155, 156, 200, 201; Fanny Dashwood, 153–54, 167, 192–96, 200–201; Henry Dashwood, 153, 179; John Dashwood, 153–54, 193, 195–96, 197, 201; Marianne Dashwood, 153, 154, 155, 158, 159, 162, 163, 171, 179, 181, 191, 200, 201, 204; Edward Ferrars, 154, 204; Mrs. Jennings, 154, 155–56, 157–59, 162–63, 173; Sir John Middleton, 163; Mr. and Mrs. Palmer, 162; Eliza Williams, 163; John Willoughby, 155, 159, 191, 201, 204
Seymour, William, 63
Shakespeare, William, 21, 158
Sham Castle (Bath, England), 60, 63, 78–83, 84, 97, 231
Silva (Evelyn), 126, 127, 129–33, 157, 158, 162; Hunter's republication of, 130–33, 152; as influence on Sense and Sensibility, 152–54. See also Deptford

Skeat, W. W., 123
Skrine, Henry, 42
Smith, Gertrude Tucker. See Tucker, Gertrude
Smith, Martin Stafford, 85, 86
Smithers, David Waldron, 168
Society of Dilettanti, 174, 187
Southam, Brian, 35, 44, 46, 122, 146, 214, 218, 223, 226, 241, 269n65
Southey, Robert, 129–30
Spence, Jon, 36, 220
Spenser, Edmund, 143
Stainborough Hall, 28, 40–41. See also Wentworth Castle
Stanhope, Sir William, 180
Stapleton, Sir Thomas, 180
Steel's Navy List, 210. See also navy lists
Sterne, Laurence, 66, 135
Stevenson, John Hall, 180
Stoneleigh Abbey, 18–19
Strafford family, 10
Stuart, Elizabeth, 32
Stuart, Lady Elizabeth, 148
Susan. See Northanger Abbey
Sutherland, Kathryn, 11

Talbot, Elizabeth, 237
Tanner, Tony, 8
Tennyson, Alfred, Lord, 228, 231
Thorpe, Thomas, 74–78, 98
Tilney/Tylney family, 103–4, 118, 256, 282n88
Tilney-Long, Catherine, 95, 117–21
Tilney-Long, Sir James, 117
Tilney-Long, James (son), 117
Tindal, Nicholas, 39
Todd, Janet, 24, 46, 121–22, 123, 269n65
Tom Jones (Fielding), 66–67
Trilling, Lionel, 35
Tristram Shandy (Sterne), 135
Tucker, Gertrude, 58, 59, 85–86
Tucker, John, 180
Tudor-Stuart conflicts, 104
Tunstall, James, 81, 82, 101–2, 107
Tyers, Jonathan, 138

Ulysses (Joyce), 24–25, 26, 91–92
Upfal, Annette, 17–18

CPSIA information can be obtained
at www.ICGtesting.com
Printed in the USA
LVOW07s1628010217
522882LV00005B/1075/P

9 781421 411910